ACADEMY
AWARD WINNING
MOVIES
1928–2020

ACADEMY AWARD WINNING MOVIES

1928–2020

How Movies Have Changed Through The Years

Dr. Diane Holloway Cheney

gatekeeper press™

Columbus, Ohio

Academy Award Winning Movies 1928-2020: How Movies Have Changed Through The Years

Published by Gatekeeper Press
2167 Stringtown Rd, Suite 109
Columbus, OH 43123-2989
www.GatekeeperPress.com

Library of Congress Control Number: 2021945872

ISBN (paperback): 9781662918933
eISBN: 9781662918940

Acknowledgements

We owe gratitude to those who have studied movies, music, and have written so many fabulous books about films. We are grateful to Ted Turner for his vision about what appealed to people. We are thankful to Turner Classic Movies (TCM) which has captured the passion of movies from ordinary people who enjoy them.

This book illustrates how movies have changed over the years--especially as more minorities are finally being included. It also introduces many ways to consider movies based on our senses, such as paying attention to the role of music in movies. As a psychologist, I know well how films impact lives as they make us want to copy the words, dress, hair styles, and actions of stars. Children grow up seeing movies at home or in theaters and we may be who we are because of those influences.

We can now analyze what effects come from good directors, movie musicians, cinematographers who know just where to point the camera, and actors who help us learn emotions like empathy through our identification with them. Movies tell stories and help us know ourselves and others better by building understanding. Each of these parts of movie making gradually evolved over the last hundred years. We are greatly indebted to the Academy of Motion Picture Arts and Sciences (AMPAS) for improving the caliber of films by increasing the perfection of craftspeople in their 24-25 categories.

Familiar music elicits long-forgotten emotions and memories, so film composers often include tunes we've heard before. Music can create a sense of community and togetherness. Drumming, used by various birds and animals, is basic to our body's heart and pulse. When drumming or noises are organized, they arouse our wish for action. As neurologist Oliver Sacks explained, hearing and action are linked in the brain of a child. (See Oliver Sacks *Musicophilia: Tales of Music and the Brain,* 2007). These things help explain why music was added to films, even in the silent era when pianists played as we watched actors and dialogue cards on the screen.

The history of Academy Award ceremonies and awards are captured with each passing year. Many may search for their favorite movies here. Photographs of movie stars take up many pages in previous books about films, but they do not enhance our understanding of why some movies are better than others. Here we sought important themes and movies of lasting value. That knowledge will add joy to those who keep this book close by as they go back to re-watch a movie to search for additional sights, sounds, and ideas.

In addition, this book will investigate the climate and history of Texas for the origin of movies from 1911 to 1940. Black movie makers were helped by local Texans long before they were included in major movie studios as actors or technicians.

It is hard to know whether the annual academy award presentations will continue to occur. So many companies are replacing big studios in film production. As viewers of the awards have decreased in recent years, changes are occurring. We may be in the era of diminishing Academy Awards. Since awards stimulate excellence in all fields, it will be interesting to see what happens over the coming years as moviemaking continues to progress.

We also acknowledge Rusty Bradshaw who was the editor for this book. In addition to work for newspapers as an editor, Rusty writes books himself. He has written *The Rehabilitation of Miss Little, Moist on the Mountain,* and, most recently, *Gorge Justice.*

This book could never had been completed without the able and extensive help from my beloved Edgar Van Cott. The beautiful cover was designed by Carolyn Van Cott.

Table of Contents

Introduction

My organizations include the American Psychological Association, Psychoanalysis Today, Society for Cognitive Studies of the Moving Image, American Medical Writers Association, American Film Institute, Academy Museum of Motion Pictures, and Sundance Institute.

What does a film institute do? The American Film Institute educates filmmakers, honors the heritage of the motion picture arts, and makes top ten and top one hundred lists of movies. For example, here was the 2008 top one hundred list ranked from best on down:

Citizen Kane, The Godfather, Casablanca, Raging Bull, Singin' in the Rain, Gone with the Wind, Lawrence of Arabia, Schindler's List, Vertigo, The Wizard of Oz, City Lights, The Searchers, Star Wars, Psycho, 2001: A Space Odyssey, Sunset Blvd., The Graduate, The General, On the Waterfront, It's a Wonderful Life, Chinatown, Some Like It Hot, The Grapes of Wrath, E.T. The extra-Terrestrial, To Kill a Mockingbird, Mr. Smith Goes to Washington, High Noon, All About Eve, Double Indemnity, Apocalypse Now, The Maltese Falcon, The Godfather Part II, One Flew Over the Cuckoo's Nest, Snow White and the Seven Dwarfs, Annie Hall, The Bridge on the River Kwai, The Best Years of Our Lives, The Treasure of Sierra Madre, Dr. Strangelove, The Sound of Music, King Kong, Bonnie and Clyde, Midnight Cowboy, The Philadelphia Story, Shane, It Happened One Night, A Streetcar Named Desire, Rear Window, Intolerance, The Lord of the Rings: The Fellowship of the Ring, West Side Story, Taxi Driver, The Deer Hunter, MASH, North by Northwest, Jaws, Rocky, The Gold Rush, Nashville, Duck Soup, Sullivan's Travels, American Graffiti, Cabaret, Network, The African Queen, Raiders of the Lost Ark, Who's

Afraid of Virginia Woolf?, *Unforgiven*, *Tootsie*, *A Clockwork Orange*, *Saving Private Ryan*, *The Shawshank Redemption*, *Butch Cassidy and the Sundance Kid*, *The Silence of the Lambs*, *In the Heat of the Night*, *Forrest Gump*, *All the President's Men*, *Modern Times*, *The Wild Bunch*, *The Apartment*, *Spartacus*, *Sunrise*, *Titanic*, *Easy Rider*, *A Night at the Opera*, *Platoon*, *12 Angry Men*, *Bringing Up Baby*, *The Sixth Sense*, *Swing Time*, *Sophie's Choice*, *Goodfellas*, *The French Connection*, *Pulp Fiction*, *The Last Picture Show*, *Do the Right Thing*, *Blade Runner*, *Yankee Doodle Dandy*, *Toy Story*, and *Ben-Hur*.

CHAPTER ONE

The Beginning of Movies

Cave artists were like cinematographers who knew that the eye focuses on movement. A director tells cinematographers where to point the camera and what lighting is desired where the most action is shown. The musical composer and arranger connects us with feelings about the story and screen action as we watch it. When we say feelings, we include emotions and body changes, such as increased heart rate, blood pressure, muscular tension, eye blinks or tears, vocalizations such as sighs or screams, and skin conductance.

Directors tell musicians what kind of music they desire to accompany certain scenes. Greeks and later physicians have found that flutes and stringed instruments decrease pain, anxiety, and depression. Music like Beethoven's "Moonlight Sonata," Debussy's "Clair de Lune," Albinoni's "Adagio in G," and Mozart's "Piano Concerto #21 Second Movement" aid breathing and increase oxygen. Jagged loud sounds raise the emotions of the viewer just as marching music arranges scenes to proceed in an orderly fashion. Swooning music may accompany love scenes with swirling sensations that accompany romance.

One has only to take their pulse and blood pressure while watching an exciting or scary movie to see changes. If the changes are disturbing, turning down the music volume will calm the viewer.

Everyone knows about Thomas Edison's inventions. The deafer he became, the more he cared about hearing and seeing. He, like

Beethoven, worked ever faster while they still had the ability to ply their arts. He began with the Edison Speaking Phonograph in 1878. Then he devised an electric incandescent light bulb in 1878 that created light twenty-four hours a day. Next, he created phonographs as dictation machines. Then he wanted to develop "an instrument which does for the eye what the phonograph does for the ear."

He demonstrated a Kinetoscope in 1888. It was a cylinder wrapped with photographs in a spiral pattern and viewed through a peephole by one person at a time. By 1889, he used celluloid film cut into strips fed across the viewing point in punched sprocket holes. It was coin-operated for people to view 20-second films through a viewer at the top of the box and listen to synchronized sound with a stethoscope-like device in their ears. Kinetoscope parlors were opened in New York in 1894. Thus, the beginning of movies with exciting motion of people on film included sound, but early filmmakers chose to produce less expensive movies without sound.

Edison conducted a public demonstration of his Kinetoscope in Paris in 1895 that inspired Antoine and Louis Lumière to invent the first commercially viable projector. Edison encouraged them to create something that more than one person could view at a time. Their first movie in 1895 was called *English Workers Leaving the Lumière Factory*.

Two other French brothers, George and Gaston Méliès, wanted to buy a Lumière projector but Antoine refused them. With the help of others, George and Gaston made a movie called *A Trip to the Moon*. The 10-minute hand-colored silent film had six old costumed astronomers handed telescopes by young people. George played the instructor describing the trip on a chalk board.

The astronomers entered a bullet-shaped capsule and were shot by a cannon to the moon. The spaceship hit the eye of the moon man's comical face as he winced. Upon landing, they saw giant mushrooms and acrobats from the Folies Bergère somersaulting about in skeleton-styled costumes. There were stars with faces of smiling girls. They returned to earth bringing back one moon character. This was the first film with a real story.

Movie history is heard in the lyrics of early charming troubadours. Perhaps the biggest song hit of 1902 was "Under the Bamboo Tree" by three black men--Bob Cole and brothers James Weldon Johnson and John Rosamond Johnson. It was sung by Judy Garland and Margaret O'Brien in the 1944 movie *Meet Me in St. Louis*.

Those Haitian brothers had professional musical training in the U.S. and London. They went on to be involved in a few movies, and James Weldon Johnson helped start the National Association for the Advancement of Colored People (NAACP). President Theodore Roosevelt named him ambassador of Venezuela and Nicaragua from 1906 to 1913. He composed "God's Trombones," about the creation of the world, in a long song best captured by the Fred Waring chorus available on the Internet. He wrote "The Autobiography of an Ex-Colored Man" about a black who passed and interacted as an equal with whites. James Weldon Johnson wrote the poem and John Rosamond Johnson wrote the lyrics and tune of the original black anthem "Lift Ev'ry Voice and Sing."

In 1910, black Cecil Mack and Lew Brown wrote "That's Why They Call Me 'Shine'," which is sometimes simply called "Shine." The song is based on a real man who was beaten to death in a race riot of 1900. The movie *Casablanca* won the Academy Award for best picture of 1942 and Sam (Dooley Wilson) played "Shine" along with other songs in the nightclub. Mack and Brown tried to show how calling people bad names affected them.

Verse: When I was born they christened me plain Samuel Johnson Brown,
I hadn't grown so very big 'fore some folks in the town

Had changed it 'round to Sambo, I was Rastus to a few,
Then Choc'late Drop was added by some others that I knew,
And then to cap the climax I was strolling down the line
When someone shouted, "Fellers, hey, come on and pipe the Shine."

Refrain:
'Cause my hair is curly, 'Cause my teeth are pearly,
Just because I always wear a smile, Like to dress up in the latest style,
'Cause I'm glad I'm living. Take troubles smiling, never whine;
Just because my color's shady, Slightly diff'rent maybe,
That's why they call me "Shine."

Verse: A rose, they say, by any other name would smell as sweet,
So if that's right, why should a nickname take me off my feet?
Why, evr'ything that's precious from a gold piece to a dime
And diamonds, pearls, and rubies ain't no good unless they shine.
So when these clever people call me "shine" or "coon" or "smoke,"
I simply smile, and smile some more, and vote them all a joke.
I'm thinking just the same, what is there in a name?

Jewish Max Steiner did the score for *Casablanca* and belonged to a people who experienced being put down. He was inspired when the movie showed black Dooley Wilson and Humphrey Bogart as equals. "Let's go fishin'," said Sam to the Bogart character, something that showed their equal relationship with each other. Steiner took a chance and inserted the "Shine" song. However, actress Ingrid Bergman's character referred to Sam as "boy"—demeaning for a grown man, but a rather common practice by Americans describing Negroes in the 1940s.

About 1913, Charlie Chaplin's antics were in a Mack Sennet one-reel slapstick Keystone Comedy. *Chicago Record-Herald* writer Arthur Brisbane saw it and wrote: "Motion pictures are just a passing fancy and aren't worth comment in this newspaper." Irving Berlin took them seriously and wrote "At the Picture Show" with E. Ray Goetz. Here are some lines:

> Hurry up, hurry up, buy your ticket now,
> Hurry up; hurry up, better come somehow;
> Ev'rybody's going: all tiptoeing to the picture show.
> Come and see the villain gay, steal the hero's girl away
> Or ponies racing, just see them chasing,
> At the picture show, owned by Marcus Loew.

The following year, movie-goers were exposed to serials. *The Perils of Pauline* ran in little segments stopping in the midst of danger to the heroine, which would be resolved in the next episode. Sometimes colors were added to the screen to make things more exciting and the next song refers to the color green. These serials kept audiences coming back to theaters to see how their star would handle close calls. This song, entitled "The Perils of Pauline" explained the ruse:

> I'm worried as can be, all the movie shows I see
> Have that awful mystery, 'Pauline and her perils.'
> On a rope they dangle her, then they choke and strangle her,
> With an axe, they may mangle her, always something new.
> To make you shake they give her Paris green.

In 1915, a silent movie called *The Birth of a Nation* was released by D. W. Griffith studio. It was based on the book *The Clansman* by Thomas Dixon, Jr. The clan was Ku Klux Klan (KKK). The 3-hour movie claimed to describe the origin of this nation. Despite inaccuracies, it was a roaring success. Dixon studied law with future president Woodrow Wilson at Johns Hopkins, and went on to become a fiery Baptist minister, lecturer, and novelist.

Griffith decided to have no black blood among the principal actors but some blacks were used as extras and housed in segregated quarters. This epic silent movie broke new ground for telling a fascinating story with huge casts and extras. Among those were Lillian Gish, Walter Huston, Donald Crisp, Wallace Reid, Monte Blue, Eugene Pallette, Jack Pickford (brother of Mary Pickford), John Ford, Raoul Walsh, Erich von Stroheim and Elmo Lincoln who became the first actor to portray Tarzan.

The movie was shown at the White House on February 18, 1915. This quotation from Dixon's book appeared on the screen during *The Birth of Nation:* "At last there had sprung into existence a great Ku Klux Klan, a veritable empire of the South, to protect the Southern country." The movie showed letters and titles and ran with music for those theaters that had sound equipment. In other theaters, cue sheets were given to a pianist or orchestras about what to play and when.

The KKK spawned many songs, such as "That's Why I'm a Klansman, Hooray," but also a spoof. College students Helen Marcell and Peggy Hedges in Ottawa, Kansas, penned "Daddy Swiped Our Last Clean Sheet and Joined the Ku Klux Klan." One song from *The Birth of a Nation* was a love song created for the romance between white actors Lillian Gish and Henry B. Walthall. It was entitled "The Perfect Song," the first theme song from a movie, and was used as the theme song for radio and TV sitcom *Amos 'n' Andy*. Incredibly, a song from a movie about the need to get rid of blacks by the KKK was the theme for a comedy show about blacks.

Suddenly, movies became the place where people experienced parts of life they might never enjoy in person. Viewers saw the seven deadly sins (wrath, greed, sloth, gluttony, pride, envy, and lust) without sinning.

They could learn the virtues (patience, charity, diligence, temperance, humility, gratitude, and chastity) by watching heroes and heroines conquer vices. They could visit foreign places, see wealth and poverty, feel humor and mockery, enjoy music and dance, and vicariously feel a variety of emotions. They could copy dress and hair styles, behavior, and sayings of stars as they wished. They could see the lives of famous and infamous people, and experience fright and fancy whenever they wanted.

What about the fantasies of young girls who went to movies? Mary Pickford played cute naïve girls. Theda Bara played a vamp who seduced the guys. Handsome Charlie Chaplin usually played a funny tramp. Billie Burke was a beauty married to Broadway producer Florence Ziegfeld, and starred on stage, in movies, and on radio. Francis X. Bushman, called "the handsomest man in the world," starred in and directed movies. By 1919, soldiers were coming back from France and World War I. The new date for couples was seeing movies.

The Four Horsemen of the Apocalypse was a movie with Rudolph Valentino that caused ladies to swoon as he sensually danced the tango and snapped a whip. He became an overnight idol in movies like *The Sheik*. From such movies came songs like 1921 "The Sheik of Araby" with lyrics by Harry Smith and Francis Wheeler and music by Ted Snyder. What female could resist the vicarious experience of leaving her dishes behind to join a sheik in a tent for a tango?

> I'm the Sheik of Araby. your love belongs to me.
> At night when you're asleep, into your tent I'll creep,
> The stars that shine above, will light our way to love,
> You'll rule this land with me, the Sheik of Araby.

That song led to another of the same year which made fun of a girl's wish to find a sheik. "Rebecca Came Back from Mecca" by Bert Kalmar and Harry Ruby was a big hit.

Since Rebecca got back from Mecca,
All day long she keeps on smoking Turkish tobecca.
With her veil upon her face, she keeps dancing 'round the place
And yesterday her father found her with a Turkish towel around
her.
Oh! Oh! Ev'ryone's worried so, they think she's crazy in the dome,
She's as bold as Theda Bara, Theda's bare but Becky's barer,
Since Rebecca came back home.

In 1922, Bessie Smith (depicted in a recent movie by Queen Latifa) belted out "Tain't Nobody's Bizness If I Do" and other songs of defiance and misery for blacks.

If I go to church on Sunday then just shimmy down on Monday,
Tain't nobody's bizness if I do do do-do.
I swear I won't call no copper if I'm beat up by my poppa.

CHAPTER TWO

The Role of Texas in Movie Production

Many early film makers were drawn to San Antonio for its history and climate since outdoor light was needed. One early movie maker was Gaston Méliès, brother of French filmmaker George Méliès. They leased 20 acres, a 2-story house, and barn that became the Star Film Ranch. In 1911, Gaston made about seventy 10-minute or less silent movies and then it closed.

The best was *The Immortal Alamo*. The actors were Edith Storey, handsome Francis Ford (older brother of future actor and director John Ford), and William Clifford. George Méliès often played a part. The *Alamo* movie didn't include the 1836 battle but used the old Alamo and 100 cadets from nearby Peacock Military Academy. (Future film director, producer, and screenwriter King Vidor was born in Galveston, Texas, and attended the Peacock Military Academy from age 6 and was 17 when *The Immortal Alamo* was made. Earlier at age six, he had seen the Galveston Hurricane of 1900 and would later direct the cyclone scene for *The Wizard of Oz* using his recollections. See *A Tree Is a Tree* by King Vidor published in 1953.) Meanwhile, the *Alamo* movie used the formula of a pretty girl, shy hero, and a villain. No copies exist but still pictures from that early film can be seen on the Internet.

Gaston moved to California as did actors like Francis Ford (who changed his name from Feeney to Ford because of the auto) and took younger brother John under his wing. Gaston, with family and friends, went to make movies in Asia and sold his half of the studios. He settled in Corsica in 1913 but did not make any more movies.

George and Gaston Méliès influenced many, such as Edison employee, Edwin S. Porter. He was hired by Edison in 1900 to work with film equipment and became a director. He realized that by cutting and pasting scenes, a vigorous story line created excitement. Porter produced *The Great Train Robbery* in 1903. He knew Americans wanted down to earth excitement with heroes like police and firemen rescuing those in danger. Filmmakers learned more when William Pinkerton addressed the International Chiefs of Police in 1904 describing his detective agency.

Porter was fired by Edison in 1909. However, Porter influenced D. W. Griffith who produced *The Birth of a Nation* to notice those exciting stories from what Pinterton had described. Griffith then did his long movie with more suspenseful scenes.

Screen credits for crafts led to rivalry and improved standards for each craft area. That led to more attention for directors. After talkies, they could make or break a picture through filming, story selection, elaborate sets, their emphasis, and music. Cecil B. DeMille did epics, Walt Disney did animation, and whites who produced movies rarely hired blacks.

Director King Vidor produced *The Big Parade,* a silent film released in 1925 that depicted the experiences of enlisted men in World War I. (It was an antiwar film that influenced the making of *All Quiet on the Western Front.)* The movie was filmed in Texas depicting trench warfare and featured John Gilbert and Renée Adorée. The story by Laurence Stallings was about a rich boy (Gilbert) who did not want to go to war but his friends persuaded him to enlist. He fell for the same girl (Adorée) as two other guys. During the war, his buddies were killed and he was shot just as he shot the German who came to finish him off. He wounded the German and the two were face to face. He could not shoot him and gave him a cigarette. Soon the German died and Gilbert was taken to a hospital. The 151-minute film was produced by Vidor and Irving Thalberg. It was the biggest hit since *The Birth of a Nation* and would remain so until *Gone with the Wind*. Music was provided by William Axt when it was re-issued in 1931 with a sound-track.

In 1927, *The Rough Riders* movie was made about the attack on the Spanish who attempted to take over Cuba but were defeated at San Juan Hill. The movie was filmed around San Antonio because that unit was significant to the Spanish American War. The Paramount movie was produced by Adolph Zukor and directed by Victor Fleming. Paramount held a big party at the St. Anthony Hotel in San Antonio at the beginning of filming. Stars included Noah Beery, Charles Farrell and Mary Astor. The battle to repel the Spanish was led by Col. Leonard Wood and Teddy Roosevelt so the movie ended with Mary Astor and family attending the inauguration of Theodore Roosevelt as president.

King Vidor produced the 1929 movie *Hallelujah*. He had always wanted an all-black movie so he used East Texas cotton fields as the setting to film a movie about Memphis. He wrote a script with the help of three black people and starred Daniel L. Haynes, Nina Mae McKinney, and William Fontaine. It was his first sound film and he used the following music: "Sometimes I Feel Like a Motherless Child," "Go Down Moses (Let My People Go)," "Old Folks at Home," "Swanee River," "Bridal Chorus," Irving Berlin's "Waiting at the End of the Road," Berlin's "Swanee Shuffle," "Swing Low, Sweet Chariot," "Get on Board Little Children," "Gimme Dat Old Time Religion," W. C. Handy's "St. Louis Woman," and "Goin' Home" from Antonin Dvorak's *Symphony #9*.

Vidor's father's sawmill in East Texas had given him the chance to see blacks singing, working, and playing together. He portrayed them as simple, promiscuous, lazy, and superstitious. While this was not as bad as their portrayal in *The Birth of a Nation,* it showed some prejudices of the day. Blacks who attended had to sit in the balcony. Few whites attended. Among the cast shown in a church, two actors known later appeared: Clarence Muse and Madam Sul-Te-Wan. The movie was banned south of the Mason-Dixon Line in most places. The actress who played a harlot was a stunning beauty nicknamed the "black Garbo." Vidor lost money on the endeavor but it demonstrated that the white public was not ready for movies about blacks.

The first movie to win an Academy Award was *Wings*, filmed at Kelly Field in San Antonio, later a U.S. Air Force Base. The 1927 film was made by William Wellman starring Clara Bow, Richard Arlen, Buddy Rogers, and Gary Cooper.

Alfred Nathaniel Sack (1896-1969) and brother Lester M. Sack from Mississippi established a theatre chain and production company for African Americans who could find little help elsewhere to make movies. They began in San Antonio where the Army and Air Force provided locations for movies such as *The Big Parade* (1925), *The Rough Riders* (1927), *Wings* (1927), etc. Alfred moved on to Dallas and worked with two of the most prominent black movie makers—Oscar Micheaux and Spencer Williams.

Spencer Williams (1893-1969) began as a stagehand for Oscar Hammerstein. He watched vaudeville black star Bert Williams before beginning college. He went to Hollywood in 1923 and appeared in 1928 *Steamboat Bill, Jr.*, 1929 *The Melancholy Dame*, and 1931 *The Public Enemy*.

Williams was hired to cast African-Americans for Gloria Swanson's *Queen Kelly* in 1928, but many of his scenes with blacks have been lost. Swanson fired director Erich von Stroheim, whose intensity prolonged scenes and increased production costs. Her lover, Joseph Kennedy, Sr., father of President John Kennedy, had financed the movie. When she found his money was only a loan, she stopped production before finishing the movie. It was about a convent girl abducted by a prince and sent to live in a brothel in Africa. Williams had located blacks, such as actress Madame Sul-Te-Wan (Nellie Wan) who loved to wear turbans and braids, and was the first black actress to land a Hollywood studio contract.

Spencer Williams produced a Sack musical called *Harlem on the Prairie* in 1937. It featured musicians such as Earl "Fatha" Hines, whom Count Basie called the "greatest piano player in the world." This first "all-colored" western musical cost less than $50,000 and was a big hit with black audiences.

Later, Williams was hired for the *Amos 'n' Andy* TV show. White players told him to say "dis here" and "dat dere" which would gain more laughs. He argued that he knew better how blacks talked. When the NAACP objected to negative black portrayals, the program ceased.

Oscar Micheaux made forty-four feature films between 1919 and 1948. He used some help from Alfred Sack and their first big hit was with a story by black director Dudley Murphy. Murphy and Sack put together one of the earliest talkies and the only recording of Bessie Smith, *Queen of the Blues*. The 1929 movie *St. Louis Blues* used the Fletcher Henderson band, and was arranged by Rosamond Johnson. Bessie belted out "St. Louis Blues," and the 26-minute movie ended when Bessie found another woman in the arms of her man.

As she sang the sorrowful W. C. Handy melody, people in the club joined in singing and waiters twirled trays. The man who played her boyfriend was an excellent fast tap-dancer in one scene. The song had a little chorus from George Gershwin's "Rhapsody in Blue." Women with skimpy clothing had hair under their arms, much as Sophia Loren did in her early Italian movies. But these films are a credit to Bessie, W. C. Handy, the Johnson brothers, Mr. Sack and Mr. Murphy. Also, the actress who beat up Bessie was Isabel Washington, the first Mrs. Adam Clayton Powell Jr. He was the first African American elected to Congress from New York.

Oscar Micheaux (1884-1951) was the grandson of a Kentucky slave and was eventually called "The Czar of Black Hollywood." He wrote about the social oppression he experienced when young. Early on, he worked as a Pullman porter and met whites who helped him buy land in South Dakota. He wrote articles and submitted them to newspapers like *The Chicago Defender.* Then, he concentrated on writing and film-making.

His stories were criticized by the Virginia Board of Censors because they portrayed black people as they lived instead of portraying them as just maids, butlers, and criminals. He moved to Chicago and produced a feature film in 1919 called *The Homesteader,* which was advertised as an all-star Negro cast shown at movie theaters for blacks. He wrote the book about a young black man who fell for a bi-racial girl, thus marriage was against the law. He married another girl, but later left her and returned to the original girl he loved.

In 1920, Micheaux produced *Within Our Gates, The Brute,* and *The Symbol of the Unconquered.* The first was an all-colored cast in a movie about a bi-racial woman who loved a black doctor. With revival of the KKK, the movie included the lynching of an innocent black man and was therefore censored. *The Brute* was an all-colored cast silent movie in which a black boxer defeated a white, but the censors removed that scene. The third movie involved a black man who discovered that his land was on an oil field. Whites tried to expel him from his property.

In 1921, *The Gunsaulus Mystery* was about the real murder of a black girl and the trial of a black janitor. The discovery of a white man who committed the crime led to exoneration of the black janitor, but the public kidnapped and lynched the black janitor so the sad tale was worth telling.

Micheaux did four silent movies in 1922 and three have been found. *Birthright* (1924) was the story of a young mulatto man written by

Pulitzer Prize winner T. S. Stribling. The young man completed a Harvard education and returned to improve racial problems in his town. The story was a social critique of the South and segregation. (See *Oscar Micheaux: The Great and Only* by Patrick McGilligan published in 2007.)

A Son of Satan (1924) is a lost film but featured musicians like Noble Sissle and Eubie Blake who had starred in the Broadway show *Shufflin' Along.* The movie was censored because of the title word "satan," the killing of a KKK leader, and miscegenation. The Board called it "blurring of racial lines in public spaces such as dance halls." Fines had to be paid whenever censored movies were shown.

Micheaux produced *Body and Soul,* a silent all-black cast movie starring Paul Robeson. Paul played two roles—an escaped prisoner who posed as a corrupt minister and his good brother, an inventor. The minister tried to swindle the congregation and the good twin fell in love with a girl. Violence ended when the girl awoke from a dream. Paul was a famous actor, singer, athlete, lawyer and social activist. The movie was selected in 2019 by the Library of Congress for preservation for being "culturally, historically, or aesthetically significant."

In 1926, Micheaux used a novel from Charles W. Chestnutt, a lawyer who became an essayist for the NAACP. Still other silent films were *The Devil's Disciple* (1926) and *The Spider's Web* (1926). The latter film had a Cuban racketeer portrayed by Juano Hernandez who starred in *The Pawnbroker* and *They Call Me Mr. Tibbs*! In the U.S., all minorities found it hard to find roles.

Meanwhile, Alfred Sack produced a 1930 movie called *Deep South* written by Jester Hairston, a Tufts and Juilliard graduate who conducted and sang with bands. The movie starred Willie Best (black musician), Clarence Muse (lawyer, choral conductor and first African American to star in a film), and Hattie McDaniel (daughter of a slave, band vocalist, radio actress, and first African American to win an Academy Award).

When snubbed by black actors for playing maids, she said, "I'd rather play a maid than be one."

Dudley Murphy and Alfred Sack produced *The Sport Parade* in 1932, starring Joel McCrea, William Gargan, and humorist Robert Benchley. That pre-code picture included a wet towel being snapped at nude McCrea by Gargan where football players were showering.

Murphy and Sack's next movie was *The Emperor Jones* (1933), a story by Eugene O'Neill about a black porter who became a boxer. He accidentally killed a man, was jailed, escaped, and went to the Caribbean where he became an emperor. The word "nigger" was used many times. (Later, Paul Robeson played the part.) The music of Rosamond Johnson helped the movie.

Sack hired Irwin and Hazel Frankly to write and produce the 1938 *Policy Man*, featuring Count Basie and his band, and Arthur White's Lindy Hoppers (named for aviator Charles Lindbergh). There was a bit of a mystery but the main draw was the band.

In 1940, Oscar Micheaux, Alfred Sack, and black aviator Hubert Julian produced *The Notorious Elinor Lee* starring Robert Earl Jones (1910-2006), father of actor James Earl Jones. The movie also had Oscar Polk who played Pork in the 1939 *Gone with the Wind* movie. Juano Hernandez, Puerto Rican star of *Intruder in the Dust* (1949) also starred. The movie was about a boxer whose corrupt promoter bet against him, but a lady ruined the plan and the boxer won.

Singing cowboy movie star Gene Autry arranged a deal between Alfred Sack's executive producer Richard C. Kahn for Herbert Jeffrey to be a singing black cowboy as the main star in some black cowboy movies. Sack's movies were sometimes called Merit Pictures.

Spencer Williams and Sack produced two films: *Harlem Rides the Range* (1939) and *Son of Ingagi* (1940). They were among many found in 1983 in a Tyler, Texas, warehouse, apparently used to collect celluloids. (See G. William Jones *Black Cinema Treasures Lost and Found* published in 1991.) Findings included black movies made from 1935 to 1956. They are now held by Southern Methodist University and are available for viewing online. There were six short films, nine feature length films, and newsreels. One is the next movie described here.

The Blood of Jesus was written and produced by Spencer Williams for Sack Amusement Enterprises. Williams played a small role in the movie, but the sound included familiar gospels throughout to add poignancy. The story was about a wife hoping her husband would come pray with her. He didn't and accidentally dropped his rifle. It shot her and she lay dying. She dreamt about the gates of heaven opening and angels talking to her. Then her prayers to a crucifix of Jesus on the wall dropped blood on her face and she arose. The movie was made for about $5,000.

Alfred Sack married Mildred Hoddy in 1941. She had a sister, Jean Hoddy, who had some interest in the black movies Alfred was financing. One 1944 movie opened: "Alfred N. Sack reverently presents *Go Down Death* inspired by a poem of James Weldon Johnson." Jean Hoddy took that poem and created a story line. That 1927 poem was a funeral sermon beginning:

> Weep not, weep not, she is not dead; She's resting in the bosom
> of Jesus. Heart-broken husband—weep no more; Grief-stricken
> son—weep no more; Left-lonesome daughter--weep no more;
> She only just gone home.

Alfred Sack helped Williams do the third movie in a trilogy that began with *The Blood of Jesus,* but the middle film has been lost. This movie was filmed in Dallas and San Antonio, Texas, but was banned in Maryland, New York and Ohio because of a scene with a woman's bare breast.

The first black actress to win an Academy Award was Hattie McDaniel for *Gone with the Wind* (1939) who won best actress in a supporting role for playing a maid. Sidney Poitier was the first black nominee for best actor in *The Defiant Ones* (1958), and the first winner for best actor in *Lilies of the Field* (1963). Dorothy Dandridge was the first black nominee for best actress in *Carmen Jones* (1954) and Halle Berry was the first black best actress winner in *Monster's Ball* (2001). The first black nominated for best actor in a supporting role was Rupert Crosse for *The Reivers* (1969) and the first black winner was Louis Gossett, Jr. in *An Officer and a Gentleman* (1982).

A black has not won best director but John Singleton was nominated for *Boyz n the Hood* (1991). The first blacks nominated for best original song were Quincy Jones and Bob Russell for "The Eyes of Love" in *Banning* (1967). The first black to win for best original song was Isaac Hayes for the "Theme from Shaft" in *Shaft* (1972). The first black nominated for best writing was Quincy Jones for *The Color Purple* (1985). The first black to win for best writing was British film-maker Sir Steven McQueen for *12 Years a Slave* (2013).

Back to Alfred Sack, he had difficulty paying his crew at the theater and producing movies. A *Boxoffice* magazine for movie producers ran an article on May 21, 1948, page 89, entitled: *Alfred Sack Faces Charge of Wage Hour Violations.* Judge T. W. Davidson's federal court put Sack on a 2-year probation. Sack's attorney asked for a probation extension until details about failure to pay overtime records could be checked. Black movies were gradually getting less patronage so Sack had to decide whether to stop producing them or showing them to black audiences or both.

Clever 50-year-old Alfred Sack invented a successful plan so he could pay his debts and remain viable. He developed the only Dallas theatre showing foreign and revival movies, using sub-titles when necessary. He took over the old Gay Theatre owned by I. Gay, which had opened in 1942. He renamed it Coronet Theatre located at 2420 N. Fitzhugh in Dallas. It opened December 18, 1948, with members of the Dallas Symphony Orchestra on hand. There was a new sound system, opera seats, special murals, an art-deco look, and five hundred seats that were insufficient for the number who wanted to attend the *Barber of Seville* and *Lucretia Borgia.*

Alfred and Lester Sack also bought the Lucas Theater at 4519 Maple Street in Dallas, which they renamed the Encore. They hired Judy Garland's mother, Ethel Gumm Garland, (Mrs. Gumm had adopted her daughter's stage name) to manage it around 1949. Audiences didn't come so the theater closed in 1951 and they let Ethel go.

Alfred and Mildred Sack had a daughter, Sarah Lee, who was born blind. They worked hard with lawyers to change Texas laws, which did not permit blind persons to attend schools. Mildred mediated with agencies so Sarah Lee could attend a public school in Dallas. They established the Dallas School for the Blind but Sarah never saw her dad's movies. This project took much money and Coronet Theatre attendees, such as this author, donated to the new school for the blind. Mildred Sack worked through the National Council of Jewish Women in Texas to lobby legislature to help blind people. Their Dallas School for the Blind opened in 1949 for their daughter, Sarah Lee, and the many other children with visual difficulties.

People met Al Sack in the early 1950s by attending his theaters. Patrons often saw the short man of five feet or so who welcomed all, often giving passes for films. He knew regular attendees on a first-name basis. His wife only came during special celebrations but they were both seen on holy days at Temple Emmanuel in Dallas. Alfred's wife died at age 44 in 1961, due to a long heart ailment. After Alfred Sack died in 1969, others ran the theatre until it was razed in 1999.

In Dallas during the 1950s, there was constant news about Baruch Lumet and his acting school. Baruch was born in 1898 in Warsaw,

Poland, and graduated from the Warsaw Academy of Dramatic and Musical Arts in 1918. He made his acting debut there and appeared in London 1920-21 and Maurice Schwartz's Yiddish Art Theater in New York City (1926-31).

Lumet appeared in these films: *One Third of a Nation* (1939), *The Interns* (19562) and *Adventures of a Young Man* (1962). He was in TV shows, including two *Alfred Hitchcock Presents* in 1961.His son, Sidney, grew up with some appearances on stage in Dallas. Baruch involved Sidney in one movie starring the two of them-- *One Third of a Nation*. That play and movie was under the Federal Theater Project. The title came from President Franklin Roosevelt's 1937 speech saying "I see one-third of a nation ill-housed, ill-clad, ill-nourished." The movie was about a New York City tenement fire and Sidney Lumet, nearly 15 years old, played the role of a boy hurt by the tenement fire, acting as the brother of film star Sylvia Sidney.

Baruch Lumet was the director of the Dallas Institute of Performing Arts and the Knox Street Theater in Dallas, Texas, (1953-1960). He advertised that he trained Jayne Mansfield, Rip Torn, and Sidney Lumet. On December 3, 1950, Gloria Vanderbilt accompanied husband Leopold Stokowski to Dallas when he was invited by Dallas Symphony Orchestra conductor Walter Hendl to be guest conductor. Gloria would next marry Sidney Lumet in 1956 for seven years.

Jayne Mansfield was born Vera Jayne Palmer. Her father died, and her mother married Harry L. Peers, and they moved to Dallas. There she was known as Vera Jayne Peers. At 17, she married Paul Mansfield and they attended Southern Methodist University to study acting in 1950. They moved to Austin, Texas, to study dramatics at the University of Texas. She became friends with actors Rip Torn and Pat Hingle at the University of Texas.

Back in Dallas in 1952, Jayne worked with Baruch Lumet as did Rip Torn. She starred in Baruch Lumet's Knox Street Theatre on

October 22, 1953, when they presented Arthur Miller's *Death of a Salesman*. Baruch called Rip and Jayne his "kids." He helped Jayne get her first screen test at Paramount in April 1954. She had small roles but when Hugh Hefner's *Playboy* featured her in February 1955, her career took off. She died in a terrible car accident in 1967 but daughter, Mariska Hargitay, was a long-time television star in *Law and Order: Special Victims Unit.*

CHAPTER THREE

Why Were Academy Awards Developed?

Louis B. Mayer was the chief at Metro-Goldwyn-Mayer. The Russian émigré had reached the big-time and wanted his wife and two daughters to have a new beach house. He decided to save money by having his own employees build it quickly, just as they did for movie sets. He discussed designs with Cedric Gibbons, the head of design at MGM.

Gibbons drew up plans, and worked out a schedule to have it built in only six weeks. The plan required three shifts of laborers per day working around the clock. However, MGM was about to sign an agreement with the International Alliance of Theatrical Stage Employees for wage and hour laws. So, production manager Joe Cohn suggested using just a few skilled people and hiring outside cheaper labor for the house to be ready in the spring of 1926.

This news worried Mr. Mayer because if laborers signed on with a union, perhaps his other employees would as well. What if actors, directors, and writers developed a union and wanted more pay, health benefits, pensions, and a cut of the profits through residuals?

Also, more movie stars were creating bad press by scandals, including murder, infidelity, drug use, and bad behavior. Charlie Chaplin, who had sex with an underage girl, tried to help her get an abortion. When that failed, he married her but they were soon divorced with her complaints of his sexual proclivities. Comedian Roscoe "Fatty" Arbuckle had sex with an actress at a party in 1921 and she died of a ruptured bladder. He was charged with manslaughter but was exonerated after a third trial. Young actress Peg Entwistle played minor roles in movies and committed suicide in 1932 by jumping from the huge H on the Hollywood sign above the city.

Mr. Mayer first signed a Studio Basic Agreement on November 29, 1926, with the labor unions. However, many friends and actors worried about the impact of these scandals on the movie-going public for the young cinema industry.

On January 1, 1927, Mayer met with the head of the Association of Motion Picture Producers (Fred Beetson), actor Conrad Nagel, and MGM director Fred Niblo. They decided to discuss a "mutually beneficial" industry organization. By May of 1927, they opened the non-profit Academy of Motion Picture Arts and Sciences, abbreviated AMPAS. They offered membership and decided to award prizes. Their goal was to discourage development of a union and convince the public that Hollywood was a wonderful place where people were doing quality work.

The group was composed of people invited on the basis of recommendations and achievements. There were members-at-large and members who worked in specific branches. AMPAS has expanded now to some 25-plus technical and creative categories. All members pay dues.

The idea of prizes caused Cedric Gibbons to sketch something on the tablecloth that looked like a man holding a sword to his feet, using it to pin down reels of film. He would later ask actor Emilio Fernandez to be the model of what would finally be called "Oscar." Mr. Fernandez can be seen playing bad guy General Mapache in director Sam Peckinpah's western *The Wild Bunch*.

The Academy Awards presentations have improved public relations for the movie industry. Now, there are health plans, pensions, and residuals for AMPAS members. (See the Barry Monush article: *The*

Lure of Oscar: A Look at the Mightiest of All Award Shows, the Academy Awards published in The Paley Center for Media.)

At the first ceremony, sound had barely arrived in movies. Warner Brothers had been near bankruptcy when they decided to bring musical stage star Al Jolson onto the screen in *The Jazz Singer.* He agreed because that movie was almost his life story as the son of a Jewish synagogue cantor. In one scene, he played the piano, telling his mother how great he was now. He went off script saying, "Wait a minute, you ain't heard nothin' yet, folks." It was a hit, and so was his stage persona in black-face singing soul-wrenching songs. Whites singing or acting in black-face became taboo later.

Sam Warner died before the movie opened, so brother Jack began to develop "talkies." When movies had sound, theater pianists were not needed. Piano composer Hoagy Carmichael's mother played piano for silent movies, and they all used cue sheets showing pianists a song or a type of music to play as silent movie dialogue cards lit up. Dialogue lines disappeared on screen when talking pictures began being shown.

Machinery was installed in theaters to coordinate action with sounds. Some voices were not good, such as John Gilbert's, whose squeaky voice ended his career. The movie *Singing in the Rain* cleverly depicted those days when sound came to movies and some acting careers ended.

The Academy decided it was not fair to let talkies compete with silent films. So, the first awards allowed only silent movies to compete. Two tied for first place. *Wings,* directed by William Wellman, was the most expensive movie of the two highest nominees for Best Picture. *Wings* was called the "best picture production" and *Sunrise,* was called the "best picture, unique and artistic production."

Emil Jannings, the German actor who won best actor for *The Last Command* and *The Way of All Flesh,* realized that his accent would be too thick for American talkie movies. Thus, he returned to Germany to make movies and was not present at the first award ceremony. However, Janet Gaynor won best actress for three movies—*7th Heaven, Street Angel,* and *Sunrise.*

Wings director, "Wild" Bill Wellman, and *Sunrise* director, F. W. Murnau, were not winners for best director. Those honors were awarded to Frank Bozage, director of *7th Heaven* (a drama) and Lewis Milestone, director of *Two Arabian Knights* (a comedy).

Charlie Chaplin was originally a nominee for best actor, best writer, and best comedy director for *The Circus.* His scandalous behavior had been bad for Hollywood, so he received just a special honorary award. He received one final honorary award in 1971.

The first award ceremony took place on May 16, 1929, at the Blossom Room of the Roosevelt Hotel in Hollywood California. AMPAS' first president and host of the ceremony was actor Douglas Fairbanks, Sr. The winners had been decided by votes three months earlier so the statuette presentations took only a few minutes for the 250 attendees who paid $10 each. Fairbanks and Al Jolson handed out the trophies in about five minutes.

The process of peaceful transition of power from one actor, director, or producer to another was difficult for many. Competition between entertainment professionals existed but transitions continued so that one winner did not continue to win year after year. Some future actors disliked the competition between cohorts and said so in Academy Award ceremonies, as will be seen.

Originally, the 230 members chose ten worthy entries for twelve different categories, then asked members from their five branches (actors, producers, directors, writers, and technicians) to cut the list down to three recommendations. Those three were given to a central board of judges of five members (one from each branch) who made the final selections of winners. The ceremony was heard only on a local Los Angeles radio station.

The goals of the Academy of Motion Picture Arts and Sciences have broadened through the years. They now list seven purposes as follows:

- Advance the arts and sciences of motion pictures
- Foster cooperation among creative leaders for culture, educational, and technological progress
- Recognize outstanding achievements
- Cooperate on technical research and improvement of methods and equipment
- Provide a common forum and meeting ground for various branches and crafts
- Represent the viewpoint of actual creators of the motion picture, and
- Foster education activities between the professional community and the public at large

AMPAS represents more than 6,000 technical and artistic members of the motion picture industry and supports diverse educational and promotional activities.

The Academy Awards always take place in the following year after the film's release. This book will mention the tagline or poster description of the best picture, story line, winning actors and actresses, which later included best supporting actors and actresses, winning directors, best song, and description of best foreign film. United States as well as British winning films are included. Notable events at the ceremonies are mentioned at the beginning of each presentation year.

1st Academy Awards

Ceremony: Historic events at the first Academy Awards were two winners for best picture, only best movie winners of the silent era, the first male kiss in movies, the first nude scene in movies, the best actor and actress winners having been nominated for more than one movie, tie for winning movie director, and the absence of best actor winner who returned to Germany assuming his accent was unacceptable in talking movies. The ceremony was conducted at the Roosevelt Hotel in Hollywood on May 16, 1929, and took only five minutes. It was broadcast on a Los Angeles radio station. Musical scoring and songs would soon be added to awards.

1928 *Wings*

Tagline: "An epic of the air." Why did *Wings* win one of the first two Academy Awards for best picture? This thrilling silent movie was made a few months after Charles Lindbergh created excitement by flying solo from the U.S. to France. He had only to overcome sleepiness for the 33.5-hour flight, maintain attention, evacuate waste products, and had nobody to talk to. The pilots in *Wings* were also fighting enemies in addition to Lindbergh's problems.

Wings was directed by French Foreign Legion pilot "Wild" Bill Wellman, wounded from combat in World War I. He walked with a limp, but knew how to direct pilot dogfights and war scenes. Wellman helped audiences by showing clouds as pilots flew so viewers got more sense of speed and adventure. It ran originally for more than two hours but was trimmed to just under that for release.

Wings was filmed at Monthans Air Force Base in Tucson, Arizona; Kelly Field in San Antonio, and Corpus Christi, Texas, where extras were hired from the Texas National Guard. The budget was $2 million but box office well exceeded costs. Three hundred pilots were involved, and 3,500 infantrymen were brought in for battlefield shots. One stunt pilot broke his neck and an Army pilot was killed during filming. Wellman's demand for reality cost more than most movies, but he turned out a very profitable blockbuster which ran for years.

Richard Arlen had been a pilot in the Canadian Flying Corps. Charles "Buddy" Rogers never flew so a real pilot sat behind him and did hand movements. Gary Cooper's part was two minutes. He was dating Clara Bow, the "It Girl" who had a nudity scene in the movie. She required Gary to be in the movie if she was to participate. The card for silent movies showed Cooper's dialogue as he faced doom. He said, "Got to go out and do a flock of figure eights before chow." As Arlen and Rogers cautioned him, he said, "Luck or no luck, when your time comes, you're going to get it." And he did.

Arlen and Rogers played buddies who both fell for Clara Bow, but treasured their relationship. Director Wellman understood that uniformed services pilots, firemen, and policemen count on each other to survive, and nobody wants to die alone. As Arlen was dying, he told Rogers not to leave. Rogers reached over and kissed him near his mouth—the first male kiss in movies. Arlen apologized for getting shot by saying, "I wanted to get one more Heinie for you."

The music was to be composed in eight weeks but reduced to four for an early opening. John Zamecnik described his process in a September 1, 1927, interview for the music magazine *The Metronome*. He went into the projection room in the morning and held a watch to the episodes and made notes for timing the action and music to fit the situation. He did not have time to do an original score, so used known tunes. He went back in the afternoons to time his pieces. Then the orchestra rehearsed until it was ready. He was a Czech and studied in Prague under Dr. Antonin Dvorak. He was chief violinist for Victor Herbert in America.

This style of composing required knowing all kinds of music and was copied by film composers up to the present time. For Allied aviator flight tunes, Zamecnik used Mendelssohn's "Midsummer's Night Dream Opus 21," which captured the exhilaration of flying. He created dance-like themes using "Little Brown Jug" for the Clara Bow character. John Philip Sousa marches were used for military scenes and the German National Anthem when the German pilots appeared. For Americans he used the "Star Spangled Banner." A Civil War song, "Marching Through Georgia," and "Over There" by George Cohan were used for victories. Café scenes had "Darktown Strutters' Ball," "I'm Forever Blowing Bubbles," and "Can Can." When French troops advanced to the front, "La Marseillaise" was played. Franz Liszt's "Les Preludes" helped the brutal war scenes and Giuseppe Verdi's "Sicilian Vespers" was heard as the hero took on German foes. "My Buddy" by Walter Donaldson and Gus Kahn brought home the sad ending with words like: "Nights are long since you went away. I think about you all through the day. My buddy, my buddy, no buddy quite so true."

1928 *Sunrise: A Song of Two Humans*

Tagline: "A song of two humans." Why did this movie also win best movie for unique and artistic picture? German director F. W. Murnau was known in his country for artistic and moody movies, including *Nosferatu* and other unusual productions. *Sunrise* was a universal story of what happens when a pretty girl tries to steal a husband away from his family. In one scene, the seductress put her arms around the man in a ghostly presence. The seductress, played by Margaret Livingston, urged the man to drown his wife, played by Janet Gaynor. The man realized in the boat that he couldn't do it. The movie dwelt poetically upon the couple finding love again.

Moody music and expressive faces often did not require dialogue. But here's a comment from the shady lady: "Do you truly love me? Sell your farm and come with me to the city!"

Austro-Hungarian Hugo Riesenfeld and Hungarian Erno Rapee did the music and sound for *Sunrise*. They used Charles Gounod's 1872 "Funeral March of a Marionette" and Frederic Chopin's "A Minor Prelude." Riesenfeld did music for earlier movies like 1920 *Dr. Jekyll and Mr. Hyde* and *The Mask of Zorro*, 1922 *Blood and Sand*, 1924 *The Thief of Baghdad;* and 1927 *The General.* Rapee was the Radio City Music Hall director and did cue sheets for silent movies, such as 1923 *King of Kings,* and 1927 *What Price Glory* and *7th Heaven.*

A cue sheet was needed by a pianist, organist, or band playing for silent movies. Here is an example of a cue sheet by Rapee for 1926 movie *What Price Glory* starring Victor McLaglen and Delores del Rio. Each line of the cue sheet had music to be played--some music composed by Rapee or from cited sources. Here is the first page of that movie cue sheet:

1 At screening—March Theme: Semper Fidelis March (Sousa) ....45 sec.

Musical notes to be played

2 (Action) Marching troops halt....25 sec.

Musical notes to be played

3 (Title) Sergeant Quirt. Marine Hymn....15 sec.

Musical notes to be played

4 (Action) Man being tattooed. Captain Theme: Down by the Winegar Woiks (Donovan) 25 sec.

Musical notes to be played

Many believe that *Sunrise* was not only one of the best movies ever made but the best silent film ever created, and it ranks highly among all movies ever made. Young Janet Gaynor's expressions of joy and George O'Brien's face and body wracked with guilt and pain pull upon the emotions of viewers. O'Brien, whose favorite director was John Ford, would be seen in later movies with John Wayne in the 1950s.

In many descriptions of Gaynor, despite her marriages and a child, she was said to have been bisexual with two partners—one of whom was her co-star in this movie, Margaret Livingston, and the other was actress and singer Mary Martin. In fact, Gaynor and her husband, movie gown designer Adrian, moved to Brazil and lived near Mary Martin and Richard Halliday. Adrian designed costumes for *The Wizard of Oz* including Judy Garland's red shoes. Adrian and Gaynor may have had a lavender (sham) marriage as did Mary Martin and Richard Halliday. Lavender marriages were not unusual in Hollywood.

Sunrise was made in Coronado and Big Bear Lake, California. It cost $200,000 but box office well exceeded budget.

Other nominees for best picture included *The Racket* and *7th Heaven*.

Emil Jannings (1884-1950) from Rorschach, Switzerland, won Best Actor for *The Last Command* and *The Way of All Flesh*. The other contender was Richard Barthelmess *(The Noose)* and *(The Patent Leather Kid)*.

Janet Gaynor (1906-1984) from Philadelphia won Best Actress for *7th Heaven, Street Angel,* and *Sunrise: A Song of Two Humans*. Other contenders were Louise Dressler *(A Ship Comes In)* and Gloria Swanson *(Sadie Thompson)*.

Frank Bozage, Director of *7th Heaven* for drama and **Lewis Milestone, Director** of *Two Arabian Knights* for comedy, thus both won Awards as Best Director.

2nd Academy Awards

Ceremony: The Ambassador Hotel in Los Angeles was the site of this ceremony hosted by epic movie producer Cecille B. DeMille. The one-hour ceremony was broadcast on a local radio station. Winners were not announced in advance so there was an aura of suspense. No film won more than one award. This year attracted attention because its Best Picture winner brought sound, singing, dancing, music, and technicolor into theaters, but copies do not remain of the beautiful colors in the original production. It also was notable for the first death of a nominee for Best Actress—Jeanne Eagels for *The Letter.*

Mary Pickford, co-founding member of the Academy of Motion Picture Arts and Sciences, and wife of its first president, Douglas Fairbanks, was told she was being considered for Best Actress. She invited judges for tea at her home hoping to influence them. Other contenders were not informed that they were under consideration. She won. This practice was soon forbidden.

1929 *The Broadway Melody*

Tagline: "Talking, singing, dancing." Some movie theaters were not yet equipped for sound so a silent version of the movie was available. But this color and talkie movie brought out audiences big-time. This best movie award was laid at the feet of young producer Irving Thalberg.

An important new song by Nacio Herb Brown and Arthur Freed was "You Were Meant for Me." The story was about a couple of girls going to Broadway, hoping to find fame. The movie opened with "Give My Regards to Broadway" by George M. Cohan. One other familiar song by Brown and Freed was the "Wedding of the Painted Doll." These songs were repeated in later musicals made about early movies.

The name of one character was Zanfield, a take-off on Ziegfeld, the most popular Broadway musical producer of that era. This movie was edited by Sam S. Zimbalist, a Russian Jewish violinist married to opera diva Alma Gluck. Their son was TV actor Efrem Zimbalist *(FBI* and *77 Sunset Strip* series). Another character named Jock Warriner was a parody on Jack Warner of Warner Brothers. In-jokes like these made the movie seem very up-to-date.

The movie included no well-known actors but had a female dancer doing tap dancing en pointe, which is extremely difficult. The ladies, in this movie before code, were a bit buxom without bras. Typical dialogue included the following lines about the Mahoney sisters—the main act:

Stage Manager: "You were great, Mahoney!"

Chorus girl: "I'll say you were! You'll be riding in a Rolls Royce by Thursday."

Stage Manager: "What a flock of Johns will be waiting at that Stage door."

Queenie Mahoney: "Go on, you can't kid me!"

Stage Manager: "I'm not kidding you. I may be there myself."

Hank Mahoney: "Well, we aren't leavin' this town 'til we get a flash of Babe Ruth and Grant's Tomb."

One more line was: "Those men aren't going to pay ten bucks to look at your face; this is Broadway!"

This first sound musical production was made before they learned how to record sound so some scenes had to be reshot. The quality of acting and singing was poor, probably because producers expected the audiences to be so thrilled by sound, dancing, and color that it would succeed. It did draw people in but is now very unpopular with viewers who complain about this and that.

The movie was shot for $379,000, using little in the way of Hollywood sets except stages. It grossed several times the budget. Its success led to sequels: *The Broadway Melody of 1936, The Broadway Melody of 1938, The Broadway Melody of 1940,* and *Two Girls on Broadway* made in 1940. Eleanor Powell was a star and dancer in most of those movies.

Other movie nominees included *Alibi, Hollywood Revue, In Old Arizona,* and *The Patriot.* Of these, *In Old Arizona* came from an odd O'Henry story and introduced a sympathetic outlaw called the Cisco Kid. It was followed by numerous entertaining Cisco Kid productions on radio, in comics, on television later, and a movie.

Warner Baxter (1891-1951) from Columbus, Ohio, won Best Actor for *In Old Arizona.* Other contenders were George Bancroft *(Thunderbolt),* Chester Morris *(Alibi),* Paul Muni *(The Valiant),* and Lewis Stone *(The Patriot).* Baxter starred in many movies and by 1936 was the highest-paid actor in Hollywood. His house was at 686 Nimes Road in the Bel Air neighborhood of Los Angeles. Jack Ryan, inventor of the talking Barbie Doll, purchased the property in late 1962 and turned the house into the greatest glittering pad in Bel-Air, which co-author Edgar Van Cott visited. He saw Warner's "secret room." The house was demolished in 1985, but Baxter's house started a trend to build a hideout room with a door concealed as a wall panel as seen in *Young Frankenstein.*

Mary Pickford (1883-1979) from Toronto, Canada, won Best Actress for *Coquette.* Other contenders were Ruth Chatterton *(Madame X),* Jeanne Eagels *(The Letter)* who had died of an overdose by the time of the award ceremony, Corinne Griffith *(The Divine Lady),* and Bessie Love *(The Broadway Melody).*

Frank Lloyd, Director of *The Divine Lady.*

3rd Academy Awards

Ceremony: The ceremony was broadcast over the radio during its hour-long length. The host was actor Conrad Nagel, president of AMPAS that year. He was one of the original founders of the awards along with Mary Pickford, Douglas Fairbanks, Richard Barthelmess, Jack Holt, Milton Sills, and Harold Lloyd. Nagel began in silent movies in 1918 and continued into sound movies until 1953. This was the first Best Movie to have both director and producer win Oscars.

1930 *All Quiet on the Western Front*

Tagline: "The greatest war picture ever made." Erich Maria Remarque's *All Quiet on the Western Front* was a 1929 best seller and movie rights were quickly bought for $40,000 by Carl Laemmle, president of Universal Studios and a Jewish émigré from Germany. Director Lewis Milestone's emphasis on the chaos and confusion on the battlefield was copied by Steven Spielberg in his 1998 movie *Saving Private Ryan*. This was the story of German school boys whose teacher persuaded them to join the Army for the glory of service to the Fatherland.

This was among the first movies that Georg Gyssling, sent to Hollywood by Nazi leaders, edited to remove things that would prevent film sales in Germany. Louis B. Mayer and producer Joseph Mankiewicz were ordered to eliminate three scenes. Mankiewicz refused the German consul's request that Nazi villains be Communist villains. Production code leader Joseph Breen seemed to go along with Gyssling's recommendations. (See *The Brothers Mankiewicz* by Sydney

Ladensohn Stern published in 2019 and *Hitler in Los Angeles* by Steven J. Ross published in 2017.)

This is one of the most important movies ever made and drew attention across the world. The author changed his German name Remark to his French side Remarque and sought asylum in Switzerland. The story was taken from his time in the German military during World War I and involved a German soldier with his six friends. It opened in a classroom where a professor was trying to get young men to go to war. On the board was a Greek saying from Homer's *Odyssey:* "Tell me, oh muse, of that ingenious hero who traveled far and wide." The young men signed up.

After basic training, the battleground and activities were chaotic and deafening. There was a lack of food, sudden deaths, amputations, and the realization that war was hell. There was little humor, one attempt to share food and companionship with French girls, and utter confusion. Actor Lew Ayres stabbed a Frenchman and the two stayed in a foxhole as the man died over several hours. Ayres gave him water, comforted him, and begged the dead body to forgive him. The actor who played the Frenchman was Raymond Griffith who could speak only a whisper due to childhood diphtheria. It was a powerful scene remembered by many moviegoers all their lives. That foxhole scene was reminiscent of the old adage, "There are no atheists in the foxholes."

The German returned to his community during recovery. He went to his school to tell what he'd seen but was considered a coward. The boy returned to battle and was killed. The final scene was his hand reaching for a butterfly, acted by director Milestone since the cast had already gone.

Some of the dialogue showed the horror of war. "Me and the Kaiser, we are both fighting, with the only difference the Kaiser isn't here." "At the next war, let all the Kaisers, presidents, generals, and diplomats go into a big field and fight it out amongst themselves. That will satisfy us and keep us at home." "You still think it's beautiful to die for country, it's better not to die at all. War is dirty. It is death." In one scene reminding viewers of The Last Supper, the Germans shared a meal of blood-soaked bread and cognac.

The film was not anti-German due to Nazi Gyssling's cuts. Its depiction of Germans still did not suit Hitler's propagandist, Joseph Goebbels, who chose to attack its Berlin premiere on December 4, 1930. Brownshirts set off stink bombs, threw sneezing powder into the audience, and sent white mice running through the theater. Nazis yelled out "Judenfilm" (Jewish film). People who looked Jewish were beaten inside and outside the theater. Nazis made owning Remarque's book a crime and destroyed thousands of volumes, raiding bookstores and homes.

At the movie's release in New York in April, 1930, a *Variety* reviewer wrote" "The League of Nations could make no better investment than to buy up the master-print, reproduce it in every language, to be show in all nations until the word 'war' is taken out of dictionaries." Thus, this movie was probably chosen because it had delivered a powerful anti-war message, perhaps the strongest ever presented in a movie. The producers chose to have no music and used only screams, the roar of artillery, mud sloshing, and natural sound effects.

The movie was filmed in various California sites, such as Irvine Ranch near Santa Ana and Balboa. The budget was $1.25 million, but it grossed much more. It ran about 2.5 hours. The Army did not cooperate in the filming. Remarque, who gave his middle name Paul to his main character, lived an interesting life involved with actresses Marlene Dietrich and Hedy Lamarr. However, he was haunted because his sister was beheaded when the German judge said she would suffer because Remarque could not be arrested.

Because of this movie, main actor Lew Ayres became a conscientious objector. He served in World War II for 3.5 years in the Medical Corps and received three battle stars.

Other movie nominees included *The Big House, The Divorcee,* and *The Love Parade.*

George Arliss (1868-1946) from London, England, won Best Actor for *Disraeli.* Other contenders were himself for *The Green Goddess,* Wallace Beery *(The Big House),* Ronald Colman *(Bulldog Drummond* and *Condemned),* Maurice Chevalier *(The Big Pond* and *The Love Parade)* and Lawrence Tibbett *(The Rogue Song).*

Norma Shearer (1900-1983) from Montreal, Canada, won Best Actress for *The Divorcee.* Other contenders were Nancy Carroll *(The Devil's Holiday),* Ruth Chatterton *(Sarah and Son),* Greta Garbo *(Anna Christie* and *Romance),* Norma Shearer *(Their Own Desire),* and Gloria Swanson *(The Trespasser).*

Lewis Milestone, Director of *All Quiet on the Western Front.*

Carl Laemmle, Producer of *All Quiet on the Western Front.*

4th Academy Awards

Ceremony: This ceremony was conducted on November 10, 1931, at the Biltmore Hotel in Los Angeles, hosted by 61-year-old British actor Lawrence Grant. These awards were for films released from August 1, 1930 through July 31, 1931. Nine-year old Jackie Cooper, nominated Best Actor in *Skippy*, fell asleep on the shoulder of Best Actress nominee Marie Dressler. When she was announced as winner, he was eased onto his mother's lap. He was the first child star to receive a nomination.

1931 *Cimarron*

Tagline: "Terrific as all creation!" After the earlier important movies winning for Best Picture, this movie was of lesser importance. It was a winner because it cost so much to make and the story was by famous author Edna Ferber. She was a Jewish American feminist who cared about land, Indians, and about portraying strong women and their abilities. The land rush scenes used thousands of extras, one of whom was the grandson of Indian leader Cochise. Two Oklahoma land rushes in 1889 led to settlers, cattlemen, and white people entering Indian land so the state nickname was Sooners. From Ferber's standpoint, she felt that landscape dictated behavior and people were responsive to it. The land made all the difference at the end of the movie.

The movie depicted settlers riding fast to put in a stake with a white flag and pick up a certificate back at the starting place. The marriage of Richard Dix (Yancey) and Irene Dunne (Sabra) was not exactly a love story because it showed the wandering adventurous nature of men and stoic womanhood that led to good child-rearing. The wanderer, who started a newspaper seeking fame, left it to his wife to run and to raise their children for years at a time. Sabra had the aid of others, including a peddler, Sol Levy, who despite portrayal as a stereotypical Jew became a trusted friend. Other racial themes included a black boy (Eugene Jackson) on a beam fanning people at a dinner table until he fell off onto a cake for a joke. He earlier played Pineapple in the *Our Gang* comedies and was the comic in this movie until he died trying to save Cravat children.

The Dix character, Yancey Cravat, was based on the son of Sam Houston, named Temple Houston. The Cravat son was named Cimarron, which meant wild and unruly. Cim displeased his mother when he married an Indian. She first disliked Indians even though Yancey accepted them, but she finally came to love Cim's wife. The relations between two races (Indian and white) involved miscegenation, which Ferber wrote about in *Showboat* between black and white lovers. For those who occupied this Osage town, the surprise was that oil was found on land retained by the Indians, which whites had declined since it wasn't fertile enough for agriculture.

Maximilian Raoul Steiner from Vienna, Austria, was hired to do music for the beginning and the ending of this movie. His father, Gabor, was in charge of the carnival and Ferris wheel shown in *The Third Man*. Max was trained by Johannes Brahms and Gustav Mahler and his godfather was Richard Strauss. Family friends included Johann Strauss, Jr. and Jacques Offenbach.

His scoring for the title was twice as long as the usual scoring for a title. First there was a fierce Indian tune in a minor key suggesting a western theme. Next came gallops preparing the audience for the land rush scenes. Then when the pictures of the actors dressed for their character were given five seconds each, the music shifted to a quiet march. Later at a dance, a somber waltz theme suggested the longings in Sabra's mind for her absent husband. A triumphant march played as a statue was unveiled of her husband. In the book, the husband is a hero at the end when he absorbs an explosion to save the lives of oil drillers. However, in the movie, he died in the arms of his wife after saving lives.

Unfortunately, the Dunne character who ran the newspaper and raised her children displayed racism apparent to movie viewers. Had the Joseph Breen code been in effect by that time, she would have been gentler with different races. Other problems for the later code might have been the saloon paintings of women with few clothes, and Yancey's defense of a prostitute. Sabra tried to make Indians accept her white values. Such ideas were changed in the 1961 remake.

Dialogue was not that special. For example: "Sugar, if we all took root and squatted, there would never be any new country." "They will always talk about Yancey. He's gonna be part of the history of the great southwest."

Westerns rarely win best picture and the next after this was *Dances with Wolves*. Edna Ferber was paid $125,000 for movie rights. It was shot around Los Angeles and the budget was $1.433 million. It lost $565,000 in box office sales. Richard Dix, an excellent actor in silent movies, overacted in some scenes. Irene Dunne may have underacted. The 131-minute movie served a purpose as it depicted the beliefs of people at the time. But it has not done well as time passed. It has the lowest rating of all best pictures according to IMDB's rating system.

Other movie nominees included *East Lynne, The Front Page, Skippy,* and *Trader Horn.*

Lionel Barrymore (1878-1954) from Philadelphia won Best Actor for *A Free Soul.* Other contenders were Jackie Cooper *(Skippy)*, Richard Dix *(Cimarron)*, Fredric March *(The Royal Family of Broadway)*, and Adolphe Menjou *(The Front Page)*.

Marie Dressler (1869-1934) from Coburg, Canada, won Best Actress for *Min and Bill.* Other contenders were Marlene Dietrich *(Morocco)*, Irene Dunne *(Cimarron)*, Ann Harding *(Holiday)*, and Norma Shearer *(A Free Soul)*.

Norman Taurog, Director of *Skippy.*

5th Academy Awards

Ceremony: This event was conducted on November 11, 1932, at the Ambassador Hotel, hosted again by Conrad Nagel. It included films screened in Los Angeles between August 1, 1931, and July 31, 1932. Walt Disney created a short animation film for the banquet called *Parade of the Award Nominees*. This year introduced short films as a new category with *Flowers and Trees* being the first color and short animation winner by Walt Disney. This year, there was a tie for Best Actor. Both Wallace Beery and Fredric March won the award.

1932 *Grand Hotel*

Tagline: "Imagine them all in one picture!" Irving Thalberg's idea of the first all-star Hollywood epic with many stars of the early 1930s was a hit. It fostered other movies, such as *Airport* (1970), *The Poseidon Adventure* (1972), *The Towering Inferno* (1974) and *Ocean's Eleven* (2001), among others. It was the first time two Barrymores (Lionel and John) played together and paved the way for a movie the next year, when they were joined by sister Ethel.

This movie followed the lives of five people for two days in a luxurious hotel in Berlin. MGM bought the rights from German author Vicki Baum, former chambermaid in two Berlin hotels, for $35,000. Her title was *People at the Hotel*. MGM hired William Drake to adapt it.

The preview screening in Monterrey, California, produced such positive reviews for new starlet Joan Crawford that producer Irving Thalberg worried she would upstage Garbo, who was being paid the most. Thus, he tried to balance their roles accordingly. Garbo was, after all, speaking with a thick Swedish accent while playing a Russian ballerina. Joan was easier to understand.

Grand Hotel flew by in less than two hours. Unusual photography allowed the hotel check-in desk to be viewed from every angle since it was the center of action for guests and hotel employees, while Strauss' "Blue Danube" was heard in the background. Many hotel guests sailed on the Danube River from the Black Sea through Vienna and south of Berlin into Munich.

This was a strange concoction of the introverted and claustrophobic Garbo, the extroverted whiskey-breathed John Barrymore, Joan Crawford determined not to be overlooked, and the egotistical old Wallace Beery, whom nobody liked. But audiences loved it. It was an omen to World War II since the facially-scarred hotel doctor, played by Lewis Stone, was injured in World War I by a grenade. His line at the beginning and end of the movie was oblivious to the dramas of the five main characters. He said "Grand Hotel. People coming, going. Nothing ever happens."

The Great Depression depicted in the movie left many with sagging futures and one terminally ill accountant played by Lionel Barrymore. He had come to live it up for a few days before death. A man down on his luck, played by John Barrymore, became a hotel thief. He met Greta Garbo while stealing her jewels. He heard her talking about suicide because her dancing career was dying away with smaller audiences. Even though she said "I want to be alone" more than once, he said: "That isn't true. You don't want to be alone."

Wallace Beery played a corrupt businessman trying to do a merger. He hired a stenographer, played by Joan Crawford in an eye-catching role as an aspiring starlet. Interactions between all the principals ended unhappily except for Jean Hersholt. He played a hotel porter whose wife finally delivered their child.

William Axt and Charles Maxwell supplied the music from other composers for the most part. "On the Beautiful Blue Danube" Opus 314, by Johann Strauss in 1867 played during the opening scene in the lobby and at the end. Strauss' 1862 song "Morning Papers," Opus 279, was heard as the morning opened.

The Garbo character rushed to the theater with "Tales from the Vienna Woods," Opus 325 by Johann Strauss. Strauss' "Artist's Life" was often played in the background. Sergei Rachmaninoff's "Second Piano Concerto in C minor" showed the Garbo character with great rapture as a has-been ballerina. She sang a bit in German (which was dubbed) from Edward Grieg's 1864 "Ich Libe Dich" which means "I love you." "Vienna, City of My Dreams" by Rudolf Sieczynski, played when John Barrymore wished to love Garbo, lamenting her declining popularity. The familiar "Love's Dream After the Ball" by Alfonse Czibulka played after Beery and Barrymore argued at the ball.

Near the end, "The King's Horses" by Noel Gay symbolically played when dying Lionel Barrymore was in his room where all the king's horses and all the king's men couldn't put Humpty Dumpty back together again. Musicians have such subtle touches in movies.

MGM used sets in Culver City, California, for the hotel and despite the big names, the movie was made for $700,000. It grossed more than twice that amount.

This movie was copied in MGM's *Dinner at Eight* (1933), *Wonder Bar* (1934), *Week-end at the Waldorf* (1945), *The Grand Budapest Hotel* (2014), *At the Grand* (1958 in Europe), and *Grand Hotel: The Musical* on Broadway (1989).

Other movie nominees included *Arrowsmith, Bad Girl, The Champ, Five Star Final, One Hour with You, Shanghai Express,* and *The Smiling Lieutenant*. Again, producer Irving Thalberg's extravaganza won Best Picture.

Wallace Beery (1885-1949) from Kansas City, Missouri, won Best Actor for *The Champ*.

Fredrick March (1897-1975) from Racine, Wisconsin, won Best Actor for *Dr. Jekyll and Mr. Hyde*.

Helen Hayes (1900-1993) from Washington, D.C. won Best Actress for *The Sin of Madelon Claudet*. Other contenders were Marie Dressler *(Emma)* and Lynne Fontanne *(The Guardsman)*.

Frank Borzage, Director of *Bad Girl*.

6th Academy Awards

Ceremony: The Awards were presented at the Ambassador Hotel on March 16, 1934. The films eligible were released from August 1, 1932, until December 31, 1933. That was the last time the eligibility period was spread over two calendar years until the 93rd Academy Awards due to the COVID-19 pandemic and necessary social distancing.

Host Will Rogers, Oklahoma humorist and movie star, goofed when announcing winners. The Best Director category had two directors in contention named Frank. When Rogers announced the winner, he said "Come up and get it, Frank!" Frank Capra, director of *Lady for a Day,* got up and walked toward the stage. However, the actual winner was Frank Lloyd who directed *Cavalcade.* To handle his mistake, Rogers invited the third nominee for best director, George Cukor to join the two Franks on stage. Poor Rogers died the following year in a plane crash.

Walt Disney became the first person to win consecutive Academy Awards, winning best short subject/cartoon for *The Three Little Pigs* after having won that award for *Flowers and Trees* the previous year.

This year began regular national radio broadcasts of the awards until they became a television broadcast in 1953.

1933 *Cavalcade*

Tagline: "The picture of the generation!" *Cavalcade* is a 1933 movie based on a 1931 play of the same name by Noel Coward. The story followed aristocratic London residents and their servants beginning in 1899 through 1933. They went through various historic events, such as the Boer War, the death of Queen Victoria, the sinking of the *Titanic,* and World War I. It has mostly an English cast headed by Diana Wynyard and Clive Brook. A young 16-year-old Betty Grable is the "Blonde on the Couch" in the 1930s, and the little girl who plays a servant's daughter is Bonita Granville. Despite all the eras covered in the thirty-four years, the black and white movie ran only 112 minutes.

A special treat was the songs from various eras, including four by Noel Coward, but none of his were big hits from this movie. A few favorite oldies were "Auld Lang Syne;" "A Bird in a Gilded Cage;" "The Blue Danube;" "Nearer My God to Thee;" "It's a Long Way to Tipperary;" "Pack Up Your Troubles in your Old Kit Bag and Smile, Smile, Smile;" "Oh, You Beautiful Doll;" "Mademoiselle from Armentieres;" "Hinky Dinky Parley Voo;" "When Johnny Comes Marching Home;" and "Over There."

Various family tragedies and historic changes took place, which now seem very dated. It was the first movie which took out bad words from Coward's play, such as "damn," "hell," and "hell of a lot," which were not thought to offend anyone during the Hays Office era. Much of the dialogue was good but not memorable. For example: "There should never be any good reason for neglecting someone that you love."

Often Coward's short novels worked much better. David Lean directed the 1945 Coward story *Brief Encounter* starring Trevor Howard, a married doctor who fell in love with a married woman. With Rachmaninoff's "Second Piano Concerto" playing in the background, this brilliant simple love story is good every time it is seen through the years. The affair, hidden from each spouse, suggested Coward's difficult life as a closeted homosexual.

The winning movie was about England and their people but was filmed in Los Angeles. However, Fox newsreel camera men went to London to record some of the original stage production to guide its adaptation.

Frank Lloyd won an Oscar for Best Director and William Darling won for Best Art Direction.

Noel Coward was paid $100,000 for the rights to the play and songs he wrote. The budget was $1.180 million. It was an instant success and more than offset expenses. It was not the sort of movie with deep emotions or cohesion and generated no sequels, but was often rated enjoyable to see and worth viewing once.

Other movie nominees include *42nd Street, A Farewell to Arms, I Am a Fugitive from a Chain Gang, Lady for a Day, Little Women, The Private Life of Henry VIII, She Done Him Wrong, Smilin' Through,* and *State Fair.* Of those movies, *42nd Street* was about putting on a musical drama and Busby Berkeley's camera was like a choreographer arranging dancers.

Charles Laughton (1899-1962) from Scarborough, England, won Best Actor for *The Private Life of Henry VIII.* Other contenders were Leslie Howard *(Berkeley Square)* and Paul Muni *(I Am a Fugitive from a Chain Gang).*

Katharine Hepburn (1907-2003) from Hartford, Connecticut, won Best Actress for *Morning Glory.* Other contenders were May Robson *(Lady for a Day),* and Diana Wynyard *(Cavalcade).*

Frank Lloyd, Director of *Cavalcade.*

7th Academy Awards

Ceremony: The awards were presented on February 27, 1935, at the Biltmore Hotel in Los Angeles, hosted by Kentuckian Irvin S. Cobb, a humorist, columnist, and author of many books made into silent movies.

This was the year that introduced a new category: Best Song written specifically for the movie. The winner was "The Continental." The title was the name of a new dance done to the music. Fred Astaire and Ginger Rogers, stars of *The Gay Divorcee,* danced to this song for seventeen minutes. The lyrics were by Herb Magidson and music by Con Conrad.

Max Steiner was in charge of providing Astaire with musicians. Once the piano score of the dance was approved, Steiner assigned it to an orchestrator. Music costs doubled as the long dance scene required many takes. That dance scene made the movie extraordinary. Steiner worked night and day and his parents were being evicted in Austria due to the Nazis. That worry and the need to send them money put pressure on him. He threatened to quit over conditions keeping him up until 3:30 a.m., but everything calmed down. (See *Music by Max Steiner,* by Steven C. Smith, Oxford University Press, 2020.)

Two other songs in the competition were "Carioca" from the movie *Flying Down to Rio,* and "Love in Bloom" from *She Loves Me Not* (which became comedian Jack Benny's theme song).

In addition, this was one of two years where write-in candidates were allowed. More new categories included Best Film Editing, Best Original Score, and the first Juvenile Award, won by six-year-old Shirley Temple.

1934 *It Happened One Night*

Tagline: "Together for the first time." *It Happened One Night,* a pre-code romantic comedy, was brimming with cute lines. Producer and Director Frank Capra worked with Harry Cohn and they turned out a script that didn't read well but sprang to life on the screen.

The story was a bit complicated because an heiress, Ellie, played by actress Claudette Colbert, planned to marry to get away from her father. But when daddy learned the man was a fortune hunter, he wanted to prevent the marriage. Angrily, the heiress ran away to find her would-be husband, but had little travel money. She ran into a reporter named Peter, played by Clark Gable, who wanted to do a story on the heiress, her journey, and get a reward her father offered.

Sometimes, studios got mad at stars who rejected roles or had affairs that got bad press. Thus, Clark Gable was sent to a minor studio, Columbia Pictures, as a punishment by MGM. He earned $2,500 per week for this four-week film. Sometimes punishments turn out well.

The movie's dialogue and the acting made this film special. When Colbert and Gable spent a night in a motel, he hung a blanket on a wire to divide the room and called it the "walls of Jericho." Ellie said: "That, I suppose, makes everything quite all right?" Peter said: "Oh this? Well, I like privacy when I retire. Yes, I'm very delicate in that respect. Prying eyes annoy me. Behold the walls of Jericho. Uh, maybe not as thick as the ones that Joshua blew down with his trumpet, but a lot safer."

Later, the reporter tried to thumb a ride on a road but had no luck after bragging of former successful thumbing. Ellie said, "Oh, you're such a smart aleck! Nobody knows anything but you. I'll stop a car and I won't use my thumb." She pulled her skirt above her knee. The next car screeched to a halt. "Well, I proved once and for all that the limb is mightier than the thumb."

Upon arriving home, the heiress thought the reporter only wanted a story and a big reward from getting her home. Her father asked how she felt about him. She said, "I don't know very much about him, except that I love him." The movie had a happy ending which the audience enjoyed.

The delightful story was by reporter Samuel Hopkins Adams. He later wrote the story for *The Harvey Girls,* which brought out Judy Garland's talents. Adams had a reputation of muckraking when he exposed patent medicines and medical frauds. His book *Night Bus* (later called *It Happened One Night*) surprised everyone, including himself.

Gable got the role when Robert Montgomery and Fredric March turned it down. Casting the heiress was difficult. Miriam Hopkins, Loretta Young, and Myrna Loy rejected the role. Constance Bennett wanted it if she could produce the film but Columbia Pictures did not agree. Bette Davis wanted the part but Warner Brothers refused to lend her. Carole Lombard was interested but it was being filmed at the same time her *Bolero* work was going on at Paramount.

Gable was reluctant to do the picture and arrived to talk with Capra while drunk, angry, and rude. When he began work the first day, he said something like, "Let's get this over with." Colbert was not happy with the role and disliked Capra after a bad movie experience with him. She and Gable disliked the script. Furthermore, she thought raising her skirt for an automobile driver was unladylike, but after seeing a double do it, said she would do it with her own leg.

She wanted to do the movie in four weeks because of a planned vacation to Sun Valley, Idaho. The studio doubled her pay from $25,000 to $50,000 for the month. With no time to build sets, real places were used along roads. Because of the production code against unmarried couples sharing a hotel room, the scene with a blanket arose. It took so much time for Gable to take off his shirt and undershirt to prepare for bed, they left off the undershirt and sales for those garments plummeted. Because they traveled across the country by bus, bus travel increased wildly.

The scene of passengers singing "The Daring Young Man on the Flying Trapeze" was intended to be strummed by two hillbillies. During practice, the extras kept joining in and finally Gable did, too. Capra left it in for a delightful scene.

It wasn't expensive to film at Thousand Oaks, California, and cost $325,000, but raked in several times that amount. The film only did medium business initially, until word-of-mouth spun its magic. Soon, everybody wanted to see it. At a time when few had money, actors riding buses, staying in a motel, a man with no undershirt, and a couple hoofing it on the road were just right.

Nominated for Best Actress, Colbert left the set describing it as the worst picture she ever made. She assumed Bette Davis would win. Not intending to stay for the Academy Awards, Harry Cohn learned she was about to get the award. He sent someone to get her off the train to Idaho, and she had on a simple two-piece suit when she received the award. To the end of her 92 years, she was shocked at its continued popularity and reputation as a classic masterpiece.

There was little music. Clark Gable sang "Who's Afraid of the Big Bad Wolf," "The Flying Trapeze" was sung by all bus passengers, and Richard Wagner's Bridal Chorus "Here Comes the Bride" from *Lohengrin* ended the movie. The music was done by composer Howard Jackson and Louis Silvers, the latter having done the music for 1927 *The Jazz Singer* starring Al Jolson, Warner Oland, and Myrna Loy. He was later in charge of the Lux Radio Theater weekly show.

This movie set a new record when it won an Oscar for Best Picture, Best Director (Capra), Best Actor (Gable), Best Actress (Colbert), and Best Writing Adaptation by Robert Riskin—called the Big Five. It only happened twice more with *One Flew Over the Cuckoo's Nest* in 1975 and *The Silence of the Lambs* in 1991.

The movie inspired *Eve Knew Her Apples* (1945), *You Can't Run Away from It* (1956), seven Indian films from 1956 to 2007, the hitchhiking scene in the 1937 Laurel and Hardy *Way Out West*, Mel Brooks 1987 *Spaceballs*, and 2001 *Bandits*.

Other movie nominees included *The Barretts of Wimpole Street, Cleopatra, Flirtation Walk, The Gay Divorcee, Here Comes the Navy, The House of Rothschild, Imitation of Life, One Night of Love, Viva Villa! The White Parade,* and *The Thin Man*. The last was Dashiell Hammett's introduction of romantic mystery with an alcoholic couple and their dog Asta. That movie generated eight movies based on the William Powell and Myrna Loy delightful dialogue.

Clark Gable (1901-1960) from Cadiz, Ohio, won Best Actor for *It Happened One Night*. Other contenders were Frank Morgan *(The Affairs of Cellini)* and William Powell *(The Thin Man)*.

Claudette Colbert (1905-1996) from Paris, France, won Best Actress for *It Happened One Night*. Other contenders were Grace Moore *(One Night of Love)*, Norma Shearer *(The Barretts of Wimpole Street)*, and Bette Davis *(Of Human Bondage)*.

Frank Capra, Director of *It Happened One Night*.

8th Academy Awards

Ceremony: The big event was conducted March 5, 1936, at the Biltmore Hotel in Los Angeles hosted by Frank Capra. This was the first year that gold statuettes, later called Oscars, were given out. A new category of Best Dance Direction was added. It was the last year for write-in votes. The best movie is historic because three cast members ran against each other for Best Actor. Clark Gable, Franchot Tone, and Charles Laughton were nominated, but none of them won.

1935 *Mutiny on the Bounty*

Tagline: "A thousand hours of hell for one moment of love!" This film was about the real mutiny aboard a ship called *Bounty* led by mid-shipman Fletcher Christian against Captain William Bligh. The captain's dastardly behavior toward his men caused most of the crew to revolt. His ship was taken over by Christian's followers and Bligh was sent off with a small crew, expected to sink. However, stalwart Bligh's boat made it to land and the British Royal Navy court-martialed the mutineers. Meanwhile, some mutineers lived on love in the Pitcairn Isle paradise with Polynesian natives.

Director Frank Lloyd expected trouble with his major stars. Gable and Tone were rivals for young actress Joan Crawford but after a quarrel, they decided they both liked women and alcohol and had fun together. Macho Gable was expected to dislike gay Charles Laughton. However, Laughton brought a burly companion as his masseuse, and they avoided confrontations with Gable. The main complaint Gable voiced with Laughton was that he avoided Gable's eyes when speaking his lines. Only later did they learn that the man felt he was fat, bad looking, and expected to be instantly repulsed by anyone who looked him in the face.

Gable's dialogue showed reasons for mutiny: "I've never known a better seaman, but as a man, he's a snake. He doesn't punish for discipline. He likes to see men crawl." Bligh's dialogue showed lack of respect and care for his men: "What's your name?" "Thomas Ellison, sir. Pressed into service. I've got a wife, a baby!" Bligh: "I asked your name, not the history of your misfortunes." Bligh said, "Discipline is the thing." Later, Bligh told Christian: "You're sending me to my doom, eh? Well, you're wrong Christian! I'll take this boat as she floats to England if I must. I'll live to see you—all of ya—hanging from the highest yard arm in the British fleet!"

There were some silly shenanigans during the filming. Joan Crawford and William Randolph Hearst's mistress, movie star Marion Davies, dressed up like two native girls (played by Movita and Mamo wearing little) fooling around between shots. Clark Gable imitated Joan for laughs.

The cast for this 132-minute film included other good actors, such as Eddie Quillan and Donald Crisp. The film cost $1,950,000 and grossed more than twice that amount. They hired 2,500 Tahitians and the scenery of that area was magnificent. Much of the movie was filmed on Catalina Island off the coast of California with many other extras, some of whom were James Cagney, David Niven, and future singer Dick Haymes. Sadly, cameraman Glenn Strong died when a barge capsized.

Bounty music was under Herbert Stothart who won an Academy Award for *The Wizard of Oz* score. He was supported by Walter Jurmann from Vienna for exciting music of winds, battles, love, and heartbreaks. Stothart had American Nat Finston and Bronislaw Kaper of Warsaw,

Poland, compose "Love Song of Tahiti" with Gus Kahn lyrics. Other songs in *Bounty* were "Rule Britannia," sung by crewmen; "Rock-a-Bye Baby," sung by Franchot Tone; "God Rest Ye Merry Gentlemen," sung by English carolers and mutineers in Tahiti; and "We Three Kings," heard during a Christmas scene.

Two other movies about the *Bounty* were made before this one. The first was a 1916 silent black and white 55-minute film made in Australia called *The Mutiny of the Bounty* with unknown actors. The second was a 60-minute travelogue made by Charles Chauval, who travelled 15,000 miles over the South Seas. Intending to record history, he sailed to Tahiti and Pitcairn Island to show what was left of the sailors who intermarried with natives some 144 years earlier. That section was a tale of the mutiny told by old sailors. The film described transporting breadfruit from Tahiti to the West Indies. The cast dress and undress attracted much attention.

Chauval's mutiny scene needed an actor for Fletcher Christian. Errol Flynn (1909-1959) was a handsome lad born in Battery Point, Tasmania. Flynn was given a horrible wig and shown in flogging and fencing scenes. Felix Mendelssohn's "Hebrides Overture" was played along with some other old songs. Despite bad acting, Flynn relocated to Hollywood later. His autobiography described his mother's ancestor, Richmond Young, as Christian's midshipman. Richmond brought home an inscribed sword from Captain Bligh that Errol claimed to play with as a child.

Some studios tried to make *Bounty* sequels in 1940 and 1945. A 1962 three-hour remake was so bad that the $19 million budget could not be covered by $13 million box office income. Marlon Brando played Christian, and Trevor Howard played Bligh in *Mutiny on the Bounty*. Another remake was in 1984 when Mel Gibson played Christian versus Anthony Hopkins as Bligh in *The Bounty*. The $20 million movie never came anywhere close to recouping its budget.

Other 1935 movie nominees included *Alice Adams, Broadway Melody of 1936, Captain Blood, David Copperfield, The Informer, The Lives of a Bengal Lancer, A Midsummer Night's Dream, Misérables, Naughty Marietta, Ruggles of Red Gap,* and *Top Hat.* The latter should be noted as the first top billing of the dancing duo Fred Astaire and Ginger Rogers. Many more movies stemmed from that movie, which contained Irving Berlin music and a flimsy story.

Victor McLaglen (1886-1959) from Tunbridge Wells, England, won Best Actor for *The Informer.* Other contenders were Clark Gable *(Mutiny on the Bounty),* Charles Laughton *(Mutiny on the Bounty),* Paul Muni *(Black Fury),* and Franchot Tone *(Mutiny on the Bounty).*

Bette Davis (1908-1989) from Lowell, Massachusetts, won Best Actress for *Dangerous.* Other contenders were Elisabeth Bergner *(Escape Me Never),* Claudette Colbert *(Private Worlds),* Katharine Hepburn *(Alice Adams),* Miriam Hopkins *(Becky Sharp),* and Merle Oberon *(The Dark Angel).*

Best Song "Lullaby of Broadway," w. Al Dubin, m. Harry Warren, from *Gold Diggers of 1935.*

John Ford, Director of *The Informer.*

9th Academy Awards

Ceremony: This event was conducted on March 4, 1937, at the Biltmore Hotel, hosted by humorist George Jessel. In 1936, the Best Supporting Actor and Actress awards originated. The winners were given plaques until 1944 when they were awarded Oscar statuettes.

This Best Picture was the first musical film in history for which one of its cast members won an Academy Award. Luise Rainer received the Best Actress award for portraying Anna Held, Ziegfeld's first wife. This Best Picture was also the longest talking film of the time—though two silent films had run longer (*The Birth of a Nation* and *Intolerance).*

1936 *The Great Ziegfeld*

Tagline: "More Stars than There Are in the Heavens." Producer Hunt Stromberg intended to have even more stars that Ziegfeld discovered but time passed before production and some stars had died, such as Will Rogers who was played by impersonator A. A. Trimble.

This movie depicted the life of theatrical impresario Florenz "Flo" Ziegfeld, Jr. played by dapper William Powell. Some of it was true to life but many liberties were taken. Flo's father, a former mayor in Germany, started the Chicago Academy of Music. He was put in charge of music for the 1893 Colombian World's Fair, to celebrate the 400-year anniversary of Christopher Columbus' voyage. The fair was also to demonstrate the city's recovery from the devastating fire of 1871. Ziegfeld's father (1841-1923) trained at university to teach classical music. His disinterested son, Flo, was more interested in popular music and entertainment.

The movie showed how young Flo introduced exciting music and acts, such as strongman Eugene Sandow, belly dancer Little Egypt, tap dancer Ray Bolger, comedian/singer Fanny Brice, and lasso comedian Will Rogers. After the movie came out, Algerian belly dancer Farida Mahzar, who played Little Egypt, sued the studio, claiming that they portrayed her as a lewd character. She died of a heart attack before the court case was concluded. She and other dancers did bump and grind numbers while shedding clothing, which were called Hoochie Koochie dances.

Flo acted as a barker himself at the fair, which set attendance records of 25 million people. The Ferris wheel, designed by George Washington Ferris, was a rival to the Eiffel Tower, costing fifty cents for a 20-minute ride in a lit-up machinery wheel. Ferris died four years later at age 37.

The fair was so successful that Flo began to gamble and lost thousands during his travels. He had a Cecil B. DeMille "bigger is better" attitude, so put on huge shows with women showing legs to weary businessmen who wanted to relax in New York City during the evening.

Ziegfeld, Jr.'s love life was depicted in part by French wife Anna Held, and by English wife Billie Burke. But there were many illicit affairs implied during the movie. Other stars were Frank Morgan, Virginia Bruce, Reginald Owen, and Nat Pendleton.

Musical events in this movie were magnificent. The $200,000 "wedding cake" scene featured a tower rotating with 175 spiral steps, weighing 100 tons. One of the extras in this scene was Pat Ryan who later became Mrs. Richard Nixon. After the beginning of George Gershwin's "Rhapsody in Blue," Dennis Morgan sang Irving Berlin's "A Pretty Girl Is Like a Melody" during the scene which won the Academy Award for Best Dance Direction by Seymour Felix. The women in this movie had terribly expensive gowns specially designed by Adrian, mentioned earlier as the husband of Janet Gaynor.

Some of the dialogue displayed Ziegfeld's many sides. He said, "I'm the funniest kind of a fellow. I love *all* the girls!" Myrna Loy as Ziegfeld's wife after Anna Held said, "He's a terrible ladies' man. I suppose that's forgivable because he's surrounded by so many beautiful women." One of Ziegfeld's discoveries was janitor Ray Bolger: Ziegfeld said, "You're better with your feet than you are with your broom."

Ziegfeld sent wife Anna Held milk for bathing and used publicity about this in real life and in this movie. Many popular songs made this movie constantly entertaining: "Won't You Come and Play with Me," "If You Knew Susie," "Shine on Harvest Moon," "Yiddle on Your Fiddle," "My Man," "When You Wore a Tulip," "Look for the Silver Lining," "Ol' Man River," Harriet Hoctor Ballet and two opera excerpts. What makes this movie rise above its excessive length and reach viewers are things like the cake dance, strongman Sandow, and the many featured stars.

Fannie Brice had played a child named Baby Snooks on radio beginning around 1937 and she was a great success. She could do comedy but the surprise in this movie was her torch song. She stood alone against a lamp post while evoking emotions singing, "My Man." It may have been true to life because she had married a gangster. She sang about how she loved her man no matter how bad he was.

Universal Pictures bought the film rights to Ziegfeld's life story from widow Billie Burke in 1933. She wanted to play herself but had just turned 50, so was hired as a technical director. She later appeared every Saturday morning on the children's radio show called *Let's Pretend,* had her own show, and was seen regularly on other radio shows, like *Duffy's Tavern.* She also appeared with Judy Garland in the 1939 *Wizard of Oz,* playing the "Good Witch." The Gumm Sisters were originally to appear in this movie but were removed as the star list multiplied.

The film was shot at MGM in Culver City, California, for a budget of $2,000,000, some $500,000 more than was intended. However, it earned something more than that. Running time was 177 minutes, unless it was the roadshow edition with overture music, entr'acte, and exit music for a total of 185 minutes.

The movie produced sequels, such as *Ziegfeld Girl* (1941) starring James Stewart, Judy Garland, Hedy Lamarr, and Lana Turner. In 1946, Vincente Minelli made *Ziegfeld Follies* with famous song and dance actors, well-known comedians, and delightful songs.

Other movie nominees included *Anthony Adverse, Dodsworth, Libeled Lady, Mr. Deeds Goes to Town, Romeo and Juliet, San Francisco, The Story of Louis Pasteur, A Tale of Two Cities,* and *Three Smart Girls.*

Paul Muni (1895-1967) from Lemberg, Austria, won Best Actor for *The Story of Louis Pasteur.* Other contenders were Gary Cooper *(Mr. Deeds Goes to Town),* Walter Huston *(Dodsworth),* William Powell *(My Man Godfrey),* and Spencer Tracy *(San Francisco).*

Luise Rainer (1910-2014) from Vienna, Austria, won Best Actress for *The Great Ziegfeld.* Other contenders were Irene Dunne *(Theodora Goes Wild),* Gladys George *(Valiant Is the Word for Carrie),* Carole Lombard *(My Man Godfrey),* and Norma Shearer *(Romeo and Juliet).*

Gale Sondergaard won Best Supporting Actress for *Anthony Adverse.*

Walter Brennan won Best Supporting Actor for *Come and Get It.*

Best Song "The Way You Look Tonight," w. Dorothy Fields, m. Jerome Kern, from *Swingtime.*

Frank Capra, Director of *Mr. Deeds Goes to Town.*

10th Academy Awards

Ceremony: Floods delayed the tenth Academy Awards ceremony by one week. It took place on March 10, 1938, at the Biltmore Hotel in Los Angeles. Host was Bob Burns, an Arkansas radio and movie entertainer, who had created a musical pipe called a Bazooka. Two categories were eliminated from the Academy Awards after this performance. One was Best Dance Direction and the other was Best Assistant Director.

When Spencer Tracy won the Oscar for Best Actor in *Captains Courageous,* he was in the hospital with a hernia operation. When his wife showed him the Oscar at the hospital, they saw it was engraved to "Dick Tracy" (the comics detective) rather than "Spencer Tracy". (See *An Affair to Remember* by Christopher Anderson, G. K. Hall & Co, Thorndike, Maine, 1997, page 145.)

Walt Disney's *Snow White and the Seven Dwarfs* was the first full-length technicolor animated movie with sound and was the first movie to publish a soundtrack. It received only a nomination for Best Score. Disney won an honorary Academy Award the next year for that movie, which pioneered a new entertainment field for motional picture cartoons. The Oscar for that movie had a usual sized Oscar and seven miniature statuettes on its base representing the seven dwarfs.

The soundtrack for *Snow White* included songs by Frank Churchill and Larry Morey. Harry Stockwell, father of child star Dean Stockwell, played The Prince and Billy Gilbert from silent movies played Sneezy. Songs included: "I'm Wishing," "One Song," "With a Smile and a Song," "Whistle While You Work," "Heigh-Ho," "Bluddle-Uddle-Um-Dum,"

"The Silly Song," and "Someday My Prince Will Come." Paul Smith and Leigh Harline composed other music.

1937 *The Life of Emile Zola*

Tagline: "Here is true greatness." This movie depicted some of the life of French author Emile Zola and his later effort to help a Jewish officer, Captain Alfred Dreyfus, defend himself against French anti-Semitism. Much of this film is historical depicting Zola, played by Austro-Hungarian Paul Muni, and Zola's relationship with French painter Paul Cézanne. Zola had successes with early novels and especially *Nana,* taken from the life of a prostitute whom he met.

Zola learned of a Jewish Frenchman whom the army decided was a spy--Captain Alfred Dreyfus (played by Joseph Schildkraut). His wife, played by Gale Sondergaard, pled with Zola to take up the cause for her husband, who was unjustly imprisoned on Devil's Island in French Guiana because he was a Jew.

The aging Zola then wrote a letter called" J'Accuse" in a popular French newspaper calling out the French authorities for anti-Semitism when a Hungarian officer was the actual spy. Zola said, "I shall tell the truth. Because if I did not, my nights would be haunted by the specter of an innocent man expiating under the most frightful torture a crime he never committed."

Zola was charged with libel. His attorney (Donald Crisp) managed to reduce Zola's sentence to a year in prison and a large fine. Zola's lawyer got 1,500 signatures of those who defended Dreyfus from doctors, physicists, anthropologists, linguists, philologists, and chemists. One chemist, Edouard Grimaux, said that "real scientific method was lacking" in the charges brought against Dreyfus. Zola fled, on advice of friends, to England to continue to plead justice for Dreyfus. Zola died of carbon monoxide in his house about when Dreyfus was exonerated due to Zola's entreaties. Zola died a hero for defending the Jew. A few years later, Captain Dreyfus was cleared of charges and reinstated in military service in 1906.

The movie received acclaim but was strangely silent on the issue of racial prejudice. Nazi Georg Gyssling had called Jack Warner telling him to remove the word "Jew" from the movie and have no celebration of a victory for Jews when Dreyfus was restored to the French Army. (See *Hitler in Los Angeles* by Steven J. Ross, Bloomsbury Publishing, 2017.)

The movie was made using Goff Island in Laguna Beach, California, as Devil's Island. Reviews described the movie as an historical film and Muni's portrayal as excellent. It was not really historical since there were numerous errors, and the word Jew was omitted to please the Germans.

Max Steiner's music foretold the death of Zola from smoke inhalation in the first scene as Emile struggled with his faulty stove. Max created a smoky sound from low flutes, a harp, and a piano, which darkened the light. Since Zola's most famous book was about a prostitute whom he called Nana (with two syllables), Steiner used a sad 2-note motif inserted in Sibelius' "Valse Triste" (sad waltz). Zola's defense of Dreyfus was triumphant. So, Max created a three-note motif as an upward leap for victory over Nana's sad theme. Steiner didn't win the Academy Award for this but wanted no publicity since his Austrian family were under Hitler's rule. He also included a rendition of the 1792 *La Marseillaise*.

The cost of making the116-minute movie was $700,000, but the profits exceeded that by several times the budget.

Other movie nominees included *The Awful Truth, Captains Courageous, Dead End, The Good Earth, In Old Chicago, Lost Horizon, One Hundred Men and a Girl, Stage Door,* and *A Star Is Born.*

Spencer Tracy (1900-1967) from Milwaukee won Best Actor for *Captains Courageous*. Other contenders were Charles Boyer *(Conquest)*, Fredric March *(A Star Is Born)*, Robert Montgomery *(Night Must Fall)*, and Paul Muni *(The Life of Emile Zola)*.

Luise Rainer won the Best Actress for *The Good Earth*. Other contenders were Irene Dunne *(The Awful Truth)*, Greta Garbo *(Camille)*, Janet Gaynor *(A Star Is Born)*, and Barbara Stanwyck *(Stella Dallas)*.

Alice Brady won Best Supporting Actress for *In Old Chicago*.

Joseph Schildkraut won Best Supporting Actor for *The Life of Emile Zola*.

Best Song "Sweet Leilani," w. m. Harry Owens, from *Waikiki Wedding*.

Leo McCary, Director of *The Awful Truth*.

11th Academy Awards

Ceremony: The awards were presented at the Biltmore Hotel on February 23, 1939, with no main host. Sir Cedric Hardwicke and Tyrone Power presented many of the Oscars. This was the first ceremony in which a foreign language film was nominated for Best Picture. That film was Jean Renoir's *Grand Illusion*. Two juvenile actors won awards: Deanna Durbin and Mickey Rooney, "for their significant contribution in bringing to the screen the spirit and personification of youth, and as juvenile players setting a high standard of ability and achievement."

1938 *You Can't Take It with You*

Tagline: "You'll love them all for giving you the swellest time you've ever had." Frank Capra won Best Picture, and this was his third Oscar as director. He described how he specifically picked out James Stewart because he thought Stewart fit his concept of idealized America.

The story is about a young fellow (Stewart) from a wealthy family who falls for a stenographer (Jean Arthur) from an eccentric poor family. Arthur's family was depicted with considerable snobbery by Stewart's family. Her grandfather, played by Lionel Barrymore with crutches (due to his arthritis), talked with Stewart's parents over a harmonica song of "Polly Wolly Doodle," telling how success in business may mean a lot in life but "you can't take it with you."

Jean Arthur's sister, played by 15-year-old Ann Miller, tap-danced to Brahms' "Hungarian Dance" played on the xylophone. One family member had fireworks that exploded during the family interaction scene. Jean Arthur's family was so eccentric that some movie critics claimed the movie was fun but not very realistic.

Music chosen by Russian Dimitri Tiomkin included Chopin's "Valse Brilliante" Op. 34, No. 2 played on the xylophone, "Just Once Again" by Walter Donaldson, "Rockin' the Town" by Johnny Green, "Gypsy Dance No. 8" by Mischa Bakaleinikoff and Ben Oakland, and "Loch Lomond" played on the harmonica by Lionel Barrymore. "Whistle While You Work" from *Snow White and the Seven Dwarfs* was included as whistled by a toy. Tiomkin knew that Capra just wanted fun music that people could dance to or play or sing along with—nothing new.

The film has not weathered well because it was slightly too long (over two hours) and had an appeal for that era of people coming out of the Great Depression, which differed from later eras and other concerns. However, there was a very natural quality in the dialogue between Stewart and Arthur.

In 1937, Harry Cohn of Columbia Pictures bought the film rights of the 1936 Pulitzer Prize-winning play from George Kaufman and Moss Hart for $200,000. The movie was shot at a Hollywood studio in two months from April 25 to June 29, 1938, with a budget of $1,644,736. It received box-office receipts more than twice that amount.

One of Barrymore's lines to Edward Arnold, who played the stenographer's father, was, "I used to be just like you. Then one morning I was going up in an elevator and it struck me that I wasn't having any fun. So, I came right down, and I never went back. That was thirty-five years ago." The movie was said to be wholesome, homespun, appealing, but some critics thought it forced gaiety and sentiment.

Other movie nominees included *The Adventures of Robin Hood, Alexander's Ragtime Band, Boys Town, The Citadel, Four Daughters, Grand Illusion, Jezebel, Pygmalion,* and *Test Pilot.*

Spencer Tracy won Best Actor for *Boys Town*. Other contenders were Charles Boyer *(Algiers)*, James Cagney *(Angels with Dirty Faces)*, Robert Donat *(The Citadel)*, and Leslie Howard *(Pygmalion)*.

Bette Davis won Best Actress for *Jezebel*. Other contenders were Fay Bainter *(White Banners)*, Wendy Hiller *(Pygmalion)*, Norma Shearer *(Marie Antoinette)*, and Margaret Sullavan *(Three Comrades)*.

Fay Bainter won Best Supporting Actress for *Jezebel*.

Walter Brennan won Best Supporting Actor for *Kentucky*.

Best Song "Thanks for the Memory," w. Leo Robin, m. Ralph Rainger, from *The Big Broadcast of 1938*.

Frank Capra, Director of *You Can't Take It with You*.

12th Academy Awards

Ceremony: The event was conducted on February 29, 1940, in the Coconut Grove at the Ambassador Hotel in Los Angeles. It was hosted by Bob Hope in the first of 19 years that he served as host. By this time, the Academy Awards of 1939 had changed the name of the prize statuette to Oscar. The name, according to rumor, was used because an Academy executive director said that the statuette looked like her Uncle Oscar.

The newspaper published the winners before the nominees entered the banquet room. The Academy then decided to use the sealed-envelope format to add suspense. This was also the first year for a new category of special effects for color and for black and white films.

Clark Gable had refused to attend the opening gala of *Gone with the Wind* because the Atlanta theater did not admit black patrons. He liked black actress Hattie McDaniel, but she begged him to attend anyway. She was not allowed to sit with others at the banquet, so she sat with her escort at a tiny corner table. The award for Best Supporting Actress went to Hattie McDaniel, the first black to win an Academy Award. Presenter, actress Fay Bainter said, "It is a tribute to a country where people are free to honor noteworthy achievements regardless of creed, race, or color."

Robert Donat won Best Actor and Spencer Tracy accepted the award for him. Honorary awards included one for Douglas Fairbanks, first president of the Academy, and one for a juvenile award to Judy Garland for *The Wizard of Oz*. The Irving G. Thalberg Memorial award went to David O. Selznick. Thalberg, MGM producer, died young in 1936 after many successful films. (See *The Jew in American Cinema* by Patricia Erens published in 1984.)

1939 *Gone with the Wind*

Tagline: "The most magnificent picture ever." It won eight Academy Awards: Best Picture, Best Actress, Best Supporting Actress, Best Color Cinematography, Best Director, Best Screenplay (Sidney Howard was listed because he died before the awards, but others, including David O. Selznick, had helped write the screenplay). The film was adapted from the 1936 novel by Margaret Mitchell, whom producer Selznick paid $50,000 for rights.

Millionaire John "Jock" Hay Whitney subsidized Selznick's productions. Jock stuttered and debated to improve speech but was never chosen for acting, only for investing. He produced Broadway shows, such as *Life with Father* and *A Streetcar Named Desire*. Jock provided funds for this movie and Selznick's *Rebecca* and another movie--*Dark Victory* starring Bette Davis, George Brent, and Ronald Reagan. Jock consented to be godfather to both of Selznick's sons. (See *Jock: The Life and Times of John Hay Whitney* by E. J. Kahn, Jr., published in 1981.)

This production was delayed because Selznick wanted Clark Gable to play Rhett Butler. The time delay allowed writers to reduce the long book into 221-minutes running time. Selznick reduced working hours for actors by providing bananas and peanuts, so they didn't stop to eat. Training of actors to portray Southern accents took much time. First Lady Eleanor Roosevelt asked for her maid to be given a screen test for the role of Mammy, but she didn't pass. Had Eleanor's maid been selected, perhaps seating would have been allowed for blacks in Atlanta.

Max Steiner's background in opera made him create theme melodies for each major character or place. He saw the movie and then designed the score in 12 weeks with two main love themes, folk and patriotic music, and ninety-nine separate pieces of music. He composed the opening minutes of the score with a Tara theme, Scarlett's (Vivien Leigh) birthplace and beloved soil, which begins and ends the movie. There was a minor theme for Ashley Wilkes (Leslie Howard) whom Steiner saw as effeminate, and a bold little used Rhett Butler (Clark Gable) theme. There was even a calm theme for Ashley's gentle wife Melanie (Olivia de Havilland). Those themes guided the viewer's expectations about each character and place in the epic melodrama.

Bonding between people in the movie was strong between Ashley Wilkes and wife Melanie, but weak between Scarlett and Rhett Butler. Scarlett was more swept away by her selfish nature, so finally her sense of belonging to anybody or anything was "gone with the wind."

There were ten songs by Stephen Foster, and others: "I Wish I Was in Dixie's Land," "Sweet and Low," "Ye Cavaliers of Dixie," "Taps," "Maryland My Maryland," "Irish Washerwoman," "Garryowen," "When Johnny Comes Marching Home," "When This Cruel War Is Over," "The Bonnie Blue Flag," "Hark the Herald Angels Sing," "Tramp Tramp Tramp," "Go Down Moses," "March through Georgia," "Battle Hymn of the Republic," "Yankee Doodle," "Stars of the Summer Night," "Bridal Chorus," "Deep River," "For He's a Jolly Good Fellow," "London Bridge Is Falling Down," "Ben Bolt," etc.

David Selznick said during the burning of Atlanta, "Dixie" should be played in a minor key to keep film auditors away from deleting "improper" Southern allegiances. (See Mervyn Cooke's 2008 *A History of Film Music*.) Also, Steiner's management of the music by themes for each character (a leitmotif) was classic and became the mode for many film composers. Leitmotif means the reappearance of an idea, person, or situation, and was especially used in Wagnerian operas.

The Hays Office used to fine producers for using the word "damn," but in November 1939, they permitted its use because it was a quotation from a literary work. Thus, Gable as Butler said, "Frankly, my dear, I don't give a damn!" In addition, the movie was filmed on the Selznick lot and the burning of Atlanta used old, abandoned sets blown up by explosives which Selznick himself operated. The cost of the production was $3.85 million.

An early problem was who should play Scarlett O'Hara against Clark Gable's Rhett Butler. Selznick built publicity by a casting call interviewing 1,400 unknowns, at a cost of $100,000. Some known stars considered were Miriam Hopkins, Tallulah Bankhead, Joan Crawford, Norma Shearer, Katharine Hepburn, Jean Arthur, Joan Bennet, Frances Dee, Paulette Goddard, Susan Hayward, Lana Turner, and English actress Vivien Leigh. Selznick's friend, Jock Whitney, dated several of those ladies during that time.

Several directors took part in the movie's early filming but the final one, Victor Fleming, won the credit and the Oscar. At the same time, he was directing *The Wizard of Oz* and had to leave work temporarily due to exhaustion. The film was done in two parts and most reviewers and audiences thought the first half, centering on the collapse of the Old South, was more interesting than the second half, which focused on relationships between the main characters.

Fickle Scarlett pretended to love Butler but really loved Ashley Wilkes (Leslie Howard) so this made the movie seem like a love story. Wilkes married Melanie, played by Olivia de Havilland, who portrayed a lady-like temperament. But Scarlett had a passionate side that Rhett could see. He told her, "You should be kissed and often, and by someone who knows how."

The author and producer focused on plantation life supported by slavery as if slaves were happy. They were depicted as very ignorant and unready for freedom. Much has been written about the different view that producers of today would take with the racial perspective to show the inhumanity of slavery.

The movie ended as the once rich Scarlett pleaded for help from a husband she had spurned. Their relationship had become extremely complicated, and love had been lost on all sides. Undaunted, after Rhett's parting words of "Frankly, my dear, I don't give a damn," the courageous and vain Scarlett decided to think about it later. She reasoned, "After all, tomorrow is another day." She sounded hopeful that she could lure him back, but the curtain closed.

David O. Selznick and wife, Jock Whitney; and film editor Hal Kern drove out to Riverside, California, to preview a rough cut of the film at the Fox Theater. The audience was told they could stay or leave for the screening of a new movie. When the title appeared on the screen, the audience cheered. After the movie ended, it received a standing ovation.

The film's premiere in Atlanta, Georgia, on December 15, 1939, was quite an event. It was the climax of three days of festivities hosted by the mayor using contributions by Jock Whitney. That included a parade of limousines with stars from the movie, receptions, a costume ball, and the governor declaring December 15 a state holiday.

In 1942, Selznick liquidated his company because John Whitney wanted to get out of movies. Selznick was exhausted from hard work on the last few movies and sold his share of the *GWTW* to Jock Whitney and his sister for $500,000. In turn, the Whitneys sold it to MGM for $4.8 million. MGM reissued it several times redoing a few shots for wider screens. It was shown on television in 1976 in a special premiere event and was watched by 47.5% of the households sampled in America. That set a record for the highest rated film to air on television.

Ted Turner, who developed Turner Classic Movies, TBS, and CNN, had a favorite movie: *Gone with the Wind.* He bought the movie but because CBS had rights, it took years to be shown. He waited and we all benefitted.

Other movie nominees included *Dark Victory, Goodbye, Mr. Chips, Love Affair, Mr. Smith Goes to Washington, Ninotchka, Of Mice and Men, Stagecoach, The Wizard of Oz,* and *Wuthering Heights.* Of these many excellent movies, all of which were overshadowed by *Gone with the Wind,* was *The Wizard of Oz.* Frank Baum's outrageously amusing story made stars out of those who appeared in it—Judy Garland, Ray Bolger, and Frank Morgan in particular.

Robert Donat (1905-1958) from Manchester, England, won Best Actor for *Goodbye, Mr. Chips.* Other contenders were Clark Gable *(Gone with the Wind),* Laurence *Olivier (Wuthering Heights),* Mickey Rooney *(Babes in Arms),* and James Stewart *(Mr. Smith Goes to Washington).*

Vivien Leigh (1913-1967) from Darjeeling, India, won Best Actress for *Gone with the Wind.* Other contenders were Bette Davis *(Dark Victory),* Irene Dunne *(Love Affair),* Greta Garbo *(Ninotchka)* and Greer Garson *(Goodbye, Mr. Chips).*

Hattie McDaniel won Best Supporting Actress for *Gone with the Wind.*

Thomas Mitchell won Best Supporting Actor for *Stagecoach.*

Best Song "Over the Rainbow," w. E.Y. Harburg, m. Harold Arlen, from *The Wizard of Oz.*

Victor Fleming, Director of *Gone with the Wind.*

13th Academy Awards

Ceremony: These awards were presented on February 27, 1941, at the Biltmore Hotel in Los Angeles, hosted by Bob Hope. This was the first year to use sealed envelopes with votes counted by Price Waterhouse. This was the first time the same producer won two consecutive Best Picture awards. *Pinocchio* was the first animated film to win competitive Oscars for Best Original Score and Best Original Song.

President Franklin Roosevelt gave a 6-minute radio message to the Academy audience from the White House. Here are some of his comments:

I'm happy to greet the motion picture industry of America, whose representatives are gathered from far and near, for the annual awards dinner of the Academy of Motion Picture of Arts and Sciences... The American motion picture is a national and international force... We've seen it reflect our civilization throughout the rest of the world. The aims and the aspirations and the ideas of a free people, and of freedom itself.

That is the real reason that some governments do not want our American films exhibited in their countries. Dictators, those who enforce the totalitarian form of government, think it is a dangerous thing for their unfortunate peoples to know that in our democracy, officers of the government are the servants—never the masters—of the people.

The assault on the democratic form of government imperils world civilization today...We have been seeking to affirm our faith in the Western world through a wider exchange of culture, and of education, and of thought, and of free expression among the various nations of this hemisphere. Your industry has and is utilizing vast resources of talent and facilities in a sincere effort to help the people of the hemisphere to come to know each other better.

Our government has invited you to do your share of the job of interpreting the people of the Western Hemisphere to one another... Tonight I want to place the chief emphasis on the service that you render in promoting solidarity among all the peoples of the Americas. For all of this, and for your splendid cooperation with all who are directing the expansion of our defense forces, I am glad to thank you.

This ceremony also gave two honorary awards: Bob Hope in recognition of his unselfish services to the Motion Picture Industry and Colonel Nathan Levinson for his outstanding service to the industry and the Army during the past nine years, which made possible the production of Army Training Films.

1940 *Rebecca*

Tagline: "The shadow of a remembered woman came between their lips, but these two had the courage to hope and to live their love." *Rebecca* is based on Daphne du Maurier's novel of the same name. The book was a romantic thriller written in the first person. An aristocratic widower (Laurence Olivier) lost his first wife under mysterious circumstances. He then married a beautiful but shy woman (Joan Fontaine) and brought her to live in his mansion on the windy coast of England. She found herself uncertain of her husband's love after his housekeeper (Judith Anderson) made comments about the dead wife as a ravishing beauty. The housekeeper's dislike of the new wife and Rebecca's former lover (George Sanders) added complications to the scenario creating numerous mysteries.

The first wife in the original story was killed by her husband who would need to pay for his sin according to the Production Code. The movie also had to avoid a possible lesbian relation between the housekeeper and the dead wife. So, Robert Sherwood and Joan Harrison developed the screenplay with those differences from the novel.

Alfred Hitchcock's direction made this a more complex and mysterious film with haunting scenes. "To make a good film," Alfred Hitchcock once said, "you need three things: the script, the script, and the script." His techniques began in silent pictures where images rather than dialogue made films popular. He believed that there was terror only in the anticipation of doom. Thus, he manipulated audiences and built suspense through a movable camera's focus, voice-overs casting mystery over a movie at the outset, suspenseful music, and unusual scenery.

This movie was shot at Selznick Studios; Big Sur, California; and Point Lobos State Natural Preserve in California. The final burning of the mansion emitted smoke that Selznick wanted to spell out "R" for *Rebecca*, but Hitchcock thought that lacked subtlety. Hitch appeared toward the end of the movie as he walked away from a phone box, facing away from the audience. Despite the complexity of the film, it took only 2.5 months to film. The movie ran just more than two hours at 130 minutes.

Editing to maintain suspense was essential to Hitchcock. He did not want to distract viewers by small things when they could be riveted to their seats through suspense. His shrewd goal was to make a picture short enough that people did not have to go to the bathroom during it. Some dialogue was in Olivier's comment to his new wife, played by Fontaine, "There's no need to be frightened, you know. Just be yourself and they'll all adore you."

Casting was easy because producer David O. Selznick and investor Jock Whitney knew Laurence Olivier, who was dating their star of *Gone with the Wind,* Vivien Leigh. Olivier and Leigh divorced their spouses and married each other August 31, 1940. In addition, they had cast Olivia De Havilland in *GWTW,* and her sister was Joan Fontaine.

Hitchcock agreed to screen test Fontaine after seeing her play a meek wife in *The Women* (1939). This movie made her a star.

Selznick wanted Steiner to do the music for Rebecca, but Max was still working on *Gone with the Wind*. Hitchcock was pleased with Polish musician/conductor Franz Waxman who used ominous and suspenseful music. Minor keys, rumbling timpani, strings, and flutes implied problems ahead. *Rebecca* made Waxman's name and he did more than 100 movies thereafter.

Hitchcock did not win Best Director, but his methods made him the master of suspense. The opening scene of *Psycho* had a camera scan downtown Phoenix, Arizona, and slowly move toward an open hotel window into a room where partly clad Janet Leigh had been in a sexual encounter with a married man. Hitchcock's camera let viewers peek into a bedroom and used that same idea in *Rear Window* where James Stewart saw a crime through a window.

The challenge with *Rebecca* was that she was dead and only lived through the musical theme used by Waxman to represent her. That was like *Laura* (the 1944 movie with Gene Tierney, Dana Andrews, and Judith Anderson) where the heroine was thought to be dead and lived only through a musical theme until she appeared. In this movie, housekeeper Mrs. Danvers (Judith Anderson) made Fontaine believe her husband (Olivier) didn't love her, despite their delightful meetings and honeymoon.

Scenes were made spooky by use of an electric organ and a modern synthesizer called Novachord. This eerie quality was later used in Alfred Hitchcock's *Spellbound*, a psychological thriller where dreams and fears were dramatized with an instrument called the theremin. A love theme was used for the early and late parts of *Rebecca*. The 132-minute movie had a budget of $1.29 million but made more than three times that amount in box office. The movie won Best Picture and Best Black and White Cinematography.

Other movie nominees included *All This and Heaven Too, Foreign Correspondent, The Grapes of Wrath, The Great Dictator, Kitty Foyle, The Letter, The Long Voyage Home, Our Town,* and *The Philadelphia Story.*

James Stewart (1908-1997) from Indiana, Pennsylvania, won Best Actor for *The Philadelphia Story.* Other contenders were Charlie Chaplin *(The Great Dictator),* Henry Fonda *(The Grapes of Wrath),* Raymond Massie *(Abe Lincoln in Illinois),* and Laurence Olivier *(Rebecca).*

Ginger Rogers (1911-1995) from Independence, Missouri, won Best Actress for *Kitty Foyle.* Other contenders were Bette Davis *(The Letter),* Joan Fontaine *(Rebecca),* Katharine Hepburn *(The Philadelphia Story),* and Martha Scott *(Our Town).*

Jane Darwell won Best Supporting Actress for *The Grapes of Wrath.*

Walter Brennan won Best Supporting Actor for *The Westerner.*

Best Song "When You Wish Upon a Star," w. Ned Washington, m. Leigh Harline, from *Pinocchio.*

John Ford, Director of *The Grapes of Wrath.*

14th Academy Awards

Ceremony: The Awards were presented on February 26, 1942, at the Biltmore Hotel in Los Angeles, hosted by Bob Hope. Some of the ceremony was broadcast on *CBS* radio. The biggest news at this event was that *Citizen Kane* did not win Best Picture. John Ford won his third Best Director award. The award for Best Actress was notable because two sisters ran against each other: Olivia de Havilland and Joan Fontaine.

This was the first year for documentaries and the first Oscar was awarded to *Churchill's Island.* That 21-minute propaganda short depicted the Royal Air Force and Royal Navy control of sea and sky around the island, and the Dunkirk evacuation.

Honorary awards went to Leopold Stokowski for *Fantasia*, and Walt Disney and his team for *Fantasia.*

1941 *How Green Was My Valley*

Tagline: "Rich is their humor. Deep are their passions. Reckless are their lives. Mighty is their story!" The movie was based on Richard Llewellyn's 1939 novel. It starred Walter Pidgeon, Maureen O'Hara, Anna Lee, Donald Crisp, and 13-year-old Roddy McDowell. It was intended to have one actor play Huw as a young boy and Tyrone Power to play him as an adult. However, producer Darryl F. Zanuck decided to see the entire story through the eyes of young Huw.

The story of a hard-working Welsh mining family of six boys and kind parents described the loss of a way of life in the South Wales coalfields and its effects on families. The fictional village was based on where the author spent summers visiting his grandfather. Zanuck intended to go to Wales to film the picture but World War II interfered.

The film began when an older Huw said, "I am packing my belongings in the shawl my mother used to wear when she went to market. And I'm going from my valley. And this time, I shall never return." Huw recalled, "If my father was the head of our house, my mother was its heart." Later, he said, "Men like my father cannot die. They are with me still, real in memory as they were in flesh, loving and beloved forever. How green was my valley then."

The coal miners in the movie fall in love, sing as they walk to and from work, and strike when their wages are decreased. Young Huw was picked on and taught to fight by two men (Rhys Williams and Barry Fitzgerald.) The church deacon (Walter Pidgeon) was denounced by citizens until a mine disaster occurred, and all were re-united as tragedies occurred.

John Ford's sentimental concern for the character of people and their determination to help each other showed up in this fine film. He built an 80-acre replica of a Welsh mining town at Brent's Crags in the Santa Monica Mountains near Malibu, California. When the Welsh choir who performed in the picture arrived and saw the site, they fell to their knees and wept. Thanks to Alfred Newman in charge of music, all songs were sung in Welsh except "God Bless the Queen." The film was made for $1.25 million and brought in four times that amount.

Other movie nominees included *Blossoms in the Dust, Citizen Kane, Here Comes Mr. Jordan, Hold Back the Dawn, The Little Foxes, The Maltese Falcon, One Foot in Heaven, Sergeant York,* and *Suspicion.* These excellent movies made choices difficult, but *Citizen Kane* was trend-setting in a way that others weren't. Orson Welles and Herman Mankiewicz were so inspired by William Randolph Hearst that they made a movie with new tricks copied by moviemakers thereafter.

(See *The Brothers Mankiewicz* by Sydney Ladensohn Stern published in 2019.) Orson and Herman chose to depict a man with splendid abilities but who was utterly corrupt. The 25-year-old Welles co-wrote, produced, directed, and starred in the film that was exciting for its boldness in a character study of one of the most important Americans during the early 1900s.

Gary Cooper (1901-1961) from Helena, Montana, won Best Actor for *Sergeant York*. Other contenders were Cary Grant *(Penny Serenade)*, Walter Huston *(The Devil and Daniel Webster)*, Robert Montgomery *(Here Comes Mr. Jordan)*, and Orson Welles *(Citizen Kane)*.

Joan Fontaine (1917-2013) born in Tokyo won Best Actress for *Suspicion*. Other contenders were her sister, Olivia de Havilland *(Hold Back the Dawn)*, Bette Davis *(The Little Foxes)*, Greer Garson *(Blossoms in the Dust)*, and Barbara Stanwyck *(Ball of Fire)*.

Mary Astor won Best Supporting Actress for *The Great Lie*.

Donald Crisp won Best Supporting Actor for *How Green Was My Valley*.

Best Song "The Last Time I Saw Paris," w. Oscar Hammerstein, m. Jerome Kern, from *Lady Be Good*.

John Ford, Director of *How Green Was My Valley*.

15th Academy Awards

Ceremony: This event as conducted on March 4, 1943, at Cocoanut Grove at the Ambassador Hotel in Los Angeles, hosted by Bob Hope. It was notable for Best Actress Greer Garson's longest (5.5 minutes) acceptance speech. *Mrs. Miniver* received 12 nominations and was the first film to have five acting nominations. Some of the ceremony was broadcast on CBS radio.

Irving Berlin presented the award for Best Song and wound up winning it for his own "White Christmas." An 8-minute Walt Disney cartoon with Donald Duck called *Der Fuehrer's Face* won for the Best Animated Short Film. It was an anti-Hitler cartoon and song, with Donald Duck having a nightmare about being a Nazi serving Hitler, Goebbels, Mussolini, etc. However, Disney withdrew it from circulation because the duck was a Nazi. It was shown again in 2004.

There was a 4-way tie for Best Documentary. Winners were: *The Battle of Midway* (US Navy), *Kokoda Front Line!* (Australian News & Information Bureau), *Moscow Strikes Back* (Artkino), and *Prelude to War* (US Army Special Services).

Honorary awards were made to three: Charles Boyer "for his progressive cultural achievement in establishing the French Research Foundation in Los Angeles as a source of reference for the Hollywood Motion Picture Industry." Noel Coward "for his outstanding production achievement in *In Which We Serve*." MGM "for its achievement in representing the 'American Way of Life'" in the production of the *Andy Hardy* series of films.

Sidney Franklin received the Irving Thalberg Memorial Awards for directing 27 films, producing three, including *Mrs. Miniver,* and acting in seven, including *Mrs. Miniver.*

1942 *Mrs. Miniver*

Tagline: "The story of all good people everywhere." This movie was based on Jan Struther's 1940 novel. It was filmed before Pearl Harbor brought the U.S. into the war. It was the first film centered on World War II to win an Academy Award for Best Picture. Mrs. Miniver (Greer Garson), her husband (Walter Pidgeon), three children, a maid, and cook lived in a large house on the Thames where their motorboat was moored.

As the war nears, their son (Richard Ney) returned from Oxford and met the granddaughter of Lady Beldon (Dame May Whitty) played by Teresa Wright. She noted the attitude of the young man and said, "I know how comfortable it is to curl up with a nice, fat book full of big words and think you're going to solve all the problems in the universe. But you're not, you know. A bit of action is required now and then." They fall in love, and he enlists in the RAF.

Mr. Miniver joined other boat owners and took his motorboat to assist the Dunkirk evacuation. He left his family thinking "it can't happen here," but it did. While gone, a wounded German pilot (Helmut Dantine) arrived and demanded food and a coat from Mrs. Miniver at gunpoint. He claimed the Nazis would overcome all enemies. She fed him, disarmed him when he fainted, and called the police. Mr. Miniver returned home to later learn of his wife's heroic acts.

Lady Beldon visited to talk Mrs. Miniver into discouraging the love between their two children, but she was reminded that she fell in love when very young. She was also the constant winner of an annual flower show. Local postmaster (Henry Travers) had developed a flower he named "Mrs. Miniver" and entered it in the show. Reluctantly, Lady Beldon announced him as winner.

As air raid sirens sound, the crowd dispersed, and Ney's wife, Teresa Wright, was killed by a bullet. Ney returned to find her dead. A church service was led by the vicar (Henry Wilcoxon) for those who died. Ney sat with Dame Whitty as they all sang "Onward Christian Soldiers."

Notable features in the movie were the gradual erosion of social classes as the war progressed. The marriage of the Minivers displayed a partnership of equal friends. When the movie came out, President Roosevelt rushed it to theaters. He said it hastened America's involvement in the war. Winston Churchill said it had "done more for the Allied cause than a flotilla of battleships."

Actor Henry Wilcoxon and director William Wyler re-wrote the sermon and it made history. President Roosevelt used it to build morale, put it in leaflets dropped over enemy and occupied territory, and it was reprinted in *Time* and *Look* magazines. Here is that sermon:

We in this quiet corner of England have suffered the loss of friends very dear to us, some close to this church. George West, choirboy. James Ballard, stationmaster and bell ringer, and the proud winner only an hour before his death of the Beldon Cup for his beautiful Miniver Rose. And our hearts go out in sympathy to the two families who share the cruel loss of a young girl who was married at this altar only two weeks ago. The homes of many of us have been destroyed, and the lives of young and old have been taken. There's scarcely a household that hasn't been struck to the heart. And why? Surely, you must have asked yourselves this question? Why, in all conscience, should these be the ones to suffer? Children, old people, a young girl at the height of her loveliness? Why these? Are these our soldiers? Are these our fighters? Why should they be sacrificed?

I shall tell you why. Because this is not only a war of soldiers in uniform. It is the war of the people, of *all* the people. And it must be fought not only on the battlefield, but in the cities and in the villages, in the factories and on the farms, in the home and in the heart of every man, woman, and child who loves freedom. Well, we have buried our dead, but we shall not forget them. Instead, they will inspire us with an unbreakable determination to free ourselves, and those who come after us, from the tyranny and terror that threaten to strike us down. This is the People's War. It is *our* war. *We* are the fighters. Fight it, then! Fight it with all that is in us! And may God defend the right.

This movie was made in Hollywood and in 2006 was ranked as the most inspiring film of all time by the American Film Institute. It did much to create America's support for its British allies. The film budget was $1.34 million but it brought in more than five times that amount. Running time was 133 minutes.

Jan Struthers was paid by MGM and bought two ambulances for the British war effort with that money. She developed Mrs. Miniver at the direction of Ian Fleming's brother, Peter, who asked her to develop columns for *The Times* (British newspaper). He said to write about "an ordinary sort of woman who leads an ordinary sort of life—rather like yourself." A sequel was made entitled *The Miniver Story* with Garson and Pidgeon. In 1960, a 90-minute TV production on CBS starred Maureen O'Hara and Leo Genn.

Joseph Goebbels, Nazi propaganda minister, wrote that the movie "shows the destiny of a family during the current war... There is not a single angry word spoken against Germany; nevertheless, the anti-German tendency is perfectly accomplished."

An American rose grower produced a "Mrs. Miniver" red rose that was propagated by English nurseries and can be seen in some public gardens in the UK and Canada. The story of Greer Garson's life was portrayed in the 1999 book *A Rose for Mrs. Miniver* by Michael Royan.

The special music in *Mrs. Miniver* included "Midsummer's Day" written by actor Gene Lockhart; "Good Night, Ladies;" "God Save the King;" "Children of the Heavenly King;" "Wedding March;" "For He's a Jolly Good Fellow;" "Onward Christian Soldiers;" and "Pomp and Circumstance."

Other movie nominees included *The Invaders, Kings Row, The Magnificent Ambersons, The Pied Piper, The Pride of the Yankees, Random Harvest, The Talk of the Town, Wake Island,* and *Yankee Doodle Dandy.*

James Cagney (1899-1986) from New York City won Best Actor for *Yankee Doodle Dandy.* Other contenders were Ronald Colman *(Random Harvest),* Gary Cooper *(The Pride of the Yankees),* Walter Pidgeon *(Mrs. Miniver),* and Monty Woolley *(The Pied Piper).*

Greer Garson (1908-1996) from County Down, Ireland, won Best Actress for *Mrs. Miniver.* Other contenders were Bette Davis *(Now, Voyager),* Katharine Hepburn *(Woman of the Year),* Rosalind Russell *(My Sister Eileen),* and Teresa Wright *(The Pride of the Yankees).*

Teresa Wright won Best Supporting Actress for *Mrs. Miniver.*

Van Heflin won Best Supporting Actor for *Johnny Eager.*

Best Song "White Christmas," w. m. Irving Berlin, from *Holiday Inn.*

William Wyler, Director of *Mrs. Miniver.*

16th Academy Awards

Ceremony: This event took place at Grauman's Chinese Theater in Los Angeles. Free passes were given to men and women in uniform. The 30-minute ceremony hosted by Jack Benny was broadcast by CBS. Jack Benny was dimly seen in *Casablanca* and ads offered free passes to those who could name the scene where he appeared. There were some 50 extras when he visited the Burbank studio as a *Casablanca* café scene was filmed. He grabbed a white coat and appeared as a waiter in the background.

When Benny announced the Best Picture, Hal Wallis got up to go to the stage, but Jack Warner rushed up to collect the Oscar. The Warner family sat blocking Wallis. He sat down, humiliated, and furious. He resigned from Warner Brothers the next month. Hal Wallis did receive the Irving Thalberg Memorial Award. He had become head of production at Warner Brothers and produced *Casablanca, Dark Victory, The Adventures of Robin Hood, The Maltese Falcon, Sergeant York* and *Now, Voyager* and many other movies.

The Tom and Jerry cartoon series won an Oscar. George Pal was given an honorary award "for the development of novel methods and techniques in the production of short subjects known as Puppetoons." Best supporting actors and actresses finally won a full-size Oscar. Also, in a new tradition, many previous winners were presenters of new awards in their category.

1943 *Casablanca*

Tagline: "They have a date with fate in Casablanca." The film was based on an unproduced play called *Everybody Comes to Rick's* by

Murray Burnett and Joan Alison. Story editor Irene Diamond found the script and convinced Hal Wallis to buy the rights in January 1942 for $20,000. It was renamed *Casablanca* due to the 1938 hit *Algiers* starring Charles Boyer and Hedy Lamarr, a movie made upon the formula of French film *Pepe Le Moko* of Algiers.

This movie has more recognizable script lines than any American movie ever made. The handling of suspense, detail, song, and beauty by Michael Curtiz was outstanding. The development of characters, intrigue and romance were beguiling.

Julius and Philip Epstein were paid $30,416 and Robert Koch was paid $4,200 for story enhancement and dialogue additions. The total budget was $1,039,000. The film was a surprise hit, making more than four times the budget. (For more about this movie, see *We'll Always Have Casablanca* by Noah Isenberg, published in 2017.)

Rick, a cynical ex-patriate (Humphrey Bogart) runs a nightclub in Casablanca during the early stages of World War II. Despite pressure from Vichy French and German occupants, his cafe became a place for refugees seeking escape to America. Ilsa, his former lover (Ingrid Bergman), and her husband (Paul Henreid) show up one day. Rick and Ilsa must decide about re-uniting and leaving for America or staying together in Morocco. The love story is tied in with the war as the French and Germans go at each other in various scenes. Corrupt characters inhabit Casablanca and the morals of each plays a part in their final actions.

Throughout history, the greatest stories describe main characters with their faults and show them try to improve when faced with challenges. This story improved that struggle with humorous dialogue, intrigue, murders, and the emergence of a code of ethics that solved problems for all involved. The movie finale had not yet been written when shooting began. But the twins Julius and Philip Epstein had a sudden thought one day that the film should end by the characters doing the right thing. Self-sacrifice held sway over love as Rick sent his dear Ilsa off with her husband, Viktor Lazlo, who was helping freedom fighters oppose the Nazis.

The final scene was shot with three little people moving about a mostly cardboard airplane seen vaguely through a fog in the distance. Those were three people from the 124 little people that Gabor Steiner (Max Steiner's father) supplied for *The Wizard of Oz* from his carnival work in Vienna by the ferris wheel in *The Third Man*. He had created Midget City in his Viennese carnival and many of them wanted to come to the U.S. to be in movies.

Everybody did the right thing in the end. French police chief Renault dismissed his officers after Rick shot Major Strasser with the phrase, "Round up the usual suspects." Thus, Renault freed Rick who said, "Louis, I think this is the beginning of a beautiful friendship."

The director, Hungarian Jew Michael Curtiz, enriched the movie by his focus on European immigrants fleeing Nazism. He cast many Europeans actors who escaped from Germany. Curtiz never got English down well. After directing swashbucklers, his orders to actors were: "Pull up your tights and light your torches," "Please make me a love nest," and "Bring on the empty horses," when he wanted to see stray horses on a battlefield. He said, "When I come here [to the U.S.], the underdog is always hero and I never forget." So, in *Casablanca,* the underdog was the hero. (See Alan K. Rode's *Michael Curtiz: A Life in Film.*)

The remarkable list of stars also included Claude Rains, Conrad Veidt, Sydney Greenstreet, Peter Lorre, S. Z. Sakall, Leonid Kinskey, Helmut Dantine, Marcel Dalio, Madeleine Lebeau, Joy Page, and Dooley Wilson, who was a drummer and singer and faked playing the piano in the movie. Other actresses considered for the role of Ilsa were Ann Sheridan, Hedy Lamarr, Luise Rainer, and Michelle Morgan. Bogart was the only person considered for his role. Paul Henreid was reluctant to take the part until he was offered top billing with Bogart and Bergman.

The only three *Casablanca* stars born in America were Bogart, Wilson, and Joy Page. Bogart had a noticeable lisp that came from a bad operation on his lower lip from a splinter of wood that had become embedded. He was an excellent chess player and *Casablanca* opened with him playing chess against himself.

Production Code Administrator Joseph Breen opposed the sexual relations of married Ilsa with Rick, until they inserted her comment that she thought her husband was dead when she had an affair with Rick. They opposed Claude Rains' Captain Renault seeking sex with women in return for visas. A young woman consulted Rick about the Captain's offer to help them if she submitted to his sexual vicissitudes. Rick heroically arranged for her husband to win at his gaming table. Whether it was the code or the writers, this movie ended by displaying good morals and values.

"Here's lookin' at you, kid," said four times in the movie, may have been a takeoff on Eddie Cantor's 1932 comment to Sid Grauman. He wrote in wet cement in front of Grauman's Theater "Here's looking at you, Sid." Another source was when Bergman, still learning English, was being shown how to play poker with cast members. Bogart would stand by and say, "Here's looking at you." It caught on so well that when Bogart and his wife attended the premiere, crowds hollered that phrase to him as they stepped from their limo to the theater.

The American Film Institute has called these among the 100 best movie quotes:

"We'll always have Paris."

"Here's looking at you, kid."

"Of all the gin joints in all the towns in all the world, she walks into mine."

"Play it, Sam. Play 'As Time Goes By'."

"Round up the usual suspects."

Also nominated was "Ilsa, I'm no good at being noble, but it doesn't take much to see that the problems of three little people don't amount to a hill of beans in this crazy world." Another good line was when Police Chief Renault (Claude Rains) was told to close Rick's café, but he needed a reason, so he said, "I'm shocked, shocked to find gambling is going on in here." The croupier handed him money, "Your winnings." Renault: "Oh, thank you very much."

Warner Brothers decided to release *Casablanca* on January 23, 1943, just after the Casablanca Conference at the Anfa Hotel on Jan. 14-24, 1943, with FDR, Churchill, De Gaulle, and Henri Giraud. The four main officials agreed to FDR's wish for unconditional surrender to end World War II. Churchill invited FDR to join him the next few days at Marrakesh in Morocco where Churchill painted the Atlas Mountains from Hotel Mamoun windows.

Music played a big part in this movie. We recall that the letters of transit in the movie were signed by De Gaulle (Free French leader) and Bogart placed them in the piano Sam played. The duel of the German and French anthems at Rick's café brought out tears shed by actors. Max Steiner may have wanted to write his own song to replace "As Time Goes By," but he didn't get it done. So, Bogart and Bergman's favorite song and variations of it were used every time Bergman appeared. Herman Hupfeld's 1931 song had wartime lyric that fit the movie scenario:

> You must remember this, a kiss is just a kiss
> A sigh is just a sigh, the fundamental things apply as time goes by
> It's still the same old story, a fight for love and glory
> A case of do or die, the world will always welcome lovers as time goes by.

Steiner was delighted that the café with musicians allowed him to pick out a variety of songs: "It Had to Be You," "Shine," "Avalon," "Perfidia," "The Very Thought of You," "Knock on Wood," "Tango de la Rosa," "Die Wacht am Rhein," and "La Marseillaise." One other song being played as Ilsa and Viktor Lazlo enter Rick's is Cole Porter's 1930 "Love for Sale." The shocking lyrics were not sung so the Hollywood Production Code was not invoked. They would have banned it if these Porter lyrics were sung:

> Love for sale, appetizing young love for sale,
> Love that's fresh and still unspoiled,
> Love that's only slightly spoiled, love for sale. Who will buy?

Many of the same stars were in other films, such as *Passage to Marseille* and *The Maltese Falcon* (1944) with Bogart, Rains, Greenstreet, and Lorre. The two pianos used in *Casablanca* were sold profitably. The piano in the Paris scene was sold in 2012 for $600,000. The piano at Rick's café where he hid the two letters of transit sold for $3.4 million in 2014.

This movie encouraged several parodies, including the Marx Brothers 1946 *A Night in Casablanca*, Neil Simon's 1978 *The Cheap Detective*, Woody Allen's 1972 *Play It Again, Sam*, several radio shows, a colorized version on television, and a real Rick's Café in Casablanca.

Rick's Café in Casablanca now has piano, singers, instrumentalists, is open for lunch and dinner, has a small roulette table, and a loop film showing the movie in the old Medina in Casablanca. It was opened in 2004 by former U.S. Embassy diplomat Kathy Kriger with investors called The Usual Suspects. She died in 2018 but left a 2012 book called *Rick's Café: Bringing the Film Legend to Life in Casablanca*.

Long-time friend, Texas journalist Lloyd C. Clark (1923-2014), wrote regular newspaper columns about *Casablanca*. He published collections of such articles as *You Must Remember This, The Usual Suspects, Here's Looking at You*, etc. from his time with the *Daily News-Sun* in Sun City,

Arizona. He also taught at Rio Salado Community College in Surprise, Arizona.

Other movie nominees included *For Whom the Bell Tolls, Heaven Can Wait, The Human Comedy, In Which We Serve, Madame Curie, The More the Merrier, The Ox-Bow Incident, The Song of Bernadette,* and *Watch on the Rhine.*

Paul Lukas (1894-1971) from Budapest, Hungary, won Best Actor for *Watch on the Rhine.* Other contenders were Humphrey Bogart *(Casablanca),* Gary Cooper *(Robert Jordan),* Walter Pidgeon *(Marie Curie),* and Mickey Rooney *(The Human Comedy).*

Jennifer Jones (1919-2009) from Tulsa, Oklahoma, won Best Actress for *The Song of Bernadette.* Other contenders were Jean Arthur *(The More the Merrier),* Ingrid Bergman *(For Whom the Bell Tolls),* Joan Fontaine *(The Constant Nymph),* and Greer Garson *(Madame Curie).*

Katina Paxinou won Best Supporting Actress for *For Whom the Bell Tolls.*

Charles Coburn won Best Supporting Actor for *The More the Merrier.*

Best Song "You'll Never Know," w. Mack Gordon, m. Harry Warren, from *Hello, Frisco, Hello.*

Michael Curtiz, Director of *Casablanca.*

17th Academy Awards

Ceremony: This event was conducted at Grauman's Chinese Theater in Hollywood, California. It took place March 15, 1945, and was hosted by Bob Hope and John Cromwell, a film and stage director and actor, and father of actor James Cromwell. The entire awards ceremony lasting 70 minutes was broadcast nationally on ABC radio.

Bob Hope won an honorary award "for his many services to the Academy." Margaret O'Brien, 8 years old, won the Academy Juvenile Award as the Outstanding Child Actress of 1944. She starred in *Meet Me in St. Louis* with Judy Garland.

This was the first year that Best Picture was limited to five pictures. This was also the only time an individual was nominated for Best Actor and Best Supporting Actor for playing the same role in the same film: Barry Fitzgerald for the character of Father Fitzgibbon. He won for Best Supporting Actor.

The Irving G. Thalberg Memorial Award went to director and producer Darryl F. Zanuck. Beginning in the silent era, he had tackled tough subjects and during his service in World War II asked for riskier assignments. By this time, he had made a star of Jennifer Jones in *Song of Bernadette*, produced the haunting *Laura*, confronted race issues in *Pinky*, and depicted unionization and destruction of the environment in *How Green Was My Valley*. He would later focus on Jews in *Gentlemen's Agreement*.

1944 *Going My Way*

Tagline: "Bing's 'little angels'-the roughest gang this side of reform school." This feel-good story was a musical comedy and drama. A new, vivacious priest (Bing Crosby) was transferred to a New York City church with Father Fitzgibbon, played by wry, warm Barry Fitzgerald. The new priest appeared unacceptable to the old because he dressed informally, enjoyed golf, and had casual friendships with priests. When elder Fitzgibbon criticized golfing, the young priest said, "A golf course is nothing, but a pool room moved outdoors."

Young O'Malley attempted to address youth who were getting in trouble with the law, whereas Fitzgibbon remained silent because the boys attended church. The Crosby priest helped the boys develop a church choir, but their practice noise disturbed the old priest. Bing tended to "Say it with music."

When the elder priest learned that he was to be replaced by the younger one, he was upset and put to bed by Crosby singing the Irish lullaby, "Too Ra Loo Ra Loo Ral." As they discussed the elder's wish to return to Ireland to see his 90-year-old mother, they drew closer. Eventually, Crosby arranged for mother and son to have a visit.

The young priest met with a couple and discussed how he chose the priesthood and enjoyed "going my way." He met an old girlfriend, played by Rise Stevens, who performed at the Metropolitan Opera. She sang the "Habanera" from *Carmen*. They devised a plan for the new boys' choir to perform at the Metropolitan to raise money to save the church from debts and bankruptcy. They decided to sing "Swinging on a Star," which won Best Song.

The only complaint viewers seemed to have was length (126 minutes) and too many songs. Additional songs included "Day After Forever," "Ave Maria," "Adeste Fideles," and "Silent Night." The Robert Mitchell

Boys Choir performed. It might not generate such wide acclaim in today's world, but it suited the war-weary world of 1944.

It was filmed at the Lakeside Country Club at Toluca Lake in Los Angeles; St. Monica Catholic Church in Santa Monica, California; Paramount Studios in Los Angeles; and the parking lot of the Shrine Auditorium in Los Angeles. This low budget ($1.3 million) film surprised all with a total box office some ten times the budget.

Other movie nominees included *Double Indemnity, Gaslight, Since You Went Away,* and *Wilson.* Some of these lasted better than *Going My Way.* "Gaslighting" has become a common phrase in politics where a manipulator tries to get people to question their own memory, perceptions, or facts. Charles Boyer sought his wife's riches upstairs when he used up some gas for lighting their attic. The gas variations made her doubt herself and think she was going crazy. Another unique picture was *Double Indemnity,* one of the first "film noir" movies made. An insurance agent learned that a woman wanted help to murder her husband for money. But apparently many looked for a crowd-pleaser with a priest who sang.

Bing Crosby (1903-1977) from Tacoma, Washington, won Best Actor for *Going My Way.* Other contenders were Charles Boyer *(Gaslight)*, Barry Fitzgerald *(Going My Way)*, Cary Grant *(None but the Lonely Heart)*, and Alexander Knox *(Wilson).*

Ingrid Bergman (1915-1982) from Stockholm, Sweden, won Best Actress for *Gaslight.* Other contenders were Claudette Colbert *(Since You Went Away)*, Bette Davis *(Mr. Skeffington)*, Greer Garson *(Mrs. Parkington)*, and Barbara Stanwyck *(Double Indemnity).*

Ethel Barrymore won Best Supporting Actress for *None but the Lonely Heart.*

Barry Fitzgerald won Best Supporting Actor for *Going My Way.*

Best Song "Swinging on a Star," w. Johnny Burke, m. Jimmy Van Heusen, from *Going My Way.*

Leo McCary, Director of *Going My Way.*

18th Academy Awards

Ceremony: The event was conducted on March 7, 1946, at Grauman's Chinese Theatre in Hollywood, hosted by Bob Hope and James Stewart. The award ceremony celebrated the end of World War II by replacing the bronze statuettes with gold plating. Joan Crawford assumed she would not win Best Actress for *Mildred Pierce* and went home. She was in bed when the award was delivered to her. She was up against excellent actresses: Ingrid Bergman, Greer Garson, Jennifer Jones, and Gene Tierney.

Honorary awards went to Walter Wanger "for his six years as President of the Academy of Motion Picture Arts and Sciences;" Republic Studios, Daniel J. Bloomberg, "for the building of an outstanding musical scoring auditorium which provides optimum recording conditions and combines all elements of acoustic and engineering design;" *The House I Live In,* a tolerance 10-minute short produced by Frank Ross and Mervyn LeRoy with screenplay by Albert Maltz and song by Earl Robinson (m) and Lewis Allan (w) starring Frank Sinatra. Playing himself, Sinatra acted as if he was taking a break from recording to step outside for a smoke. He saw some boys chasing a Jewish boy and intervened. He told them we are "all" Americans, and one American's blood is as good as another's, and all our religions are to be respected equally. He sang "The House I Live In" with words by Abel Meeropol, who would later adopt the two sons of Julius and Ethel Rosenberg who were electrocuted in 1953. In later years, Meeropol's second verse referring to "my neighbors white and black" was sung by Paul Robeson, Mahalia Jackson, and Josh White. (See *Paul Robeson: A Biography* by Martin Abuml Duberman, published in 1989.) Sinatra sang the song at a Nixon White House dinner later. Ronald Reagan used it in his 1985 inaugural ceremonies. Meeropol also wrote "Strange Fruit," which was sung and recorded by Billie Holiday in 1939 to protest the lynchings of black Americans in lyrics that compared victims to the hanging fruit of trees.

Peggy Ann Garner, age 14, received the award for Outstanding Child Actress of 1945. She had starred *in Jane Eyre, The Keys of the Kingdom, A Tree Grows in Brooklyn,* and *Junior Miss.*

1945 *The Lost Weekend*

Tagline: "How daring can the screen dare to be?" This movie was unusual in so many ways. No movie had dealt seriously with an addiction and health issue like alcoholism. In fact, movies had shown William Powell and Myrna Loy in *The Thin Man* series of Dashiell Hammett detective stories drinking alcohol almost constantly.

To tackle this semi-autobiographical book by Charles R. Jackson was quite a feat. First, they considered casting and decided that to sell this kind of movie, it would take a matinee idol. But actors might consider it suicide for their career. They selected Ray Milland and he took on the role with hesitation since he had only done movies in light comedy earlier.

Milland, from Wales, usually played an Englishman but now he was a man whose life was wrecked by drinking. He prepared for the role by spending a night at Bellevue in the alcoholic ward. He also lost eight pounds for the role and the experience caused his marriage to suffer a bit. After completion of the film, he and his wife took a holiday in Canada and all healed.

The actress who would try to save the drunkard was Jane Wyman, married to Ronald Reagan. A search for a more famous actress like

Katharine Hepburn or Jean Arthur was unsuccessful. This role led to Wyman's greater success and Best Actress award later. The Ray Milland character's brother, who supported him when unable to hold a job, was played by Phillip Terry.

Other characters were Lillian Fontaine, mother of Olivia de Havilland and Joan Fontaine, who played Wyman's mother. The savvy realistic bartender who tried to stop customers from over-drinking was played by Howard da Silva, son of Russian parents who knew well the dreadful history of drinking in Russia. Unfortunately, that actor's reputation was stained by the House Un-American Activities Committee accusations and his talent was lost from films from 1951 to 1961.

The story is about four days and began with a scene like Alfred Hitchcock used in *Psycho* as the camera gradually zoomed in over a cityscape to a window where a bottle of whisky was hanging below a window. The bottle was would-be writer Milland's attempt to hide alcohol from his brother and girlfriend. He had decided to visit a farm and start a book called *The Bottle* about an alcoholic and was to begin it on this weekend.

In the throes of addiction, he promised brother and girlfriend to spend this weekend away from all temptations. But too ravaged by his need and without money, he attempted to pawn things for drinks or get them at the local bar where he cozied up to a lady wanting attention and stole her purse. The camera followed as he walked up Third Avenue in New York City to P. J. Clarke's, a tavern often frequented by author Charles Jackson. The local bar was copied and made at Paramount Studios and some actors like Robert Benchley stopped by for drinks during filming.

Don (Milland) wound up in Bellevue Hospital in the alcoholic unit nicknamed "Hangover Plaza." He escaped from the ward but at home, having DTs (delirium tremens) he saw a mouse crawling through a wall, a flying bat diving at him, and the bat killed the mouse as blood ran down the wall. During this scene, we hear some eerie music implying mental confusion. It is played on an instrument that one does not touch but moves one's fingers about through electronic wires emitting weird sounds. The instrument ordered by Miklós Rózsa was a theremin, invented by a Russian in the 1920s. It was also used in *Spellbound, The Day the Earth Stood Still, Forbidden Planet,* and other eerie movies.

The movie had some music, such as the drinking song in *La Traviata* by Verdi, and songs played in the bar, including "It Was So Beautiful," "Louise," and "Somebody Stole My Gal."

In the movie finale, the Jane Wyman character learned from the pawn shop that her boyfriend hocked his typewriter for a gun and seemed to plan suicide. (He committed suicide in the book.) He used Henry David Thoreau's line, "Most men lead lives of quiet desperation. I can't take quiet desperation!"

The movie had her confront him about suicide. Within a few minutes, he decided to give up drinking and write his book about his compulsion for alcohol. This slick ending of a grueling 101-minute film was not very believable but the realism about addiction was riveting for audiences. Never had a movie had so little time in which to do so much.

This film was produced on a budget of $1.25 million and grossed a surprising ten times that amount at the box office. It was selected by the National Film Registry for preservation due to the "uncompromising look at the devastating effects of alcoholism."

There was an increase in Alcoholics Anonymous (AA) from 1945 with 12,986 members and 556 groups to 1950 with 96,475 members and 3,527 groups. The movie did not focus on that sort of help, but many have credited the movie with people seeking more help with their alcoholic problems. Billy Wilder wanted to do this film because he had worked with Raymond Chandler, a recovering alcoholic. Chandler was notable for his film noir stories.

This was the first "film noir" to win an Academy Award. What is that? It's a mood movie filmed darkly, low budget, in a seedy part of a large city, with lower class people, and many actors with cynical attitudes. There is usually one good and one bad woman or femme fatale. The hero may be an ordinary guy or a private detective with faults, but his heart is usually in the right place.

Turner Classic Movies has had specialty showings of film noirs for some time. Certain directors, producers, and actors preferred these movies and here is a partial list of such films: *The Big Sleep, The Big Heat, D.O.A., The Invisible Man, The Maltese Falcon, The Naked City, The Postman Always Rings Twice, Double Indemnity, Mildred Pierce, Murder My Sweet, Little Caesar, Scarface, High Sierra, The Killers, Touch of Evil, Kiss Me Deadly, The Third Man, Sunset Boulevard, They Live By Night, They Drive by Night, Rififi, Le Diabolique, Crossfire, The Hitchhiker, Laura, Shadow of a Doubt, Notorious*, and *White Heat*.

Other movie nominees included *Anchors Aweigh, The Bells of St. Mary's, Mildred Pierce*, and *Spellbound*.

Ray Milland (1907-1986) from Neat, Wales, won Best Actor for *The Lost Weekend*. Other contenders were Bing Crosby *(The Bells of St. Mary's)*, Gene Kelly *(Anchors Aweigh)*, Gregory Peck *(The Keys of the Kingdom)*, and Cornel Wilde *(A Song to Remember)*.

Joan Crawford (1904-1977) from San Antonio, Texas, won Best Actress for *Mildred Pierce*. Other contenders were Ingrid Bergman *(The Bells of St. Mary's)*, Greer Garson *(The Valley of Decision)*, Jennifer Jones *(Love Letters)*, and Gene Tierney *(Leave Her to Heaven)*.

Anne Revere won Best Supporting Actress for *National Velvet*.

James Dunn won Best Supporting Actor for *A Tree Grows in Brooklyn.*

Best Song "It Might as Well Be Spring," w. Oscar Hammerstein II, m. Richard Rodgers, from *State Fair.*

Billy Wilder, Director of *The Lost Weekend.*

19th Academy Awards

Ceremony: This gala event was conducted March 13, 1947, at the Shrine Auditorium in Los Angeles. For the first time, the public was allowed to buy tickets. Jack Benny hosted the event and every category had at most five nominations. Claude Jarman, Jr., was awarded the Outstanding Child Actor of 1946 for the 12-year-old's performance in *The Yearling*.

Honorary awards were given to several. First, to Laurence Olivier "for his outstanding achievement as actor, producer and director in bringing *Henry V* to the screen." Second, to Harold Russell "for bringing hope and courage to his fellow veterans through his appearance in *The Best Years of Our Lives.*" It had been thought he would not win Best Supporting Actor, so he made history by receiving two Oscars for one role. Third, to Ernst Lubitsch "for his distinguished contributions to the art of the motion picture." The German-born director came to the U.S. in 1922 and began in Mary Pickford silent movies. He was nominated three times for director and directed *Design for Living, Ninotchka, The Merry Widow, The Shop Around the Corner, To Be or Not to Be,* and *Heaven Can Wait.* He became ill and couldn't finish a picture so the award may have been due to illness. He died of his sixth heart attack eight months later.

Many good films were being made in other countries. A decision was made to open the doors to foreign films the following year if they met the requirements of the Academy.

1946 *The Best Years of Our Lives*

Tagline: "So true, so dramatic, so heart-warming." The story of World War II veterans returning home from overseas came from MacKinlay Kanter, who interviewed troops as a U.S. newspaper war correspondent. Samuel Goldwyn hired him to write a screenplay about this. He sold the movie rights and screenwriter Robert Sherwood adapted it. It was renamed *The Best Years of Our Lives.* Despite Kanter's disappointment with the film changes, he went on to write best-seller *Andersonville* about a confederate prisoner of war camp.

Sherwood's good script often gave director William Wyler the chance to just pause and let the looks on Fredric March, Myrna Loy, Dana Andrews, Teresa Wright, Virginia Mayo, Harold Russell, Cathy O'Donnell, and Hoagy Carmichael faces deliver the messages. Three veterans returned to a town and tried to assimilate back home. March was welcomed by wife, Myrna Loy, and children but had trouble at work. He gave a vet with no collateral a loan. He told his boss, "His collateral is in his hands, his heart and his guts." Andrews' wife, Virginia Mayo, cared little to continue life with a man who could not find a respectable job. She said, "I gave you the best years of my life, and what have you done. You flopped. Couldn't even hold that job at the drugstore."

Russell returned with a permanent handicap, the loss of two hands, and worried whether his fiancé would pity him more than love him. Russell asked his fiancé to see him to bed and began to undress to let her know what life with him would be like. "This is when I know I'm helpless. My hands are down there on the bed. I can't put them on again without calling to somebody."

Harold Russell was no actor. He came to the U.S. from Nova Scotia and jumped at military opportunities. As a sergeant, he trained soldiers in explosives, but a TNT explosion burned off his hands. He was seen by director Wyler in a training film for vets with injuries to show how to return to normal life using hooks for hands. Starring in this movie led to future work as chairman of the President's Commission on Employment of the Handicapped.

The three men went to a bar run by Hoagy Carmichael who played Harold Russell's uncle. His music was song therapy where the vets consoled each other and enjoyed camaraderie. Hoagy's songs included "Among My Souvenirs;" "Toot, Toot, Tootsie;" "Beer Barrel Polka;" "Bridal Chorus;" and his own "Lazy River." Hoagy played "Chopsticks" with Russell using his hooks. Russell later recalled that Hoagy was conscientious, patient, and made him realize he could do more than he knew with his hooks. (See *Stardust Melody: The Life and Music of Hoagy Carmichael* by Richard M. Sudhalter published in 2002.)

This movie stays fresh because it has the reactions of all veterans returning home from war: post-traumatic stress disorder, flash backs, personality changes between loved ones, difficulty finding a decent job and making a living, and handling war wounds that change one's life. It brought home the theme that things and people are different than in the past.

It was shot at Los Angeles County Arboretum and Botanical Gardens; Ontario Army Airfield in California; Cincinnati, Ohio; and studios. Actors worked in their own clothes, not costumes. The budget was $2.1 million, and box office was ten times that amount. The movie was 170-minutes but was so good it won nine Oscars: Samuel Goldwyn for Best Picture, William Wyler for Best Director, Fredric March for Best Actor, Harold Russell for Best Supporting Actor, Robert Sherwood for Best Screenplay, Daniel Mandell for Best Film Editing, Hugo Friedhofer for Best Scoring of a Dramatic Picture, and honorary awards for Russell and Goldwyn.

Other movie nominees included *Henry V, It's a Wonderful Life, The Razor's Edge,* and *The Yearling.*

Fredric March (1897-1975) from Racine, Wisconsin, won Best Actor for *The Best Years of Our Lives.* Other contenders were Laurence Olivier *(Henry V),* Larry Parks *(The Jolson Story),* Gregory Peck *(The Yearling)* and James Stewart *(It's a Wonderful Life).*

Olivia de Havilland (1916-2020) from Tokyo won Best Actress for *To Each His Own.* Other contenders were Celia Johnson *(Brief Encounter),* Jennifer Jones *(Duel in the Sun),* Rosalind Russell *(Sister Kenny),* and Jane Wyman *(The Yearling).*

Anne Baxter won Best Supporting Actress for *The Razor's Edge.*

Harold Russell won Best Supporting Actor for *The Best Years of Our Lives.*

Best Song "On the Atchison, Topeka and the Santa Fe," w. Johnny Mercer, m. Harry Warren, from *The Harvey Girls.*

William Wyler, Director of *The Best Years of Our Lives.*

20th Academy Awards

Ceremony: The Academy Awards were presented March 20, 1948, at the Shrine Auditorium in Los Angeles, hosted by Agnes Moorhead and Dick Powell. Shirley Temple was awarded an Oscar as a child star. She said: "Thank you very much. Mommy, can we go home now?" At age 71, Edmund Gwenn was the oldest Oscar-winner up to that time, winning Best Supporting Actor for playing Santa Claus in *Miracle on 34th Street.*

Academy president Danish actor Jean Hersholt began in silent movies, went on to talkies, and his *Dr. Christian* radio show. He said:

There can be no more fitting moment than this 20th anniversary to look back through the years, far beyond the beginning of the Academy, far beyond the great industry that we know exists today, to those first days when the arts and sciences of making films were born. How fortunate we are that our profession is so young that we may honor tonight men still living who were pioneers. We take a happy pause in this sentimental journey to pay tribute to four of these men who, as far back as 1895, had faith in what we have become today. Their names are Colonel William N. Selig, Albert E. Smith, George K. Spoor, and Thomas Armat."

Two recipients who came were Colonel Selig and Albert E. Smith. Selig, age 84, said he "saw the movies when they were in their swaddling clothes.... I feel very proud and very happy to have seen that little child in swaddling clothes grow up to be such a big and beautiful lady. And I want to thank everyone ... for remembering the 'forgotten man'."
He had produced early documentaries of the West with cowboy stars

like Tom Mix. He improved nickelodeons with *The Count of Monte Cristo* and *Dr. Jekyll and Mr. Hyde.* Then he added jungle-zoo wild animals that inspired the first movie theme park in 1914. Albert Smith, age 73, was notable for presenting magic, magic lanterns, drawings, ventriloquism, and recitations for Thomas Edison's Vitagraph in 1897.

Thomas Armat invented a motion picture projector that he sold to Thomas Edison for his Kinetoscope. George K. Spoor with Gilbert "Broncho Billy" Anderson discovered stars, such as Wallace Beery, Francis X. Bushman, Ben Turpin, Gloria Swanson, and Charlie Chaplin. Spoor hired Louella Parsons as a screenwriter, and she later became a Hollywood gossip columnist. He built the Magniscope 35 mm movie projector, later produced the world's first newsreel, and invented an early 65 mm widescreen process for films produced from 1926-1930.

Jean Hersholt began the Motion Picture Relief Fund creating a hospital and nursing home for sick and indigent movie personnel. He sponsored the humanitarian award that was issued to humanitarians for years. Also, the new category of Best Foreign Language Film began.

Another honorary award was given to black actor/singer James Baskett "for his able and heart-warming characterization of Uncle Remus, friend and storyteller to children in Walt Disney's *Song of the South.*" Disney met him and was so impressed that he asked him to play Uncle Remus, the voice of Br'er Fox, and sing "Zip-a-Dee-Doo-Dah" in the movie, which won for Best Song, but he couldn't attend the movie's premiere in segregated Atlanta. The NAACP boycotted the movie and criticized Baskett for accepting the demeaning stereotyped role.

1947 *Gentlemen's Agreement*

Tagline: "Polite anti-Semitism." Film producer Darryl Zanuck joined the Los Angeles Athletic Club as a way of gaining access to people in the movie business. His application initially was rejected on the mistaken anti-Semitic assumption that someone named Zanuck must be Jewish. During his heyday at 20th Century-Fox, Mr. Zanuck and Walt Disney were two white Anglo-Saxon Protestant tycoons at the summit of the movie business. Later, Mr. Zanuck took the initiative of adapting *Gentleman's Agreement* to the screen over the objections of several Jewish colleagues, who feared that a movie attacking anti-Semitism would merely stir up the anti-Semites. This drama was based on Laura Hobson's 1947 best-selling novel of the same name.

Writer Philip Green (Gregory Peck) was recruited by a national magazine producer (Albert Dekker) to write a series of articles about anti-Semitism in America. Green decided to handle this by pretending to be a Jew and was shocked by the results. When checking into a New York hotel. the clerk said, "Well, we have a very high-class clientele." Green: "Then you do restrict your guests to Gentiles?" Clerk: "Well, I would hardly say that, and in any event, there seems to have been some mistake made because we don't have a single free room in the entire hotel."

Green was engaged to Kathy (Dorothy McGuire), niece of the publisher who assigned Green to this series. The controversies affected their relationship. Kathy said, "You think I'm an anti-Semite." Phil: "No, I don't. But I've come to see lots of nice people who hate it and deplore it and protest their own innocence."

Phil discussed his noticeable rebuffs with Jewish friend Dave (John Garfield). Phil: "You mean you get indifferent to it in time?" Dave: "No, but you're concentrating a lifetime into a few weeks. You're not changing the facts; you're just making them hurt more."

Even Phil's secretary (June Havoc) admitted that she was a Jew but lied on her application form to get a job. Phil's son (a young Dean Stockwell) got into a fight with kids who thought he was a Jew. Phil discussed his feelings with his mother played by Anne Revere. He also discussed these problems with a good friend played by Celeste Holm.

Elia Kazan and Moss Hart wrote the screenplay for this movie with a message. Hart came from a poor Jewish family writing plays for the Young Men's Hebrew Association. He joined up with George F. Kaufman and they received the Pulitzer Prize for the 1938 winner *You Can't Take It with You.* Alfred Newman, son of Russian Jewish parents, composed the music. He composed music for the shocking 1931 movie *Street Scene and* re-used his haunting song in *Gentlemen's Agreement.* Newman, Max Steiner, and Dimitri Tiomkin were called the "three godfathers of film music." That song, the sounds of busy streets, gave the movie a George Gershwin touch, since all three composers revered Gershwin.

This 118-minute movie was filmed in New York City and Darien, Connecticut; for a budget of $1,985,000, and earned double the amount with $3.9 million in rentals in 1948 and more later. It was dated due to references to World War II, but its message has continued through the years. The message is probably "all humans are equal, but some are more equal than others" due to prejudices. The role of Green was first offered to Cary Grant, but he turned it down. Peck accepted even though his agent advised him to refuse for fear it would endanger his career.

The movie upset the House Un-American Activities Committee. Elia Kazan, Darryl Zanuck, Anne Revere, and John Garfield were called to testify before the committee. Revere refused and although Garfield appeared, he did not name names. Both were placed on the Hollywood Blacklist. Garfield was called again to testify against his wife, former member of the Communist Party, but he died of a heart attack at the age of 39 before his second hearing date.

Other movie nominees included *The Bishop's Wife, Crossfire, Great Expectations,* and *Miracle on 34th Street.*

Ronald Colman (1891-1958) from Richmond, England, won Best Actor for *A Double Life.* Other contenders were John Garfield *(Body* *and Soul)*, Gregory Peck *(Gentleman's Agreement)*, William Powell *(Life with Father)*, and Michael Redgrave *(Mourning Becomes Electra)*.

Loretta Young (1913-2000) from Salt Lake City, Utah, won Best Actress for *The Farmer's Daughter.* Other contenders were Joan Crawford *(Possessed)*, Susan Hayward *(Smash-Up, the Story of a Woman)*, Dorothy McGuire *(Gentleman's Agreement)*, and Rosalind Russell *(Mourning Becomes Electra)*.

Celeste Holm won Best Supporting Actress for *Gentleman's Agreement.*

Edmund Gwenn won Best Supporting Actor for *Miracle on 34th Street.*

Best Song "Zip-A-Dee-Doo-Dah," w. Ray Gilbert, m. Allie Wrubel, from *Song of the South.*

Elia Kazan, Director of *Gentleman's Agreement.*

The new category of Best Foreign Language Film: *Shoe-Shine,* director Vittorio De Sica, Italy, Italian/English. The story was about a post-World War II orphan boy and his best friend who saved money from shining shoes in Rome to buy a horse. The friend's brother told them how to con money from a local fortune teller. Thus, the boys were able to purchase the horse. But they ended up in a juvenile detention center where they are driven apart by police demanding one of them to rat on the other about the money for their horse. This tragic end left many viewers crying.

The British Film Academy (BFA) was founded in 1947. The Guild of Television Producers and Directors merged with it to create the Society of Film and Television Arts (SFTA). In 1959, the Royal Family became involved, and Prince Philip was appointed its first president. In 1976, the opening of new headquarters was attended by the Queen; husband Prince Philip's daughter Princess Anne; and Prince Philip's uncle, Earl Mountbatten of Burma. The British Academy of Film and Television Arts (BAFTA) was henceforth connected with members of the royal family except during the term of actor/producer Lord Richard Attenborough. Thus, the British Best Film, Best Director, Best Producer, will be mentioned for the forthcoming years. Best British Actor and Actress will be mentioned after those categories were developed in 1952.

British Best Film: *Odd Man Out,* director and producer Carol Reed.

21st Academy Awards

Ceremony: The event was moved from the Shrine Auditorium to the Academy's theater because of rumors that some studios may have tried to influence votes. It was conducted at The Academy Theater, Hollywood, California, on March 24, 1949, hosted by Robert Montgomery.

Montgomery was an actor, director, and producer of film and TV since 1929. He testified before HUAC over concern about communist influences in Hollywood. He was president of the Screen Actors Guild 1935-1938 and 1946-1947, succeeded by Ronald Reagan. When General Dwight Eisenhower decided to run for president, he hired Montgomery to be his TV coach and gave him an office at the White House during his administration. His daughter, Elizabeth Montgomery, played Samantha on the TV series *Bewitched*.

When Jane Wyman was announced as Best Actress for her role as a mute in *Johnny Belinda*, she said, "I accept this very gratefully for keeping my mouth shut for once. I think I'll do it again," and then she sat down.

Several honorary awards were bestowed by Jean Hersholt on people who had made a difference in the movie industry. Sid Grauman was honored for "raising the standard of exhibition of motion pictures." Sid created the Chinese Theatre and the Egyptian Theatre and invited stars to put their hands and feet in wet cement in front of his Chinese theater. He was one of the original 36 founders of the Academy of Motion Picture Arts and Sciences.

Adolph Zukor was honored for "his services to the industry over forty years." The Austro-Hungarian film producer began with the first ever feature-length film, *The Prisoner of Zenda*, in 1913. He was one of the three founders of Paramount Pictures Corporation, and his private estate is now the Paramount Country Club. He signed early stars, like Mary Pickford, Roscoe "Fatty" Arbuckle, Douglas Fairbanks, Gloria Swanson, Pola Negri, and Rudolph Valentino. He produced 1926 *Beau Geste,* 1927 *Wings,* 1931 *Dr. Jekyll and Mr. Hyde,* and many other films.

Walter Wanger, a film producer since the 1910s, was president of the Academy from 1939-1940, 1941-1945, and produced a very high-quality film about Joan of Arc starring Ingrid Bergman. Her personal life may have interfered with nominations for the movie. When Wanger was given the honorary award for "service to the industry in adding to its moral stature in the world community by his production of the picture *Joan of Arc,*" he refused it. He was angry that this excellent work was not nominated for Best Picture.

Ivan Jandl received the Academy Juvenile Award for his portrayal of a 9-year-old boy trying to find his mother in concentration camps after World War II. The boy had polio at age three and was not expected to walk but pulled through and was found by producer Fred Zimmerman. He spoke no English but memorized English lines to play this role in *The Search.* However, young Jandl was prevented by communists in Prague, Czechoslovakia, from attending the ceremonies. He was not permitted by the government to keep the award in his home.

Jerry Wald received the Irving G. Thalberg Memorial Award. He became an American screenwriter and producer of films and radio shows. He produced the 1941 *The Man Who Came to Dinner,* 1942 *All Through the Night,* 1943 *Destination Tokyo,* 1944 *The Very Thought of You,* 1945 *Mildred Pierce,* 1946 *Humoresque,* 1947 *Dark Passage,* 1948 *Key Largo* and 1948 *Johnny Belinda.*

1948 *Hamlet*

Tagline: "One of the screen's most exciting experiences." This amazing British film was adapted, directed, produced, and acted by Laurence Olivier. Many have concluded that Olivier was the best actor of all during his lifetime. He had a vision of how he wanted to make *Hamlet,* perhaps the best depiction of revenge ever written by the masterful William Shakespeare. Olivier wanted it to be of tolerable length with exciting dialogue, excluding unnecessary characters to shorten running time, and to depict the eerie atmosphere of Elsinor in Denmark.

The film opened with Olivier's voice saying, "This is the tragedy of a man who could not make up his mind." The movie began with the clash of ocean waves against the stone cliffs of Elsinor and the ominous discords of William Walton's score. We are warned that we are about to see the inner workings of a mind full of passion, anger, and film noir touches through dark shadows, steep stairways, fog, noises, pulsing heartbeats, and storms. Music included bells tolling with discord, Hamlet's tortured mind is accompanied by disharmonic music. Ophelia's madness is heard through oboes, folk ballads, and violins. The body of Hamlet was carried up the steps by silhouetted soldiers marching in time to the funeral march ending with a final bass tone.

Olivier surrounded himself with English actors: Basil Sidney, Felix Aylmer, Peter Cushing, Christopher Lee, Jean Simmons, Niall MacGinnis, Eileen Herlie, Anthony Quayle, Stanley Holloway, etc. Through moving cameras nosing about the castle and into his mother's bedroom ala Sigmund Freud, emotions were captured in close-ups of main figures like Hamlet. Muir Matheson conducted the score by looking at the large movie screen and conducting the orchestra facing him as the conductor. Many conductors watched the movie while conducting the music.

The sudden death of Hamlet's father, immediate marriage of his mother to his father's murderer, accidental murder of his girlfriend's father, and Hamlet's inability to avenge these wrongs absorb him. The phrase "to be or not to be" becomes a suicidal theme. The creation of a play within a play to push his mother and new stepfather to openly confess their scheme failed. He was banished from Denmark, but pirates disrupted the voyage and he returned.

The final scene with poison in a drink and on his sword turned out to be suicidal for his mother and deadly for him. He remained noble throughout the story and was carried off militarily at the end. Revenge and possible oedipal love for his mother, whom he kissed on the lips several times, moved the masterpiece into the psychological realm. The sensitive scene of his bad treatment of Ophelia and her insanity and suicide added to the tension toward the end.

Some have criticized the removal of speeches to a single statement, and the deletion of somewhat comical characters, such as Fortinbras, Rosencrantz, and Guildenstern. Others have appreciated a running time of only 154 minutes compared to four plus hours for the entire play. The bland treatment of so much dialogue in other Hamlet movies and plays is replaced by this passionate production. Shakespeare's Globe Theatre never had such scenery, sounds, and close-ups.

Hamlet won Academy Awards for Best Picture (J. Arthur Rank-Two Cities Film and producer Olivier), Best Actor (Olivier), and Best Costume Design, Black-and-White (Roger Furse). It was the first non-American film to win Best Picture.

The movie was shot at Elsinore and England at Pinewood Studios in the village of Iver Heath in Buckinghamshire. This movie was very popular in Great Britain and made a profit of £779,700 over a budget of £527,530. It was distributed by Rank Film Distributors in the UK and Universal-International in the U.S. The U.S. box office was $3,250,000.

Other movie nominees were *Johnny Belinda, The Red Shoes, The Snake Pit,* and *The Treasure of the Sierra Madre.* Some had worthwhile messages because World War II left veterans, wives, and families searching for more meaning in their lives. The most unusual of these nominees was *The Red Shoes,* with stunning color, music, choreography, and filmmaking. A beautiful dancer tried to use her dance gift to find personal happiness. Those searches made her "burn her candle at both ends so that it would not last the night." Audiences had never seen so much beauty and emotion in a movie, and it inspired new dancers and ballet for some time.

Laurence Olivier (1907-1989) from Surrey, England, won Best Actor for *Hamlet.* Other contenders were Lew Ayres *(Johnny Belinda),* Montgomery Clift *(The Search),* Dan Dailey *(When My Baby Smiles at Me),* and Clifton Webb *(Sitting Pretty).*

Jane Wyman (1914-2007) from St. Joseph, Missouri, won Best Actress for *Johnny Belinda.* Other contenders were Ingrid Bergman *(Joan of Arc),* Olivia de Havilland *(The Snake Pit),* Irene Dunne *(I Remember Mama),* and Barbara Stanwyck *(Sorry, Wrong Number).*

Claire Trevor won Best Supporting Actress for *Key Largo.*

Walter Huston won Best Supporting Actor for *The Treasure of the Sierra Madre.*

Best Song "Buttons and Bows," w. Ray Evans, m. Jay Livingston, from *Paleface.*

John Huston, Best Director of *The Treasure of Sierra Madre.*

Best Foreign Language Film: *Monsieur Vincent,* director Maurice Cloche, France, French. This French movie starred Pierre Fresnay as Vincent de Paul. The story of his sweeping changes in the church dealing with poverty and developing charities and hospitals produced the French welfare state. The church canonized Vincent in 1737 after he had been stoned and called names earlier. He developed the Congregation of the Mission, the Ladies of Charity and the Daughters of Charity. The movie was shot by Claude Renoir and the screenplay was by dramatist Jean Anouilh. It offered a redemptive message of Christian love and reconciliation to French audiences who had undergone occupation and liberation during World War II.

British Best Film: *The Fallen Idol,* director, and producer Carol Reed.

22nd Academy Awards

Ceremony: This event was conducted at the RKO Pantages Theatre in Hollywood, California on March 23, 1950, hosted by actor Paul Douglas. Bobby Driscoll won the juvenile award for *The Window* and *So Dear to My Heart*. The 13-year-old thanked God for his parents.

This was the last year when all five Best Picture nominees were filmed in black and white. An honorary award was given to Cecil B. DeMille as a distinguished motion picture pioneer and for his 37 years of brilliant showmanship. He began in silent films and created large budget spectaculars, was good at directing thousands of extras, and focused on westerns and Biblical themes. He influenced Alfred Hitchcock, Stephen Spielberg, and appeared or did prologues for some 21 of his films.

Jean Hersholt received an award for his four terms as president of the Academy from actor Ronald Reagan. Hersholt said he made his first picture in 1906 in Denmark, and it took only four hours to make, citing how things had changed.

1949 *All the King's Men*

Tagline: "These people were in his hip pocket next to the whisky, the blackjack, and the gin." The title came from Mother Goose, who said:

Humpty Dumpty sat on a wall, Humpty Dumpty had a great fall; all the king's horses and all the king's men, couldn't put Humpty together again.

This movie was based on 1946 Robert Penn Warren's Pulitzer Prize-winning novel focusing on the rise and fall of a southern politician named Willie Stark. He was played by Broderick Crawford, and resembled Louisiana governor Huey Long. Mercedes McCambridge, Joanne Dru, John Ireland, John Derek and Sheppard Strudwick rounded out the main cast.

This film noir movie depicted a politician who became as corrupt as his political opponents once he gained power. As the saying goes, "Power tends to corrupt and absolute power corrupts absolutely." The movie action was seen through the eyes of a journalist (John Ireland). Many people were gunned down in the movie. Nobody in the movie was given a script. They looked at the script once and it was taken away. Crawford said, "We had to stay on our toes."

The movie was shot in California using residents and an old courthouse, which was demolished not long after the movie was released. The movie originally ran 250 minutes and the director told editors to chop all scenes and leave the center of each scene. Thus, the 109-minute movie ran like a documentary with jagged edges for greater effect. Its turbulence and naturalness won acclaim.

The dark film dealt with graft, corruption, love, drink, and one line was, "There's something on everybody. Man is conceived in sin and born in corruption." Stark also said in a speech: "Now, shut up! Shut up all of you. Now listen to me, you hicks. Yeah, you're hicks too, and they fooled you a thousand times like they fooled me. But this time, I'm going to fool somebody. I'm going to stay in this race. I'm on my own, and I'm out for blood."

Such political campaigns were familiar in America and generated much enthusiasm among voters. That was how Willie Stark got elected, but it also foretold his downfall because he was not a good man. John Wayne was offered this role but found it unpatriotic and refused it. It was the last Best Picture winner to be based on a Pulitzer Prize-winning novel.

Music was composed by Russian pianist Louis Gruenberg, and he used other well-known songs and singers to fit the time and the place. Those included "Hail, Hail, the Gang's All Here," Hank Williams' "Long Gone Lonesome Blues," Andy Razaf and Fats Waller's "If It Ain't Love," Sidney Bechet's "Si Tu Vois Ma Mere," and some classical numbers, such as Beethoven's "Fur Elise," Mozart's "The Marriage of Figaro," and "Cosi fan Tutte."

The movie made between $2 million and $9 million at the box office with a budget of $50 million, so it was considered a king-sized collapse.

Other movie nominees included *Battleground, The Heiress, A Letter to Three Wives,* and *Twelve O'Clock High.*

Broderick Crawford (1911-1986) from Philadelphia won Best Actor for *All the King's Men.* Other contenders were Kirk Douglas *(Champion),* Gregory Peck *(Twelve O'Clock High),* Richard Todd *(The Hasty Heart),* and John Wayne *(Sands of Iwo Jima).*

Olivia de Havilland won Best Actress for *The Heiress.* Other contenders were Jeanne Crain *(Pinky),* Susan Hayward *(My Foolish Heart),* Deborah Kerr *(Edward, My Son),* and Loretta Young *(Come to the Stable).*

Mercedes McCambridge won Best Supporting Actress for *All the King's Men.*

Dean Jagger won Best Supporting Actor for *Twelve O'Clock High.*

Best Song "Baby, It's Cold Outside," w. m. Frank Loesser, from *Neptune's Daughter.*

Joseph L. Mankiewicz, Director of *A Letter to Three Wives.*

Best Foreign Language Film: *The Bicycle Thief,* director Vittorio De Sica, Italy, Italian. This sad movie described a father trying to support his family in post-World War II Italy. He applied for a job pasting advertisements but needed a bicycle. The family sold belongings to purchase one but while he was working, a young man stole it. Police didn't help but the father saw a bicycle and tried to steal it. The owner saw the man, felt pity for him, and told people to release him. Father and son walked off together. De Sica used ordinary people instead of professional actors. Sergio Leone, a later movie producer of spaghetti westerns, was an uncredited seminary student in one scene. The heart-wrenching story of a man trying to help his family without aid from police or others won many awards and some voted it the best movie ever made. It intimated that poor people might be good despite stealing.

British Best Film: *The Third Man,* director, and producer Carol Reed. *The Third Man* used music from street musician Anton Karas using a zither. Many say that zither theme song is one of the main reasons this movie was so notable. The historic ferris wheel ridden by Orson Welles and Joseph Cotton also made it special.

23rd Academy Awards

Ceremony: This event was conducted on March 29, 1951, at the RKO Pantages Theatre in Hollywood, hosted by Fred Astaire. Academy Honorary Awards were given to actor George Murphy "for his services in interpreting the film industry to the country at large." Louis B. Mayer received an award "for distinguished service to the motion picture industry." The Irving G. Thalberg Memorial Award was given to Darryl F. Zanuck because he learned how to adapt to changing screen sizes, tackle social issues that other studios avoided, and made box office hits out of difficult movies.

Presenters of awards ranged through actors, actresses, and the first African American to receive the 1950 Nobel Peace Prize, Ralph Bunche, for his mediations in Israel. He was involved in the formation and administration of the United Nations and peacekeeping. He presented the award for the Best Motion Picture.

1950 *All About Eve*

Tagline: "It's all about women and their men." This story was written and directed by Joseph L. Mankiewicz and produced by Darryl F. Zanuck. It was based on *The Wisdom of Eve*, a 1946 short story by Mary Orr. It featured many stars, including Bette Davis, Anne Baxter, George Sanders, Celeste Holm, Gary Merrill, Hugh Marlowe, Thelma Ritter, Gregory Ratoff, Walter Hampden, and Marilyn Monroe in one of her earliest movies. This film set the mold for movies about movies, because it showed the common problem with aging female stars as younger and more beautiful ladies replace them.

Bette Davis was the perfect example of an aging beauty and did not realize that her understudy (Anne Baxter) wanted to replace her. She knew she had critics, so at a party she said, "Fasten your seatbelts. It's going to be a bumpy night." Mary Orr, the author of this story, had experienced just such a problem with a conniving girl who stole her place in acting.

It was first thought that Susan Hayward would play the aging actress, but Zanuck thought she was "too young." Marlene Dietrich was shunned as "too German." Gertrude Lawrence was considered but she did not like to drink or smoke in films. Zanuck found that Barbara Stanwyck was unavailable, and Tallulah Bankhead and Joan Crawford were considered but not chosen. Finally, Claudette Colbert was set to star but became injured, withdrew, and Ingrid Bergman was briefly considered before the role was given to Bette Davis. With her casting, the character was re-written as more abrasive.

Anne Baxter, architect Frank Lloyd Wright's granddaughter, had only played supporting roles. She had won Best Supporting Actress for *The Razor's Edge* and became the bitchy dishonest character rivaling Davis in this movie. Witty sharp-tongued dialogue in smoky rooms set Davis apart from other stars in this movie.

Baxter had studied with Russian actress Maria Ouspenskaya who starred in 1936 *Dodsworth,* 1939 *Love Affair,* 1940 *Waterloo Bridge,* 1941 *The Wolf Man,* 1942 *King's Row, 1943 Frankenstein Meets the Wolf Man,* 1945 *Tarzan and the Amazons,* 1946 *I've Always Loved You,* 1947 *Wyoming,* and 1949 *A Kiss in the Dark.* Ouspenskaya brought the practices of Russian actor Konstantin Stanislavsky to the U.S. He had worked with writers Leo Tolstoy and Anton Chekov. American actors who studied Stanislavsky's method acting included Stella Adler, Marlon Brando, Lee Strasberg, and Gregory Peck.

Zanuck tried to improve Joseph L. Mankiewicz' screenplay and chose the title after the George Sanders' character who said he would tell "more about Eve—all about Eve." Hence, the title was changed. Sexy Marilyn Monroe was described by the Sanders' character hilariously as a "graduate of the Copacabana School of Dramatic Art." She got the role because she seemed better suited to comedy than Angela Lansbury, who was considered. Monroe was so intimidated by Bette Davis that she left the set to vomit, and it took 11 takes to complete the scene.

The movie was described by critic Roger Ebert of the *Chicago Sun Times* as Davis' best role with her depiction of ambition in the movie industry. The movie ran 138 minutes, had a budget of $1.4 million, and exceeded $8.4 million at the box office. The movie was made in Los Angeles studios, but to get close to theatres, some scenes were shot in the theatre district of Manhattan. The John Golden Theatre at 252 W. 45th Street at 8th Avenue was one scene. Another was the interior of the Curran Theatre at 445 George Street in San Francisco. But the most intriguing scene of all was at the 21 Club in New York City at 21 W. 52nd Street.

The 21 Club was also prominent in the movie *Rear Window* with James Stewart, whose character had a broken leg and was unable to go anywhere. His girlfriend, played by Grace Kelly, ordered him a Caesar salad and a lobster from the 21 Club, and those recipes are online today.

Why was the 21 Club featured in *All About Eve?* Begun in 1922, it became an unusual restaurant with two features—antique toys donated by guests hanging from the ceiling and jockeys with distinctive colors ordered by breeders and elites, with some 35 jockeys lined up on the stairs and landing of the restaurant, and two inside the front door. That began in the 1930s with a rich horse breeder named Mr. Van Urk, who had a dessert named for him at the 21. He was so impressed that he donated the first jockey statuette. During prohibition and after, the restaurant had secret stashes of alcoholic beverages for customers like American presidents, world leaders, and actors and actresses.

The music for this movie was arranged by Alfred Newman. He did not favor tunes for individual actors and used a single theme he composed throughout the movie, shifting it to fit the scenes. He did include songs by others, such Liszt's "Liebestraum," Richard Rodgers' "Manhattan" "Blue Moon" and "Thou Swell," Nat Simon's "Poinciana," Debussy's "Beau Soir," Harold Arlen's "That Old Black Magic" and "Stormy Weather," Anton Bruckner's "Symphony No. 4 in E-flat major," and Vincent Rose's "Linger Awhile."

Other movie nominees included *Born Yesterday Father of the Bride*, *King Solomon's Mines*, and *Sunset Boulevard*. It was unusual that two movies in the same year were made about fading female movie stars— *All About Eve* and *Sunset Boulevard*.

Jose Ferrer (1909-1992) from Santurce, Puerto Rico, won Best Actor for *Cyrano de Bergerac*. Other contenders were Louis Calhern *(The Magnificent Yankee)*, William Holden *(Sunset Boulevard)*, James Stewart *(Harvey)*, and Spencer Tracy *(Father of the Bride)*.

Judy Holliday (1922-1965) from New York City won Best Actress for *Born Yesterday*. Other contenders were Anne Baxter *(All About Eve)*, Bette Davis *(All About Eve)*, Eleanor Parker *(Caged)*, and Gloria Swanson *(Sunset Boulevard)*.

Josephine Hull won Best Supporting Actress for *Harvey*.

George Sanders won Best Supporting Actor for *All About Eve*.

Best Song "Mona Lisa," w. Ray Evans, m. Jay Livingston, from *Captain Carey, U.S.A.*

Joseph L. Mankiewicz, Director of *All About Eve*.

Best Foreign Language Film: *The Walls of Malapaga,* director Rene Clement, France/Italy, French, Italian. The aging French actor, Jean Gabin, starred in this movie, speaking French while involved with an Italian actress and her daughter (who both spoke Italian in the movie). The movie was considered a re-make of Gabin's famous role in 1937 *Pepe Le Moko,* about a French criminal who hid in the Casbah in Algiers. Morocco and Algeria were quite famous in movies of the 1930s and 1940s.

British Best Film: *The Blue Lamp.* Director Basil Dearden. Producer Michael Balcon.

24th Academy Awards

Ceremony: This event was conducted at the RKO Pantages Theatre in Hollywood on March 20, 1952, hosted by actor Danny Kaye.

The Academy gave two honorary awards. One went to Gene Kelly for "his versatility as an actor, singer, director and dancer, and his choreography of *An American in Paris*." The other was for Best Special Effects in *When Worlds Collide*.

The Irving G. Thalberg Memorial Award was presented by Darryl Zanuck to Arthur Freed for *An American in Paris*, where he was both lyricist and film producer. His songwriting went back to early appearances with the Marx Brothers after he met their mother, Minnie Marx. The Academy awarded Freed for Best Picture by name instead of by studio, breaking their old tradition.

Vivien Leigh was unable to attend and receive the Oscar for *A Streetcar Named Desire* due to appearing in a New York play. Greer Garson accepted the award saying, "It's an honor and a thrill to accept this for you, Vivien. I hope you're listening in New York. We're all very excited about it. God bless you and congratulations." Word had circulated that Leigh was unwell.

1951 *An American in Paris*

Tagline: "Romance. Adventure. Gershwin." Paris evoked memories for many. Ernest Hemingway said, "If you were lucky enough to have lived in Paris as a young man, then wherever you go, it stays with you, for Paris is a moveable feast."

Perhaps Gene Kelly felt similarly. His role in this movie was about a struggling artist living in Paris with a pianist friend, played by Oscar Levant (who had been a friend of the Gershwin brothers). Kelly said, "Back home everyone said I didn't have any talent. They might be saying the same thing over here, but it sounds better in French." One of Levant's lines was, "I'm a concert pianist. That's a pretentious way of saying I'm unemployed now." They had another friend, a French singer played by George Guetary.

A society woman played by Nina Foch bought some paintings by the Kelly figure and invited the artist to a party. Kelly met French Leslie Caron. They dated and danced by the Seine River near Notre Dame Cathedral. They wanted to dance all over Paris to the tune of "An American in Paris." The movie had them dance in all kinds of sites and with much passion. Car horns were included in George Gershwin's music and were heard as the two dancers embraced.

Arthur Freed came up with the idea when attending a production of Gershwin's music and his 1928 "An American in Paris" number. He wanted to buy the rights to "An American in Paris." George's brother, Ira, would sell if only Gershwin numbers were used in the movie. Audiences were lucky to hear "Embraceable You," "Nice Work If You Can Get It," "By Strauss," "I Got Rhythm," "Tra-la-la," "Love Is Here to Stay," "I'll Build a Stairway to Paradise," "Concerto in F for Piano and Orchestra," "S'Wonderful," and "An American in Paris." Ira was paid $56,250 as a consultant. Some movie composers, like Max Steiner, were George Gershwin's friends as well. (See *Music by Max Steiner* by Steven C. Smith published in 2020.)

Gene Kelly wanted a French girl to play the role of the dancer opposite him and met Leslie Caron in Paris after seeing her in a ballet. She hardly knew English when she began, and due to malnutrition during World War II could not dance every day. Filming therefore took longer. Kelly wanted more scenes in Paris but budgets and timing reduced final filming. Gene Kelly danced on Oscar Levant's piano, and cheered up the old, depressed pianist whose fingers were, in real life, succumbing to arthritis that ended his career.

The last twenty minutes of the film have only dancing without dialogue. That cost the studio around $500,000 to film on 44 sets. The background reflections of French painters took six weeks to build and kept 30 painters working nonstop. Filming was lengthened because actress Nina Foch developed chicken pox and had to stop filming toward the movie ending, as makeup artists had trouble covering the pockmarks. Later, Nina Foch went on to teach others how to act.

MGM was surprised they won the Oscar for Best Picture. They took out a full-page age in *Variety* with their Leo the Lion mascot saying, "Honestly, I was just sitting in the sun, waiting for a streetcar." That referred to two nominees *A Place in the Sun* and *A Streetcar Named Desire*.

The movie ran 113 minutes and the budget of $2.7 million was high, but the film earned more than $7 million in the U.S., Canada, and Europe.

Other movie nominees included *Decision Before Dawn, A Place in the Sun, Quo Vadis,* and *A Streetcar Named Desire.*

Humphrey Bogart (1899-1957) from New York City won Best Actor for *The African Queen.* Other contenders were Marlon Brando *(A Streetcar Named Desire),* Montgomery Clift *(A Place in the Sun),* Arthur Kennedy *(Bright Victory),* and Fredric March *(Death of a Salesman).*

Vivien Leigh won Best Actress for *A Streetcar Named Desire.* Other contenders were Katharine Hepburn *(The African Queen),* Eleanor Parker *(Detective Story),* Shelley Winters *(A Place in the Sun),* and Jane Wyman *(The Blue Veil).*

Kim Hunter won Best Supporting Actress for *A Streetcar Named Desire.*

Karl Malden won Best Supporting Actor for *A Streetcar Named Desire*.

Best Song "In the Cool, Cool, Cool of the Evening," w. Johnny Mercer, m. Hoagy Carmichael, from *Here Comes the Groom*.

George St evens, Director of *A Place in the Sun*.

Best Foreign Langue Film: *Rashomon,* director Akira Kurosawa, Japan, Japanese. Rashomon, city gate of ancient Kyoto, was an action-packed movie. It used camera angles, closeups, and flashbacks to show how four people described the same event: a man's murder and the rape of his wife. The movie demonstrated how justice intersected with human nature and different views of the same events. Kurosawa's model for music for this film came from Ravel's tense *Bolero*.

British Best Film: *The Lavender Hill Mob*. Director Charles Crichton. Producer Michael Balcon.

25th Academy Awards

Ceremony: This event was conducted on March 19, 1953, at the RKO Pantages Theatre in Hollywood and had a hook-up at the NBC International Theatre. Bob Hope emceed the Hollywood portion. Conrad Nagel and Fredric March emceed the New York City portion. Special guests were Governor Earl Warren and soon to be Chief Justice of the U.S. Supreme Court and the Los Angeles mayor and his wife.

The big surprise was *High Noon's* loss to *The Greatest Show on Earth*. Cecil B. DeMille began as an actor and was involved with epic movies in the silent movie era. He directed crowd scenes hollering directions from a height with a bull horn. People enjoyed his movies for the moment but did not necessarily remember them for decades.

This was the 25th anniversary of the Oscars and was first year of the annual television broadcast of the Oscars ceremonies. The TV audience was estimated at 40 million viewers watching the movie industry's "biggest show on earth." Two-time winner Vivien Leigh was hospitalized with a nervous breakdown. The two male best actors (Gary Cooper and Anthony Quinn) were in Mexico shooting a new picture together. Gloria Grahame was the only winning actress to accept her Oscar there. When John Wayne accepted the Oscar for Best Actor Gary Cooper, he said:

Ladies and gentlemen, I'm glad to see that they're giving this to a man who is not only most deserving but has conducted himself through his years in our business in a manner that we can all be proud of. Coop and I have been friends, hunting and fishing, for more years than I like to remember. He's one of the nicest fellows I know. I don't know anybody any nicer. And our kinship goes further than that friendship because we both fell off of horses in pictures together. Now that I'm through being such a good sport, spouted all this good sportsmanship, I'm gonna go back and find my business manager, and agent, and producer, and find out why I didn't get *High Noon* instead of Cooper.

Honorary awards went to George Alfred Mitchell "for the design and development of the camera that bears his name" in the field of cinematography; Joseph M. Schenck "for long and distinguished service to the motion picture industry;" Merian C. Cooper "for his innovations and contributions to the art of motion pictures." Harold Lloyd won for "master comedian and good citizen," and Bob Hope won for "his contribution to the laughter of the world, his service to the motion picture industry, and his devotion of the American premise." Cecil B. DeMille won the Irving G. Thalberg Memorial Award.

1952 *The Greatest Show on Earth*

Tagline: "Technicolor—truly marvelous color, we repeat—this huge motion picture of the big-top is the dandiest ever put upon the screen." This movie was set in the Ringling Brothers and Barnum & Bailey Circus. Two main stars, Betty Hutton, and Cornel Wilde studied and practiced working with trapeze artists to play their roles. Charlton Heston was the circus manager running the show. James Stewart starred as a mysterious clown with medical background and was never seen without his clown face make-up. Some fourteen hundred people, hundreds of animals and 60 railroad cars of equipment and tents composed the movie with circus acts. Dorothy Lamour, Gloria Grahame, and Lyle Bettger rounded out the cast.

Equipment failure, dangerous falls, revenge, and love with all the wrong people make up the excitement that builds throughout the movie. One line is, "Listen, sugar, the only way that you can keep me warm is to wrap me up in a marriage license." DeMille was the narrator for the movie.

Surprise cameo appearances in circus attendees add to the enjoyment. They include Bob Hope, Bing Crosby, William Boyd in his Hopalong Cassidy attire, Danny Thomas, Van Heflin, Leon Ames and the voice of Edmond O'Brien. The fact that this was chosen as the Best Picture may have had something to do with Senator Joseph McCarthy pursuing Communists in Hollywood, since *High Noon* producer Carl Foreman soon wound up on the Hollywood blacklist.

The movie score was arranged by Victor Young and Ned Washington with John Ringling North's contribution of "Luawana Lady." Other rousing effective songs were "Be a Jumping Jack," "Popcorn and Lemonade," "A Picnic in the Park," "Sing a Happy Song," "Dream Lover," "Only a Rose" and "Standby March."

The movie ran 152 minutes, had a budget of $4 million and made $36 million at the box office. The success influenced a television series starring Jack Palance in Heston's role. It ran for thirty episodes in 1963-1964. The movie influenced director Steven Spielberg to make film his career. He liked the train crash scene and his 2005 movie *War of the Worlds* showed two kids looking at the train-wreck from this movie as they channel-surfed on their TV.

Other movie nominees included *High Noon, Ivanhoe, Moulin Rouge,* and *The Quiet Man.* The theme for *High Noon* played when Gary Cooper could find nobody to stand with him against bad guys. Sometimes movies that lost have lasted better over the years than the year's winner.

Gary Cooper won Best Actor for *High Noon.* Other contenders were Marlon Brando *(Viva Zapata!),* Kirk Douglas *(The Bad and the Beautiful),* Jose Ferrer *(Moulin Rouge),* and Alec Guinness *(The Lavender Hill Mob).*

Shirley Booth (1907-1992) from New York City won Best Actress for *Come Back, Little Sheba*. Other contenders were Joan Crawford (*Sudden Fear*), Bette Davis *(The Star)*, Julie Harris *(The Member of the Wedding)*, and Susan Hayward *(With a Song in My Heart)*.

Gloria Grahame won Best Supporting Actress for *The Bad and the Beautiful*.

Anthony Quinn won Best Supporting Actor for *Viva Zapata!*

Best Song "High Noon," w. Ned Washington, m. Dimitri Tiomkin, from *High Noon*. This movie went nowhere in review audiences until the song was introduced. Tiomkin's music even heralded a clock ticking down to the shootout.

John Ford, Director of *The Quiet Man*.

Best Foreign Language Film: *Forbidden Games,* director Rene Clement, France, French. A little Parisian girl about six is orphaned when her parents were killed in a Nazi air raid. She joined an older peasant boy and they tried to make sense of their chaotic world by creating burial grounds for animals like the little girl's pet dog. Their forbidden game was creating these animal cemeteries and stealing crosses from real cemeteries for them. The boy's father heard angry local citizen responses. That caused separation between the little girl from the boy and her future ended bleakly. The haunting tune played throughout the movie may be one of the most beautiful songs ever written, called "Romance." Critics described the film thusly: "As an indictment of war, it is unsurpassed." "With its mixture of tones, its multiple plots, and its important use of the Spanish guitarist Narciso Yepes, it is very much its own film."

British Best Film: *The Sound Barrier,* director, and producer David Lean. The new categories of actors were added in this year. **British Best Actor:** Ralph Richardson in *The Sound Barrier.* **British Best Actress:** Vivien Leigh in *A Streetcar Named Desire.*

26th Academy Awards

The Ceremony: This event of March 25, 1954, was televised at Hollywood's RKO Pantages Theatre in Hollywood and NBC Century Theatre in New York City. Donald O'Connor hosted in Los Angeles and Fredric March in New York City. Some 43 million viewers enjoyed the awards.

Fred Zinnemann directed *From Here to Eternity*, which received 13 nominations and won eight Oscars. William Holden's speech for Best Actor in *Stalag 17* had time to say only "Thank you" and he published a full-page ad to thank everyone he wanted to thank that night.

Walt Disney won four awards setting a record for the most Oscars won in the same year. Honorary awards included Pete Smith "for his witty and pungent observations on the American scene in his 'Pete Smith Specialties,'" and Joseph Breen "for his conscientious, open-minded, and dignified management of the Motion Picture Production Code."

George Stevens won the Irving G. Thalberg Memorial Award. His career began by directing *Laurel and Hardy* shorts in 1929, and working as director, producer, screenwriter, and cinematographer. He won Oscars for directing *A Place in the Sun* and *Giant*. In World War II he headed filmmaking from 1943-46 under General Eisenhower, documenting D-Day, the liberation of Paris, horrific scenes from Dachau concentration camp, and presentation of such scenes at the Nuremburg Trials.

1953 *From Here to Eternity*

Tagline: "The original Pearl Harbor Story." The movie opened in 1941 where Robert Prewitt (Montgomery Clift) requested an Army transfer. Sent to Schofield Army Base in Hawaii, his new captain heard of his boxing skill and wanted him to represent the company. Having ruined the eyesight of a man in boxing, he did not want to box anymore and was now a bugler. His friend, (Frank Sinatra) ran into problems with a sadistic stockade sergeant (Ernest Borgnine).

Prew (Clift) fell for a social club hostess (Donna Reed) before the bombing of Pearl Harbor. He went AWOL but learned of the bombing and was killed as he went back to join his troops. The sergeant (Burt Lancaster) made passionate love to the wife of the captain on a special beach scene just before Pearl Harbor. Other characters filled out the roles described by the movie author, James Jones, who boxed during his Army term in World War II.

Some special lines included "Nobody ever lies about being lonely." Also, Prew told his sergeant (Lancaster), "A man don't go his own way, he's nothing." The sergeant said, "Maybe back with days of the pioneers a man could go his own way, but today you got to play ball." Many lines against the Army and profanity were deleted. The social club was a brothel in James Jones' book and the hostesses were prostitutes.

Casting against type made for an interesting movie. Ava Gardner campaigned for husband Frank Sinatra to get the role of the soldier tormented by Borgnine's character and he received a mere $8,000 for his small role. Sinatra was grateful to Clift for teaching him more about acting. Deborah Kerr had been cast in restrained lady roles and sought something sexier. Joan Crawford wanted the role, but required her own photographer so was rejected.

The sergeant played by Lancaster was a role Robert Mitchum wanted but his boss, Howard Hughes, said "no." Ronald Reagan and Walter Matthau were considered for that role. Lancaster was awed by Clift's skill and admitted he shook when he began to play his role. Eventually, he got more into the role than many he played. Clift, Sinatra and author Jones became drinking buddies during the movie. Jones was chatting with hostesses in the scene where Borgnine played the piano. George Reeves played a role 11 months after his TV series of *Superman* began.

Director Zinnemann had the song "Re-enlistment Blues," described in Jones' book, included in the movie. He hoped it would become a theme, such as the song in *High Noon*. The song is sung twice, by Merle Travis with his guitar and with Clift tooting a bugle (he had trained bugling and boxing for this movie) and is quite melodious but never became a big hit.

The 118-minute movie required cutting many excellent side stories. Jones was paid $82,000 for book rights, and the total budget was $1,650,000. The world box office was 18.5 times the budget, so the movie was a huge success. It was shot at Kuhlo Beach, Kalakaua Venue, Honolulu; Oahu, Hawaii; and the Lancaster-Kerr beach love site is now a tourist site.

The title came from Rudyard Kipling's 1892 poem "Gentlemen-Rankers" about British soldiers that killed so many they lost their way and were "damned from here to eternity."

Other movie nominees included *Julius Caesar, The Robe, Roman Holiday,* and *Shane.*

William Holden (1918-1985) from O'Fallon, Illinois, won Best Actor for *Stalag 17*. Other contenders were Marlon Brando *(Julius Caesar),* Richard Burton *(The Robe),* Montgomery Clift *(From Here to Eternity),* and Burt Lancaster *(From Here to Eternity).*

Audrey Hepburn (1929-1993) from Brussels won Best Actress for *Roman Holiday.* Other contenders were Leslie Caron *(Lili),* Ava Gardner *(Mogambo),* Deborah Kerr *(From Here to Eternity),* and Maggie McNamara *(The Moon Is Blue).*

Donna Reed won Best Supporting Actress for *From Here to Eternity.*

Frank Sinatra won Best Supporting Actor for *From Here to Eternity.*

Best Song "Secret Love," w. Paul Francis Webster, m. Sammy Fain, from *Calamity Jane.*

Fred Zinnemann, Director of *From Here to Eternity.*

Best Foreign Language Film: No award given.

British Best Film: *Genevieve,* director, and producer Henry Cornelius. **British Best Actor:** John Gielgud in *Julius Caesar.* **British Best Actress:** Audrey Hepburn in *Roman Holiday.*

27th Academy Awards

Ceremony: The awards were presented at RKO Pantages Theatre in Hollywood and NBC Century Theatre in New York City on March 30, 1955. Bob Hope was the Hollywood host and actress Thelma Ritter hosted the New York City event.

Honorary awards included Greta Garbo "for her unforgettable screen performances;" Danny Kaye "for his unique talents, his service to the Academy, the motion picture industry, and the American people;" and Jon Whiteley and Vincent Winter for their "outstanding juvenile performance in *The Little Kidnappers.*"

Dorothy Dandridge became the first African American actress to receive a nomination for Best Actress. When Eva Marie Saint went up to claim the Best Supporting Actress for *On the Waterfront,* she was nine months pregnant. She said, "I may have the baby right here." Then she thanked all the longshoremen in the movie.

1954 *On the Waterfront*

Tagline: "This man lived by the jungle law of the docks." This movie arose from *New York Sun's* reporter, Malcolm Johnson, who won the Pulitzer Prize for his 24-article series called "Crime on the Waterfront" in 1948. The movie, written by Budd Schulberg and developed by director Elia Kazan, placed Terry Malloy in the middle of the dock workers union of New York. Terry wanted to be a prize fighter but tended pigeons and ran errands for the boss of the union.

One day he saw a murder by two thugs of his boss. Upon meeting the dead man's sister named Edie, he felt guilty for the death. She introduced him to a priest who tried to convince him to testify in court so the dock racketeers would be stopped. Terry told him, "If I spill, my life ain't worth a nickel." Father Barry said, "And how much is your soul worth if you don't?"

Thus, the film depicted union violence and corruption among longshoremen, and racketeering on the waterfront of Hoboken, New Jersey. In this setting of toughness, Terry's surprising internal gentleness gave his character great depth. When Terry recalled a fixed fight where his career might have risen, he said, "I coulda' had class. I coulda' been a contender... Instead of a bum, which is what I am—let's face it." Perhaps Terry's self-hatred destroyed him.

When Terry finally testified, he no longer had friends or a job and was beaten badly. Finally, he was joined by other workers and the criminals were undone. The movie and its depiction of the priest created attention to crime among the immigrants and poor people nearby who worked at jobs that threatened life and limb.

There were problems for those involved with the movie. Elia Kazan was criticized for identifying eight former communists before the House Committee on Un-American Activities in 1952. Arthur Miller, who wrote the first script, was unhappy when asked to rewrite it with Communists as the antagonists. When he refused, Schulberg replaced him.

Marlon Brando first refused the role and Frank Sinatra asked for it. Paul Newman (born in Ohio as the son of Hungarian Jews) as Terry plus wife Joanne Woodward in the Eve Marie Saint role performed a love scene. But they were not chosen and the Brando approval infuriated Sinatra. Then he tried to take the role of the priest, but Karl Malden was chosen. The Edie role was also offered to Grace Kelly, who turned it down to make *Rear Window*.

The movie ran 108 minutes. The budget was $910,000 and the box office was $9.6 million. It was filmed on 36 days at docks, slum dwellings, bars, alleys, and roof tops located in Hoboken. The church in that city used for some exterior scenes was Our Lady of Grace built in 1874.

Leonard Bernstein created the score with shocking and heroic music. Sometimes Bernstein had to change music due to Brando's grunts. Many actors continue to point to Brando's performance as the greatest they have ever seen. Brando was trained by Stella Adler, who was trained by the wonderful Russian actress, Madame Maria Ouspenskaya, who brought the Russian Stanislavski method acting to America. What was this training that Brando undertook?

An actor was taught to learn where I am, when action happens, who am I, what relationships do I have, and with these "given circumstances" they understand and create their character. Emotions of face and body convey their inner struggles and build empathy. Brando acted so the audience could almost read his mind. Madame Maria taught actors Stella and Luther Adler, Lee Strasburg, Sanford Meisner, Elia Kazan, Clifford Odets, Franchot Tone, Morris Carnovsky, and John Garfield. Adler taught Marlon Brando, and Meisner taught Robert Duvall and Diane Keaton. Marlon Brando and his older sister, Jocelyn, who became an actress, grew up in a family that helped Henry Fonda get his start in acting, thus Fonda was a good friend of the Brandos.

Other movie nominees included *The Caine Mutiny, The Country Girl, Seven Brides for Seven Brothers,* and *Three Coins in the Fountain.*

Marlon Brando (1924-2004) from Omaha, Nebraska, won Best Actor for *On the Waterfront.* Other contenders were Humphrey Bogart *(The Caine Mutiny),* Bing Crosby *(The Country Girl),* James Mason *(A Star Is Born),* and Dan O'Herlihy *(Robinson Crusoe).*

Grace Kelly (1928-1982) from Philadelphia won Best Actress for *The Country Girl.* Other contenders were Dorothy Dandridge *(Carmen Jones),* Judy Garland *(A Star Is Born),* Audrey Hepburn *(Sabrina),* and Jane Wyman *(Magnificent Obsession).*

Eva Marie Saint won Best Supporting Actress for *On the Waterfront.*

Edmond O'Brien won Best Supporting Actor for *The Barefoot Contessa.*

Best Song "Three Coins in the Fountain," w. Sammy Cahn, m. Jule Styne, from *Three Coins in the Fountain.*

Eliz Kazan, Director of *On the Waterfront.*

Best Foreign Language Film: *Gate of Hell,* director Teinosuke Kinugasa, Japan, Japanese. In this movie, a samurai performs a heroic act by rescuing a pretty lady from a riot. He falls in love with her but learns she is already married. He is so obsessed with her that he gradually grows unstable and wants to have her no matter the consequences.

British Best Film: *Hobson's Choice,* director, and producer David Lean. **British Best Actor:** Kenneth More in *Doctor in the House.* **British Best Actress:** Yvonne Mitchell in *The Divided Heart.*

28th Academy Awards

Ceremony: The event was conducted on March 21, 1956, at RKO Pantages Theatre in Hollywood and NBC Century Theatre in New York City. Jerry Lewis hosted the California segment. Claudette Colbert and Joseph Mankiewicz hosted the New York segment. Italian Anna Magnani won for Best Actress. Lewis kidded about how difficult it was to read Italian sub-titles when someone like Gina Lollobrigida was on the screen.

James Dean was the second actor who was nominated for an Academy Award after his death. Dean died in a car accident at the age of 24 on September 30, 1955. His nomination was for his role in *East of Eden,* and he was again nominated the following year for his role in *Giant.*

Among the many presenters of awards was Grace Kelly, who presented the award for Best Actor to Ernest Borgnine. That was her last appearance before she departed the U.S. to marry Prince Rainier of Monaco. Olivia de Havilland had arranged a meeting of the two a year earlier. They married on April 18, 1956, and had three children.

Walt Disney won an Oscar for a documentary. Jokes were made about Disney's small budgets since they paid no salaries to animals or cartoons. Disney opened Disneyland in Anaheim, California, in July 1955. *Speedy Gonzales* produced by Edward Selzer won Best Cartoon Short Subject. The voice of Mel Blanc as the Mexican mice trying to cross the border for cheese and avoiding a cat was charming. It was an innocent reminder of the problems about crossing the border between the United States and Mexico that continued in recent years.

1955 *Marty*

Tagline: "The other guys wanted dames. He wanted a girl." *Marty* was the first Hecht-Lancaster production and won Best Director for Delbert Mann, Best Screenplay for Paddy Chayefsky, and Best Actor for Ernest Borgnine. Chayefsky had noticed a sign at a ballroom entrance: "Girls, dance with the man who asks you. Remember, men have feelings, too." He wanted to write about a man who goes to a ballroom, and he hoped to make it "the most ordinary love story in the world."

An Italian American butcher who is unmarried at age 34 assumed he would never marry after all his siblings had married and settled down. Marty said, "Ma, sooner or later, there comes a point in a man's life when he's gotta face some facts. And one fact I gotta face is that whatever it is that women like, I ain't got it."

Music was arranged by Roy Webb who used the talents of Harry Warren and others. After an opening with a brass fanfare, music quieted down. When Marty heard of other girls, he was reminded that he had no girls. When he called a girl, a voice was absent because the music told viewers that he was brushed off. Flute, clarinet, and oboe sounded the end of his quest for a girl.

His mother pushed him to go to the Stardust Ballroom one night. He reluctantly went and ran into a teacher, crying after a blind date abandoned the plain-looking woman. He talked with her, they danced, walked, and talked at a diner and enjoyed an evening together. Soft love themes were heard as he helped her on with her coat. At home, his mother and aunt worried that if he married, they would be left alone. So, he did not call Clara back as he had promised to do.

Suddenly, Marty realized he was giving up someone he liked and who liked him. His friend asked what he was doing. Marty said:

"You don't like her, mother don't like her, she's a dog and I'm a fat, ugly man! Well, all I know is I had a good time last night! I'm gonna have a good time tonight! If we have enough good times together, I'm gonna get down on my knees and I'm gonna beg that girl to marry me!"

He then went to a phone booth and joyful music was heard as he called Clara for a happy ending. This simple movie was made in 19 days at local areas around the Bronx and New York City for $343,000. It generated about $3 million at the box offices. Lyrics were sung by male voices at the end with music by Harry Warren and George Bassman.

United Artists wanted to cast Marlon Brando as Marty. But when Borgnine's name was mentioned, Burt Lancaster favored him since they worked on *From Here to Eternity*. Even though Lancaster was not in *Marty*, he was in the movie trailer to garner more attention for it. The campaign for the film included getting news announcer Walter Winchell to call the film one of the biggest sleepers in Hollywood history.

The role of Clara was being considered for Nancy Marchand, but Gene Kelly interrupted things. He was married to Betsy Blair, who had been blacklisted due to communist sympathies and was having trouble finding work. When Kelly argued for her consideration, he was said to have refused to continue filming *It's Always Fair Weather*. Blair got the role and was good enough to be nominated for Best Supporting Actress. Jerry Orbach was in his first movie as a ballroom patron. Author Paddy Chayefsky played Leo in a short scene. The success of this movie made many decide to explore more television plays.

Other movie nominees included *Love Is a Many-Splendored Thing*, *Mister Roberts*, *Picnic*, and *The Rose Tattoo*.

Ernest Borgnine (1917-2012) from Hamden, Connecticut, won Best Actor for *Marty*. Other contenders were James Cagney *(Love Me or*

Leave Me), James Dean *(East of Eden)*, Frank Sinatra *(The Man with the Golden Arm)*, and Spencer Tracy *(Bad Day at Black Rock)*.

Anna Magnani (1908-1973) from Rome won Best Actress for *The Rose Tattoo*. Other contenders were Susan Hayward *(I'll Cry Tomorrow)*, Katharine Hepburn *(Summertime)*, Jennifer Jones *(Love Is a Many-Splendored Thing)*, and Eleanor Parker *(Interrupted Melody)*.

Jo Van Fleet won Best Supporting Actress for *East of Eden*.

Jack Lemmon won Best Supporting Actor for *Mister Roberts*.

Best Song "Love Is a Many-Splendored Thing," w. Paul Francis Webster, m. Sammy Fain, from *Love Is a Many-Splendored Thing*.

Delbert Mann, Director of *Marty*.

Best foreign language film: *Samurai, The Legend of Musashi*, director Hiroshi Inagaki, Japan, Japanese. The most famous Japanese actor of the time, Toshiro Mifune, played the main role. He and his best friend joined the Army thinking of fame and glory, but their side was defeated. They were called traitors and when about to be executed, a Buddhist priest offered help. He began training the young hero to be a samurai. He also falls for a beautiful girl. The movie depicted a young man searching for identity and purpose in life.

British Best Film: *Richard III*, director, and producer Laurence Olivier. **British Best Actor:** Laurence Olivier in *Richard III*. **British Best Actress:** Katie Johnson in *The Ladykillers*.

29th Academy Awards

Ceremony: This event of March 27, 1957, was the last time the awards were conducted in both Hollywood and New York City. Thereafter, it has been in only California, making for some very sleepy East Coast viewers the next day. These awards were hosted in Hollywood by Jerry Lewis and in New York by actress Celeste Holm.

For the first time, every nominated Best Picture was in color. The major award winners were epics, and that trend was followed for some years. James Dean became the only actor to receive a second posthumous nomination for acting. This was the first time that the Best Foreign Language Film was competitive instead of just a Special Achievement Award.

The Oscar for Best Original Story went to Robert Rich for *The Brave One.* There was no Robert Rich because that was a pseudonym for Dalton Trumbo, who was blacklisted and unable to receive the award under his own name. Another award for adapted screenplay nominated for *Friendly Persuasion* did not have a name to credit. Michael Wilson wrote the screenplay but because of communist affiliations was omitted. The error was corrected December 19, 2002.

Actor/singer Eddie Cantor received an Honorary Award "for distinguished service to the film industry" and helped found The March of Dimes. Buddy Adler received the Irving G. Thalberg Memorial Award for his work as producer at 20th Century Fox where he produced *From Here to Eternity, Love Is a Many Splendored Thing,* and *Bus Stop.* He also began the Fox Talent School with a $1 million budget for new talent.

Y. Frank Freeman received the Jean Hersholt Humanitarian Award for his work as head of Paramount where his studio made *The War of the Worlds, The Naked Jungle, Conquest of Space,* and other productions.

1956 *Around the World in 80 Days*

Tagline: "Hop on a sailing railroad across the West! Be attacked by fierce prairie Indians! Rescue a Princess in India! Sail a burning Atlantic paddle-wheeler! Fight bulls in Spain!" This blockbuster movie was based on Jules Verne's 1872 classic *Around the World in Eighty Days.* This was Mike Todd's only movie production and was shown in the Todd-AO curved screen.

The story involved Englishman (David Niven) who wagered Robert Morley that he could go around the world in 80 days. Losing this £20,000 bet would ruin him financially. With much ingenuity, he created ways to take an assistant Passepartout (Cantinflas) and get back just in time to win. Noel Coward said of Niven, "Mad dogs and Englishmen go out in the midday sun."

There were no opening credits, and the movie began with newsman Edward R. Murrow showing a short history of flight. Here are a few quotations from the movie:

Phileas Fogg: "Crisis or no, nothing should interfere with tea."

Princess Aouda: "Mr. Fogg, why must you be so… so British?"

Princess Aouda: "Have there been any women in his life?" Passepartout: "I assume he had a mother, but I am not certain."

Victor Young's music was traditional music of English origin. He was nominated 22 times but never won an Oscar until this movie resulted in a posthumous award. Young died the previous November of a cerebral hemorrhage at age 57. Young did excellent compositions about Paris,

India, Japan, and bullfights. He threw in known works, such as "Rule Britannia," "Yankee Doodle Dandy," "La Cucaracha," and "William Tell's Overture" when the cavalry rode in.

The budget was an estimated $6 million, and the box office was $42 million. This movie ran 167 minutes but some versions, including the entr'acte and exit music, made it 183 minutes. The movie set many records, such as running for three years straight (1956-1959) at the Rivoli Theatre in New York City in Todd-AO.

Casting was simple when Cary Grant turned down the main role and David Niven accepted. Fernandel would have had to learn English, but Mexican comedian Cantinflas knew English and did a wonderful job in his role as Fogg's assistant. Shirley MacLaine did not distinguish herself in this role, but she soon did in other movies. Robert Newton, according to David Niven's book *Bring on the Empty Horses,* was in liver failure. He agreed to drink nothing during filming and died before seeing the movie, wherein he played an amusing Scotland Yard detective who thought Fogg robbed the Bank of England.

Here are some of the actors in cameo scenes, a few of whom donated their services: Finlay Currie, Robert Morley, Noel Coward, Sir John Gielgud, Trevor Howard, Charles Boyer, Evelyn Keyes, Jose Greco, Gilbert Roland, Cesar Romero, Sir Cedric Hardwicke, Ronald Colman, Peter Lorre, George Raft, Marlene Dietrich, John Carradine, Frank Sinatra, Buster Keaton, Col. Tim McCoy, Joe E. Brown, Andy Devine, John Mills, Glynis Johns, and many more.

The movie took 75 days to film, used 112 locations in 13 countries, included 68,894 people, nearly 8,000 animals, and 74,685 costumes (the most ever used in a Hollywood production). The success enabled Mike Todd to repay his debts. He threw a one-year anniversary party at Madison Square Garden attended by 18,000 people, featured on television. When he died March 22, 1958, he left ownership of this movie to widow, Elizabeth Taylor, who sold it in later years.

Other movie nominees included *Friendly Persuasion, Giant, The King and I,* and *The Ten Commandments.*

Yul Brynner (1915-1985) from Vladivostok in eastern Russia won Best Actor for *The King and I.* Other contenders were James Dean *(Giant),* Kirk Douglas *(Lust for Life),* Rock Hudson *(Giant),* and Laurence Olivier *(Richard III).*

Ingrid Bergman won Best Actress for *Anastasia.* Other contenders were Carroll Baker *(Baby Doll),* Katharine Hepburn *(The Rainmaker),* Nancy Kelly *(The Bad Seed),* and Deborah Kerr *(The King and I).*

Dorothy Malone won Best Supporting Actress for *Written on the Wind.*

Anthony Quinn won Best Supporting Actor for *Lust for Life.*

Best Song "Que Sera, Sera," w. Ray Evans, m. Jay Livingston, from *The Man Who Knew Too Much.* This song was something like a lullaby, one of the original origins of music. It was designed in the movie to be heard by a child who would realize his mother was nearby. It also conveyed fate in the words "What will be, will be."

George Stevens, Director of *Giant.*

Best Foreign Language Film: *La Strada,* director Federico Fellini, Italy, Italian. This movie featured Anthony Quinn, Richard Basehart and Giuletta Masina (Fellini's wife). It was the sad story of a young girl who was bought by a strongman (Quinn) who entertains people. He humiliated, neglected, and persecuted the girl (Masina) and killed a clown (Basehart) who tried to help her. The movie used music by Nino Rota whose music was used in the *Godfather* movies. He included brisk circus-type music in the movie. Fellini worked well with Rota, describing what kind of music he wanted. Then Rota would do his own composing and play songs for Fellini until the director picked one.

British Best Film: *Reach for the Sky.* Director Lewis Gilbert. Producer Daniel Angel. **Best Actor:** Peter Finch in *A Town Like Alice.* **Best Actress:** Virginia McKenna in *A Town Like Alice.*

30th Academy Awards

Ceremony: This event was conducted at the RKO Pantages Theatre in Hollywood, California. It was hosted by Bob Hope, Rosalind Russell, David Niven, James Stewart, and Jack Lemmon.

This was the first time that all five Best Picture nominees included nominations for Best Director as well. The honorary awards included Charles Brackett "for outstanding service to the Academy," B. B. Kahane "for distinguished service to the motion picture industry," the Society of Motion Picture and Television Engineers "for their contributions to the advancement of the motion picture industry," and Gilbert M. "Broncho Billy" Anderson, "motion picture pioneer, for his contributions to the development of motion pictures as entertainment."

Samuel Goldwyn received the Jean Hersholt Humanitarian Award for his writing, library, and hospital. Among his movies were *Arrowsmith, The Hurricane, Dodsworth, Dead End, Wuthering Heights, The Little Foxes,* and *The Best Years of Our Lives.* This was also the first Oscar for an Asian, when Miyoshi Umeki won Best Supporting Actress for *Sayonara.*

Rock Hudson and Mae West sang "Baby, It's Cold Outside." Mae, age 65, wore a huge headdress. During their song, Rock lit a cigarette and handed it to her saying, "It's king-sized." She added at the end of the song, "As I've always said, it's not the men in your life, it's the life in your men." They kissed to much applause.

When the program ran short by 20 minutes, emcee Jerry Lewis and the conductor encouraged everyone on stage to keep singing "There's No

Business Like Show Business." Some paired off to dance to keep the home audience entertained.

1957 *The Bridge on the River Kwai*

Tagline: "A magnificent moving film." The movie is more about the Alec Guinness character and the other individuals than it is about war.

Frenchman Pierre Boulle had been a prisoner of war in Thailand and created the role played by Alec Guinness from his memories of French officers. Boulle also wrote *Planet of the Apes* and *Mirrors of the Sun,* about an ill-fated attempt of the French to develop solar energy using mirrors. He did not speak English, so Carl Foreman wrote the screenplay, but because he was a Communist from 1938-1942, Foreman received no credit.

The day before Foreman died of a brain tumor in 1984, he was told he would receive an Oscar for *The Bridge on the River Kwai.* He had earlier written the screenplay for *High Noon* because his theme was a loner for a good cause against a group. Gary Cooper defended him when producers wanted to kick him out of the industry.

Directors considered for this movie were John Ford, William Wyler, Howard Hawks, Orson Welles, and Fred Zinnemann. David Lean was chosen but argued with Guinness on how his role should be played. Guinness won, believing the movie should show that men can enslave men and how the enslaved person reacts should serve as a model.

The movie was about Englishmen taken prisoner by the Japanese. They argued about the Geneva Conventions that exempt officers from manual labor. But the movie about their leader, Guinness, was the core of the movie. The prisoners were told, "You British prisoners have been chosen to build a bridge across the River Kwai. It will be pleasant work, requiring skill, and officers will work as well as men. The Japanese

Army cannot have idle mouths to feed. If you work hard, you will be treated well, but if you do not work hard, you will be punished."

When the British lieutenant colonel (Guinness) complained to the Japanese colonel about officers doing labor, he was beaten and placed in an iron box, and officers were made to stand all day in intense heat. The lieutenant colonel was after many weeks released because his men were sabotaging a bridge for dignitaries who would soon arrive by train. He was removed from the box after promising that his men would build the bridge by the required date. Guinness said he based his walk when released from the "oven" on his 11-year-old son's walk, when the boy was recovering from polio after paralysis from the waist down.

An American prisoner (William Holden) had escaped but was convinced by a British officer (Jack Hawkins) to return and maneuver a way to blow up the bridge. The day dignitaries were to arrive showed Guinness discovering wires exposed by low water. He went down and found they led to explosives. Holden tried to warn him, was shot, and Guinness was shot but fell on the detonator saying, "What have I done?" The audience knew the Japanese colonel would commit hara-kiri; an ancient ritual suicide developed by the Samurai soldiers for losing face.

The movie ran 167-minutes and is often shown with an intermission. It was mainly made in Ceylon (Sri Lanka) and the bridge was near Kitulgala. Some Japanese audiences disliked the depiction of their race as inept engineers.

British composer Malcolm Arnold had ten days to write forty-five minutes of music and a marching song that troops whistled. The "Colonel Bogey March" was composed in 1914 by a British Army bandmaster and golfer who whistled it instead of shouting "Fore" while teeing off. Bogey is a golf term meaning "one over par." The last 20 minutes had no music. That "Bogey March" occasionally appeared in other movies and television programs.

The movie was a massive success at the box office, earning $18 million the first year and $15 million the following year, far outweighing its budget of $2.8 million. It opened in London with the three top stars on October 2, 1957, and again on October 11, 1957, to the public. Prince Philip, whom Queen Elizabeth had just given the title "prince," was sitting in the loge. He thanked the audience for coming and spoke about the movie at the intermission when tea and pastries were being served to all. This set a tradition for British movie openings for years.

Other movie nominees included *12 Angry Men, Peyton Place, Sayonara,* and *Witness for the Prosecution.*

Alec Guinness (1914-2000) from London won Best Actor for *The Bridge on the River Kwai.* Other contenders were Marlon Brando *(Sayonara),* Anthony Franciosa *(A Hatful of Rain),* Charles Laughton *(Witness for the Prosecution),* and Anthony Quinn *(Wild Is the Wind).*

Joanne Woodward (1930-?) from Thomasville, Georgia, won Best Actress for *The Three Faces of Eve.* Other contenders were Deborah Kerr *(Heaven Knows, Mr. Allison),* Anna Magnani *(Wild Is the Wind),* Elizabeth Taylor *(Raintree County),* and Lana Turner *(Peyton Place).*

Miyoshi Umeki won Best Supporting Actress for *Sayonara.*

Red Buttons won Best Supporting Actor for *Sayonara.*

Best Song "All the Way," w. Sammy Cahn, m. Jimmy Van Heusen, from *The Joker Is Wild.*

David Lean, Director of *The Bridge on the River Kwai.*

Best Foreign Language Film: *Nights of Cabiria,* director Federico Fellini, Italy, Italian. Giuletta Masina (Fellini's wife) played an eternally optimistic streetwalker in Rome with a heart of gold and a head of cotton candy. This funny, poignant movie inspired the American movie "Sweet Charity," a Bob Fosse musical.

British Best Film: *The Bridge on the River Kwai.* Director David Lean. Producer Sam Spiegel. **British Best Actor:** Alec Guinness in *The Bridge on the River Kwai.* **British Best Actress:** Heather Sears in *The Story of Esther Costello.*

31st Academy Awards

Ceremony: The event was conducted on April 6, 1959, at the Pantages Theatre in Hollywood, California, and was broadcast by NBC. Hosts included Jerry Lewis, Bob Hope, David Niven, Mort Sahl, Tony Randall, and Laurence Olivier. Because David Niven won Best Actor for his role in *Separate Tables,* it made him the only host to have won an award in the same ceremony.

Maurice Chevalier received an honorary award for 50 years in show business and movies. The Irving G. Thalberg Memorial Award went to Jack Warner. Jack and his brothers, who began in the movie industry during the silent era, developed movies with causes and messages.

All nominations for *Gigi* resulted in Oscars. Winners were Arthur Freed for Best Picture, Vincente Minnelli for Best Director, Frederick Loewe and Alan Jay Lerner for Best Original Song, Andre Previn for Best Scoring, Cecile Beaton for Best Costume Design, Alan Jay Learner for Best Adapted Screenplay, Adrienne Fazan for Best Film Editing, and William A. Horning, Preston Ames, Henry Grace, and Keogh Gleason for Best Art Direction.

1958 *Gigi*

Tagline: "Thank heaven for Gigi." Gigi was based on Yola Letellier who was raised to be a companion for older men—a prostitute. She married a man 49 years older but had relations with others, including Lord Louis Mountbatten, Viceroy of India. Before his boat was blown up by the IRA in 1979, Mountbatten had an open marriage with his wife and

Yola was like a family friend. French writer Sidonie Gabrielle Colette (1873-1954) wrote the novella entitled *Gigi* in 1944.

Colette chose Audrey Hepburn to play the role on Broadway, which ran from November 1951 to May 1952. When the movie was made, the rights to the book were purchased from Colette's widowed husband and Anita Loos. That led to a fight ending Hollywood's Hays Production Code because producer Arthur Freed had to show that Gigi rejected the courtesan lifestyle. Gigi was raised by her aunt (Isabel Jeans) and grandmother (Hermione Gingold), both aging courtesans. Their goal was to make her a poised beautiful lady to show off as a companion.

Gigi, a bit boyish, was a friend with young aristocrat Gaston. He (Louis Jourdan) sang about how boring his life was. Maurice Chevalier's character warned him, "Youth is the thing, Gaston. Youth. Stay close to the young and a little rubs off."

Chevalier carried the show as he sang "Thank Heaven for Little Girls," "I Remember It Well" with Hermione Gingold, and "The Gossips." The songs, all in a happy major key, offset the lurking sadness in the life of a prostitute. People who grew up in Europe and America were conditioned to think happy thoughts when they heard the major keys and sad thoughts when they heard the minor keys. People in eastern countries did not grow up with that orientation and minor keys were often seen as happy.

Jourdan, not a singer, was encouraged by seeing Rex Harrison's singing/talking a role in *My Fair Lady*. So, he sang well with "It's a Bore," "She Is Not Thinking of Me," and other songs. Gigi, (Leslie Caron) made a choice about being a courtesan. She assumed that the Jourdan character would fool around. She said, "I would rather be miserable with you than without you."

Having been filmed in Paris, when Gaston walked away from Gigi's house, he was silhouetted by the real Place de la Concorde fountain.

He thought a bit and returned to ask for Gigi's hand in marriage. One scene was at the famous Parisian restaurant, Maxim's, with eye-catching mirrors.

Casting wanted Dirk Bogarde but he was unavailable, so the role of Gaston went to Jourdan. Audrey Hepburn was considered for Gigi but was busy and Caron had perfected her English. Despite being a ballerina, this was a non-dancing role. Irene Dunne turned down the distasteful role of the aunt preferring to continue her work as a U.S. delegate to the U.N. The budget was $3.3 million but box office was $13.2 million making the 115-minute movie a huge hit.

Other movie nominees included *Auntie Mame, Cat on a Hot Tin Roof, The Defiant Ones,* and *Separate Tables.*

David Niven (1909-1983) from Kirriemuir, Scotland, won Best Actor for *Separate Tables.* Other contenders were Tony Curtis *(The Defiant Ones),* Paul Newman *(Cat on a Hot Tin Roof),* Sidney Poitier *(The Defiant Ones),* and Spencer Tracy *(The Old Man and the Sea).*

Susan Hayward (1918-1975) from Brooklyn won Best Actress for *I Want to Live.* Other contenders were Deborah Kerr *(Separate Tables),* Shirley MacLaine *(Some Came Running),* Rosalind Russell *(Auntie Mame),* and Elizabeth Taylor *(Cat on a Hot Tin Roof).*

Wendy Hiller won Best Supporting Actress for *Separate Tables.*

Burl Ives won Best Supporting Actor for *The Big Country.*

Best Song "Gigi," w. Alan Jay Lerner, m. Frederick Loewe, from *Gigi.*

Vincente Minnelli, Director of *Gigi.*

Best Foreign Language Film: *Mon Oncle,* director Jacques Tati, France, French. This colorful comedy is about an uncle, Monsieur Hulot, played by Tati, and his relationship with his 9-year-old nephew. The boy's parents were materialistic and tried to improve their status with possessions. Hulot lived in a run-down area and got about by walking or riding a motor bike. The French were tempted by American materialism to be better than their neighbors. Americans who lived in France at that time were seen as shallow, unable to enjoy a casual life where stores closed for three hours in the afternoon to relax. The actors were non-professionals. There was a pleasant but monotonous musical score.

British Best Film: *Room at the Top.* Director Jack Clayton. Producers James and John Woolf. **British Best Actor:** Trevor Howard in *The Key.* **British Best Actress:** Irene Worth in *Orders to Kill.*

32nd Academy Awards

Ceremony: This event was conducted on April 4, 1960, at the RKO Pantages Theatre in Hollywood. It was hosted by Bob Hope and ran on NBC for one hour and forty minutes.

The best movie, *Ben-Hur*, won eleven Oscars, breaking the record of nine for *Gigi* the year before. Director William Wyler became the third person to win more than two Best Director awards (following Frank Capra and John Ford). He had directed *Mrs. Miniver* and *The Best Years of Our Lives* earlier. Sam Zimbalist, producer of *Ben-Hur*, died in Rome of a heart attack on November 4, 1958, and was the only producer of a Best Picture awarded a posthumous Oscar.

Honorary awards went to actor Buster Keaton "for his unique talents which brought immortal comedies to the screen" and Lee De Forest "for his pioneering inventions which brought sound to the motion pictures." Bob Hope was given the Jean Hersholt Humanitarian Award for his GI shows and his work for the Oscars.

1959 *Ben-Hur*

Tagline: "The entertainment experience of a lifetime." This movie began with an aristocratic Jew named Judah Ben-Hur (Charlton Heston) whose best friend was a Roman named Messala (Stephen Boyd). The Roman had become an important tribune of Pontius Pilate. Childhood friends, Messala told Judah, "Either you help me, or you oppose me. You have no other choice. You're either for me or against me." Judah: "If that is the choice, then I am against you."

After an accidental roof tile is knocked off by Ben-Hur's sister and kills a Roman in a parade, Judah, his sister and his mother were taken to prison. During three years of servitude, he was once given water by a man he later learned was Jesus. While rowing in a galley, the ship captain (Jack Hawkins) told Judah, "Your eyes are full of hate. That's good. Hate keeps a man alive. It gives him strength." Later, Judah saved the life of that captain and was rewarded with freedom.

Judah fell for Esther (Haya Harareet) who learned that his mother and sister were no longer in prison but in a leper colony. He practiced entering a chariot race to avenge the wrongs of Messala for punishing him, his mother, and his sister. Judah dealt with many about the race, including a sheik (Hugh Griffith) who had a whimsical way of looking at marriage. He told Judah, "One wife? One God, that I can understand, but one wife! That is not civilized. It is not generous."

When Judah returned to his beloved Esther, she said, "I've seen too much what hate can do. My father was burned up with it. But I've heard of a young rabbi who says that forgiveness is greater and love more powerful than hatred." After Christ's crucifixion, Judah told his love, "Almost at the moment he died, I heard him say, 'Father, forgive them for they know not what they do.'" She said, "Even then?" Judah: "Even then. And I felt his voice take the sword out of my hand."

The movie was based on the Civil War general and governor of New Mexico Lew Wallace's book *Ben-Hur: A Tale of the Christ*. It was first made in 1925 starring Ramon Navarro as Judah Ben-Hur. Navarro was invited to the opening of the new movie. MGM was in dreadful financial shape, and after the success of Cecil B. DeMille's *The Ten Commandments,* director William Wyler vowed to save the company by outdoing DeMille with this epic. He summoned many writers to create the script, including Gore Vidal, Karl Tunberg, S. N. Berhman, Maxwell Anderson, and Christopher Fry. Fry gave the dialogue a more formal tone without being stilted.

It was filmed in Libya, Rome, Arizona, and California. MGM roaring Leo the Lion was the wrong mood for the opening sacred nativity scene, so Leo was shown as quiet. Casting for Judah Ben-Hur considered Stewart Granger, Robert Taylor, Marlon Brando, Burt Lancaster, Paul Newman, Rock Hudson, Leslie Nielsen, and Kirk Douglas. Heston was finally the choice. Stephen Boyd was chosen for Messala who played his friend and later enemy. Charlton and Stephen both had blue eyes, so Boyd was given some brownish contact lenses for his eyes.

Director William Wyler's sister-in-law, Cathy O'Donnell, was cast as Judah's sister. Judah's mother was played by Martha Scott after another actress could not cry on cue. Sam Jaffe and Finlay Currie were cast, and Wyler wanted Jack Hawkins to play the captain whom Heston rescued. Reluctant after *The Bridge on the River Kwai,* Hawkins screen time was reduced. Hugh Griffith was cast as the colorful and mischievous sheik who enriched his every scene.

Jesus was played by Claude Heater, an American opera singer, who was performing in Rome with the Vienna State Opera. His role was mostly filmed from behind, so viewers did not see his face. He was a handsome young man who died in 2020 after a career in opera. Director Wyler said, "I spent sleepless nights trying to find a way to deal with the figure of Christ…I wanted to be reverent and yet realistic. Crucifixion is a bloody, awful, horrible thing, and a man does not go through it with a benign expression on his face. I had to deal with that."

Music by Hungarian Miklós Rózsa was the longest score ever composed for a film. The majestic sounds and rapid pace increased the excitement during the movie and were influential in movies such as *Jaws, Star Wars,* and *Raiders of the Lost Ark.* Rózsa did not compose a main theme or leitmotif but did switch from full orchestra to a pipe organ whenever Jesus appeared.

Seven thousand extras were hired to cheer in the stands. In addition, many wealthy citizens of Rome were allowed to act as extras in the villa scenes. The day of shooting the chariot scenes found poor people seeking work as extras and when turned away they assaulted the gates and had to be dispersed by police.

There were 300 sets scattered over 148 acres, and the chariot race covered 18 acres. An identical racetrack was built to train horses for the race. Andalusian and Lipizzan horses were used and 18 chariots, nine for practice, were made. Heston and Boyd had to learn how to drive a chariot from stunt director Yakima Canutt, and Heston was given special contact lenses to prevent grit from injuring his eyes. Dynamite charges were used for Boyd's chariot with sharp wheels intended to grind through the wheels of the nearest chariot. Andrew Marton and Yakima Canutt directed the nine-minute chariot scene, and one of their directors was Sergio Leone, who went on later to make spaghetti westerns in Italy and Spain. A near-fatal accident came when Yakima's son, Joe Canutt, was tossed into the air by accident, but fortunately he only had a chin injury.

Stuntman Andrew Marton created a scene showing Ben-Hur being thrown off but remounting his chariot. In the background, Canutt's accident can be seen when he was tossed in the air. In some scenes, dummies were used as bodies that were trampled by horses during the race.

Camels, elephants, horses, and other animals used during filming were distributed to zoos when the movie was completed. Marketing dollars were used to survey 2,000 high schools in 47 American cities who were given study guides to create interest. Candy, items of jewelry, men's ties, perfume bottles, toy armor, and Ben-Hur novels were sold to promote the film.

The budget was $15.2 million and $14.7 million was spent on marketing the movie. It brought in box office receipts of more than $146.9 million and did save MGM from going under. Ben-Hur ran 212 minutes and was shot using the new MGM Camera 65.

Other movie nominees included *Anatomy of a Murder, The Diary of Anne Frank, The Nun's Story,* and *Room at the Top.*

Charlton Heston (1923-2008) from Evanston, Illinois, won Best Actor for *Ben-Hur.* Other contenders were Laurence Harvey *(Room at the Top),* Jack Lemmon *(Some Like It Hot),* Paul Muni *(The Last Angry Man),* and James Stewart *(Anatomy of a Murder).*

Simone Signoret (1921-1985) from Wiesbaden, Germany, won Best Actress for *Room at the Top.* Other contenders were Doris Day *(Pillow Talk),* Audrey Hepburn *(The Nun's Story),* Katharine Hepburn *(Suddenly, Last Summer),* and Elizabeth Taylor *(Suddenly, Last Summer).*

Shelley Winters won Best Supporting Actress for *The Diary of Anne Frank.*

Hugh Griffith won Best Supporting Actor for *Ben-Hur.*

Best Song "High Hopes," w. Sammy Cahn, m. Jimmy Van Heusen, from *Hole in the Head.*

William Wyler, Director of *Ben-Hur.*

Best Foreign Language Film: *Black Orpheus,* director Marcel Camus, France, Portuguese. This musical movie features dancers, singers, and the excitement of a Rio carnival. The story is a modern take-off on the Greek tragedy of Orpheus, the lute player whose music brought the dawn each day, and his beloved beautiful Eurydice.

They fell for each other despite a girlfriend and attended a costume ball, so others did not know who they were. One dancer at the ball was Death. Eurydice fled Death. Orpheus, unaware that Eurydice grabbed a power line to escape, electrocuted her. Death said, "Now, she's mine."

Orpheus searched for her down a spiral staircase to the underworld. In Hades, a man told Orpheus to sing to his love. He found her dead body and carried her up and out. His former girlfriend threw a stone at him, and he fell off a cliff with Eurydice in his arms. Some children picked up his guitar and played so the sun rose as the children danced. The glorious soundtrack inspired Vince Guaraldi to do several albums on jazz impressions of *Black Orpheus*. The film was notable because of the happy and poignant music, the colorful costumes and sets, and the tragic story of unrequited love. Shortly after opening, the movie was shown at the annual conference of the American Psychoanalytic Association and generated much consideration about patients suffering the loss of loved ones and death.

British Best Film: *Sapphire.* Director Basil Dearden. Producer Michael Relph. **British Best Actor:** Peter Sellers in *I'm All Right Jack*. **British Best Actress:** Audrey Hepburn in *The Nun's Story.*

33rd Academy Awards

Ceremony: The event was conducted on April 17, 1961, at the Santa Monica Civic Auditorium in Santa Monica, California. It was hosted by Bob Hope and broadcast by ABC television, lasting two hours and ten minutes. This was the last Academy Awards ceremony where juveniles were recognized because they would compete with adults in the future. Hayley Mills, age 14, was recognized for her performance in the Walt Disney production of *Pollyanna*.

Gary Cooper was the year's honorary recipient "for his many memorable screen performances and the international recognition he has gained for the motion picture industry." James Stewart, his close friend, accepted the Oscar on his behalf. Stewart's emotional speech hinted dire illness and Cooper had cancer. He died less than four weeks later May 13, 1961, at age 60.

Stan Laurel, the idea man for the Laurel and Hardy comedies, was honored "for his creative pioneering in the field of cinema comedy." The Jean Hersholt Humanitarian Award went to Sol Lesser, who transitioned to sound films with major pictures and stars. In 1933 he bought screen rights to Edgar Rice Burroughs' *Tarzan of the Apes* starring Buster Crabbe. Later those films starred Johnny Weissmuller and Lex Barker. His films included *Our Town* and *Stage Door Canteen*. In later life, he restored many of his early productions and then retired in 1958.

1960 *The Apartment*

Tagline: "You'll simply fall apart with laughter." Billy Wilder and Izzy A. L. Diamond wrote the screenplay. *The Apartment* was about insurance clerk (Jack Lemmon) who climbed the corporate ladder by allowing executives to use his apartment for illicit affairs. He liked employee (Shirley MacLaine) whom he soon learned was having an affair with his boss (Fred MacMurray).

With a scene coming from I. A. L. Diamond's own life, Lemmon found MacLaine in his bed after trying to commit suicide with sleeping pills when she learned MacMurray did not plan to marry her. MacLaine said while crying over her affair with MacMurray, "When you're in love with a married man, you shouldn't wear mascara."

Lemmon got his neighbor, a doctor played by Jack Kruschen, to save her. The neighbor assumed Lemmon was a playboy. With comic relief by the doctor's wife (Naomi Stevens), who provided some Jewish penicillin (chicken soup), the MacLaine character survived. Lemmon then gave his resignation and carried on with the MacLaine character. He told the MacMurray character, "I decided to become a mensch," meaning a person of integrity and honor.

This dark comedy or morality tale was told extremely well with other minor characters including Edie Adams, who told MacMurray's wife what her husband was doing. MacMurray was then kicked out of his house by his wife. The MacLaine character stood up for herself as did the Lemmon character. When Lemmon asked MacLaine over a card game in the final scene about MacMurray, she said, "We'll send him a fruitcake every Christmas."

The tagline about laughter is not the reaction we had to Laurel and Hardy comedies when they erred. Laughter in this movie showed an acceptance of MacLaine's and Lemmon's failure to cope successfully and brought about empathy from others to heal from shame.

The idea of the movie came from Noël Coward's one-act play called *Still Life*, made into the movie *Brief Encounter*. That movie starred Celia Johnson and Trevor Howard who had an affair. The play depicted an affair of two married people in an apartment. The British movie skipped that bit leaving to viewer's imagination any consummation of love. In that movie, Coward was the train station announcer and David Lean directed. The music in *Brief Encounter* was Rachmaninoff's 2nd Piano Concerto, whereas the music in *The Apartment* was by Adolph Deutsch and Charles Williams, originally entitled "Jealous Lover."

The music included "Adeste Fideles," "Capriccio Italien" by Tchaikovsky, "Auld Lang Syne," "There's a Tavern in the Town," "Little Brown Jug" and "Jingle Bells." The movie was later made into the 1968 musical *Promises, Promises* with the help of Burt Bacharach, Hal David and Neil Simon. This movie ran 125-minutes, had a budget of only $3 million and box office brought in $24.6 million. Despite its subject matter, it was nominated for ten awards and won five, including Best Picture, Best Director (Billy Wilder), and Best Screenplay by Wilder and Diamond.

Other movie nominees included *The Alamo, Elmer Gantry, Sons and Lovers,* and *The Sundowners*.

Burt Lancaster (1913-1994) from New York City won Best Actor for *Elmer Gantry*. Other contenders were Trevor Howard *(Sons and Lovers)*, Jack Lemmon *(The Apartment)*, Laurence Olivier *(The Entertainer)*, and Spencer Tracy *(Inherit the Wind)*.

Elizabeth Taylor (1932-2011) from London won the Best Actress for *Butterfield 8*. Other contenders were Greer Garson *(Sunrise at Campobello)*, Deborah *Kerr (The Sundowners)*, Shirley MacLaine *(The Apartment)*, and Melina Mercouri *(Never on Sunday)*.

Shirley Jones won Best Supporting Actress for *Elmer Gantry*.

Peter Ustinov won Best Supporting Actor for *Spartacus*.

Best Song "Never on Sunday," w. m. Manos Hadjidakis, from *Never on Sunday*.

Billy Wilder, Director of *The Apartment*.

Best Foreign Language Film: *The Virgin Spring*, director Ingmar Bergman, Sweden, Swedish. Devout Christians played by Max von Sydow and Birgitta Valberg send their only daughter (Birgritta Pettersson) and their foster daughter (Gunnel Linblom) to deliver candles to a distant church. On their way through the woods, they encounter savage goat herders who rape and murder their real daughter while the foster daughter hid. When the killers sought refuge in the farmhouse of the girls' parents, the father plotted a fitting revenge.

British Best Film: *Saturday Night and Sunday Morning*. Director Karel Keisz. Producer Tony Richardson. **British Best Actor:** Peter Finch in *The Trials of Oscar Wilde*. **British Best Actress:** Rachel Roberts in *Saturday Night and Sunday Morning*.

34th Academy Awards

Ceremony: This event occurred on April 9, 1962, at the Santa Monica Civic Auditorium in Santa Monica, California. It was hosted by Bob Hope for his 13th time, and broadcast by ABC for two hours and ten minutes.

Foreigners won more awards. Federico Fellini won Best Director nomination for *La Dolce Vita,* Maximilian Schell won Best Actor for *Judgment at Nuremberg,* Sophia Loren won Best Actress in *Two Women,* and Hispanic Rita Moreno won Best Supporting Actress for *West Side Story.*

Honorary awards went to three men: William L. Hendricks "for his outstanding patriotic service in the conception, writing, and production of the Marine Corps film, *A Force in Readiness,* which has brought honor to the Academy and the motion picture industry;" Fred L. Metzler "for his dedication and outstanding services to the Academy;" and Jerome Robbins "for his brilliant achievements in the art of choreography on film."

The Irving G. Thalberg Memorial Award went to Stanley Kramer, director and producer of many message films. To find funding for movies, he tried to find movies that had something to say. The Jean Hersholt Humanitarianism Award went to screenwriter, playwright, film producer, and theatre director George Seaton. He was the Academy Awards director for three terms beginning in 1955. Some of his films were *A Day at the Races, The Wizard of Oz, That Night in Rio, The Song of Bernadette, Coney Island, Junior Miss, Miracle on 34th Street, Apartment for Peggy, Berlin Airlift, For Heaven's Sake, The Country Girl,*

The Bridges at Toko-Ri, Teacher's Pet, But Not for Me, The Pleasure of His Company, The Hook, Mutiny on the Bounty, and *Airport.*

1961 *West Side Story*

Tagline: "Unlike other musicals, *West Side Story* grows younger." This movie was inspired by Shakespeare's *Romeo and Juliet.* In 1947, Jerome Robbins, Leonard Bernstein, and Arthur Laurents wanted to do a modern musical based on that old love story. First, they thought of Irish and Jewish families living in Manhattan with anti-Semitism as the reason people fought each other. They put the idea away for five years. Then Laurents and Bernstein were chatting about juvenile delinquent gangs in New York, a new phenomenon due to child labor laws restricting those under 16 from work, and Puerto Ricans who became U.S. citizens in 1917.

Bernstein and Laurents were blacklisted for alleged communist activity, but they wanted to work with Robbins despite his cooperation with the HUAC. They worked with a title called *East Side Story,* but it was soon changed to *West Side Story.*

Nobody wanted to finance such a dark musical. But the promise of more dancing than any former show, and cheap sets making it look like authentic streets where gangs congregated, began to sell backers. They wanted to cast James Dean for one gang leader, but he soon died.

Laurents met Stephen Sondheim at a party where they talked about the venture and Oscar Hammerstein believed in the project and encouraged them. They worked on the balcony scene of the doomed lovers and introduced some comic relief by police officers. Songs were developed, such as "America," "I Feel Pretty," "Gee, Officer Krupke," "Maria," and "Tonight." One song forecast the future: "One Hand, One Heart" with the words "Make of our hearts one heart. Make of our vows one last vow. Only death will part us now."

It became a hit on Broadway in 1957. So, they made the movie. The 1961 movie of *West Side Story* was directed by Robert Wise and Jerome Robbins, and starred Natalie Wood, Richard Beymer, Rita Moreno, George Chakiris, and Russ Tamblyn. Chakiris and Moreno won Best Supporting Actor and Actress.

The tragic musical tale featured two gangs, the Jets (whites) and the Sharks (Puerto Rican) who insulted each other, fought, and disrupted the community requiring police to quell problems. One night there was to be a "rumble" and Natalie's (Maria) character asked boyfriend Beymer (Tony) to go and calm it. He promised to do so but the boys pulled out knives and two were killed.

Much intervention and anger persisted, and Moreno's angry character told the boys that Maria was dead. Beymer was shattered and called out to the bad boys to come and kill him, since he had nothing to live for. Just as he was killed, he found that Maria was alive. She ended by saying, "Now I can kill too, because now I have hate!" But she could not fire the gun she picked up. All the gang members surrounded her and her dead beloved Tony whom they carried away, suggesting that the feud was over.

The dancers loved being considered real characters in this movie. The dancing was exciting, and the music heightened the emotions of the audience. Some of the songs linger in memory for viewers but the excitement and pitch were the draws of this movie. Again, the Puerto Rican characters were not played by Natives but by studio casting. Some have said that the main themes were violence breeds violence and that the film depicted cultural misunderstanding and the lack of society to integrate young people constructively. The *Romeo and Juliet* story made the audience understand that the movie would end badly but audiences loved the dancing and the excitement and took the tragedy in stride.

The movie budget was $6.75 million, and the box office brought in $44.1 million. The running time was one hundred fifty-two minutes, and the story has been remade and redone over the years.

Other movie nominees included *Fanny, The Guns of Navarone, The Hustler,* and *Judgment at Nuremburg.*

Maximillian Schell (1930-2014) from Vienna won Best Actor for *Judgment at Nuremburg.* Other contenders were Charles Boyer *(Fanny),* Paul Newman *(The Hustler),* Spencer Tracy *(Judgment at Nuremberg),* and Stuart Whitman *(The Mark).*

Sophia Loren (1934-?) from Rome won Best Actress for *Two Women.* Other contenders were Audrey Hepburn *(Breakfast at Tiffany's),* Piper Laurie *(The Hustler),* Geraldine Page *(Summer and Smoke),* and Natalie Woods *(Splendor in the Grass).*

Rita Moreno won Best Supporting Actress for *West Side Story.*

George Chakiris won Best Supporting Actor for *West Side Story.*

Best Song "Moon River," w. Johnny Mercer, m. Henry Mancini, from *Breakfast at Tiffany's.*

Robert Wise and Jerome Robbins, Directors of *West Side Story.*

Best Foreign Language Film: *Through a Glass Darkly,* director Ingmar Berman, Sweden, Swedish. This eerie movie uses photography, especially of people's faces, to show that they are apart when they intend to be together. This story of a young lady with schizophrenia showed her staring into space and not connecting with others because she was hearing and seeing things—like believing God was a spider.

Those who have visited Sweden and Russia and other places have seen that at certain seasons there is very little dark and at others there is very little light. This is summer where the light lasted nearly twenty-four hours. When the young lady's brother, who was an adolescent with sexual urges, tried to come close to his sister, there are hints of incest. The movie is deep, dark, and helps the audience understand the major problems of mental illness and the difficulties of family members to help or be close to those who are so ill. Rarely has a movie shown so clearly the distance of the mentally ill from those trying to help them.

British Best Film: *A Taste of Honey.* Director and producer: Tony Richardson. **British Best Actor:** Peter Finch in *No Love for Johnnie.* **British Best Actress:** Dora Bryan in *A Taste of Honey.*

35th Academy Awards

Ceremony: This event was conducted April 8, 1963, at Santa Monica Civic Auditorium in Santa Monica, California. It was hosted by Frank Sinatra and broadcast by ABC television.

The winning movie, *Lawrence of Arabia,* had ten nominations and won seven. It was the longest movie that won Best Picture, being some two minutes longer than *Gone with the Wind.*

Musical director Alfred Newman was honored. He would eventually win nine Academy Awards, was nominated 45 times, and composed the 20th Century Fox screen logo at the beginning of each of their films. He conducted and arranged music for George Gershwin, Charlie Chaplin, and Irving Berlin. These Russian Jewish composers, Newman, Max Steiner, and Dimitri Tiomkin were called the "three godfathers of film music." Alfred was the head of a household of great musicians composed of brothers, sons, daughter, nephews, etc.

Alfred composed scores for *Gunga Din, Beau Geste, Wuthering Heights, The Hunchback of Notre Dame, The Mark of Zorro, How Green Was My Valley, The Song of Bernadette, Captain from Castile, The Robe, All About Eve, Love Is a Many Splendored Thing, Anastasia, The Diary of Anne Frank,* and later movies including *How the West Was Won, The Greatest Story Ever Told,* and *Airport.* Newman borrowed musical themes and even used his own over and over. He composed music for the shocking 1931 movie *Street Scene* and re-used his haunting song "Street Scene" in *Gentlemen's Agreement, I Wake Up Screaming, The Dark Corner, Cry of the City, Kiss of Death,* and *Where the Sidewalk Ends.* Newman died about seven years after this appearance.

Ingrid Bergman, in Paris, introduced the Foreign Picture category, and actor Wendell Corey, in Santa Monica, named the winner, *Sundays and Cybele.* The role of foreign movies in world film fare was increasing with every year.

The Jean Hersholt Humanitarian Award went to Steve Broidy, who entered the film industry as a salesman for Universal Studios in 1926. He worked for Warner Brothers Studios, Monogram Pictures, Allied Artists Productions, and formed his own company called Motion Pictures International. He was the founding life chairman of Cedars-Sinai Medical Center in Los Angeles and was on the Motion Picture Arts and Sciences Board of Governors from 1960 to 1969.

1962 *Lawrence of Arabia*

Tagline: "A mighty motion picture of action and adventure." This movie was considered by most people to be one of the greatest movies ever made. It was based on T. E. Lawrence's book, *Seven Pillars of Wisdom,* the rights of which were purchased from the author's brother, Arnold Lawrence, for £25,000. However, after the movie came out, Arnold denounced it saying that it was false because his brother was "one of the nicest, kindest, and most exhilarating people I've known." The title of Lawrence's book came from the *Book of Proverbs* 9:1 "Wisdom hath builded her house, she hath hewn out her seven pillars." He wrote about seven great cities of the Middle East and his experiences during the Arab Revolt of 1916-1918.

Casting for Lawrence considered Albert Finney, Marlon Brando, Anthony Perkins, Montgomery Clift, and Alec Guinness. When Peter O'Toole was chosen, author/actor Noel Coward said, "If you had been any prettier, the film would have been called Florence of Arabia." Although O'Toole's face resembled Lawrence, the actor was nine inches taller than Lawrence. In earlier years, Alexander Korda considered filming *Seven Pillars of Wisdom* with Laurence Olivier, Leslie Howard, Robert Donat, or Dirk Bogarde. The project fell through, however. The panoramic desert scenes and complex emotions of the main character from revenge to loyalty, from love of adventure to hate for his job, make this movie extraordinary. Many emotions were famously directed by David Lean to be shown through pauses and non-verbal actions.

In this movie, the Alec Guinness role of Prince Faisal considered Laurence Oliver first, but he dropped out. Anthony Quinn's role made the actor so excited he spent hours using make-up to look like the real Auda, whom he impersonated. Omar Sharif's role was offered to Horst Bucholz and Alain Delon, but Sharif was already a star in the Middle East so was chosen to play Sherif Ali. Some criticized using caucasians for Arabic roles.

Jack Hawkins played General Allenby, but Cary Grant and Laurence Olivier were considered. Anthony Quayle as Colonel Brighton and Claude Rains as Ambassador Bryden had no competition. Jose Ferrer as the Turk had only a five-minute role so demanded payment of $25,000 and a Porsche, exceeding the amounts paid to O'Toole and Sharif together.

The role of the American newsman, Lowell Thomas, who made Lawrence known, was run by Kirk Douglas and Edmond O'Brien, but Arthur Kennedy was selected. Thomas was looking for a hero and loved pictures of Lawrence in his flowing white garb, head covering, and curved dagger at his waist. Other roles were easier to cast. The crew of 200 and the cast and extras numbered more than 1,000 people working on the film.

The beginning of the movie is the death of T. E. Lawrence as he dodged young people on bicycles and his motorcycle crash caused his death on May 19, 1935. People were discussing whether he deserved a high-level burial. His remarkable actions and the question of whether he was good or bad were the subjects of the movie.

The movie skipped over his early work as an archaeologist for the British Museum on digs with David. G. Hogarth and Leonard Woolley in Carchemish and Flinders Petrie in Egypt. He learned Arabic, French, and Greek, and did maps, searches, contacts, and briefings for British military intelligence officers. While covered in only one sentence, he was a bastard child because his parents did not marry. That was a grave disgrace in Great Britain at that time, so he felt like a second-class citizen in his early years.

He was chosen by officers to investigate and assist the Arabs in their war against the Turkish Ottomans, which would lessen threats and protect the recently built Suez Canal. He was sent to Mesopotamia where the Arabs might conquer Syria's four great cities: Damascus, Homs, Hama, and Aleppo. It was thought that Prince Faisal was the best person to lead the revolt, so Lawrence was sent to find him. That plan worked and Faisal set the Arabs to work under Lawrence. He had learned the ways of the Bedouins and desert life, and eventually was given desert clothing, hat, and dagger.

In real life, actor O'Toole hated the desert, and was nearly killed when he fell off his camel, but the camel stood over him and running horses in the scene missed him. O'Toole got a big piece of foam rubber to place on the seat of his camel so it would be more comfortable.

Lawrence took Faisal's troops and captured Aqaba, using guerilla warfare. He then began to blow up trains in the Wadi Rum area of Jordan. He seemed to enjoy it so much that he might have thought that "power was the greatest aphrodisiac." Tourists can now visit that area, hear about Lawrence and the Arabs, chat in yurts with tea and sweets, and walk carefully along walls with aged old petroglyphs drawn on the rocks.

At Dera'a, Lawrence and others were captured by the Ottoman military, and O'Toole was beaten badly. That experience, plus early shots showing how he burned his fingers with fire, suggested that he was masochistic, and his enjoyment of killing showed the other side of masochism, which is sadism. These sexual features are purposely made vague in the movie but stronger in Lawrence's book *Seven Pillars of Wisdom*. He wrote: "In Dera'a that night, the citadel of my integrity had been irrevocably lost."

The movie dwelt little with Lawrence's life after the fall of Damascus and the end of Lawrence's dream of an independent Arabia. He returned to work for the British government, a full colonel, attended the Paris Peace Conference on May 17, 1919, as part of Faisal's delegation, and survived a plane crash that killed the pilot and co-pilot. Lawrence served as an advisor to Winston Churchill, enlisted in the RAF having changed his name, but was found out. He left the service with regret at the end of his RAF service in March 1935.

He owned as many as eight motorcycles, corresponded with Churchill, E. M. Forster, Lady Astor, George Bernard Shaw, Edward Elgar, Robert Graves, Noel Coward, and Joseph Conrad. He adopted the name of T. E. Shaw and was asked to do a more vigorous translation of Homer's *Odyssey*. His study of ancient Greek enabled him to publish the 28th translation of the epic, which was published in 1932 and excited readers more than any other translation.

The movie is so remarkable that it has inspired many, such as Steven Spielberg, to become a filmmaker. It has influenced George Lucas, Sam Peckinpah, Stanley Kubrick, Martin Scorsese, Ridley Scott, Brian De Palma, and Oliver Stone. That was thanks to the film's visuals, musical score, excellent screenplay, and the performance of Peter O'Toole. In one scene, O'Toole wrote a promissory note to Auda (Quinn) writing right to left as the Arabs wrote, not left to right.

The grand visuals in the desert, thanks to director David Lean, featured a tiny speck of black in the desert riding from great distance to the well where O'Toole was drinking. The figure was followed as it gradually arrived with Omar Sharif on a camel. Crowd scenes of attacks, gritty scenes of traversing seemingly impossible distances on rocks and sand, and the energy of all performers caught up audiences.

Maurice Jarre was little known but was called in at the last moment to compose two hours of music in only six weeks. Producer Sam Spiegel asked him to score two themes to show the Eastern side and the British side for the film. The theme for the Eastern side, when Lawrence was dressed in his white desert garb, was in minor unresolved chords that played beautifully, and the British side was in major uncomplicated chords that had a military fervor.

Desert scenes were shot in Jordan, Morocco, and Spain. King Hussein was helpful and often visited sets in Jordan. The movie ran two hundred twenty-seven minutes, had a budget of $15 million, and made $70 million and much more later. The movie was shortened to one hundred eighty-seven minutes for some versions. Some comments follow. To illustrate the creative screenplay, a few quotations are mentioned here.

The reporter (Kennedy): "What is it, Major Lawrence, that attracts you personally to the desert?"

Lawrence (O'Toole): "It's clean."

Lawrence: "So long as the Arabs fight tribe against tribe, so long will they be a little people, a silly people—greedy, barbarous, and cruel as you are."

Lawrence added: "The best of them won't come for money; they'll come for me."

Other movie nominees included *The Longest Day, The Music Man, Mutiny on the Bounty,* and *To Kill a Mockingbird.* The latter film, conspicuous by its absence from the Oscars, was Gregory Peck's favorite of all his movies. The theme carried many messages but basically said, "Hear no evil, see no evil, speak no evil" to those who accused others of bad acts.

Gregory Peck (1916-2003) from La Jolla, California, won Best Actor for *To Kill a Mockingbird*. Other contenders were Burt Lancaster *(Birdman of Alcatraz)*, Jack Lemmon *(Days of Wine and Roses)*, Marcello Mastroianni *(Divorce Italian Style)*, and Peter O'Toole *(Lawrence of Arabia)*.

Anne Bancroft (1931-2005) from The Bronx won Best Actress for *The Miracle Worker*. Other contenders were Bette Davis *(What Ever Happened to Baby Jane?)*, Katharine Hepburn *(Long Day's Journey into Night)*, Geraldine Page *(Sweet Bird of Youth)*, and Lee Remick *(Days of Wine and Roses)*.

Patty Duke won Best Supporting Actress for *The Miracle Worker*.

Ed Begley won Best Supporting Actor for *Sweet Bird of Youth*.

Best Song "Days of Wine and Roses," w. Johnny Mercer, m. Henry Mancini, from *Days of Wine and Roses*.

David Lean, Director of *Lawrence of Arabia*.

Best Foreign Language Film: *Sundays and Cybele*, director Serge Bourguignon, France, French. This French movie starred German actor Hardy Kruger. It was the tragic tale of a young girl who was befriended by an emotionally disturbed veteran of the French Indochina War. He believed he might have killed a young girl while landing his stricken plane. He saw her, Cybele, being dropped at an orphanage and tried to help her. He shared his Sundays with her for months. The vet had a girlfriend and a nurse, in addition to his beloved little girl, Cybele. His nurse learned of this odd relationship and told the veteran's doctor. The vet wanted to give Cybele a Christmas present so took a knife and cut down a metal rooster from the top of a nearby church. He took it to Cybele just as police, called by a doctor, arrived, and killed him dead to protect the child from his knife. Maurice Jarre, who arranged the music for *Lawrence of Arabia*, also arranged the somber music for this film and was nominated for it.

British Best Film: *Lawrence of Arabia.* Director: David Lean. Producer: Sam Spiegel. **British Best Actor:** Peter O'Toole in *Lawrence of Arabia.* **British Best Actress:** Leslie Caron in *The L-Shaped Room.*

36th Academy Awards

Ceremony: The awards event was on April 13, 1964, at Santa Monica Civic Auditorium in Santa Monica, California. Jack Lemmon was the host, and the awards were on ABC television.

The Best Picture winner, *Tom Jones,* was the only film to have three Best Supporting Actress nominations. The Best Actress Oscar went to Patricia Neal for *Hud* despite very little time on screen. Margaret Rutherford, age 71, was the oldest winner for Best Supporting Actress. Sidney Poitier, Bahamian American, was the first black actor to win Best Actor. His *Lilies of the Field* role came five years after a 1958 nomination for *The Defiant Ones.*

Sammy Davis, Jr. read the five names for Best Music Score for an Adaptation. He was given the envelope and announced that the winner was John Addison for *Tom Jones* who was not in the list of nominees. He quickly said, "I was given the wrong envelope. Wait till the NAACP hears about this." Then he got the right winner. He then announced the five names for Best Music Score. Then he said to the audience, "I bet you know who the winner is."

Sam Spiegel received the Irving G. Thalberg Memorial Award. He was the producer of Oscar-winning movies such as *Bridge on the River Kwai, Lawrence of Arabia,* and *On the Waterfront.*

1963 *Tom Jones*

Tagline: "The whole world loves Tom Jones." This movie is an enjoyable romp based on Henry Fielding's 1749 *The History of Tom Jones, a*

Foundling. That book, composed of some eighteen small books, was said by many to be the first novel produced in England. It is about the romantic and chivalrous adventures of an adopted bastard. It began with two male cousins who grew up together but were opposites in nature. Tom was kind, randy, and defended those whom he believed. His cousin was a sourpuss, vengeful, and pretentiously pious. Tom fell in love with a high-born girl whom he could not approach due his low class.

The hilarious film exposed British hypocrisy, spoofing a foxhunt with jumpy pictures of chasing a deer, and an eating scene between Tom and a lady that simulated sexually eating each other. Tom's gusto playboy role with witty narration made him likable in this lampoon of manners in a raunchy irreverent comedy. Director Tony Richardson, husband of Vanessa Redgrave, used a light touch but the movie content made some feel it was trashy. This movie came out during the time when England was producing similar spoofs of aristocracy through the *Monty Python* and Benny Hill satires.

The movie began with the Squire finding a baby in his bed and assuming it was from one of his maids and his barber. The Squire raised Tom along with his own son. At the movie's end, Tom learned the Squire's widowed sister bore him illegitimately. There was a hint of Oedipal feelings when the lady whom Tom ate with and bedded was thought to be his mother.

The casting of Albert Finney as Tom Jones was ideal. His beloved Sophie was the charming Susannah York. Hugh Griffith played the Squire, whose real-life inebriation displayed a losing battle with alcoholism, but made his manic scenes fun for audiences. Joan Greenwood is amusing as the high society lady trying to seduce Tom, which was very easy to do.

The comical style of moviemaking had a narrator, characters who sometimes talked to the camera, and subtitles as in a silent movie. The theme was portrayed in one quotation: "Happy the man, and happy he alone, who can call today his own. He who, secure within, can say, 'Tomorrow, do thy worst, for I have lived today.'"

John Addison arranged a delightful score played on period instruments. At a tremendous pace, a clavichord rippled along merrily as an undressed Finney escaped out of a window, running away, and keeping viewers panting until the next scene. Tom and Mrs. Wilkins enjoy a raucous good meal, eating lasciviously of lobster, chicken, pears, and oysters, but delightfully eating each other up with their glistening eyes. They rushed to bed as the scene concluded. Musicians surely had a twinkle in their eyes performing this movie.

The movie was one hundred twenty-eight minutes, a budget of $1 million, and box office of $37.6 million.

Other movie nominees included *America America, Cleopatra, How the West Was Won,* and *Lilies of the Field.*

Sidney Poitier (1924-?), born in Miami but raised in the Bahamas, won Best Actor for *Lilies of the Field.* Other contenders were Albert Finney *(Tom Jones),* Richard Harris *(This Sporting Life),* Rex Harrison *(Cleopatra),* and Paul Newman *(Hud).*

Patricia Neal (1926-2010) from Packwood, Kentucky, won Best Actress for *Hud.* Other contenders were Leslie Caron *(The L-Shaped Room),* Shirley MacLaine *(Irma la Douce),* Rachel Roberts *(The Sporting Life),* and Natalie Wood *(Love with the Proper Stranger).*

Margaret Rutherford won Best Supporting Actress for *The V.I.P.s*

Melvyn Douglas won Best Supporting Actor for *Hud.*

Best Song "Call Me Irresponsible," w. Sammy Cahn, m. Jimmy Van Heusen, from *Papa's Delicate Condition.*

Tony Richardson, Director of *Tom Jones.*

Best Foreign Language Film: *8½,* Federico Fellini, Italy, Italian. The story is about a filmmaker (Marcello Mastroianni) who was trying to launch a new movie. But he kept thinking of his loves, past and present, some of which appeared as fantasies. His style is to have some unusual master shots, often shocking, to set a scene in this comedy-drama, which also starred Claudia Cardinale and Anouk Aimee.

British Best Film: *Tom Jones.* Director and producer Tony Richardson. **British Best Actor:** Dirk Bogarde in *The Servant.* **British Best Actress:** Rachel Roberts in *This Sporting Life.*

37th Academy Awards

Ceremony: The event took place on April 5, 1965, at the Santa Monica Civic Auditorium in Santa Monica, California. It was hosted for the 14th time by Bob Hope. This was the first time that three films got twelve or more nominations—*Becket, My Fair Lady,* and *Mary Poppins.*

A new category was added for make-up and William Tuttle won an Honorary award for "his outstanding make-up achievement for *7 Faces of Dr. Lao.* This was the last year that ABC televised the Academy Awards in black and white.

Cole Porter had died of kidney failure on October 15, 1964, in Santa Monica, so Judy Garland sang a Cole Porter medley. The Academy Awards Orchestra ended the evening with "That's Entertainment."

1964 *My Fair Lady*

Tagline: "The loverliest motion picture of them all." The movie's name came from the rhyme "London Bridge is falling down, my fair lady." It was based on George Bernard Shaw's 1913 play *Pygmalion.* That was based on a Greek myth about the King of Cyprus who saw female prostitutes. Thus, he wanted no women and carved an ivory statue of a woman. He fell in love with the statue and kissed her. Aphrodite granted his wish and she kissed him back. A 1938 *Pygmalion* movie starred Leslie Howard and Wendy Hiller. Similar stories included *Pinocchio,* a puppet made of wood who became a boy when he perfected his behavior for his creator, Gepetto. *Cinderella* had a hard-working girl transformed into a beauty until she violated a curfew, and a kiss by a prince turned her back into a beauty.

This movie began in London when phonetics scholar Professor Henry Higgins (Rex Harrison) met phonetics expert Colonel Hugh Pickering (Wilfrid Hyde-White). Higgins boasted he could teach anyone to speak so well that he could pass them off as a duke or duchess at an embassy ball--even flower seller Eliza Doolittle with a Cockney accent (Audrey Hepburn). Pickering offered to pay all expenses if Higgins succeeded. Eliza rebelled, "I don't want no gold and no diamonds! I'm a good girl, I am."

Eliza Doolittle and her father (Stanley Holloway) were in a poor area and daddy wanted money for loaning his daughter to Higgins. Higgins said, "You mean to say you'd sell your daughter for fifty pounds?" Pickering: "Have you no morals, man?" Alfred Doolittle: "Nah, Nay, can't afford 'em, guv'nor. Neither could you, if you was as poor as me." He settled for £5. After much hard work at the hands of her mentor, Eliza finally learned to speak very well. Here are some songs sung and voiced by the actors that tracked her changes: "Why Can't the English?" "Wouldn't It Be Loverly," "I'm an Ordinary Man," "With a Little Bit of Luck," "The Rain in Spain," "I Could Have Danced All Night," "On the Street Where You Live," "Get Me to the Church on Time," "Why Can't a Woman Be More Like a Man?" and "I've Grown Accustomed to Her Face."

Music was the key to this spectacular production. Alan Jay Lerner and Frederick Lowe were challenged because Richard Rodgers and Oscar Hammerstein II had tried to do a musical *Pygmalion* years before and gave up. There was no love story or understory, and their cast could not sing properly. Lerner and Lowe wrote Higgins' role specifically for Harrison to talk on pitch. Lerner spent sleepless nights to compose an emotional "love" song for an unemotional gent to sing to Eliza. One night, Lerner's wife brought him tea to calm him. As she entered, he thanked her and said, "I guess I've grown accustomed to you...I've grown accustomed to your face." His eyes lit up. His wife sat down and watched him write that song in one sitting.

Most big movies of that era began with an overture. Usually, that was heard while theatre lights were on, curtains were still closed, and credits were running. But this overture was longer than the screen credits, so the overture began with pictures of flowers (since Eliza sold them) and continued through the screen credits.

The movie had an unusual finish. Eliza was a big hit at an embassy ball and danced with both a prince and one who claimed to be a speech expert, played by Theodore Bikel. He opined that she was a Hungarian princess. Higgins won the wager with Pickering. The movie could not end with a marriage of the 60-odd year-old Higgins and 19-year-old Eliza, but she blew up at Higgins for giving her no credit and left. He begged her to return so they could continue their friendship. After all, they had grown "accustomed to each other's faces."

Casting was interesting. Peter O'Toole, Cary Grant, Noel Coward, Rock Hudson, Sir Michael Redgrave, and George Sanders were considered for the Professor Higgins role before Harrison was chosen. O'Toole was popular after *Lawrence of Arabia* and asked for $400,000, but Harrison accepted $200,000. Cary Grant said he turned down the role because he talked more like Eliza Doolittle. He told producer Jack Warner he wouldn't play the role and wouldn't even go to the movie if Harrison did not play the role. James Cagney was offered the role of Eliza's father but when he pulled out, Holloway had played the role on Broadway and got it, becoming the only star who sang with his own voice.

Eliza was played on Broadway by Julie Andrews, and nobody had to dub her outstanding voice. But producer Jack Warner thought she wasn't well enough known to be a draw. Mary Martin declined the role when offered. When Hepburn learned that 90% of her singing would be dubbed, she walked off the stage. She returned the next day and apologized to everyone. She struggled with her role and lost eight pounds, partially due to problems with husband Mel Ferrer, who was working on a nearby set at Warner Brothers. Director George Cukor had to shoot around her for a week so she could regain her health. Cukor, who won Best Director, was second choice to Vincente Minnelli who had demanded too much money.

The film was shot from August to December of 1963 on Warner Brother studio lots in Burbank. Cecil Beaton was inspired to make the library scenes look like the opulent Chateau de Groussay, Montfort-l'Amaury in France.

Sadly, actor Henry Daniell died on October 31, 1963, after shooting his last scene in this movie as the Ambassador escorting the Queen of Transylvania. George Cukor thought he looked unwell. The 69-year-old actor died of a heart attack a few hours later. During filming on November 22, 1963, Audrey Hepburn announced on the set that she had just heard that President John Kennedy was dead, and a pall fell over everyone.

William Paley, head of CBS, paid for the original Broadway production and Warner Brothers bought the film rights in 1962 for $5.5 million plus 47.5 percent of the gross over $20 million. The film budget was $17 million, and it made $72 million in box office sales. This was the most expensive film made up to this time. The film ran one hundred seventy minutes of pure joy. This movie motivated others to create more transitions in the personality of main characters as in *Educating Rita, Trading Places, Pretty Woman, Mighty Aphrodite,* and *She's All That.*

Other movie nominees were *Becket, Mary Poppins, Zorba the Greek,* and *Dr. Strangelove or How I Learned to Love the Bomb.*

The latter film starred zany Peter Sellers playing three roles. He tried to stop a crazed general (Sterling Hayden in a sparkling role) who wanted to start World War III because the government was trying to rob him of his bodily essences. George C. Scott broke up audiences in his role. The movie ended with Slim Pickens riding the A-bomb down to Russia with multiple bombs exploding while the audience heard England's wartime song: "We'll meet again, don't know where, don't know when, but I know we'll meet again some sunny day."

Rex Harrison (1908-1990) from Hyton, England, won Best Actor for *My Fair Lady.* Other contenders were Richard Burton *(Becket),* Peter O'Toole *(Becket),* Anthony Quinn *(Zorba the Greek),* and Peter Sellers *(Dr. Strangelove).*

Julie Andrews (1935- ?) from Walton-on-the Thames, England, won Best Actress for *Mary Poppins.* Other contenders were Anne Bancroft *(The Pumpkin Eater),* Sophia Loren *(Marriage Italian Style),* Debbie Reynolds *(The Unsinkable Molly Brown),* and Kim Stanley *(Séance on a Wet Afternoon).*

Lila Kedrova won Best Supporting Actress for *Zorba the Greek.*

Peter Ustinov won Best Supporting Actor for *Topkapi.*

Best Song "Chin Chin Cher-ee," w.m. Richard M. Sherman, Robert B. Sherman, from *Mary Poppins.* This song returned to one of the origins of music, to soothe and placate children.

George Cukor, Director of *My Fair Lady.*

Best Foreign Language Film: *Yesterday, Today and Tomorrow,* director Vittorio De Sica, Italy, Italian. This was three stories in one, each starring Sophia Loren and Marcello Mastroianni. The first was about a woman (Sophia) who supported her unemployed husband (Marcello) by selling black market cigarettes. A lawyer helped her avoid imprisonment by being a pregnant woman. She kept her husband busy but after seven children in eight years, he was exhausted, and she would go to jail. She gave him a choice of keeping her pregnant, letting a neighbor man impregnate her, or going to jail. While in jail, neighbors gathered money, petitioned for her pardon, and she was reunited with husband and children. In the second story, Sophia was married to a wealthy man, but had a lover (Marcello). While driving her Rolls-Royce with Marcello, they avoided hitting a child and the expensive car crashed. She hated the damage so got into the car of a passing driver and left her lover on the road as she returned home. The third story was about a prostitute (Sophia) who serviced high class customers, including wealthy. A young seminary student fell for her. She got a wealthy customer to watch her do a striptease, so the boy returned to his studies.

British Best Film: *Dr. Strangelove or How I Learned to Love the Bomb.* Director and producer Stanley Kubrick. **British Best Actor:** Richard Attenborough in *Guns at Batasi* and *Séance on a Wet Afternoon.* **British Best Actress:** Audrey Hepburn in *Charade.*

38th Academy Awards

Ceremony: The awards event on April 18, 1966, took place at Santa Monica Civic Auditorium in Santa Monica, California, and was the first broadcast live in color on ABC. Lynda Bird Johnson, daughter of President Lyndon B. Johnson, attended the Academy Awards escorted by actor George Hamilton. Bob Hope received an honorary award "for unique and distinguished service to our industry and the Academy."

The Jean Hersholt Humanitarian Award went to Edmond L. DePatie, the vice president and general manager of Warner Brothers. He succeeded Jean Hersholt as president of the Motion Picture Relief Fund in 1955 and tried to establish a Motion Picture Hall of Fame to bring in revenue for the Motion Picture Relief Fund Country House and Hospital, developed when the untimely deaths of several destitute Hollywood stars shook the community. His efforts spurred stars and others to donate money to the effort.

Arthur Freed, AMPAS president, presented the Irving G. Thalberg Memorial Award to William Wyler. The director and producer had done three Best Picture Oscar winners: *Mrs. Miniver, The Best Years of Our Lives,* and *Ben-Hur.* He helped make Oscar winners of Audrey Hepburn, Barbra Streisand, Olivia de Havilland, Laurence Olivier, and Bette Davis. He developed their performances by having numerous re-takes until they discovered something extra in the character they played. He worked with cinematographer Gregg Toland to photograph scenes with the illusion of depth, making the scene truer to real life.

1965 *The Sound of Music*

Tagline: "The happiest sound in all the world." An Austrian lady named Maria (Julie Andrews) was training to be a nun in the 1930s but wasn't suitable. Navy Captain Georg Von Trapp (Christopher Plummer) needed a governess for his seven mischievous children after his wife died. The children resisted Maria first but her fun with them brought all together. The captain was engaged to a baroness (Eleanor Parker) but he soon noted the governess and found his children singing. Maria and Georg married soon. Austria was invaded by the Germans, and they tried to enlist the captain, who resisted. Thus, the family soon escaped from a Salzburg festival and fled to another country to find a new life involving singing.

In real life, this story was based on Maria von Trapp's memoir written to promote her family's singing after her husband's death. The captain lost his first wife after 11 years to scarlet fever. One child was ill and could not go to school, so he hired Maria to help teach his child. He was 25 years older than Maria but married her and they had three more children. They traveled in various countries and settled in the U.S. In 1956, Maria was paid $9,000 for film rights.

Paramount Pictures wanted to produce the musical with Audrey Hepburn or Mary Martin as Maria. Richard Rodgers and Oscar Hammerstein II developed the songs from the book by Howard Lindsay and Russel Crouse. The 1959 musical ran for 1,443 performances. In June 1960, 20th Century Fox purchased the film adaptation rights for $1.25 million. Several directors were considered before Robert Wise was selected. They included Stanley Donen, Vincent Donahue, George Roy Hill, William Wyler, and Gene Kelly.

Julie Andrews signed on. Plummer was not happy with his minimal role. Others considered for his role were Bing Crosby, Yul Brynner, Sean Connery, and Richard Burton, but Wise preferred Plummer and promised him a plumper role. Children interviewed for the movie were Mia Farrow, Patty Duke, Lesley Ann Warren, Geraldine Chaplin, Teri Garr, Kurt Russell, and The Osmonds. Charmian Carr, a model, was chosen by Robert Wise for poise and charm.

The European locations widened the scenes and story in ways that could not be done on the stage. It became a glorious musical that outgrossed *Gone with the Wind*. While not an accurate account of the family, the sweep of songs, Andrews' voice, and scenery produced a winner. The running time was 174 minutes, budget was $8.2 million, and box office was $286 million. Most critics reviewed it positively, but it was considered too long for children to sit through.

The real Maria von Trapp had a brief cameo as a passerby, with two of her children, during the song scene "I Have Confidence." Some quotes were: "You need someone older and wiser, telling you what to do" and "When the Lord closes a door, somewhere he opens a window." The movie opened with Maria singing "The hills are alive with the sound of music with songs they have sung for a thousand years." Most of the cast had their singing dubbed.

Other movie nominees included *Darling, Doctor Zhivago, Ship of Fools,* and *A Thousand Clowns.*

Lee Marvin (1924-1987) from New York City won Best Actor for *Cat Ballou*. Other contenders were Richard Burton *(The Spy Who Came in from the Cold)*, Laurence Olivier *(Othello)*, Rod Steiger *(The Pawnbroker)*, and Oskar Werner *(Ship of Fools)*.

Julie Christie (1940-?) from Chabua, India, won Best Actress for *Darling*. Other contenders were Julie Andrews *(The Sound of Music)*, Samantha Eggar *(The Collector)*, Elizabeth Hartman *(A Patch of Blue)*, and Simone Signoret *(Ship of Fools)*.

Shelley Winters won Best Supporting Actress for *A Patch of Blue*.

Martin Balsam won Best Supporting Actor for *A Thousand Clowns*.

Best Song "The Shadow of Your Smile," w. Paul Francis Webster, m. Johnny Mandel, from *The Sandpiper*.

Robert Wise, Director of *The Sound of Music*.

Best Foreign Language Film: *The Shop on Main Street,* directors Jan Kadar and Elmar Klos, Czechoslovakia, Slovakia. A nice shy carpenter was named "Aryan comptroller" of a button store for sewing needs owned by a nearly deaf old Jewish widow. The Nazi-occupied small Slovakian town lived in fear with constant intimidation. The carpenter's new post at the shop had a salary and good reputation despite the town's corrupt leaders. Outstanding camera work carefully showed facial and body gestures of all characters. Actions demonstrated the man's struggle with greed and guilt as he and the Jewish widow came to help each other. But when the Nazis ordered all Jews to be rounded up and sent away, he was torn. Should he have her taken away or should he save her? As he tried to protect her, tragedy happened. After a dream sequence of happier times, the ending fit the terrible chaos that was taking place. Since this movie was made just as the Communists were creating a reign of terror like Nazism, this movie was important and successful in Czechoslovakia.

British Best Film: *The Ipcress File.* Director Sidney Furie. Producer Harry Saltzman. **British Best Actor:** Dirk Bogarde in *Darling*. **British Best Actress:** Julie Christie in *Darling*.

39th Academy Awards

Ceremony: This event almost did not take place due to a strike involving the American Federation of Television and Radio Artists. An hour before the event, the strike was settled. The awards took place on April 10, 1967, at Santa Monica Civic Auditorium in Santa Monica, California. Bob Hope hosted the Awards, which were broadcast on ABC for two hours and thirty-one minutes. Because California Governor Ronald Reagan and wife Nancy attended, Hope suggested a new category of Best Performance by a Governor.

Vanessa and Lynn Redgrave were both nominated for Best Actress 25 years after two other sisters were nominated in that category—Olivia de Havilland and Joan Fontaine in 1941. Actress Patricia Neal made her first Hollywood appearance since a near-fatal stroke two years earlier and received a standing ovation from the audience.

Yakima Canutt received an honorary award "for achievements as a stunt man and for developing safety devices to protect stunt men everywhere." He was a champion rodeo rider, actor, stuntman, and action director. Rodeo star Tom Mix invited him to be in his pictures. Yakima perfected the leapfrog over the horse's rump into the saddle and taught it to Douglas Fairbanks and John Wayne. Duke copied Canutt's manner with drawling, hesitant speech, and hip-rolling walk. Canutt improved rigs, handholds, and cables that helped crashes and excitement scenes be safer for people and animals. John Ford hired him for *Stagecoach,* and he directed action for many movies, including both *Ben-Hur* productions.

Robert Wise received the Irving G. Thalberg Memorial Award. He directed and produced *West Side Story* and *The Sound of Music*. He edited *Citizen Kane* and directed and produced *The Sand Pebbles*. He was president of the Director Guild of America from 1971 to 1975, and president of the Academy of Motion Picture Arts and Sciences from 1985 to 1988. George Bagnall received the Jean Hersholt Humanitarian Award because after being an agent and publicist, he became president of the Motion Picture Relief Fund from 1956 to 1978.

1966 *A Man for All Seasons*

Tagline: "A motion picture for all times." This British drama was based on Robert Bolt's 1960 play of the same name. Bolt borrowed the title from Sir Thomas More's contemporary, Robert Whittington, who wrote this of More in 1520:

More is a man of an angel's wit and singular learning. I know not this fellow…And, as time requireth, a man of marvelous mirth and pastimes… A man for all seasons.

The movie and play showed the years of 1529 to 1535 about Sir More, Lord Chancellor of England. He infuriated the King (Robert Shaw) by refusing to sign a letter asking the Pope to annul Henry VIII's marriage to Catherine of Aragon or take an Oath declaring Henry VIII Supreme Head of the Church of England. Paul Scofield played More in the play and the film. His wife was played by Wendy Hiller and daughter by Susannah York. Orson Welles played the Chancellor whom More replaced. Other stars were Nigel Davenport, Leo McKern, Corin Redgrave, and John Hurt. In a brief scene, Corin's sister, Vanessa, played Anne Boleyn.

Friends of the king urged More to sign those letters for "fellowship." More responded, "And when we die, and you are sent to heaven for doing your conscience, and I am sent to hell for not doing mine, will you come with me, for fellowship?"

Gradually, everyone was against More and he was imprisoned in the Tower of London. His family begged him to go along with the wishes of Henry VIII. There was a final brief trial and he was sentenced to be executed. He exhibited grace under pressure throughout the proceedings. At his execution he said, "I die his Majesty's good servant, but God's first." He tipped the man who cut off his head. The character played by John Hurt became Chancellor of England.

Producers thought that Scofield was unknown and considered Richard Burton and Lawrence Olivier. Cardinal Wolsey, whom More succeeded, was offered to Alec Guinness but Orson Welles was chosen. Peter O'Toole and Richard Harris were considered for the king, but Robert Shaw was chosen in his small role. Vanessa Redgrave was to play More's daughter, but other commitments allowed little time, so she played Anne Boleyn and took no credit or money. Actors took salary cuts and kept the budget under $2 million. The movie was a box office success making more than $28 million in just U.S. sales. The movie ran 120 minutes. It was filmed in Oxfordshire, England, at Sir Thomas More's home in Horton Hill.

The music was composed and arranged by Frenchman George Delerue. This was a movie of dialogue so little music was added. Fanfares and special scenes were well done by Delerue, who became a composer due to scoliosis, having earlier been a clarinet and piano performer.

Other movie nominees included *Alfie; The Russians Are Coming, the Russians Are Coming; The Sand Pebbles;* and *Who's Afraid of Virginia Woolf?*

Paul Scofield (1922-2008) from Birmingham, England, won Best Actor for *A Man for All Seasons.* Other contenders were Alan Arkin *(The Russians Are Coming, the Russians Are Coming),* Richard Burton

(Who's Afraid of Virginia Woolf?), Michael Caine *(Alfie)*, and Steve McQueen *(The Sand Pebbles)*.

Elizabeth Taylor (1932-2011) from London won Best Actress for *Who's Afraid of Virginia Woolf?* Other contenders were Anouk Aimee *(A Man and A Woman)*, Ida Kaminska *(The Shop on Main Street)*, Lynn Redgrave *(Georgy Girl)*, and Vanessa Redgrave *(Morgan!)*.

Sandy Dennis won Best Supporting Actress for *Who's Afraid of Virginia Woolf?*

Walter Matthau won Best Supporting Actor for *The Fortune Cookie*.

Best Song "Born Free," w. Don Black, m. John Barry, from *Born Free*.

Fred Zinnemann, Director of *A Man for All Seasons*.

Best Foreign Language Film: *A Man and a Woman*, director Claude Lelouch, France. This French love story between two who tragically lost spouses featured Anouk Aimée and Jean-Louis Trintignant. It was written and directed by Claude Lelouch and shot beautifully with segues of full color to black and white to sepia tones. With music by Francis Lai, the theme song has been used in Finland on TV and for decades on their cruise ferry Silja Line.

British Best Film: *The Spy Who Came in From the Cold*. Director and producer Martin Ritt. **British Best Actor:** Richard Burton for *The Spy Who Came in From the Cold* and *Who's Afraid of Virginia Woolf?* **British Best Actress:** Elizabeth Taylor for *Who's Afraid of Virginia Woolf?*

40th Academy Awards

Ceremony: This event was postponed two days due to the assassination of Martin Luther King, Jr. on April 4, 1968. Many African American stars who were to be in the ceremony withdrew in mourning for Dr. King. Thus, they moved the date to April 10, 1968, at the Santa Monica Civic Auditorium in California. It was hosted by Bob Hope. Gregory Peck pushed acting nominees to be present at the ceremony and 18 out of 20 were there. Only ailing Katherine Hepburn and the late Spencer Tracy, who died June 10, 1967, and was nominated posthumously, did not attend.

This was a good night to deal with a movie that displayed strong prejudices toward blacks following King's assassination. The Jean Hersholt Humanitarian Award went to actor Gregory Peck, the current Academy of Motion Picture Arts and Sciences president. He invited people to make humanitarian contributions to the Southern Christian Leadership Conference for their non-violent work by contacting the Martin Luther King, Jr. Fund in Atlanta, Georgia.

When Rod Steiger received the Oscar for Best Actor, he thanked the Academy, Norman Jewison, and Sidney Poitier for giving him an understanding of prejudice to play his role in the movie. He ended saying, "We shall overcome." That came from a 1901 gospel hymn used by the civil rights movement. The song said, "We shall overcome, and we shall live in peace someday."

Alfred Hitchcock received the Irving G. Thalberg Memorial Award from Robert Wise. Hitchcock said, "Thank you very much indeed."

Arthur Freed was presented with an honorary Oscar for distinguished service to the Academy and production of six top-rated Award telecasts.

1967 *In the Heat of the Night*

Tagline: "They call me Mister Tibbs!" Well-dressed Poitier was sitting at the depot waiting for a train when a white police officer said, "On your feet, boy!" When they got to the police chief's office, Steiger said, "Got a name, boy?" Poitier said, "Virgil Tibbs." Chief: "Virgil? Well, I don't think we're going to have any trouble, are we, Virgil?" He presumed the black man had killed a wealthy white man, but Tibbs explained he was just waiting for a train after visiting his mother.

In the small town of Sparta, Mississippi, the chief asked Tibb's how much money he made. Tibbs said, "I earned that money, ten hours a day, seven days a week." Chief: "Colored can't earn that kind of money…Hell, that's more than I earn in a month!" When he talked to Tibbs' supervisor, he learned that the black man was the top homicide expert and might aid the chief.

Tibbs learned of a suspect who was arrested. He told the chief, "When I examined the deceased, it was obvious that the fatal blow was struck from an angle of 17 degrees to the right, which makes it almost certain the person who did it was right-handed." Chief: "So what?" A local man said, "Ol' Harv's left-handed, Chief. Everyone in town knows that." Chief: "Well, you're pretty sure of yourself, ain't you, Virgil? Virgil—that's a funny name for a nigger boy that comes from Philadelphia. What do they call you up there?" Tibbs: "They call me Mr. Tibbs!"

Later when the mayor talked to the Chief, he said, "Bill, what's made you change your mind about Tibbs?" Chief: "Who says I have?" Mayor: "Last chief we had—he'd have shot Tibbs one second after he slapped Endicott and claimed self-defense." Tibbs had slapped a wealthy male suspect when the suspect slapped him for asking questions.

Tibbs helped identify the killer who needed some money for an abortionist because his girlfriend said she was pregnant (which she wasn't). The killer was arrested, and the police chief escorted Tibbs to the train and wished him well.

Despite major prejudices shown in the way the local police talked to Tibbs, the chief reluctantly asked his help to solve the crime. The victim had come to build a new factory, and his widow was overwhelmed with grief. She soon realized that Tibbs was doing more to find out who the real killer was than the local police officers, so she demanded that he stay on the case.

Tibbs had to defend himself against local whites who chased or killed blacks who interfered in their little town. Several times the police chief (Rod Steiger) and local officials presumed they had the killer, but Tibbs found reasons why the suspects were not guilty.

The movie was based on John Ball's mystery novels about an African American police detective named Virgil Tibbs. Ball did 11 books about Tibbs and 18 other mystery books. He was a part-time reserve deputy for the Los Angeles County Sheriff's Office, a semi-professional magician, and a great fan of Sherlock Holmes mysteries.

Director Norman Jewison wanted Sidney Poitier to star but Sidney said he did not want to go south of the Mason-Dixon line. He recounted a bad experience when he and Harry Belafonte were in Georgia, where their car was chased, and they were threatened by some whites. Jewison then started looking for another city and came up with Sparta, Illinois. That eased Poitier and he consented. However, after shooting some three weeks, Jewison told Poitier that he couldn't find a cotton plantation north of the Mason-Dixon line but found one in Dyersburg, Tennessee. He said he would shoot the two needed scenes in two days. He also promised to protect Poitier and set up the hotel reservation at Holiday Inn, the only hotel that accepted African Americans.

Jewison wanted Rod Steiger to play a police chief because he looked the role, whereas others thought George C. Scott would do it well. The musical score of 16 songs was composed and conducted by Quincy Jones, with some lyrics by Alan and Marilyn Bergman. The title song was sung by Ray Charles, and one number was Glen Campbell singing and playing the banjo.

Whites were upset because Martin Luther King, Jr. had just led a big march in Selma, Alabama. So, Jewison told Poitier that this would be an important movie. He would play a role where he dressed well, spoke well, and was a very strong personality who was smarter than the prejudiced small-town police chief played by Steiger. Poitier agreed and things went well. Director Jewison told Rod to chew gum for his role. Rod claimed that he chewed 263 packages of gum as an imitation of a southern sheriff who chewed tobacco.

Later, Jewison was in Sun Valley Idaho, skiing with his family when his son broke a leg. Bobby Kennedy's son broke his leg there and the two of them chatted while sitting in a tiny hospital. Jewison described the story. Kennedy said it could be a very important film, and said that timing was everything—in politics, art, and life itself. When the film came out, it won a New York Film Critics Circle Award, and the award was given by Robert Kennedy. As Jewison walked up to get the award, Kennedy said something like, "I told you, the timing was right."

Producer Walter Mirisch was so worried the movie might not play in the South that he did some accounting and showed how it could still make a profit.

Rod Steiger, a method actor, got into his role so well he won Best Actor. He and other actors had tutoring by long-time Hollywood script supervisor from the South named Meta Wilde. It was well known that she and author William Faulkner were lovers when he came to do movie work in Hollywood. (See *A Loving Gentleman* by Meta Carpenter Wilde and Orin Borstem published in 1976.) But her job with this movie was to train Steiger and others about southern accents to handle script writer Sterling Silliphant's excellent dialogue. Steiger's role was the key to building empathy for the Civil Rights struggles during that era.

The movie ran 109 minutes. The film's budget was $2 million, and the box office was a surprising $24.2 million.

Other movie nominees included *Bonnie and Clyde, Doctor Dolittle, The Graduate,* and *Guess Who's Coming to Dinner.*

Rod Steiger (1925-2002) from Westhampton, New York, won Best Actor for *In the Heat of the Night.* Other contenders were Warren Beatty *(Bonnie and Clyde),* Dustin Hoffman *(The Graduate),* Paul Newman *(Cool Hand Luke),* and Spencer Tracy *(Guess Who's Coming to Dinner).*

Katharine Hepburn won Best Actress for *Guess Who's Coming to Dinner.* Other contenders were Anne Bancroft *(The Graduate),* Faye Dunaway *(Bonnie and Clyde),* Edith Evans *(The Whisperers),* and Audrey Hepburn *(Wait Until Dark).*

Estelle Parsons won Best Supporting Actress for *Bonnie and Clyde.*

George Kennedy won Best Supporting Actor for *Cool Hand Luke.*

Best Song "Talk to the Animals," w. m. Leslie Bricusse, from *Doctor Dolittle.*

Mike Nichols, Director of *The Graduate.*

Best Foreign Language Film: *Closely Watched Trains,* Director Jiří Menzel, Czechoslovakia, Czech/German. In a small town occupied by the Germans as World War II's downfall was beginning, an apprentice train-watcher was oblivious to the war. He looked forward to his first sexual experience. When he tried to have sex with his new love, a train conductor, he failed and considered suicide. He was urged to find an experienced woman and was successful sexually. She urged him to fight the Nazis and join the Resistance fight. Just as he found love, Nazis began shooting. The first girl he tried to seduce carried his cap back to his people. There were many special moments, such as when he proudly wore his new train uniform, and when Czechs were called "laughing hyenas" by Nazis, which had happened during the war.

British Best Film: *A Man for All Seasons.* Director and producer Fred Zinnemann. **British Best Actor:** Paul Scofield in *A Man for All Seasons.* **British Best Actress:** Edith Evans in *The Whisperers.*

41st Academy Awards

Ceremony: The Awards were presented on April 14, 1969, the first to be staged at the Dorothy Chandler Pavilion in Los Angeles. This Awards program was notable for the first and only tie for Best Actress. Katharine Hepburn for *The Lion in Winter* and Barbra Streisand for *Funny Girl* both received 3,030 votes. Streisand said as she was handed the Oscar, "Hello Gorgeous." Hepburn could not attend but sent word if she won saying, "If you live as long as I have, anything is possible." The rules stated that if any nominated film or artist came within three votes of winning, the result would be considered a tie.

Stanley Kubrick received the Academy Award for Best Visual Effects for *2001: A Space Odyssey*. Bob Hope presented comedian Martha Raye with the Jean Hersholt Humanitarian Award for her shows uplifting spirits for soldiers during World War II, the Korean War, and the Vietnam War. She was nicknamed Colonel Maggie.

Honorary awards went to John Chamber with an Oscar for outstanding makeup for *Planet of the Apes* and Onna White an Oscar for outstanding choreography for *Oliver!*

A combination of Ingrid Bergman, Diahann Carroll, Jane Fonda, Rosalind Russell, and Natalie Wood presented Sir Carol Reed with an Oscar for Best Director for *Oliver!* Don Rickles presented Mel Brooks an Oscar for Best Story and Screenplay Written Directly for the Screen for *The Producers*. Tony Curtis presented an Oscar to Ruth Gordon for *Rosemary's Baby*. The 73-year-old actress and writer Ruth said, "The first film I was ever in was in 1915 and now it's 1969. I don't know why it took me so long."

1968 *Oliver!*

Tagline: "The first Disney movie with attitude." This musical drama was by Vernon Harris, based on the 1960 stage musical based on Charles Dicken's 1838 *Oliver Twist*. Mark Lester played orphan Oliver, Ron Moody was Fagin, Oliver Reed (nephew of director Carol Reed) played Bill Sikes, Shani Wallis was Nancy, Harry Secombe played Bumble, Jack Wild acted the Artful Dodger, and Hugh Griffith was the Magistrate. A quote: "Mother came to us destitute. Brings a child into the world, takes one look at him and promptly dies, without leaving so much as a forwarding name and address!" Dickens satire portrayed criminals, cruel treatment of orphans, child labor, domestic violence, and recruitment of children as criminals.

The book was quite grim, but the musical made a more delightful rendition suitable for children and adults. Critics considered the way it dealt with injustice. One Englishman said, "Hell is other people." The music by Lionel Bart and John Green made it a genuine joy to behold. The names of songs depict much action in the movie: "Food, Glorious Food," "Boy for Sale," "Where Is Love?" "Consider Yourself," "You've Got to Pick a Pocket or Two," "It's a Fine Life," "I'd Do Anything," "Be Back Soon," "Who Will Buy," "As Long as He Needs Me," and "Reviewing the Situation."

Several considered for the role of Fagin were Peter Sellers, Dick Van Dyke, and Peter O'Toole. Director Reed considered Elizabeth Taylor, Julie Andrews, Shirley Bassey, and Georgia Brown for the role of Nancy. The movie ran 153 minutes, had a budget of $10 million and a box office of $77.4 million. It was filmed at Shepperton Studios in Surrey, England.

Other movie nominees included *Funny Girl, The Lion in Winter, Rachel, Rachel,* and *Romeo and Juliet.*

Cliff Robertson (1925-2011) from La Jolla, California, won Best Actor for *Charly.* Other contenders were Alan Arkin *(The Heart Is a*

Lonely Hunter), Alan Bates *(The Fixer),* Ron Moody *(Oliver!),* and Peter O'Toole *(The Lion in Winter).*

Katharine Hepburn tied for Best Actress for *The Lion in Winter.* **Barbra Streisand** (1942-?) from Brooklyn tied for Best Actress for *Funny Girl.* Other contenders were Patricia Neal *(The Subject Was Roses),* Vanessa Redgrave *(Isadora),* and Joanne Woodward *(Rachel, Rachel).*

Ruth Gordon won Best Supporting Actress for *Rosemary's Baby.*

Jack Albertson won Best Supporting Actor for *The Subject Was Roses.*

Best Song "The Windmills of Your Mind," w. Alan and Marilyn Bergman, m. Michel Legrand, from *The Thomas Crown Affair.*

Carol Reed, Director of *Oliver!*

Best Foreign Language Film: *War and Peace,* director Sergei Bondarchuk, Soviet Union, Russian/French/German. Russians wanted to outdo the Americans in a novel by one of their own after Americans made this movie. This 431-minute movie was made in four parts at a cost far exceeding $50 million dollars.

First, Bezukhov, an illegitimate son of a rich man, lived in high society. His friend Andrei was an aide-de-camp in the coalition against Napoleon. Bezukhov fell for Helene and married her, but learned she was unfaithful. His friend was badly wounded and returned just in time to see his wife die in childbirth. Second, young Natasha wanted to marry Andrei, then a widower, but he traveled abroad. She met another man, Anato. Andrei stopped seeing her and she had a nervous breakdown. Third, the Tsar appointed Field Marshal Kutuzov to defend the country and asked Andrei to be a staff officer. Andrei was wounded. The French Army forced the Russians to retreat, and Napoleon advanced to Moscow. Fourth, Moscow was set ablaze. Russians took their wounded compatriots and left. Andrei was brought home, forgave Natasha on his deathbed, and she married another.

Well, as Woody Allen said after taking a speedreading course, "I read *War and Peace* in 20 minutes. It was about Russia."

British BAFTA awards from this year forward included all films and actors, but sometimes added comments about outstanding British made films. **Best Film:** *The Graduate*. Director: Mike Nichols. **Best Actor:** Spencer Tracy in *Guess Who's Coming to Dinner*. **Best Actress:** Katherine Hepburn in *Guess Who's Coming to Dinner*.

42nd Academy Awards

Ceremony: This event was conducted on April 7, 1970, at the Dorothy Chandler Pavilion in Los Angeles, California. ABC broadcast the show internationally. This was the highest rated of the televised Academy Awards ever, according to Nielsen ratings up to 2020. *Midnight Cowboy* was the first X-rated film to win Best Picture.

Bob Hope presented the Jean Hersholt Humanitarian Award to George Jessel, an actor/singer who entertained troops and hosted many ceremonies. He had been given a watch by General Omar Bradley and a walking stick by President Harry Truman who had appointed him Toastmaster General for the U.S. During his USO shows, a helicopter jump injured him, and he received the Purple Heart. His show business start came at age 9 in a vaudeville boy trio with Walter Winchell, who later became a gossip columnist and newspaper reporter.

Cary Grant received an honorary award for his acting career. Grant received a standing ovation and said, "We all need each other. No greater honor can come to any man than the respect of his colleagues." John Wayne received the Best Actor for *True Grit* where he played Rooster Cogburn wearing an eye patch. He said, when handed the Oscar, "Wow! If I'd known that, I'd have put that patch on 35 years earlier." Fred Astaire did an unexpected dance accompanied by the orchestra after Bob Hope asked if he would ever dance again.

1969 *Midnight Cowboy*

Tagline: "Whatever you hear about *Midnight Cowboy* is true!" This unusual drama was based on a book of the same name by James

Herlihy. He wrote three novels, five plays, and two short story collections. Herlihy was a close friend of Tennessee Williams, and the two gay men spent much time in Florida when James was the protégé of Williams. Herlihy acted in three movies and sponsored a protest against the Vietnam War by not paying income tax. The film starred Dustin Hoffman, Jon Voight, Sylvia Miles, John McGiver, Brenda Vaccaro, Bob Balaban, etc.

Joe Buck (Voight) quit his dishwasher job and dressed as a cowboy to go to New York City and be a hustler seducing middle-aged rich women. As a male prostitute, he found it hard to find the right places to go. He met a con man "Ratso" Rizzo (Hoffman) who had a limp and wanted $20 to send him to a pimp. That person turned out to be a religious homosexual and Joe fled to get even with Ratso. When he found him living in a condemned building, they shared the room and food and became buddies. Joe had sexual liaisons with both males and females in the movie.

Flashbacks gave Joe's background enabling viewers to know how his lifestyle came about. One scene had someone take his picture and invite him to a party of drug-using weirdos. He took Ratso but nobody liked a stinky coughing guy, so they left. Ratso, was a coughing tubercular patient, feverish, and wasting away. He imagined going by bus to live in Florida for a better life. Joe nearly killed a male customer to get the money for the bus trip and some new clothes for both. He shed his cowboy attire and they took the bus south until Ratso died. Joe put his arm around Ratso for the rest of the trip where he sounded as if he might try to find a better job.

The movie was shot in Big Spring, Texas, New York City at several locations in Manhattan, and at the studio. Music enhanced this movie beginning with John Barry's score, Fred Neil's song "Everybody's Talkin,'" Bob Dylan's "Lay Lady Lay," "Midnight Cowboy" played on harmonica, and Randy Newman doing "Cowboy." Many were shocked at the movie with little to recommend either the people or the lifestyle portrayed. There was something in both men that people cannot abide but the performances were so good that they shined through the bleak movie. Perhaps that's the way it was in that urban lifestyle.

The film budget was $3.2 million, and the box office return was $44.8 million. Running time was 113 minutes.

Other movie nominees included *Anne of the Thousand Days; Butch Cassidy and the Sundance Kid; Hello, Dolly;* and *"Z."*

John Wayne (1907-1979) from Winterset, Iowa, won Best Actor for *True Grit.* Other contenders were Richard Burton *(Anne of the Thousand Days),* Dustin Hoffman *(Midnight Cowboy),* Peter O'Toole *(Goodbye, Mr. Chips),* and Jon Voight *(Midnight Cowboy).*

Maggie Smith (1934-?) from Ilford, England, won Best Actress for *The Prime of Miss Jean Brodie.* Other contenders were Genevieve Bujold *(Anne of the Thousand Days),* Jane Fonda *(They Shoot Horses, Don't They?),* Liza Minnelli *(The Sterile Cuckoo),* and Jean Simmons *(The Happy Ending).*

Goldie Hawn won Best Supporting Actress for *Cactus Flower.*

Gig Young won Best Supporting Actor for *They Shoot Horses, Don't They?*

Best Song "Raindrops Keep Fallin' on My Head," w. Hal David, m. Burt Bacharach, from *Butch Cassidy and the Sundance Kid.*

John Schlesinger, Director of *Midnight Cowboy.*

Best Foreign Language Film: *Z,* Director Costa-Gavras, Algeria, French/Russian/English.

This movie was named Z because it was the Greek protest slogan for "He lives." The movie began with the murder of a deputy (Yves Montand) in a seeming traffic accident, but the autopsy showed things differently. Jean-Louis Trintignant was the investigator who sorted through liars and the death of witnesses to find the assassins. Greek actress Irene Papas played the dead deputy's widow. A photojournalist played by Jacque Perrin uncovered the conspiracy and murder causing more problems. There were many clues that this was about an actual assassination of democratic Greek politician Grigoris Lambrakis in 1963. Director Jore Semprun Costa-Gavras directed this movie using a 1966 book called Z about the real murder by Vassilis Vassilikos. Viewers were on the edge of their seats. The soundtrack by Mikis Theodorakis stimulated the movie. The composer was under house arrest but gave director Costa-Gavras permission to use his music, some including bouzouki instruments.

British BAFTA awards: Best Film: *Midnight Cowboy.* Director John Schlesinger. **Best Actor:** Robert Redford in *Butch Cassidy and the Sundance Kid, Downhill Racer,* and *Tell Them Willie Boy Is Here.* **Best Actress:** Katherine Ross in *Butch Cassidy and the Sundance Kid* and *Tell Them Willie Boy Is Here.*

43rd Academy Awards

Ceremony: The event was conducted on April 15, 1971, at Dorothy Chandler Pavilion in Los Angeles, California. NBC broadcasted the Awards internationally on television. In the audience, retired General Omar Bradley and his wife sat near Karl Malden, who had played Bradley's role in *Patton*.

An Honorary Award went to 78-year-old Lillian Gish, who began in silent movies. She accepted for herself and sister, Dorothy, and complimented movies as a place for the mind and heartbeats. Swedish writer/director Ingmar Bergman received the Irving G. Thalberg Memorial Award for his influence across the world with his consistent excellence in movie ideas and productions.

Orson Welles received an honorary Oscar for his "genius" in directing movies like *Citizen Kane*. He said on TV from Spain that he appreciated this award coming from people who loved movies and made them their profession. The Jean Hersholt Humanitarian Award went to Frank Sinatra for his many international contributions for orphanages, medical centers, treatment, and living quarters for crippled and blind children, Martin Luther King College, and assistance for minority groups.

1970 *Patton*

Tagline: "The epic American war movie that Hollywood has always wanted to make but never had the guts to do before." To develop the screenplay for *Patton*, screenwriters Francis Ford Coppola and Edmund

H. North used General Omar Bradley's memoirs and other military contemporaries to reconstruct Patton's ideas and motives. Bradley disliked Patton and they were less close than in the movie. Patton sought glory, was vain, and not obedient to orders.

The movie described General George Patton, tank commander during World War II. It started with his career in North Africa, went through the invasion of Europe, and the fall of Germany. Patton had a bad temper, was insubordinate, and chose actions to ensure that he would be seen as a hero. He parted company with those who said, "Don't let's be beastly to the Germans." He was told by General Dwight Eisenhower to apologize to soldiers whom he slapped, called cowards, and sent to the front because they were shell-shocked. He saw such men as expendable—dead. He was ordered to apologize to them, and to doctors and patients who heard him berate the men, and to the troops.

Patton had great knowledge of historic battles where he was sent, felt he had been there in some sense of reincarnation, and strongly inspired men to fight. The powerful opening speech of the movie includes these words: "I want you to remember that no bastard ever won a war by dying for his country. He won it by making the other poor dumb bastard die for his country." Such words and foul language made his men feel he was one of them and they fought hard for him. When forced to apologize and demoted with his command taken away, he showed contrition. The movie alluded to a poem he wrote (in 1922) at age 34 called *Through a Glass Darkly*. The last line of the poem was: "So forever in the future, shall I battle as of yore, dying to be born a fighter, but to die again once more."

In the last scene, Patton walked off with his dog while talking to himself about how glory is fleeting. The movie ended just before his death. On his last day in Europe, he wanted to go pheasant hunting with his aide, General Hobart, and a 19-year-old PFC driver. They crashed into an Army truck that made a quick left-hand turn. Patton fell to the side bleeding from a head wound saying, "I'm having trouble breathing. Work my fingers." He was paralyzed from a broken neck and died a few days later of a massive pulmonary embolism.

Jerry Goldsmith was a frequent nominee for movie music, but this movie had a special feature--Patton's belief in reincarnation. The composer looped recorded sounds of "call to war" with trumpets that represented Patton's belief that he had been there before. The main theme was a symphonic march with a pipe organ representing Patton's religiosity.

This well-made movie was admired by politicians, military officials, critics, and the public. Scott turned down his Oscar saying he didn't believe in competition between actors. Producer Frank McCarthy had served under General George Marshall and placed his Oscar in the George C. Marshall Foundation, where it is on display in Pinehurst, North Carolina.

Patton will always be remembered. The General George S. Patton Memorial Museum on I-10 in Chiriaco Summit, California, was erected in tribute to him on the entrance of Camp Young, part of the Desert Training Center of World War II. It contains tanks used in World War II and the Korean War, as well as memorabilia from Patton's life and career. There is a video detailing his service and the creation of the Desert Training Center where one million troops were trained for Africa.

The movie ran 170 minutes. It had a budget of $12.6 million and made over $61 million.

Other movie nominees included *Airport, Love Story, Five Easy Pieces,* and *MASH.* The latter two movies displayed a growing upheaval in making irreverent films.

George C. Scott (1926-1999) from Wise, Virginia, won Best Actor for *Patton.* Other contenders were Melvyn Douglas *(I Never Sang for My*

Father), James Earl Jones *(The Great White Hope),* Jack Nicholson *(Five Easy Pieces),* and Ryan O'Neal *(Love Story).*

Glenda Jackson (1936-?) from Birkenhead, England, won Best Actress for *Women in Love.* Other contenders were Jane Alexander *(The Great White Hope),* Ali MacGraw *(Love Story),* Sarah Miles *(Ryan's Daughter),* and Carrie Snodgress *(Diary of a Mad Housewife).*

Helen Hayes won Best Supporting Actress for *Airport.*

John Mills won Best Supporting Actor for *Ryan's Daughter.*

Best Song "For All We Know," w. Arthur James, Robb Wilson, m. Fred Karlin, from *Lovers and Other Strangers.*

Franklin J. Schaffner, Director of *Patton.*

Best Foreign Language Film: *Investigation of a Citizen Above Suspicion,* director Elio Petri, Italy, Italian. This suspenseful melodrama is a satire about how law enforcement can be misused. A newly appointed Italian police inspector murdered his mistress and was part of the homicide investigation. He tested his officers by planting clues, even those that could point to him. The gist of this movie is that one cannot always be safe in the hands of police who are supposed to enforce safety. There is a dream sequence that makes the movie even more interesting.

British BAFTA awards: Best Film: *Butch Cassidy and the Sundance Kid.* Director George Roy Hill. **Best Actor:** Robert Redford in *Butch Cassidy and the Sundance Kid, Downhill Racer,* and *Tell Them Willie Boy Is Here.* **Best Actress:** Katherine Ross in *Butch Cassidy and the Sundance Kid* and *Tell Them Willie Boy Is Here.*

44th Academy Awards

Ceremony: This event was conducted on April 10, 1972, at the Dorothy Chandler Pavilion in Los Angeles. It was hosted by Helen Hayes, Alan King, Sammy Davis, Jr., and Jack Lemmon.

An honorary award went to Charlie Chaplin for "the incalculable effect he has had in making motion pictures the art form of this century." He came to the U.S. to re-market his old films and receive this award. He had a 12-minute standing ovation, the longest in Academy Awards history and blew kisses to everyone. "Thank you so much. Thank you for the honor of inviting me here. You sweet people." He put on his iconic hat and carried his cane, as his character "the little tramp." The orchestra performed "Smile," created by Chaplin for his 1936 movie *Modern Times*. The tune, beginning "Smile though your heart is aching," has been recorded by many singers, such as Johnny Mathis, Judy Garland, Sammy Davis Jr., Michael Jackson, Jimmy Durante, etc.

Singer/dancer Betty Grable and singer Dick Haymes sang and presented awards for best musical scores. Grable felt very ill and saw a doctor the next day who diagnosed lung cancer. With no health insurance due to her husband, alcoholic bandleader Harry James, she had to keep making appearances to cover her medical costs and died 14 months later at age 56.

1971 *The French Connection*

Tagline: "Doyle is bad news but a good cop." This thrilling action movie was based on Robin Moore's 1969 non-fiction book of the same name, telling the story of New York narcotics officers. Jimmy "Popeye" Doyle (Gene Hackman) and Buddy "Cloudy" Russo (Roy Scheider) portrayed the real officers—Eddie Egan and Sonny Grosso. The real bad guy, French heroin smuggler Alain Charnier, was played by Fernando Rey.

This movie showed the dangerous methods needed to find bad guys who shipped heroin across the world. It involved perhaps the most exciting chase scene ever seen in movies, as Popeye followed perpetrators by car through roads, elevated tracks and on foot. The terrible ending told viewers the true results of the real events—cases were dismissed for lack of proper evidence, a sentence was reduced to a misdemeanor, and the main smuggler was never found.

This nearly documentary film was due to director William Friedkin, having been influenced by the movie *Z*. Friedkin tried to cast Paul Newman, Jackie Gleason, Peter Doyle, Steve McQueen, Charles Bronson, Rod Taylor, and columnist Jimmy Breslin in the Popeye role before Hackman was hired. Another Spanish actor was considered before Fernando Rey, who spoke English, but his French had to be dubbed.

The movie had realistic language like: "All right, Popeye's here! Get your hands on your heads, get off the bar, and get on the wall!" "Lock them up and throw away the key." It was thrilling with action and chases enhanced by the director using a Fleetwood Mac song "Black Magic Woman" during editing to keep the runaway pace in the movie. The jazz score had thrilling tension, repeating chords, and drums and bass keeping up a high momentum to the end. The movie was shot on many New York streets and locations, as well as places in Marseille, France, where the movie begins. The budget was $1.8 million, and the box office was $75 million. It runs 104 minutes and resembles a film-noir with its gritty, dark scenes and stunt drivers in speeding cars. Critics were mixed because while extremely tense and entertaining, its message was that the cops had problems as well as the bad guys.

Other movie nominees included *A Clockwork Orange, Fiddler on the Roof, Nicholas and Alexandra*, and *The Last Picture Show.*

Gene Hackman (1931-?) from San Bernadino, California, won Best Actor for *The French Connection.* Other contenders were Peter Finch *(Sunday Bloody Sunday)*, Walter Matthau *(Kotch)*, George C. Scott *(The Hospital)*, and Topol *(Fiddler on the Roof)*.

Jane Fonda (1937-?) from New York City won Best Actress for *Klute.* Other contenders were Julie Christie *(McCabe & Mrs. Miller)*, Glenda Jackson *(Sunday Bloody Sunday)*, Vanessa Redgrave *(Mary, Queen of Scots)*, and Janet Suzman *(Nicholas and Alexandra)*.

Cloris Leachman won Best Supporting Actress for *The Last Picture Show.*

Ben Johnson won Best Supporting Actor for *The Last Picture Show.*

Best Song "Theme from Shaft," w. m. Isaac Hayes, from *Shaft.*

William Friedkin, Director of *The French Connection.*

Best Foreign Language Film: *The Garden of the Finzi Continis,* director Vittorio De Sica, Italy, Italian. This Vittorio De Sica Italian movie has no easily recognizable stars, but an interesting story based on a 1962 novel of the same name by Georgio Bassani.

Set in the late 1930s, Italian and Jewish friends have happy times together until Mussolini's edicts begin to change where Jews can go and who they can see. As Jews begin to be deported to concentration camps, families and friends are torn apart. The movie ends with an empty tennis court where they all once played, and a Jewish lament for the dead is heard in the background.

British BAFTA awards: Best Film: *Sunday, Bloody Sunday.* Director John Schlesinger. **Best Actor:** Peter Finch in *Sunday, Bloody Sunday.* **Best Actress:** Glenda Jackson in *Sunday, Bloody Sunday.*

45th Academy Awards

Ceremony: This event was conducted on March 27, 1973, at the Dorothy Chandler Pavilion in Los Angeles, California. It was hosted by Carol Burnett, Michael Caine, Charlton Heston, and Rock Hudson. It lasted two hours and twenty-eight minutes and was broadcast by NBC with some 85 million viewers. This was the first time that two African American women were nominated for Best Actress— Diana Ross and Cicely Tyson. Marlon Brando won Best Actor but sent Sacheen Littlefeather to explain that he would not accept the Oscar because Hollywood does not correctly use and depict Native Americans.

English actor Sir Charlie Chaplin had received honorary awards in 1929 and 1972. This time he received a competitive award for Best Original Dramatic Score for his 20-year-old film *Limelight.* It was eligible because it did not screen in Los Angeles until 1972. He was in trouble in America for being with girls who were 16 or younger and for his socialistic political views. After arrests and criticism, he moved to Switzerland and came back only for the award. He was knighted in 1975 in England and died in 1977 in Switzerland.

Charlton Heston had a flat tire on the way to the awards, so Clint Eastwood began to present the Best Picture. Charlton Heston ran in at the last minute to present the award. Romanian actor Edward G. Robinson had died on January 26, 1973. He had learned that he would receive an honorary award for his greatness in a cinematic lifetime. His widow received his honorary award and told the audience that he was very grateful.

The Godfather poignant ethnic theme was by Nino Rota, used in an earlier film so was ineligible. That was discovered at the last minute, so the balloting was called a "mix-up."

1972 *The Godfather*

Tagline: "An offer you can't refuse!" This movie was based on the 1969 Mario Puzo novel of the same name. Francis Ford Coppola did both screenplay and directing to make it more ethnic. Coppola hired family members, such as sister Talia Shire, daughter Sofia, wife, mother, two sons, and father—composer Carmine Coppola for additional music beyond Nino Rota's main theme. Additional music was from *The Marriage of Figaro* to convey the Italian feel and the tragedy within the film.

Paramount lost money on recent pictures. Producer Albert Ruddy was hired because he had a reputation for films being under budget. Paramount wanted this movie to appeal to a wide audience with enough violence to make it exciting. So, themes of culture, character, power, and the family made it a movie of the Italian culture. The Italian American civil Rights League wanted the words "mafia" and "Cosa Nostra" removed from the script, and the money from the premiere was donated to The Boys Club of New York.

Casting for the godfather role included Laurence Olivier, George C. Scott, Richard Conte, Anthony Quinn, Orson Welles, and Marlon Brando. Brando stuck cotton balls in his cheeks, darkened his hair with shoe polish, rolled his collar and was chosen to play Vito Corleone. He took a lower salary, bonded so his temper would not delay production, and received $1.6 million.

Robert Duval, Diane Keaton, John Cazale, and Gianni Russo were selected. The godfather's successor son, Michael Corleone, had to be cast. Other roles were crime boss Richard Conte, Abe Vigoda as a Corleone crime family boss, Talia Shire as Vito's only daughter, Sterling

Hayden as a corrupt police captain, John Marley as a Hollywood film producer, and Richard Castellan as Sonny's godfather.

Coppola and cinematographer Gordon Willis chose "tableau formats" looking like paintings. This resulted in images that are remembered well by viewers. A shocking scene of a severed horse's head in the bed of Vito's enemy was obtained from a dog-food company where the horse was to be killed anyway. The scene of Sonny's assassination was on a toll-road with billboards and his car had holes drilled in it to resemble bullet holes—a 3-day scene costing more than $100,000.

The plot involved godfather Vito Corleone's (Brando) family among criminals who competed for business and used vengeance against each other treading on their turf. Vito said, "I'm going to make him an offer he can't refuse." When visiting Paramount Studios, among the pictures on their wall was Marlon Brando reading some lines taped across Robert Duvall's chest on his shirt, since Brando could not remember his lines.

The movie opened with the wedding of Corleone's daughter (Shire) where his youngest son Michael (Al Pacino), a Marine during World War II, introduced his girlfriend (Keaton). Don Corleone refused to deal in narcotics and sent one of his enforcers to spy on them. He was killed, the lawyer was kidnapped, and Vito was gunned down. Oldest son Sonny took command. Vito survived but son Michael's jaw was broken when the police captain (Hayden) hit him. Michael met and shot the police captain and killed the rival gang's enforcer.

Killing the police captain caused Michael to take refuge in Sicily, where he fell for a young girl who died in a car explosion meant for Michael. He returned after a year and reunited with his girlfriend (Keaton), whom he married. He became the godfather after Veto died of a heart attack. Even though he denied to his wife that he ordered killings, the final scene showed him being kissed on the hand for favors done.

This 177-minute movie had a budget of $6-7 million and a box office of $246-287 million. It was a blockbuster and became the best-selling ever gangster film. Brando played the lead role well, but many believe that Coppola made this film the hit it became. Brando turned down his award, as was mentioned earlier, and Pacino did not attend the ceremony because he was insulted that his part was larger than Brando but was nominated as a supporting role. The movie was so good that parodies of roles were popular, and a second and third "Godfather" films were made.

Other movie nominees included *Cabaret, Deliverance, The Emigrants,* and *Sounder.*

Marlon Brando won Best Actor for *The Godfather.* Other contenders were Michael Caine *(Sleuth),* Laurence Olivier *(Sleuth),* Peter O'Toole *(The Ruling Class),* and Paul Winfield *(Sounder).*

Liza Minelli (1946-?) from Hollywood, California, won Best Actress for *Cabaret.* Other contenders were Diana Ross *(Lady Sings the Blues),* Maggie Smith *(Travels with My Aunt),* Cicely Tyson *(Sounder),* and Liv Ullman *(The Emmigrants).*

Eileen Heckart won Best Supporting Actress for *Butterflies Are Free.*

Joel Grey won Best Supporting Actor for *Cabaret.*

Best Song "The Morning After," w. m. All Kasha, Joe Harschorn, from *The Poseidon Adventure.*

Bob Fosse, Director of *Cabaret.*

Best Foreign Language Film: *The Discreet Charm of the Bourgeoisie,* director Luis Bunuel, France, French. This 101-minute French film starred Fernando Rey and was directed by the revered Luis Bunuel. People were lured toward fine dinners, expecting to be pampered despite everyone being corrupt. People were not who they assumed because they had different clothing in different scenes. Dreams were interspersed with scenes. The director appeared to toy with his actors, his scenes, and the audience as he played one trick after another on all.

British BAFTA awards: Best Film: *Cabaret*. Director Bob Fosse. **Best Actor:** Gene Hackman in *The French Connection* and *The Poseidon Adventure*. **Best Actress:** Liza Minnelli in *Cabaret*.

46th Academy Awards

Ceremony: The awards were conducted on April 2, 1974, at the Dorothy Chandler Pavilion in Los Angeles, California. Hosts were Burt Reynolds, Diana Ross, John Huston, and David Niven. It was shown on NBC television for three hours and twenty-three minutes to some 44.7 million viewers. This ceremony may be best remembered for the streaker (Robert Opel) who ran naked across the stage while showing a peace sign with his hand shaped like a Vee. Host David Niven quipped, "Isn't it fascinating to think that probably the only laugh that man will ever get in his life is by stripping off and showing his shortcomings."

Samuel Goldwyn died at age 94 three months earlier and this event was in his honor. He had produced *Arrowsmith, Dodsworth, Dead End, Wuthering Heights, The Little Foxes, The Best Years of Our Lives* and *Porgy and Bess.* Known for his trouble with English, he said, "A verbal contract is not worth the paper it's written on." A book he wanted to make into a film would be impossible because it was about lesbians, he was told, so he said, "We'll make them Hungarians."

An honorary award went to Groucho Marx "in recognition of his brilliant creativity and for the unequalled achievements of the Marx Brothers in the art of motion picture comedy." Groucho was helped to walk to the microphone. He said, "I wish Harpo and Chico could be here. I wish Margaret Dumont could be here because she always said, 'Why are they laughing?'"

Katherine Hepburn presented the Irving G. Thalberg award to Lawrence Weingarten. She received a standing ovation. Her voice and head were shaky from her essential tremor, which could be seen in some of her last movies, such as *On Golden Pond*. Weingarten, a movie mogul, modestly said he learned his craft from Thalberg. He produced Biblical films, comedies involving Hepburn in *Adam's Rib* and *Pat and Mike;* other movies, such as *A Day at the Races, I'll Cry Tomorrow,* and *Cat on a Hot Tin Roof,* etc. Weingarten was so impressed with producer Thalberg that he suggested this award for the most outstanding producers, and now he won it.

Alfred Hitchcock presented the Jean Hersholt Humanitarian Award to Lew Wasserman. He said that award was given not for what someone does but for who that person is. Wasserman began as a talent agent and created the star system. He began with Bette Davis, James Stewart, and Ronald Reagan, whom he helped become the Screen Actors Guild (SAG) president.

1973 *The Sting*

Tagline: "All it takes is a little confidence." This film is in distinct sections with title cards to suggest a 1930s timeframe. Each time a new section and title card were introduced, Scott Joplin music was played, especially from "The Entertainer" to evoke the 1930s.

Two grifters (played by Paul Newman and Robert Redford) shared tricks about how to con others for money. Their friends were played by Eileen Brennan and Robert Earl Jones. Their problem was how to foil the FBI (Dana Elcar), a policeman (Charles Durning), and a crime boss (Robert Shaw). One line from the movie said by the FBI agent was, "Sit down and shut up, will ya? Try not to live up to all my expectations." Quick dialog accentuated the pace of the movie.

Redford spent the night with a seeming café waitress and the next day she was walking toward him. Suddenly, she was shot by Newman's friend, and fell revealing a gun she intended to use on Redford. The male relationships received more attention than male-female relations and "one upmanship" motivated most actions between the men.

After cheating at card tables, the grifters devised a method called "the wire." Their friends helped set up a fake off-track betting parlor with actor Ray Walston reading a wire from a real race as if it were happening now. That looked like the real thing to the crime boss. After a couple of successes where Shaw made bets on winning horses, they suggested to boss Shaw that he bet $500,000. He learned at the last minute that he bet on a horse to win rather than to place in a surprise ending. The camaraderie of the two grifters, and ragtime Scott Joplin ragtime music, made the movie unique. It was a stylish good-natured comedy.

This movie was based on a 1940 book by David Maurer called *The Big Con: The Story of the Confidence Man,* and a 1958 *Maverick* TV episode called "Shady Deal at Sunny Acres." The movie portrayed crime boss Robert Shaw walking with a limp. That came from a fall the week before filming began and he was wearing a leg brace in the film. Hill decided not to use extras, used a color scheme of browns and maroons, and had Edith Head create period costumes.

The film was shot on Universal Studios backlot; Wheeling, West Virginia; the Santa Monica pier carousel; and Chicago's Union Station. The budget for the 129-minute film was $5.5 million and the movie netted $159.6 million at the box office. Old cars made street scenes seem like period pieces and Tony Bill's 1935 Pierce Arrow served as Robert Shaw's vehicle in the movie.

Other movie nominees included *American Graffiti, Cries and Whispers, The Exorcist,* and *A Touch of Class.*

Jack Lemmon (1925-2001) from Newton, Massachusetts, won Best Actor for *Save the Tiger.* Other contenders were Marlon Brando *(Last Tango in Paris),* Jack Nicholson *(The Last Detail),* Al Pacino *(Serpico),* and Robert Redford *(The Sting).*

Glenda Jackson (1936-) from Birkenhead, England, won Best Actress for *A Touch of Class*. Other contenders were Ellen Burstyn *(The Exorcist)*, Marsha Mason *(Cinderella Liberty)*, Barbra Streisand *(The Way We Were)*, and Joanne Woodward *(Summer Wishes, Winter Dreams)*.

Tatum O'Neal won Best Supporting Actress for *Paper Moon*.

John Houseman won Best Supporting Actor for *The Paper Chase*.

Best Song "The Way We Were," w. Allan and Marilyn Bergman, m. Marvin Hamlisch, from *The Way We Were*.

George Roy Hill, Director of *The Sting*.

Best Foreign Language Film: *Day for Night*, director Francois Truffaut, France, French. Director Francois Truffaut starred in the movie along with Jacqueline Bisset, Valentina Cortese, and Jean-Pierre Aumont. Several vignettes described romances, break-ups, and problems with a film crew and their director, ending with the death of the director.

British BAFTA awards: Best Film: *Day for Night*. Director Francois Truffaut. **Best Actor:** Walter Matthau in *Charley Varrick* and *Pete 'n' Tillie*. **Best Actress:** Stephane Audran in *The Discreet Charm of the Bourgeoisie* and *Just Before Nightfall*. **Best Supporting Actor:** John Gielgud in *Murder on the Orient Express*. **Best Supporting Actress:** *Ingrid Bergman in Murder on the Orient Express*.

47th Academy Awards

Ceremony: This event was conducted on April 8, 1975, at Dorothy Chandler Pavilion in Los Angeles, California. It was hosted by Bob Hope, Shirley MacLaine, Sammy Davis Jr., and Frank Sinatra. This was the last year it was televised by NBC because ABC secured future broadcasting rights.

Godfather II was the first sequel to win Best Picture. It received twice as many Oscars as the first *Godfather* movie. Father and son Carmine and Francis Ford Coppola won four awards. Carmine won Best Original Dramatic Score (with Nino Rota). Francis won Best Picture, Best Director, and Best Screenplay Adapted from Other Material (with author Mario Puzo).

French director Jean Renoir received an honorary award for five decades of masterpieces, depicting individuality, compassion, and so many expressions of humanity. Author James Michener presented awards for the Best Screenplay and the Best Original Screenplay. The Jean Hersholt Humanitarian Award went to Arthur J. Krim, president of United Artists for 18 years building minds and hearts through Columbia University and developing nations of Africa.

John Wayne presented an honorary award to director Howard Hawks who had directed four films starring Wayne, and many more films. Hawks said he and John Ford were very close and as Ford was dying, they shared what they had stolen from each other. Hawks envied Ford for receiving awards. Ford told him that one day he would receive an award, too. So, Hawks thanked the Academy for making Ford's prediction come true.

1974 *The Godfather Part II*

Tagline: "Like father, like son." This crime film was produced by Francis Ford Coppola with screenplay from Mario Puzo. Some stars from the first *Godfather* were used, such as Al Pacino, Robert Duvall, Diane Keaton, Talia Shire, and John Cazale, James Caan was shown as his oldest son who was killed in the first *Godfather*. This movie went down two tracks using flashbacks of how the godfather (Brando) began life as a young man (played by Robert De Niro). The story of Michael Corleone (Pacino) had risen to the point of having constant enemies. In an early scene, he said, "There are many things my father taught me here in this room. He taught me: keep your friends close, but your enemies closer."

The worst enemies were the Rosato brothers, who worked for Hyman Roth (Lee Strasberg). When Michael learned that his brother Fredo shared information about him with Roth, he felt betrayed. He let Fredo (Cazale) live until their mother died, after which his fate was sealed. Michael learned that his wife (Diane Keaton) had an abortion rather than bringing another child into this family of crime. He sent her away ending communication with her and their children.

Michael ordered Roth to be killed. One of the plotters against Michael Corleone was reminded by family consigliere (Duvall) that failed plotters against the Roman Emperor sometimes committed suicide, but their family was always taken care of. So, the man slit his wrists in a bathtub and Fredo was killed. The film ended with Michael pondering his future.

The music included the earlier poignant *Godfather* theme and additional music by Nino Rota, to capture an authentic sound from the old country of Italy. Rota was undoubtedly influenced by Italian opera composers like Verdi. This movie was shot in Santo Domingo, Dominican Republic, and the Sicilian village in Messina called Forza d'Agro.

The running time was 200 minutes. The budget was $13 million, and the box office was $48 million in the U.S. and $88 million worldwide. The producers made a third *Godfather* film. They packaged all three into *The Godfather Saga* for television, and finally made *The Godfather Trilogy* for home viewing, including scenes that were deleted from the earlier movies.

Other movie nominees included *Chinatown, Lenny, The Towering Inferno,* and *The Conversation.*

Art Carney (1918-2003) from Mount Vernon, New York, won Best Actor for *Harry and Tonto.* Other contenders were Albert Finney *(Murder on the Orient Express)*, Dustin Hoffman *(Lenny)*, Jack Nicholson *(Chinatown)*, and Al Pacino *(The Godfather Part II).*

Ellen Burstyn (1932-?) from Detroit, Michigan, won Best Actress for *Alice Doesn't Live Here Anymore.* Other contenders were Diahann Carroll *(Claudine)*, Faye Dunaway *(Chinatown)*, Valerie Perrine *(Lenny)*, and Gena Rowlands *(A Woman Under the Influence).*

Ingrid Bergman won Best Supporting Actress for *Murder on the Orient Express.*

Robert DeNiro won Best Supporting Actor for *The Godfather Part II.*

Best Song "We May Never Love Like This Again," w.m. Al Kasha, Joel Hirschorn, from *The Towering Inferno.*

Francis Ford Coppola, Director of *The Godfather Part II.*

Best Foreign Language Film: *Amarcord,* director Federico Fellini, Italy, Italian. The title of this film means "I remember." The story is a year in the life of a small Italian coastal village in the 1930s. It is funny, dream-like, naughty, and sentimental. Fellini is being somewhat autobiographical and even while depicting macabre things, it is still upbeat. One funny line was a man who raised his glass to a lady and said, "She's found her Gary Cooper."

British BAFTA awards: Best Film: *Lacombe Lucien.* Director Roman Polanski. **Best Actor:** Jack Nicholson in *Chinatown* and *The Last Detail.* **Best Actress:** Joanne Woodward in *Summer Wishes, Winter Dreams.* **Best Supporting Actor:** Fred Astaire in *The Towering Inferno.* **Best Supporting Actress:** Ellen Burstyn in *Alice Doesn't Live Here Any More.*

48th Academy Awards

Ceremony: This event was conducted on March 29, 1976, at the Dorothy Chandler Pavilion in Los Angeles, California. It was hosted by Walter Matthau, Robert Shaw, George Segal, Goldie Hawn, and Gene Kelly.

An 80-year-old George Burns won Best Supporting Actor in *The Sunshine Boys*. He became the oldest actor and the last person born in the 19th century to receive an acting award. Walter Mirisch presented an Honorary Award to 84-year-old Mary Pickford at her famous Pickfair mansion (from her marriage with Douglas Fairbanks) to give her the Oscar. Mirisch said she was "America's Sweetheart" starring in 160 films. She tearfully said, "You've made me very, very happy. I shall treasure it always." Her husband, Buddy Rogers, star of *Wings,* ten years younger, sat in the audience as the film of Mary's award ran.

The Irving G. Thalberg Memorial Award went to Mervyn LeRoy, director, writer, and producer who began with producing 22 silent films. He produced 75 talking films and launched new stars like Loretta Young, Clark Gable, Jane Wyman, Lana Turner, Audrey Hepburn, Robert Mitchum, and Sophia Loren. He used Dalton Trumbo as a writer on *Thirty Seconds Over Tokyo,* despite Trumbo being blacklisted in the Hollywood Ten during HUAC hearings.

The Jean Hersholt Humanitarian Award went to Dr. Jules C. Stein, an ophthalmologist who specialized in blindness. He afforded medical school by booking bands and early Hollywood stars. He described how rewarding was his experience to help the blind to finally see movies and ceremonies like this one through scientific progress.

1975 *One Flew Over the Cuckoo's Nest*

Tagline: "One flew east, one flew west; one flew over the cuckoo's nest." The Jack Nicholson (McMurphy) character got in trouble with the law. He was sentenced to a psychiatric ward to escape prison. Other patients were there voluntarily. He said, "You guys complain how much you hate it here, and don't even have the guts to leave! You're all crazy."

When he saw the oppressive Nurse Ratched, he encouraged inmates to rebel against the appalling treatment by her. His personality brought humor, hope, and possibilities to the disturbed patients in the mental hospital. Milos Forman directed this exceptional movie. The audience came to see the mental state of each patient because of the excellent acting by all characters. Nicholson did an imaginary commentary of the World Series for patients who weren't allowed to watch the game on TV. He helped patients deviate from hospital routine and drove them in a bus to a fishing hole. He arranged for a couple of women to see a boy who was too shy to approach women, but he had sex with one. However, when the nurse told the boy she would report it to his mother, a disaster occurred.

Louise Fletcher played a rule-bound nurse, determined to run the unit against the will of the patients. McMurphy did not realize that she would make decisions that would affect him forever. The Chief, a large man who admitted to McMurphy that he was not crazy but just didn't know how to handle stereotypes became his closest friend. After making promises together, when the "Chief" saw that McMurphy had been lobotomized, he made his escape.

This movie was shot at Oregon State Mental Hospital in Salem, Oregon. The fishing scene was filmed in Depoe Bay, Oregon. The movie budget was $3 million, and the box office was $108 million. This film was popular in many countries but not Communist countries. The last thing they wanted patients to do was to investigate their minds and disagree with those who were running things.

Other movie nominees included *Barry Lyndon, Dog Day Afternoon, Jaws*, and *Nashville.*

Jack Nicholson (1937-?) from Neptune City, New Jersey, won Best Actor for *One Flew Over the Cuckoo's Nest.* Other contenders were Walter Matthau *(The Sunshine Boys),* Al Pacino *(Dog Day Afternoon),* Maximillian Schell *(The Man in the Glass Booth),* and James Whitmore *(Give 'em Hell, Harry!).*

Louise Fletcher (1934-?) from Birmingham, Alabama, won Best Actress for *One Flew Over the Cuckoo's Nest.* Other contenders were Isabelle Adjani *(The Story of Adele H),* Ann-Margret *(Tommy),* Glenda Jackson *(Hedda),* and Carol Kane *(Hester Street).*

Lee Grant won Best Supporting Actress for *Shampoo.*

George Burns won Best Supporting Actor for *The Sunshine Boys.*

Best Song "I'm Easy," w. m. Keith Carradine, from *Nashville.*

Milos Forman, Director of *One Flew Over the Cuckoo's Nest.*

Best Foreign Language Film: *Dersu Uzala,* director Akira Kurosawa, Soviet Union, Russian. The Russian Army sent an explorer to Siberia. He joined as a local hunter about 1902. The poor hunter, whose name was the film title, tried to show how capable he was as a hunter and saved the life of the captain. The grateful captain took Dersu to his city, but that life was unnatural to the old hunter. Dersu returned to his land with the captain's best rifle, but fate changed everything.

British BAFTA awards: Best Film: *One Flew Over the Cuckoo's Nest.* Director Milos Forman. **Best Actor:** Jack Nicholson in *One Flew Over the Cuckoo's Nest.* **Best Actress:** Louise Fletcher in *One Flew Over the Cuckoo's Nest.* **Best Supporting Actor:** Brad Dourik in *One Flew Over the Cuckoo's Nest.* **Best Supporting Actress:** Jody Foster in *Bugsy Malone* and *Taxi Driver.*

49th Academy Awards

Ceremony: This event took place on March 28, 1977, at the Dorothy Chandler Pavilion in Los Angeles, California. The program was broadcast on ABC and lasted three hours and thirty-eight minutes. It was hosted by Richard Pryor, Ellen Burstyn, Jane Fonda, and Warren Beatty.

The Best Actor award went posthumously to Peter Finch, who died January 14, 1977, of a heart attack at age 60, and was given to his widow. This was the first posthumous Best Actor Oscar and the first to an Australian. The two producers of *Rocky* for Best Picture took Sylvester Stallone on stage with them to receive their Oscars. Stallone was given the microphone. He said, "To all those Rockys in the world, I love ya."

Unusual presenters were author Norman Mailer, who honored Paddy Chayefsky for writing *Network,* Jeanne Moreau honored Jack Avildsen as Best Director for *Rocky,* Pearl Bailey for presenting the Best Foreign Film called *Black and White in Color,* and author Lillian Hellman who presented the Best Documentary award. Hellman said she came to the event because she liked documentaries and had a mischievous pleasure in finally being seen as respectable. She was referring to her Communist sympathies, blacklisting, and living with mystery writer Dashiell Hammett, who claimed he wrote *The Thin Man* for her.

The Irving G. Thalberg Memorial Award went to Pandro S. Berman, producer of some seventy-five films, many of which were very popular. Berman thanked his co-workers through the years and to the Academy for forgetting the bad and remembering the good films. This event was also notable for the first-ever female nominee for Best Director—Lina Wertmuller for *Seven Beauties*. Barbra Streisand received her second

Oscar for composing the music for "Evergreen," the first woman to be honored as a composer, and the only person to win awards for both acting and songwriting.

1976 *Rocky*

Tagline: "His whole life was a million-to-one shot!" Sylvester Stallone wrote this in 3.5 days after watching a championship match between Muhammad Ali and Chuck Wepner on March 24, 1975. Some scenes were from real-life boxers like Joe Frazier, Ali, and Rocky Marciano.

Rocky Balboa (Sylvester Stallone) was a small-time boxer from Philadelphia. When the world heavyweight champion, Apollo Creed (Carl Weathers), learned that his opponent was injured, he offered everyone the opportunity to box with him. Rocky applied and was accepted. He trained with Mickey Goldmill (Burgess Meredith). "The world ain't all sunshine and rainbows...But it ain't how hard you get hit; it's about how hard you get hit and keep moving forward."

He began an affair with Adrian (Talia Shire), the shy sister of his pal, Paulie (Burt Young). The main theme of the *Rocky* music played could be summed up as, "I've got a beautiful feeling, everything's going my way." Rocky practiced running up and down the steps of the Philadelphia Museum of Art. The music composed by Bill Conti played the triumphant tunes as he ascended steps and met his goals for practice. At the big fight, despite numerous injuries to each other, Rocky and Apollo slugged it out to the 15th round.

Stallone wrote the story and wanted to play the part. United Artists wanted Robert Redford, Ryan O'Neal, Burt Reynolds, or James Caan who might draw more viewers. They wanted boxer Ken Norton to play Creed but gave the role to Weathers. They wanted someone else to play Adrian but chose Shire. They kept the budget under a million dollars by using Stallone family members for several roles, real broadcasters, and news anchors for several roles. During the filming of the fight, Stallone and Weathers suffered minor injuries. The scene of ice skating was shot at night because it cost too much to have skaters on the ice during daytime hours. They kept the fee for music at $25,000, yet the music adds such zest to the finale that it is remembered by viewers who saw the movie.

The world box office was $225 million. This caused seven sequels of Rocky movies and many other reminders. The steps to the Philadelphia Museum of Art are now called "Rocky steps" and a statue of the boxer with arms up is located by the steps. Philadelphia City Commerce Director Dick Doran said Stallone and *Rocky* had done more for the city's image than "anyone since Ben Franklin." Video games of Rocky were generated, and a musical was made years later.

Other movie nominees included *All the President's Men, Bound for Glory, Network,* and *Taxi Driver.*

Peter Finch (1916-1977) from London won Best Actor for *Network.* Other contenders were Robert De Niro *(Taxi Driver),* Giancarlo Giannini *(Seven Beauties),* William Holden *(Network),* and Sylvester Stallone *(Rocky).*

Faye Dunaway (1941-?) from Bascom, Florida, won Best Actress for *Network.* Other contenders were Marie-Christine Barrault *(Cousin Cousine),* Talia Shire *(Rocky),* Sissy Spacek *(Carrie),* and Liv Ullmann *(Face to Face).*

Beatrice Straight won Best Supporting Actress for *Network.*

Jason Robards won Best Supporting Actor for *All the President's Men.*

Best Song "Evergreen," w. Paul Williams, m. Barbra Streisand, from *A Star Is Born.*

John G. Avildsen, Director of *Rocky.*

Best Foreign Language Film: *Black and White in Color,* director Jean-Jacques Annaud, Ivory Coast, French. This movie was a satire on French soldiers using their servants in Africa to fight German soldiers, and Germans using their servants as soldiers. Made on the Ivory Coast, this funny anti-war movie makes fun of racists, religion, and nationalists with virtually unknown but good actors. The tagline for the 90-minute movie was "The picture that marches to a different drummer."

British BAFTA awards: Best Film: *Annie Hall.* Director Woody Allen. **Best Actor:** Peter Finch in *Network.* **Best Actress:** Diane Keaton in *Annie Hall.* **Best Supporting Actor:** Edward Fox in *A Bridge Too Far.* **Best Supporting Actress:** Jenny Agutter in *Equus.*

50th Academy Awards

Ceremony: This event was conducted on April 3, 1978, at Dorothy Chandler Pavilion in Los Angeles, California. It was hosted by Bob Hope, televised on ABC, and ran three hours and twenty minutes.

Perhaps the most notable moment came when Vanessa Redgrave won Best Supporting Actress for *Julia*. That movie dealt with Jewish author Lillian Hellman's memory of a friend who transported money to help Jews during the Holocaust. Outside the theater, members of the Jewish Defense League had been protesting. So, here is some of Redgrave's speech:

> My dear colleagues, I thank you very much for this tribute to my work. I think that Jane Fonda and I have done the best work of our lives, and I think this is in part due to our director, Fred Zinnemann, and I salute that record and I salute all of you for having stood firm and dealt a final blow against that period when Nixon and McCarthy launched a worldwide witch hunt against those who tried to express in their lives and their work the truth that they believe in. I salute you and I thank you and I pledge to you that I will continue to fight against anti-Semitism and fascism.

Later, as writer Paddy Chayefsky announced screenplay winners, he began:

> There's a little matter I'd like to tidy up, at least if I expect to live with myself tomorrow morning. I would like to say,

opinion of course, that I'm sick and tired of people exploiting the occasion of the Academy Awards for the propagation of their own personal political propaganda.

Charlton Heston was awarded the Jean Hersholt Humanitarian Award. Stanley Kramer presented the Irving G. Thalberg Memorial Award to Walter Mirisch. Special Achievement awards went to Frank Warner for sound effects in *Close Encounters of the Third Kind,* Ben Burtt for creating alien creatures in *Star Wars* that included cute R2-D2 and C-3PO creatures with voices, and Margaret Booth for film editing for 44 years beginning in 1915.

A special tribute went to those who died during the past year, including Richard Carlson, Zero Mostel, Peter Finch, Stephen Boyd, Roberto Rossellini, Howard Hawks, Joan Crawford, Bing Crosby, Elvis Presley, Groucho Marx, and Charlie Chaplin. This began a tribute awards section.

1977 *Annie Hall*

Tagline: "A nervous romance." Woody Allen co-wrote this story with Marshall Brickman. It was a search for the reasons why his relationship with a lady (Diane Keaton) failed. It was Allen's first attempt at seriousness following his movie comedies. In another sense, the movie struggled with some parts of his own life, such as his Jewish identity, the findings of his psychoanalysis, and the modern world.

Allen filled the movie with an assortment of people, including Tony Roberts, Carol Kane, Paul Simon, Shelley Duval, Christopher Walken, Marshall McLuhan, Truman Capote, Jeff Goldblum, Beverly D'Angelo, Sigourney Weaver, and Colleen Dewhurst. He also chose cinematographer Gordon Willis with whom he made some interesting creative cinematography. Sometimes, characters spoke directly to the audience, sometimes their thoughts were put into captions, such as when Keaton was talking but the caption showed her thoughts "He probably thinks I'm a yoyo." Sometimes the camera followed a character walking from one room to another showing walls, and at one point he had a cartoon version of himself.

The film's music included Allen favorites like "It Had to Be You," "Seems Like Old Times," a Christmas medley, Mozart's "Jupiter Symphony," "Sleepy Lagoon," and "A Hard Way to Go." Diane Keaton's attire influenced fashions with her look of oversized clothes, mannish blazers, billowy trousers, a man's tie, and boots. Comments were, "I want the Annie Hall look."

Other movie nominees included *The Goodbye Girl, Julia, Star Wars,* and *The Turning Point.*

Richard Dreyfuss (1947-?) from Brooklyn won Best Actor for *The Goodbye Girl.* Other contenders were Woody Allen *(Annie Hall),* Richard Burton *(Equus),* Marcello Mastroianni *(A Special Day),* and John Travolta *(Saturday Night Fever).*

Diane Keaton (1946-?) from Los Angeles won Best Actress for *Annie Hall.* Other contenders were Anne Bancroft *(The Turning Point),* Jane Fonda *(Julia),* Shirley MacLaine *(The Turning Point),* and Marsha Mason *(The Goodbye Girl).*

Vanessa Redgrave won Best Supporting Actress from *Julia.*

Jason Robards won Best Supporting Actor from *Julia.*

Best Song "You Light Up My Life," w.m. Joseph Brooks, from *You Light Up My Life.*

Woody Allen, Director of *Annie Hall.*

Best Foreign Language Film: *Madame Rosa,* director Moshe Mizrahi, France. This French movie was directed by Moshe Mizrahi, adapted from the 1975 novel by Romain Gary called *La Vie Devant Soi,* or *The Life Before Us.* A Jewish survivor of the Holocaust was formerly a highly successful prostitute (Madame Rosa played by Simone Signoret) but in old age ran a boarding home for the children of prostitutes. Since France, and especially Paris, has many Algerians, Tunisians, and Moroccans, one of her favorite children was an Algerian boy named Momo. She took him for training in religion, French literature, and Arabic. As their bond developed, Momo realized the old woman was unwell and asked her doctor (Claude Dauphin) to help her die. Meanwhile, she urged Momo to never prostitute himself. His father (Costa-Gavras) tried to collect the boy, but Madame Rosa tricked him into believing she raised Momo as a Jew, whereas she raised him as a Muslim. Signoret debated whether to star in this film because she would have to gain a lot of weight. Husband, Yves Montand, urged her to reject it but she decided that the film had an important message

British BAFTA awards: Best Film: *Annie Hall.* Director Woody Allen. **Best Actor:** Peter Finch in *Network.* **Best Actress:** Diane Keaton in *Annie Hall.* **Best Supporting Actor:** Edward Fox in *A Bridge Too Far.* **Best Supporting Actress:** Jenny Agutter in *Equus.*

51st Academy Awards

Ceremony: This event was conducted on April 9, 1979, at the Dorothy Chandler Pavilion in Los Angeles, California, hosted by talk show emcee Johnny Carson on an ABC televised program lasting three hours and twenty-five minutes, watched by 46.3 million viewers.

An honorary award was presented to Laurence Oliver for his lifetime achievement. Olivier had to stop the standing ovation by throwing kisses to the audience. He was bearded, balding, and handsome, as he described the "pure human kindness" of the award and thanked all for "this great gift."

John Wayne announced the Best Picture. He was a gaunt, haggard man walking forward to a standing ovation and everyone saw a man dying of stomach cancer. He had made his last picture while ill—*The Shootist* with Lauren Bacall two years earlier. He described how he and Oscar both came to Hollywood in 1928. "We're both a little weather-beaten but we're still here and plan to be around for a while." He died three months later at age 72. President Jimmy Carter posthumously awarded John Wayne the Presidential Medal of Freedom. Carter said, "He was a symbol of many of the qualities that made America great—the ruggedness, the independence, the sense of personal conviction and courage that reflected the best of our national character."

Director King Vidor won an honorary Oscar for "his incomparable achievements as a cinematic creator and innovator." Jack Valenti awarded Leo Jaffe, chairman of Columbia Pictures from 1973 to 1981, the Jean Hersholt Humanitarian Award. Jaffe had, among other contributions, taken a position against an employee who had embezzled $61,000 and set Colombia back on a good track after the scandal.

1978 *The Deer Hunter*

Tagline: "One of the most important and powerful films of all time." There is much to be said about this movie as it opened a new era of war movies. Many say it paved the way for violent war films such as *Platoon, Saving Private Ryan,* and Clint Eastwood's two Iwo Jima films.

The film was partly based on an unproduced screenplay by Louis Garfinkle and Quinn Redeker called "The Man Who Came to Play." That was about a man who went to Las Vegas to play Russian roulette. That dangerous game was written by writer/director Michael Cimino and Deric Washburn into a story of the Vietnam War. The movie began with steelworker friends and wives who lived in a Russian town, who attended a Russian cathedral, sang, and danced to Russian tunes, and hunted deer in their past-time activities.

Cimino wanted to create companionship and solidarity between the main characters. So, six of the male characters carried a photo of them altogether as children in his back pocket. They were also given special IDs, driver's licenses, and medical cards made for each of them.

Casting the buddies and their lovers was not very difficult. Robert De Niro was popular due to his recent *Godfather* films. Roy Scheider was the first choice, and his negative response opened the door for De Niro, who created his persona by socializing and visiting steelworkers. Christopher Walken was the choice for Corporal Nick and won a Best Supporting Actor for his role. John Savage was cast as Corporal Steven Pushkov, who got married just before going to Vietnam, and returned having lost his legs and one arm.

John Cazale, who had been in the *Godfather* as Fredo with De Niro, was cast as Stan ("Stosh"). When director Cimino learned Cazale was terminally ill with lung cancer, he shot all scenes with Cazale first. He died before seeing the movie. His real lover was Meryl Streep. She wanted to be near to care for Cazale so she was given a small role and Cimino told her to write her own lines. The other buddy was George Dzundza who played John Walsh. In real life, his mother was a Ukrainian and he learned to play the piano and sing Russian songs for this movie. The steelworks factory foreman was not an actor, but they decided to cast him in the movie as well.

The buddies decided to go to war and serve together. Before they left, John Savage played the part of a young man who married his girlfriend, and his wedding displayed the camaraderie of the families. One buddy said, "A man who says no to champagne says no to life." Shortly before they left home, the Walken character asked the De Niro character to never leave him over there in Vietnam if things got rough. That promise played out in the finale.

In terrible scenes about the Russian buddies being captured and tortured and forced to play Russian roulette where people bet on who would die, the Americans escaped. The Savage character came home with terrible handicaps. His wife showed De Niro money that was coming by mail to her husband. De Niro realized the Walken character must have stayed in Vietnam and engaged in Russian roulette, risking his life to send money to his friend. De Niro returned to Saigon, found his friend, and had difficulty getting the dazed man to return to normality. After the tragedy, De Niro returned with the body of his friend. The funeral reunited the families and the final scene had all in the bar singing "God Bless America" in honor of Nick.

The budget for this movie was $15 million and box office $49 million. Due to Cazale's deadly illness, he was not insurable. De Niro, according to Streep, paid his medical bills and helped the actor get through the end of his life making this film. Some scenes were filmed at the historic St. Theodosius Russian Orthodox Cathedral in Cleveland, Ohio, and the wedding reception was filmed at the nearby Lemko Hall. Extras for the wedding-dance scenes were asked to bring their own wrapped boxes as if they were wedding presents, and some contained real gifts.

Other movie nominees included *Coming Home, Heaven Can Wait, Midnight Express,* and *An Unmarried Woman.*

Jon Voigt (1938-?) from Yonkers, New York, won Best Actor for *Coming Home.* Other contenders were Warren Beatty *(Heaven Can Wait),* Gary Busey *(The Buddy Holly Story),* Robert De Niro *(The Deer Hunter),* and Laurence Olivier *(The Boys from Brazil).*

Jane Fonda won Best Actress for *Coming Home.* Other contenders were Ingrid Bergman *(Autumn Sonata),* Ellen Burstyn *(Same Time, Next Year),* Jill Clayburgh *(An Unmarried Woman),* and Geraldine Page *(Interiors).*

Maggie Smith won Best Supporting Actress for *California Suite.*

Christopher Walken won Best Supporting Actor for *The Deer Hunter.*

Best Song "Last Dance," w.m. Paul Jabara, from *Thank God It's Friday.*

Michael Cimino, Director of *The Deer Hunter.*

Best Foreign Language Film: *Get Out Your Handkerchiefs,* director Bertrand Blier, France, French. This romantic sex comedy is clever but concerning. A kindly husband (Gerard Depardieu) believes his wife is so depressed that he tried to cheer her up by finding a lover for her. The man he found had no interest in helping her, so the husband continued to worry about her. Finally, the lady finds her own help through a 13-year-old boy with whom she shares a bit too much. While the audience laughs at some of the antics, audiences may worry about the impact of all this on such a young juvenile.

British BAFTA awards: Best Film: *Julia.* Director Alan Parker. **Best Actor:** Richard Dreyfuss in *The Goodbye Girl.* **Best Actress:** Jane Fonda in *Julia.* **Best Supporting Actor:** John Hurt in *Midnight Express.* **Best Supporting Actress:** Geraldine Page in *Interiors.*

52nd Academy Awards

Ceremony: This event was conducted on April 14, 1980, at the Dorothy Chandler Pavilion in Los Angeles, California. It was hosted by Johnny Carson and televised by ABC for three hours and twelve minutes. Remarkable age differences occurred among actors. The Best Supporting Actor nominees included 8-year-old Justin Henry for *Kramer vs. Kramer* and 79-year-old Melvyn Douglas who won for *Being There*. Douglas was not present at the ceremony because his wife, Helen Gahagan, was ill and died two months later. He died the following year.

The Academy presented an honorary award to Alec Guinness. He said he was discovered by Sir John Gielgud and starred in 39 movies after serving in World War II. After a standing ovation, he said he'd learned "to do nothing at all" so would take the Oscar "while the going was good." Dustin Hoffman won Best Actor and looked at the Oscar and said, "He has no genitalia and he's holding a sword. Thank you all and I thank my parents for not practicing birth control."

1979 *Kramer vs. Kramer*

Tagline: "There are three sides to this love story." Ted Kramer (Dustin Hoffman), a workaholic, came home to tell his wife Joanna (Meryl Streep) of a promotion. She told him she was going to leave him because he cared more about work than home life. She did not think she could handle caring for her son (Justin Henry) while getting a job and starting a new life. Despite the boy's loss of mother, the boy and father were distant until they bonded. Ted told the boy when he said he didn't like his dad, "And I hate you back, you little shit!"

Ted then took care of their son, cooked, did housekeeping, and tried to hold down a job with growing responsibilities. Despite their earlier difficulties, the boy and father gave each other love which succeeded because the feelings were mutual. Ted and his neighbor (Jane Alexander) discussed how she had urged Joanna to leave him, but she came to see how he cared for his little boy. When the child fell from a playground jungle gym and needed medical care, Ted ran him to the care center and stayed with his son through pain and stitches.

Ted was demoted because of caring for their son during illnesses and schooling. His wife returned after 15 months and wanted to take their son back. Ted's lawyer (Howard Duff) told him the judges sympathized more with mothers getting custody than fathers. Joanna won custody. When she went to pick up her son, she realized that the little boy had a home. She told Ted she would not take him away.

The movie brought new ideas about parenting into view without taking sides. It fit the new issues of divorce, child custody, and care of children. The movie was based on Avery Corman's 1977 novel of the same name. Kate Jackson, Faye Dunaway, Jane Fonda, and Ali MacGraw were considered for the role played by Meryl Streep. Hoffman wanted to cast Streep using her depression after the death of her boyfriend, actor John Cazale. He wanted her to be emotional and the good reviews of the movie showed that she and Hoffman played their roles very believably and well.

The movie budget was $8 million and box office returns were $175 million. The 105-minute movie was filmed in Central Park in New York City and a few other places.

Other nominees included *All That Jazz, Apocalypse Now, Breaking Away,* and *Norma Rae.*

Dustin Hoffman (1937-?) from Los Angeles, California, won Best Actor for *Kramer vs. Kramer*. Other contenders were Jack Lemmon *(The China Syndrome)*, Al Pacino *(...And Justice for All)*, Roy Scheider *(All That Jazz)*, and Peter Sellers *(Being There)*.

Sally Field (1946-?) from Pasadena, California, won Best Actress for *Norma Rae*. Other contenders were Jill Clayburgh *(Starting Over)*, Jane Fonda *(The China Syndrome)*, Marsha Mason *(Chapter Two)*, and Bette Midler *(The Rose)*.

Meryl Streep won Best Supporting Actress for *Kramer vs. Kramer*.

Melvyn Douglas won Best Supporting Actor for *Being There*.

Best Song "It Goes Like It Goes," w. m. Norman Gimbel, David Shire, from *Normal Rae*.

Robert Benton, Director of *Kramer vs. Kramer*.

Best Foreign Language Film: *The Tin Drum,* director Wolker Schlondorff, West Germany. This story by Gunter Grass depicted a child who did not want to grow up surrounded by the violence and cruelty of Nazism. Instead, he banged his drum when he disliked things as his only protest to the chaos around him. The German cast is mostly unknown except for singer Charles Aznavour. The movie is complicated but is very strong.

British BAFTA awards: Best Film*: Manhattan*. Director Francis Ford Coppola. **Best Actor:** Jack Lemmon in *The China Syndrome*. **Best Actress:** Jane Fonda in *The China Syndrome*. **Best Supporting Actor:** Robert Duvall in *Apocalypse Now*. **Best Supporting Actress:** Rachel Roberts in *Yanks*.

53rd Academy Awards

Ceremony: This event took place March 31, 1981, at the Dorothy Chandler Pavilion in Los Angeles, hosted by Johnny Carson. It was broadcast on ABC for three hours, thirteen minutes. It was postponed due to the assassination attempt on President Ronald Reagan. The president had a TV set in his hospital room. He and Nancy shared the interests of the attendees. He said with amusement that film is forever and that he'd "been trapped in some films forever." Could he have meant *Bedtime for Bonzo?*

The ages of actors winning Oscars were all under 40. Best Actor Robert De Niro was 37, Best Actress Sissy Spacek was 31, Best Supporting Actor Timothy Hutton was 20, and Best Supporting Actress Mary Steenburgen was 28. Timothy Hutton had been on television, but this was his first role in a movie. The 19-year-old actor had lost his 45-year-old father, actor Jim Hutton, to cancer two years earlier. He accepted the award as Best Supporting Actor and thanked everyone, especially Robert Redford. Then he said, "I wish my father could be here."

Henry Fonda, age 76, was awarded an Academy Honorary Award and received the Academy Award for Best Actor the following year. Robert Redford presented his Oscar and said that Fonda had worked in 86 films for 46 years playing an American character, "the face of our country." He came to the stage during a standing ovation with a cane and glasses, spoke of his luck to have the opportunity to work with the best producers, writers, actors, etc.

Lillian Gish, 88 years old, was greeted with a standing ovation when she came to announce the Best Picture. She spoke of one of her first films, the 1912 *Birth of a Nation,* before announcing that *Ordinary People* won the Oscar. The Nicolas Brothers ages 60 and 67 came out, danced, tap-danced, and caught their breaths. They could still do the amazing splits and put their legs back together to rise to a standing pose. They said in the old days, they were never short of breath. They announced the Best Original Score from *Fame.*

1980 *Ordinary People*

Tagline: "Everything is in its proper place... except the past." This movie was based on Judith Guest's 1976 novel of the same name. It described what happened to a family when the older son died in a boating accident. Conrad, the surviving younger son (Timothy Hutton) attempted suicide and underwent psychiatric treatment. The father, portrayed by Donald Sutherland, tried to bring the three family members back together. He told his son, "Don't admire people too much. They might disappoint you."

The mother was played by Mary Tyler Moore in a complex role quite different from her earlier television comedies. She appeared to love the boy who died much more than the one who survived. She did not visit Conrad in the psychiatric hospital. Omissions are not accidents. He said, "She would have come if Buck was in the hospital." His mother said, "Buck never would have been in the hospital."

Conrad had difficulty getting along with old friends and started a new relationship with a girl (Elizabeth McGovern) but had some awkward experiences. He learned that a co-patient from his hospital committed suicide. His mother's distancing and his survivor guilt made challenges for the family. The well-played psychiatrist (Judd Hirsch) put just the right spin on his role. Many times, professionals giving psychological treatment are not depicted accurately, but Hirsch played his role with humor and realism.

Director Robert Redford brought out character variations without being maudlin. A famous tune from earlier centuries, "Pachelbel's Canon in D," gave the movie a quiet greater depth. A final confrontation between the boy's parents cleared the air about their differences and their future.

Redford was impressed with Guest's book. One day he saw Mary Tyler Moore at the beach looking sad. Earlier, he had thought of Ann-Margaret for the mother's role, but this view of Moore made him ask and she accepted. Redford first asked Richard Dreyfuss to play the psychiatrist but he declined. Then Redford saw a sort of craziness and jerky lines in Judd Hirsch's television series *Taxi* and the casting worked. Redford also asked Donald Sutherland to play the psychiatrist, but he preferred to play the husband, so Redford canceled a plan to ask Gene Hackman to play that role. The movie was shot on the North Shore of Chicago.

The 124-minute movie budget was $6.2 million, and it made $90 million at the box office.

Other movie nominees were *Coal Miner's Daughter, The Elephant Man, Raging Bull* and *Tess.*

Robert De Niro (1943- ?) from New York City won Best Actor for *Raging Bull.* Other contenders were Robert Duvall *(The Great Santini),* John Hurt *(The Elephant Man),* Jack Lemmon *(Tribute),* and Peter O'Toole *(The Stunt Man).*

Sissy Spacek (1949-?) from Quitman, Texas, won Best Actress for *Coal Miner's Daughter.* Other contenders were Ellen Burstyn *(Resurrection),* Goldie Hawn *(Private Benjamin),* Mary Tyler Moore *(Ordinary People),* and Gena Rowlands *(Gloria).*

Mary Steenburgen won Best Supporting Actress for *Melvin and Howard.*

Timothy Hutton won Best Supporting Actor for *Ordinary People.*

Best Song "Fame," w. Dean Pitchford, m. Michael Gore, from *Fame*.

Robert Redford, Director of *Ordinary People*.

Best Foreign Language Film: *Moscow Does Not Believe in Tears,* director Vladimir Menshov, Soviet Union, Russian. The title came from a Russian proverb that meant, "Don't complain. Solve your problems by yourself." President Ronald Reagan watched this movie before meeting Mikhail Gorbachev to gain more understanding of "the Russian soul." It was about three young girls who went to Moscow from their smaller towns. They tried to work, become educated, find good husbands, and raise children. There were various successes and heartbreaks for each of them. The movie ended with one of the young ladies saying, "I have been looking for you for so long…" The 140-minute film brought mixed reviews and had several songs, one of which was "Bésame Mucho."

British BAFTA awards: Best Film*: The Elephant Man*. Director Akira Kurosawa. **Best Actor:** John Hurt in *The Elephant Man*. **Best Actress:** Judy Davis in *My Brilliant Career*. No actors for supporting role were awarded.

54th Academy Awards

Ceremony: This event was conducted on March 29, 1982, at the Dorothy Chandler Pavilion in Los Angeles, California, hosted by Johnny Carson. It was aired on ABC television lasting three hours and forty-four minutes. *Chariots of Fire* won Best Picture and that was the first time in thirteen years since a British film won that category. Henry Fonda won Best Actor for *On Golden Pond*. His co-star, Katharine Hepburn, won a fourth Best Actress award, which was the most wins for any actress in that category. Neither star could attend the ceremony, but Jane Fonda made a moving acceptance speech for her father.

This was a year of older actor winners: Best Actor Henry Fonda was 77 and died six months after the ceremony. Upon his death, President Ronald Reagan, who knew Fonda, said, "He graced the screen with a sincerity and accuracy which made him a legend." Best Actress Katharine Hepburn was 75. Best Supporting Actor was Sir John Gielgud who was 78 and did not travel from England for the ceremony. Best Supporting Actress was Maureen Stapleton who was 57 years old.

Liberace, aged 63, dressed in white, played a piano surrounded by candelabras and orchestra, doing a medley of nominated scores. The winner was the theme song from the movie *Arthur*. Barbara Stanwyck won an honorary Oscar. She was 75 and recalled a time when she and William Holden (who died four months earlier) stood together at the Oscars when Holden said she saved his career. She had starred in *Golden Boy*, his first movie, and defended him when some wanted to fire him. She said Holden always wished she had an Oscar, so she waved the Oscar and said, "I miss you, my Golden Boy. You've got your wish!"

Danny Kaye, aged 71, won the Jean Hersholt Humanitarian Award. Kaye had used his comical and musical gifts to bring music and humor to cheer adults and children and had traveled the world for UNICEF to raise money for children and their illnesses. Kaye said, "Thanks to Dag Hammarskjold, early secretary general of UNICEF...I love this, and I love you all."

Albert (Cubby) Broccoli was presented an honorary Oscar by Roger Moore who had played James Bond in some of Broccoli's Ian Fleming movies. Albert had begun with Howard Hughes in *The Outlaw* starring Jane Russell and had produced 40 pictures. The Gordon E. Sawyer Award was presented posthumously to cinematographer Joseph B. Walker, who died seven months earlier, but had worked on 145 films and developed more than 20 patents for camera inventions.

Loretta Young presented the award for Best Picture to *Chariots of Fire*. The 69-year-old actress had begun in movies at age 2 and played an Arab child of 8 in the 1921 silent movie *The Sheik* with Rudolph Valentino.

1981 *Chariots of Fire*

Tagline: "A winner all the way." The producers of this movie were looking for a story like *A Man for All Seasons,* which featured integrity. They wanted to make a movie of a noble struggle between men of uncommon ability. The title of the movie came from the William Blake poetic line, "Bring me my Chariot of fire!"

In reading through books about the Olympics, producer David Puttnam found Eric Liddell's story. He asked screenwriter Colin Welland to research the 1924 Olympics. Ads ran for memories of that event and Welland even attended the funeral of Harold Abrahams in 1978. Liddell and Abrahams ran in the same race once. The story did not need to be a documentary but an inspiring story of men with a conscience.

Ian Charleson was chosen to play Liddell. He researched the *Bible* to create a more inspirational speech than the screenwriter's version. He played a Scottish athlete who ran for the glory of God. Ben Cross was selected to play a Jew who ran to overcome prejudice. The remarkable music, which began and ended the movie and ran through it, was developed by a Greek composer named Evangelos Odysseas Papathanassiou, known by a shortened version of his first name: "Vangelis." His electronic music modernized the movie from the 1924 Olympics to the 1980s. He composed the main theme saying, "My father is a runner, and this is an anthem to him." The composer knew that running games and Olympics began in 776 B.C. in Greece.

The film makers decided to cast unknowns, like Charleson and Cross, with veterans like Ian Holm, John Gielgud, Patrick Magee, and others. The movie was shot in Kent, St. Andrews 18th hole of the Old Course in Scotland, Eton College, and Liverpool Town Hall. Some scenes depicting the five Gilbert and Sullivan operas were filmed in Liverpool as well.

All actors who portrayed runners went through three months of training to develop their abilities and to build a bond of camaraderie. There was an actual refusal by Liddell to race on a Sunday and his refusal made headlines. The actor said, "I believe God made me for a purpose, but he also made me fast. And when I run, I feel his pleasure."

This British movie ran 124 minutes, had a budget of $5.5 million, and made $59 million in U.S. box office.

Other movie nominees included *Atlantic City, On Golden Pond, Raiders of the Lost Ark,* and *Reds.*

Henry Fonda (1905-1982) from Grand Island, Nebraska, won Best Actor for *On Golden Pond.* Other contenders were Warren Beatty *(Reds),* Burt Lancaster *(Atlantic City),* Dudley Moore *(Arthur),* and Paul Newman *(Absence of Malice).*

Katharine Hepburn won Best Actress for *On Golden Pond.* Other contenders were Diane Keaton *(Reds),* Marsha Mason *(Only When I Laugh),* Susan Sarandon *(Atlantic City),* and Meryl Streep *(The French Lieutenant's Woman).*

Maureen Stapleton won Best Supporting Actress for *Reds.*

John Gielgud won Best Supporting Actor for *Arthur.*

Best Song "Arthur's Theme (Best That You Can Do)," w. and m. Peter Allen, Burt Bacharach, Christopher Cross, from *Arthur.*

Warren Beatty, Director of *Reds.*

Best Foreign Language Film: *Mephisto,* director Istvan Szabo, Hungary, Hungarian. This Hungarian film followed a German stage actor who put on a Faustian stage production just as Nazis took power in the late 1930s. Klaus Maria Brandauer (known to Americans from *Out of Africa*) played the main role as the actor. The movie had him playing Mephistopheles but gradually ignoring his conscience to appease Nazis and improve his fame. His wife and loved ones protested the new regime and went into exile, while he aimed to help them. However, he slowly became Faust, who sold his soul to the devil (Mephisto— the role he played on stage). There were English and German versions available.

British BAFTA awards: Best Film*: Chariots of Fire.* Director Louis Malle. **Best Actor:** Burt Lancaster in *Atlantic City.* **Best Actress:** Meryl Streep in *The French Lieutenant's Woman.* **Best Supporting Actor:** Ian Holm in *Chariots of Fire.*

55th Academy Awards

Ceremony: This event was conducted April 11, 1983, at Dorothy Chandler Pavilion in Los Angeles, California. It was hosted by Liza Minelli, Dudley Moore, Richard Pryor, and Walter Matthau. It was televised by ABC and ran three hours and fifteen minutes.

The ceremony was notable because Louis Gossett Jr. was the first African American to win Best Supporting Actor. He accepted the Oscar and said he wished his son sitting in the audience would share it with him. He added that he had been raised by his great-grandmother, who lived to age 117 and next he was most grateful to his agent for their 17-year relationship.

Jessica Lange was the first in 40 years to receive nominations for both Best Actress and Best Supporting Actress. This was the only time George C. Scott attended the Oscar ceremony. Charlton Heston presented the Jean Hersholt Humanitarian Award to Walter Mirisch.

Mickey Rooney received an honorary Oscar. He said, "When I was 19 years old, I was the number one star of the world for two years. When I was 40, nobody wanted me." The 5'2" balding actor described his favorite stars "who enjoyed playing together like kids," including Judy Garland of the *Andy Hardy* series, but she had died fourteen years earlier.

1982 *Gandhi*

Tagline: "His triumph changed the world forever." This movie about the life of Mahatma Gandhi had been in mind for years by director/

producer Richard Attenborough (a former British actor) since 1942. Despite numerous difficulties over 15 years, the film was finally produced. Attenborough dedicated it to Indian civil servant Motilal Kothari, Lord Louis Mountbatten, and J. Nehru. Attenborough largely used Louis Fischer's biography of Gandhi.

His cast choices began with Ben Kingsley to play Gandhi, because Ben was not only an excellent English actor but was part Indian through his father. His birth name was Krishna Bhanji. When David Lean and Sam Spiegel considered a Gandhi film before embarking on *Lawrence of Arabia,* they considered Alec Guinness as Gandhi. The woman who played Gandhi's wife, Rohini Hattangadi, was the first Indian actress to win a British Academy Film award.

More than 300,000 extras were used for the funeral scene, more than for any film. The funeral in Delhi was estimated at one million people. The movie opened with Gandhi's assassination and continued by recounting his life. It started when Gandhi was thrown off a train despite a first-class ticket because of the color of his skin. He was challenged to make sure rules were not biased against Indians and started a non-violent protest for the rights of all Indians. One of Gandhi's lines was, "They may torture my body, break my bones, even kill me; then they will have my dead body. Not my obedience."

Attenborough chose Ravi Shankar to do the music with songs and his sitar, a 16th century long lute with 18 to 21 strings. Although Shankar's music was popular to many during the 1950s, its special emotional qualities enhanced the scenes with Gandhi.

Attenborough filled the movie with other stars, but Ben Kingsley's portrayal was the big attraction. Others were Candice Bergen as reporter Margaret Bourke-White, Edward Fox as Brigadier General Reginald Dyer, John Gielgud as the 1st Baron Irwin, Martin Sheen as a journalist, Trevor Howard as the Judge at Gandhi's sedition trial, John Mills as the 3rd Baron Chelmsford, Ian Charleson as Rev. Charles Freer

Andrews, Ian Bannen as Senior Officer Fields, and Daniel Day-Lewis as Colin, who insulted Gandhi.

His non-violent campaigns and fasts were so successful that finally his imprisonments caused changes. India won its independence, and the religious divisions resulted in the new country of Pakistan, formed where Muslims were the majority. His non-violent methods of improving social justice were used by Martin Luther King, Jr. to improve justice for African Americans.

The budget was $22 million and the box office $128 million, including the largest movie box office sales ever in India. Outside of the U.S., the movie grossed $75 million.

Other movie nominees included *E.T. the Extra-Terrestrial, Missing, Tootsie,* and *The Verdict.*

Ben Kingsley (1943-?) from Snainton, England, won Best Actor for *Gandhi.* Other contenders were Dustin Hoffman *(Tootsie),* Jack Lemmon *(Missing),* Paul Newman *(The Verdict),* and Peter O'Toole *(My Favorite Year).*

Meryl Streep (1944- ?) from Summit, New Jersey, won Best Actress for *Sophie's Choice.* Other contenders were Julie Andrews *(Victor/Victoria),* Jessica Lange *(Frances),* Sissy Spacek *(Missing),* and Debra Winger *(An Officer and a Gentleman).*

Jessica Lange won Best Supporting Actress for *Tootsie.*

Louis Gossett, Jr. won Best Supporting Actor for *An Officer and a Gentleman.*

Best Song "Up Where We Belong," w. Will Jennings, m. Jack Nitszche, Buffy Sainte-Marie, from *An Officer and a Gentleman.*

Richard Attenborough, Director of *Gandhi.*

Best Foreign Language Film: *To Begin Again,* director Jose Luis Garci, Spain, Spanish. This movie described a Spanish professor who taught literature in a California university and won the Nobel Prize for his work. He traveled to accept the prize and decided to visit his native Spain for a few days before returning home. He visited an old friend, and then found an old love. In a melancholy musical rekindling of their romance, they enjoyed Cole Porter's "Begin the Beguine" interspersed with "Pachelbel's Canon." The film ran ninety-three minutes and may have been a bit too repetitive musically.

British BAFTA awards: Best Film: *Gandhi.* Director Richard Attenborough. **Best Actor:** Ben Kingsley in *Gandhi.* **Best Actress:** Kathryn Hepburn *in On Golden Pond.* **Best Supporting Actor:** Jack Nicholson in *Reds.* **Best Supporting Actress:** Maureen Stapleton in *Reds.*

56th Academy Awards

Ceremony: This event took place on April 9, 1984, at Dorothy Chandler Pavilion in Los Angeles, California. Johnny Carson hosted and ABC televised the three hour, forty-two minute program.

The Best Supporting Actress winner was Linda Hunt, who played the part of a Chinese-Australian man who was a photographer in *The Year of Living Dangerously*.

When receiving her Oscar for Best Actress in *Terms of Endearment,* Shirley MacLaine said, "Films and life are like clay, waiting for us to mold it." Robert Duvall won Best Actor for *Tender Mercies* where he played a country and western singing star. Joe Tompkins was the first African American to be nominated in the Best Costume Design category.

Jackie Cooper and George "Spanky" McFarland presented an Honorary Award to Hal Roach for his involvement with movies since 1912 and "Our Gang" style comedies. Mr. Roach said that in those days everyone received a dollar a day, two sandwiches and a banana. He described how they collected their banana peels for film pranks saving them a little money. Cooper described how many people Roach spotted and brought to fame, such as Laurel and Hardy.

Screenwriter Horton Foote earlier won an Oscar for Best Adapted Screenplay for *To Kill a Mockingbird* in 1963. This time he won Best Original Screenplay for *Tender Mercies*.

1983 *Terms of Endearment*

Tagline: "Come to laugh, come to cry, come to care, come to terms." This was Texan Larry McMurtry's 1975 novel of the same name about a widow named Aurora (Shirley MacLaine) living in Houston, Texas. She had a daughter (Debra Winger) with whom she struggled to both care for and dominate. She had little faith in her daughter's husband (Jeff Daniels) who played a college professor with an eye for the ladies. Throughout the daughter's older years, Aurora had some male friends (Danny DeVito, John Lithgow, and next-door neighbor Jack Nicholson). Aurora and Jack (in a part written for Nicholson as a retired astronaut) decided to date each other from time to time. It began when neighbor (Nicholson) said, "Aurora, you're not fun by any chance are you?" Aurora responded, "I don't really think we should think about that right now. Impatient boys sometimes miss dessert!"

The tragic part of the movie was when Aurora's daughter acquired cancer, despite affairs, and she was dying with two children to be raised. Aurora accepted the children and the movie ended with her male friends, including the Nicholson character, making friends with the two kids.

Rank Mills' music included sad to triumphant and even Cole's Porter's "Anything Goes." Leonard Bernstein put all the music together with a rich score. Much of the movie was filmed at Aurora's home, three miles from Rice University where author McMurtry received his M.A. The budget was $8 million, and the movie netted $164.2 million at the box office. It ran 132 minutes with wonderful humor, heartache, and excellent acting.

Other movie nominees included *The Big Chill, The Dresser, The Right Stuff,* and *Tender Mercies.*

Robert Duvall (1931- ?) from San Diego, California, won Best Actor for *Tender Mercies.* Other contenders were Michael Caine *(Educating*

Rita), Tom Conti *(Reuben, Reuben)*, Tom Courtenay *(The Dresser)*, and Albert Finney *(The Dresser)*.

Shirley MacLaine ((1934- ?) from Richmond, Virginia, won Best Actress for *Terms of Endearment*. Other contenders were Jane Alexander *(Testament)*, Meryl Streep *(Silkwood)*, Julie Walters *(Educating Rita)*, and Debra Winger *(Terms of Endearment)*.

Linda Hunt won Best Supporting Actress for *The Year of Living Dangerously*.

Jack Nicholson won Best Supporting Actor for *Terms of Endearment*.

Best Song "Flashdance (What a Feeling)," w. m. Irene Cara, Keith Forsey, Giorgio Moroder, from *Flashdance*.

James L. Brooks, Director of *Terms of Endearment*.

Best Foreign Language Film: *Fanny and Alexander,* director Ingmar Bergman, Swedish. Often Bergman's Swedish movies seem to have little life in them. This one was special because two adolescents had an extremely open relationship with their relatives and friends. There is empathy for characters who are under great stress. That made the movie seem very real. One line is, "They no longer wish to hear the songs of giants. They are content with the tunes of dwarfs." The usual theatrical version ran 188 minutes, but the director's version was 312 minutes.

British BAFTA awards: Best Film: *Educating Rita,* director Bill Forsyth for *Local Hero*. **Best Actor:** Michael Caine in *Educating Rita* and Dustin Hoffman in *Tootsie*. **Best Actress:** Julie Walters in *Educating Rita*. **Best Supporting Actor:** Denholm Elliott in *Trading Places*. **Best Supporting Actress:** Jamie Lee Curtis in *Trading Places*.

57th Academy Awards

Ceremony: This event took place on March 25, 1985, at the Dorothy Chandler Pavilion in Los Angeles, California, hosted by Jack Lemmon and produced by Gregory Peck, Robert Wise, Larry Gelbart, and Gene Allen. It was televised by ABC and lasted three hours and ten minutes.

A Cambodian surgeon without acting experience, Haing S. Ngor, won the Best Supporting Actor for *The Killing Fields*. The only other actor without professional experience to win an acting award was Harold Russell in *The Best Years of Our Lives*. This was also the first time that more than one African American won an Oscar because both Prince and Stevie Wonder won for their work on *Purple Rain* and *The Woman in Red*. Peggy Ashcroft, age 77, received an Oscar for Best Supporting Actress in *A Passage to India,* making her the oldest winning actress in that category. Sally Field won Best Actress for *Places in the Heart* and had won in 1980 with *Norma Rae.* She said, "The first time I didn't feel it, but this time I feel it, and I can't deny the fact that you like me, right now, you like me!"

Sir Laurence Olivier came to the microphone to announce the Best Picture. He reacted to a standing ovation saying that he thanked the audience more than he had ever thanked anyone. Then he said he hoped he wouldn't let the occasion down too badly. He then simply opened the envelope for Best Picture award but forgot to announce the nominees. He glanced at the note and said, "The winner is *Amadeus!*" Olivier had been ill with dementia, forgetfulness, and medical problems that took him later. Fortunately, producer Saul Zaentz came to the stage for his Oscar and mentioned the other nominated movies.

Some honorary Oscars were awarded to David L. Wolper, a TV and film producer, who had just arranged the opening and closing of the XXIIIrd Olympiad in Los Angeles in 1984. A very special Honorary award was given James Stewart by Cary Grant who died of a stroke the following year. Cary said, "To James Stewart, for his fifty years of memorable performances, for his high ideals both on and off the screen, and with the respect and affection of his colleagues." Stewart received a standing ovation, thanked everybody, especially director Frank Capra, and then thanked the audience. "All you wonderful folks out there. Thank you for being so kind to me over the years. You've given me a wonderful life. God bless you. Thank you."

1984 *Amadeus*

Tagline: "The man, the music, the madness, the murder, the motion picture." This movie was taken from a fictional story written by Peter Shaffer for his 1979 stage play *Amadeus.* He came up with a rivalry between Wolfgang Amadeus Mozart and an Italian composer named Antonio Salieri. Unlike in the movie *Amadeus,* real-life Salieri was a married man with eight children and a probable mistress.

Miloš Forman couldn't get Mark Hamill because he was making another movie so chose Tom Hulce. Tom used tennis player John McEnroe's mood swings to portray the unpredictable Mozart. Meg Tilly was to be his wife, but she had a leg accident and was replaced by Elizabeth Berridge.

The movie began with Salieri (F. Murray Abraham) being committed to a psychiatric hospital after he tried to commit suicide. Salieri had spied on Mozart and learned how obscene and immature he was. Young Mozart had a very silly weird laugh throughout the movie.

Salieri saw Mozart in dalliances with young girls. He tried to expose that side of the musical genius to investors, but they paid little attention.

Mozart said, "Forgive me, Majesty. I'm a vulgar man. But I assure you, my music is not." Salieri planned to kill Mozart but when the young composer collapsed from overwork, he tried to help him. Mozart mistook him for a friend. Mozart, always in need of money, was buried in a mass grave in the rain. As Salieri was wheeled down the hall at his institution, he heard the eerie Mozart laugh.

Throughout the movie, Mozart's music was heard and only one short piece was by Salieri. The film was shot mostly in Prague, Czechoslovakia. Forman collaborated with American choreographer Twyla Tharp to stage the movements of people during musical scenes. She was a versatile ballet director (she worked with the Joffrey Ballet on "As Time Goes By") and had worked with Forman on *Hair* and *Ragtime*.

Since Miloš Forman was Czech, he wanted to use the very opera house that Mozart used two centuries earlier—the Count Nostitz Theatre. This was during the Russian occupation of Prague, so he had to pay the Russian bureaucracy to produce this musical there, and additionally spent much to revitalize the famous old theatre. The end of *Don Giovanni* was filmed there. All the original torches were used, which required extra insurance, and Forman had to sign an agreement that he would go back to his hotel every night since he was seen as a political opponent (non-communist).

The movie budget was $18 million, and the box office was $90 million. It ran 161 minutes, but some versions included more music. No major studio wanted to finance the film about classical music, wigs, costumes, and long names. But Forman made it happen with musical conductor Neville Marriner conducting the Academy of St. Martin in the Fields Orchestra, their chorus and other choristers and singers.

Other best movie nominees included *The Killing Fields, A Passage to India, Places in the Heart,* and *A Soldier's Story.*

F. Murray Abraham (1939- ?) from Pittsburgh won Best Actor for *Amadeus*. Other contenders were Jeff Bridges *(Starman)*, Albert Finney *(Under the Volcano)*, Tom Hulce *(Amadeus)*, and Sam Waterston *(The Killing Fields)*.

Sally Field won Best Actress for *Places in the Heart*. Other contenders were Judy Davis *(A Passage to India)*, Jessica Lange *(Country)*, Vanessa Redgrave *(The Bostonians)*, and Sissy Spacek *(The River)*.

Peggy Ashcroft won Best Supporting Actress for *A Passage to India*.

Haing S. Ngor won Best Supporting Actor for *The Killing Fields*.

Best Song "I Just Called to Say I Love You," w.m. Stevie Wonder, from *The Woman in Red*.

Miloš Forman, Director of *Amadeus*.

Best Foreign Language Film: *Dangerous Moves*, director Richard Dembo, Switzerland, French. This French/Swiss movie with Michel Piccoli, Leslie Caron, and Liv Ullman tells of two Russians, a 52-year-old Soviet Jew with a chess champion title playing a 35-year-old genius who defected to the West earlier. The two-generation men play with different world views, but the propaganda and money paled beside their love of the chess game.

British BAFTA awards: Best Film: *The Killing Fields*. Director William Wenders. **Best Actor:** Haing S. Ngor in *The Killing Fields*. **Best Actress:** Maggie Smith in *A Private Function*. **Best Supporting Actor:** Denholm Elliott in *A Private Function*. **Best Supporting Actress:** Liz Smith in *A Private Function*.

58th Academy Awards

Ceremony: The event occurred on March 24, 1986, at the Dorothy Chandler Pavilion in Los Angeles, California. It was hosted by Alan Alda, Jane Fonda, and Robin Williams. It was televised by ABC and lasted three hours and eleven minutes.

John Huston was the oldest nominee for Best Director at age 79. His father, Walter Huston and his daughter Anjelica, won Best Supporting Actor and Actress. The three generations of Hustons winning Oscars made history.

The Jean Hersholt Humanitarian Award was given to Charles "Buddy" Rogers. Bob Hope listed the many organizations that Rogers has assisted over the years. Having begun in *Wings,* the first winner of the Academy Awards, the handsome white-haired actor said, "I'm thrilled. They say old actors never die; they just lose their parts. Bob, thanks for the memories."

Don Ameche won Best Supporting Actor and received a standing ovation. The 78-year-old actor began as a vaudevillian, radio actor, and finally was given a movie contract in 1935. He thanked everyone who helped make *Cocoon* and the Academy for giving him their love and respect. Paul Newman, 61 years old, also received an honorary award but was in Chicago. The award by the Academy mentioned Newman's integrity and his record of great achievements in television, stage, and movies. He said the award gave him permission to do his best work down the road.

Alex North was honored for his "brilliant artistry in the creation of memorable music for many distinguished pictures." The 76-year-old composer did music for *A Streetcar Named Desire, Death of a Salesman, Viva Zapata, The Rainmaker, Spartacus, The Misfits, Cleopatra,* and *Who's Afraid of Virginia Woolf,* etc.

1985 *Out of Africa*

Tagline: "Here I am where I belong." The movie was loosely based on the 1937 book of the same name by Isak Dinesen, pseudonym of Danish author Karen Blixen. Some material was added from Dinesen's 1960 book *Shadows on the Grass.*

Meryl Streep played Blixen, Robert Redford played Denys Finch Hatton, and Klaus Maria Brandauer played Baron Blixen, Karen's husband. The gist of the movie was that Blixen learned her husband had spent her money to develop a coffee farm, but at an elevation too high for best production. He preferred to lead safaris and she came to love the African people. She developed a school, medical help, and close friendships with the natives and realized that her husband had other sexual relationships.

Her relationship with pilot Denys deepened as they flew together, and he began to stay with her. When she learned that he had another relationship, she realized he did not desire marriage and refused to be tied down. "I'm with you because I choose to be with you. I don't want to live someone else's idea of how to live. Don't ask me to do that. I don't want to find out one day that I'm at the end of someone else's life." She soon learned that his airplane had crashed.

After his funeral, she made plans to return to Denmark. The all-male club where she was first shunned welcomed her to complete her arrangements for a forwarding address. She had sad partings with the natives whom she loved. She began to write about her life and her first line was, "I had a farm in Africa, at the foot of the Ngong Hills."

Much of the movie was filmed in Nairobi and her actual house, which is now the Karen Blixen Museum. Pollack knew he wanted Brandauer for the husband but was unsure about who would play Karen Blixen. When Streep appeared with a low-cut blouse and a push-up bra, she had the sexual look that fit the role. He decided against an English actor for the Denys role and found that Redford could do well enough to make the love affair work.

The music of English composer John Barry worked with some outside numbers from Mozart and African traditional songs. Barry designed his own love song and won an Oscar for it. The movie ran 161 minutes with a budget of $28 million and box office was $227.5 million.

Other movie nominees included *The Color Purple, Kiss of the Spider Woman, Prizzi's Honor,* and *Witness.*

William Hurt (1950- ?) from Washington, D.C., won Best Actor for *Kiss of the Spider Woman.* Other contenders were Harrison Ford *(Witness),* James Garner *(Murphy's Romance),* Jack Nicholson *(Prizzi's Honor),* and Jon Voight *(Runaway Train).*

Geraldine Page (1924-1987) from Kirksville, Missouri, won Best Actress for *The Trip to Bountiful.* Other contenders were Anne Bancroft *(Agnes of God),* Whoopi Goldberg *(The Color Purple),* Jessica Lange *(Sweet Dreams),* and Meryl Streep *(Out of Africa).*

Anjelica Huston won Best Supporting Actress for *Prizzi's Honor.*

Don Ameche won Best Supporting Actor for *Cocoon.*

Best Song "Say You, Say Me," w. m. Lionel Ritchie, from *White Nights.*

Sydney Pollack, Director of *Out of Africa.*

Best Foreign Language Film: *The Official Story,* director Luis Puenzo, Argentina, Spanish. This movie deals with the forced disappearances of people during Argentina's military dictatorship (1976-1983). A couple adopted a child and learned it might be an illegal adoption. While it was a thriller, it was also a tragedy because the family fell apart as the 5-year-old girl became the subject of an intense investigation. While illustrating a country's terrorism, some criticized the director for manipulating the emotions of movie viewers.

British BAFTA awards: Best Film: *The Purple Rose of Cairo.* Director William Wenders. **Best Actor:** William Hurt in *Kiss of the Spider Woman.* **Best Actress:** Peggy Ashcroft in *A Passage to India.* **Best Supporting Actor:** Denholm Elliott in *Defense of the Realm.* **Best Supporting Actress:** Rosanna Arquette in *Desperately Seeking Susan.*

59th Academy Awards

Ceremony: This event happened on March 30, 1987, at the Dorothy Chandler Pavilion in Los Angeles, California. It was hosted by actors Chevy Chase, Goldie Hawn, and Paul Hogan. It was televised by ABC and lasted three hours and twenty-five minutes and was watched by thirty-seven million people. Goldwyn wanted to shorten the length of the show because attendance had been declining. He gave winners forty-five second with blinkers for acceptance speeches that shut them off after sixty seconds.

Marlee Matlin was the first deaf performer who won an Oscar. She was also the youngest, at age 21, to win Best Actress. She used American Sign Language when introduced and signed that she didn't prepare for this speech. She also signed to thank everyone and especially William Hurt (her co-star). She ended, "I love you."

Paul Newman, despite having won an honorary Oscar a year earlier, won Best Actor. Since his wife, Joanne Woodward, had won Best Actress in 1957 for *The Three Faces of Eve,* they became the second married couple to win acting Oscars. Ralph Bellamy received an Honorary Academy Award for his contributions to film from 1933-1988 and was one founder of the Screen Actors Guild and well respected by his peers. He made 100-plus films--the last was 1990 *Pretty Woman.*

Director producer Steven Spielberg won the Irving G. Thalberg Memorial Award. Spielberg thanked everybody, including the "audience out there in the dark." He said he was inspired by Cecil B. De Mille, William Wilder, Alfred Hitchcock, George Stevens, Ingmar Bergman, Robert Wise, etc. He said writers are story tellers and use images, performers, and music. "Movies were the literature of my life," and he encouraged all to "renew our romance of the word."

1986 *Platoon*

Tagline: "The first casualty of war is innocence." This was the first Oliver Stone movie in a trilogy about war, which included *Born on the Fourth of July* and *Heaven & Earth*. Stone said the film was based on his experience as an infantryman in Vietnam. He wanted to counter the war as portrayed in John Wayne's *The Green Berets*. Filming took place on Luzon and Manilla in the Philippines starring Tom Berenger, William Dafoe, Charlie Sheen, Keith David, Forest Whitaker, Johnny Depp, and others.

The cinematography was stunning, the battle scenes were extremely realistic, the shootings of the wrong people aroused emotions, and the actions of American veterans to stop terrible rapes and dreadful events in this unwinnable war were the themes. The view of corpses in the final scene was an image with a voiceover that a rescued veteran vowed never to forget. One character said, "The war is over for me now, but it will always be there, the rest of my days." Some said the depiction of black troops was stereotyped.

The musical score was done by George Delerue with the unexpected Samuel Barber's "Adagio for Strings" along with other music, such as "White Rabbit" by Jefferson Airplane, and "Okie from Muskogee" by Merle Haggard, "The Tracks of My Tears" by Smokey Robinson and The Miracles. The soundtrack also includes "Sitting on the Dock of the Bay" by Otis Redding. Some said that Barber's "Adagio" had been done in so many movies that it bored them. Why was Barber's 1936 music used? It was played at President Franklin Roosevelt's funeral, for the 9/11 observance by BBC, and in some 18 movies, including *The Elephant Man, Lorenzo's Oil, Amelie*, etc. That song may outlast the movie because it is a passionate catharsis. A catharsis provides relief of pent-up emotion, often through drama and music. The music worked well in this movie as it swept viewers into partnership with actors experiencing pain and devastation from a war without end. The music swelled with violins, then cellos, ascending upward with two chords that seemed to change from pain to a moment of joy, such as an Amen.

The violence planned for this movie caused many actors to turn down roles. Actors who accepted roles trained for 30 days in military-type indoctrination with limited food and water. Stone said he was trying to get actors so tired that they didn't care what happened. Stone made a cameo appearance in the final battle. The film was dedicated to those who fought and died in Vietnam. The budget was $6 million, and the box office was $138.5 million. The movie ran 120 minutes.

Other best movie nominees included *Children of a Lesser God, Hannah and Her Sisters, The Mission,* and *A Room with a View.*

Paul Newman (1925-2008) from Shaker Heights, Ohio, won Best Actor for *The Color of Money.* Other contenders were Dexter Gordon *(Round Midnight),* Bob Hoskins *(Mona Lisa),* William Hurt *(Children of a Lesser God),* and James Woods *(Salvador).*

Marlee Matlin (1965-?) from Morton Grove, Illinois, won Best Actress for *Children of a Lesser God.* Other contenders were Jane Fonda *(The Morning After),* Sissy Spacek *(Crimes of the Heart),* Kathleen Turner *(Peggy Sue Got Married),* and Sigourney Weaver *(Aliens).*

Dianne Wiest won Best Supporting Actress for *Hannah and Her Sisters.*

Michael Caine won Best Supporting Actor for *Hannah and Her Sisters.*

Best Song "Take My Breath Away," w. Tom Whitlock, m. Giorgio Moroder, from *Top Gun.*

Oliver Stone, Director of *Platoon.*

Best Foreign Language Film: *The Assault,* director Fons Rademakers, Netherlands, Dutch/Swedish/French. A Dutch man who collaborated with Nazis was killed by other Dutch people because of his betrayals. The collaborator's family wanted protection, so they drug the body next door. That night, the people in that household were taken to prison because they supposedly sheltered the dead man. Their little boy, Anton, was comforted by a barely visible woman in the dark prison, but his family was executed. The film covered forty years of the boy's life. Despite his education and marriage, he still searched for answers to that terrible night. Each person he questioned brought a little more information. So, he lived knowing that terrible things happened during war. People, each with their own reasons, hurt and affected the lives of others. One lady who played his wife in later life was the woman who comforted him in prison that awful night.

British BAFTA awards: Best Film: *A Room with a View.* **Director** Woody Allen for *Hanna and Her Sisters.* **Best Actor:** Bob Hoskins in *Mona Lisa.* **Best Actress:** Maggie Smith in *A Room with a View.* **Best Supporting Actor:** Ray McAnally in *The Mission.* **Best Supporting Actress:** Judi Dench in *A Room with a View.*

60th Academy Awards

Ceremony: This event happened on April 11, 1988, at the Shrine Auditorium in Los Angeles, California. It was hosted by Chevy Chase. It lasted three hours and thirty-three minutes and was watched on ABC television by 42.2 million people. The ceremony was moved for larger seating capacity. The 1988 strike of the Writers Guild of America hindered dialogue, so comedians were used for jokes. Best Supporting Actor winner Sean Connery said, "If such a thing as a wish accompanied this award, mine would be that we ended the writers' strike."

Billy Wilder received the Irving G. Thalberg Memorial Award. He thanked many who were gone but not forgotten: Ernst Lubitsch, Charles Brackett, Arthur Hornblower, Don Harrison, Harold Mirisch, Gary Cooper, Tyrone Power, Gloria Swanson, Humphrey Bogart, Marilyn Monroe, Maurice Chevalier, Charles Laughton, Erich von Stroheim, and Edgar G. Robinson. He talked of Hollywood's vacillation between despair and fear as they dealt with sound, television, pornography, cassettes, microchips, but ended with how irreplaceable all of them were.

Wilder wanted to thank someone else but couldn't remember the name. He said when he was a Polish Jew living in the Austro-Hungarian Empire, the Nazis began their invasions. He moved to Vienna. Paul Whiteman brought a jazz concert there and Billy became a taxi dancer for Whiteman, dancing (for pay) with women at those concerts. When they went to Berlin, he began writing German movies. Suddenly, Wilder learned he was to be arrested and fled to the U.S. on a 6-month visa. He was writing in Hollywood and wanted to stay in America. He went to the consulate in Mexicali. The consul had nothing to go on, but his word and they stared at each other. The consul then said, "What do you do?" He said, "I write movies." The consul stamped his visa and said, "Go write the best movies you can write." Wilder was forever grateful to him.

Some of his most famous films were *Ninotchka, Double Indemnity, The Lost Weekend, A Song Is Born, Stalag 17, The Seven Year Itch, The Spirit of St. Louis, Love in the Afternoon, Witness for the Prosecution, Some Like It Hot, The Apartment, Irma La Douce, The Fortune Cookie,* and his 1941 movie *Hold Back the Dawn,* where he described some of the story of his own life.

1987 *The Last Emperor*

Tagline: "He was the Lord of Ten Thousand Years, the absolute monarch of China. He was born to rule a world of ancient tradition. Nothing prepared him for our world of change."

This is the life of Pu-Yi, the last emperor of Manchuria. He was captured by the Red Army and called a war criminal in 1950. While in prison, he recalled his youth in the Forbidden City, with great luxury but unaware of the real world. He was only a puppet ruler for the Japanese. After being re-educated and thus reformed, he was released and wound up working as a gardener in the Beijing Botanical Gardens. The movie is based on his 1964 autobiography. Peter O'Toole played a Scottish tutor who helped him understand the world. For example, Pu Yi at 15 said, "Who is this, George Washington?" Tutor: "A famous American, your majesty. A revolutionary general, the first American president." Pu Yi: "Ah, like Mr. Lenin in Russia?" Tutor: "Not quite." Pu Yi: "Does he have a car?" Tutor: "He lived a long time ago, your majesty."

Director Bernardo Bertolucci obtained permission to make this first ever film of the Forbidden City. He used 19,000 extras from the People's Liberation Army The beauty of the inside (9,999 rooms because the

Chinese believed that only heaven had 10,000 rooms) and outside of the Forbidden City, customs, costumes, and lives of transition from imperialism to communism made this movie gorgeous, fascinating, and informative. Orchestral music was played as Pu-Yi saw a children's parade with pentatonic music on accordions. Other music included "Am I Blue?" "Auld Lang Syne," "China Boy," and "Emperor Waltz" by Johann Strauss. The 163-minute movie budget was $23.8 million and box office was much more than twice that.

Other movie nominees included *Broadcast News, Fatal Attraction, Hope and Glory,* and *Moonstruck.*

Michael Douglas (1944- ?) from New Brunswick, New Jersey, won Best Actor for *Wall Street.* Other contenders were William Hurt *(Broadcast News),* Marcello Mastroianni *(Dark Eyes),* Jack Nicholson *(Ironweed),* and Robin Williams *(Good Morning, Vietnam).*

Cher Sarkisian (1946- ?) from El Centro, California, won Best Actress for *Moonstruck.* Other contenders were Glenn Close *(Fatal Attraction),* Holly Hunter *(Broadcast News),* Sally Kirkland *(Anna),* and Meryl Streep *(Ironweed).*

Olympia Dukakis won Best Supporting Actress for *Moonstruck.*

Sean Connery won Best Supporting Actor for *The Untouchables.*

Best Song "I've Had the Time of My Life," w. Franke Previte, m. John DeNicola, Donald Markowitz, and Franke Previte, from *Dirty Dancing.*

Bernardo Bertolucci, Director of *The Last Emperor.*

Best Foreign Language Film: *Babette's Feast,* director Gabriel Axel, Denmark, Danish/Swedish/French. This movie was from a short story by Karen Blixen who wrote *Out of Africa.* This was the first Danish film to win an Oscar. The director found French actress Stephane Audran and hired Bibi Andersson and Jarl Kulle, two of Ingmar Bergman's favorite actors. The movie, filmed in Blixen's native Denmark, described two sisters who tended their father, an old minister with only a few old church members left. One day Babette arrived with a letter recommending her as a housekeeper. The sisters couldn't pay so she worked free. She won a lottery of 10,000 francs and used it to thank the sisters and the congregation with a feast on the pastor's hundredth birthday. To create a "real French dinner" she spent her winnings for French ingredients. A famous general was a guest and said he had only tasted such extraordinary food at the famous Café Anglais in Paris. The meal created trust between attendees, righted old wrongs, rekindled old loves, and made a redemption over the table. Babette revealed that she was once head chef of the Café Anglais (demolished in 1913). One sister told her she would be poor the rest of her life. She said, "An artist is never poor." The other sister said, "In paradise you will be the great artist God meant you to be—Oh, how you will enchant the angels!" The meal consisted of turtle soup, buckwheat pancakes with caviar and sour cream, quail in puff pastry with foie gras and truffle sauce, endive salad, rum sponge cake with figs and candied cherries, cheeses and fruits served with sauterne wines, and coffee with champagne and cognac.

British BAFTA awards: Best Film: *The Last Emperor*. **Director** Louis Malle for *Goodbye Children*. **Best Actor:** John Cleese in *A Fish Named Wanda*. **Best Actress:** Maggie Smith in *The Lonely Passion of Judith Hearne*. **Best Supporting Actor:** Michael Palin in *A Fish Named Wanda*. **Best Supporting Actress:** Judi Dench in *A Handful of Dust*.

61st Academy Awards

Ceremony: This event was at the Shrine Auditorium in Los Angeles, California on March 29, 1989. It was on ABC television for three hours and nineteen minutes, watched by 42.7 million people in the U.S., the most viewed ceremony up to that date and a 1 percent increase from the previous year.

Best Actor was Dustin Hoffman. He first thanked the other contenders and said that his father recently became disabled and was at a rehab center with new friends who were watching the show in tuxedos and drinking champagne out of cups. His mother was from Romania and his father was an Ashkenazi Jew from Kiev. His father worked as a set decorator for Columbia Pictures before a later career. His mother had named him after the silent film star Dustin Farnum, whose picture she saw on a magazine near the time of his birth in 1937.

This ceremony was the final appearance for Lucille Ball. Bob Hope and she were given a standing ovation. She died a month after the ceremony at age 77 from an aortic aneurysm. Three actors (Sean Connery, Michael Caine, Roger Moore) of the United Kingdom presented Kevin Kline with the Oscar for *A Fish Called Wanda,* a primarily English comedy. Canadians Donald and Kiefer Sutherland presented the National Film Board of Canada with an honorary award.

1988 *Rain Man*

Tagline: "A journey through understanding and fellowship." The story is of a selfish young hustler (Charlie played by Tom Cruise) who got in trouble with the law and learned that his father left $3 million to his unknown brother. That brother was an autistic savant (Dustin Hoffman) who lived in an institution. Charlie kidnapped his brother to take him on a trip to get the inheritance since all his father left him was only a car and some rose bushes. Writers Barry Morrow and Ronald Bass created a character based on meeting a real savant. The Hoffman character had strict routines, excellent memory, but showed little emotion unless he was distressed. He would not fly so they took a car trip and Charlie learned his brother excelled at math. Charlie vaguely remembered somebody who once comforted him and saved him from a scalding bath, so he called him "Rain Man."

Charlie's car was taken, and he was in debt. He decided they would go to a casino and win money by brother Raymond counting cards at blackjack. Along their way, Charlie told Ray, "I'm gonna let ya in on a little secret, Ray. K-Mart sucks." They left the casinos with thousands of dollars. When offered $250,000 to leave Raymond, Charlie said he wanted to have a relationship with his brother. They went to a train station to return Raymond to his institution, and Charlie promised to visit him in two weeks, so the relationship was going to continue.

German film composer Hans Zimmer used an intriguing film score of new music and old favorites. The old ones included Harry Warren's 1941 "At Last," 1948 "Bouncin' the Blues" and 1948 "Shoes with Wings On;" Hoagy Carmichael's 1927 "Stardust;" James Weldon Johnson's 1927 "Dry Bones;" George and Ira Gershwin's 1937 "They Can't Take That Away from Me;" and John Lennon and Paul McCartney's 1963 "I Saw Her Standing There."

Tom Hanks, Robin Williams, and Dustin Hoffman were considered for the role of the hustler Charlie. Several, including Bill Murray, were considered for the role of Raymond before the decision was made for Hoffman to play the autistic savant. The movie did not receive rave reviews, but most thought it a good story of two isolated humans who form a deep attachment. The movie played a strong role in changing misperceptions about autism for the better. The 134-minute movie budget was $25 million, and it netted $354.8 million at the box office.

Other best movie nominees included *The Accidental Tourist, Dangerous Liaisons, Mississippi Burning,* and *Working Girl.*

Dustin Hoffman won Best Actor for *Rain Man.* Other contenders were Gene Hackman *(Mississippi Burning),* Tom Hanks *(Big),* Edward James Olmos *(Stand and Deliver),* and Max von Sydow *(Pelle the Conqueror).*

Jodie Foster (1962- ?) from Los Angeles won Best Actress for *The Accused.* Other contenders were Glenn Close *(Dangerous Liaisons),* Melanie Griffith *(Working Girl),* Meryl Streep *(A Cry in the Dark),* and Sigourney Weaver *(Gorillas in the Mist).*

Geena Davis won Best Supporting Actress for *The Accidental Tourist.*

Kevin Kline won Best Supporting Actor for *A Fish Called Wanda.*

Best Song "Let the River Run," w. m. Carly Simon.

Barry Levinson, Director of *Rain Man.*

Best Foreign Language Film: *Pelle the Conqueror,* director Bille August, Denmark, Scanian/Danish/Swedish. Carl Adolph "Max" von Sydow, born in Sweden, who later became a French citizen, played the father of a young boy named after Pelle the Conqueror. The movie was based on a 1910 novel of the same name by Danish writer Martin Andersen Nexo. It described how a father and son left Sweden to start a new life in Denmark after the mother died.

They worked on a farm where employees were mistreated by the managers. The boss had affairs with female employees who had children. One was a boy who helped Pelle learn Danish. Pelle helped a Swedish boy who was constantly harassed and wanted to visit America, China, and Negroland (Africa). The boss was finally castrated by his wife for impregnating young women! Pelle's father began an affair with a woman presumed to be a widow but whose husband returned from a voyage. Pelle's father became depressed and alcoholic, was criticized by young employees, but after seeing Pelle get a promotion, sent his son on to live, travel, and work because he was too old to travel with or defend the boy anymore.

British BAFTA awards: Best Film: *The Last Emperor*. **Director** Louis Malle for *Goodbye Children*. **Best Actor:** John Cleese in *A Fish Named Wanda*. **Best Actress:** Maggie Smith in *The Lonely Passion of Judith Hearne*. **Best Supporting Actor:** Michael Palin in *A Fish Named Wanda*. **Best Supporting Actress:** Judi Dench in *A Handful of Dust*.

62nd Academy Awards

Ceremony: This event took place on March 26, 1990, at the Dorothy Chandler Pavilion in Los Angeles, California. It was hosted by Billy Crystal and aired over ABC television in three hours and thirty-seven minutes to forty million U.S. citizens. This was a 5 percent decrease from the previous year. Jessica Tandy won the Oscar for Best Actress and her Canadian actor and husband, Hume Cronyn, gave her a kiss as she got up. The 80-year-old English actress thanked her director, Australian Bruce Beresford, for this chance and called it a "miracle." She held up the Oscar and said, "I'm on Cloud Nine." She was the oldest person to win an acting Oscar up to that time.

George Lucas and Steven Spielberg, who produced eight of the ten all-time grossing movies, presented an honorary award to 80-year-old Akira Kurosawa. He had produced 27 films with a search for why people can't be happier together. Howard W. Koch received the Jean Hersholt Humanitarian Award. He began producing movies in 1947 and some of his works were *Plaza Suite, The Odd Couple, Manchurian Candidate, Airplane,* and *Airplane 2.* He was president of the Academy from 1977-79 and was known for aiding benevolent causes that helped all Academy members.

Irving Berlin died on September 22, 1989, at age 101. The evening following the announcement of his death, the marquee lights of Broadway theatres were dimmed before curtain time. President George H. W. Bush said, "Berlin was a legendary man whose words and music will help define the history of our nation." He joined a crowd of thousands to sing Berlin's "God Bless America." Former President

Ronald Reagan, who co-starred in Berlin's 1943 musical *This Is the Army*, said, "Nancy and I are deeply saddened by the death of the wonderfully talented man whose musical genius delighted and stirred millions and will live on forever."

Musicians were finally getting more recognition. Max Steiner had won the first Oscar for music in *The Informer*, won an Oscar for scoring *Now Voyager*, and Irving Berlin won an Oscar for best song, "White Christmas" from *Holiday Inn*. Steiner was born May 10, 1888, and Irving Berlin was born one day later. Max, "the father of film music," composed and scored 300-plus films, including *King Kong, Casablanca, Gone with the Wind,* and *The Searchers* before his death in 1971.

1989 *Driving Miss Daisy*

Tagline: "The funny touching and totally irresistible story of a working relationship that becomes a 25-year friendship." Daisy (Jessica Tandy) was a 72-year-old Jewish widow and retired schoolteacher in Atlanta, Georgia. She has a black housekeeper and after she had a car accident, her son (Dan Akroyd) bought her a new car and hired a black chauffeur (Morgan Freeman) named Hoke.

As Hoke and Daisy spent time together, she asked him to do the cooking as well as driving after her housekeeper died. One day, he drove her to her synagogue just as it was bombed. She had trouble accepting that anti-Semitic prejudices were responsible. Another time, she attended a dinner where Dr. Martin Luther King Jr. spoke but she had only asked her black driver to take her there. He was insulted for not being asked until they arrived if he wanted to attend. He did not go in but listened on the radio.

As time passed, Hoke arrived one morning and found Miss Daisy worried, believing she was back teaching and seemed demented. Hoke notified her son who arranged for her to enter a retirement center.

As Hoke loses his eyesight and cannot drive, his visits to Daisy become less frequent. Her son picked up Hoke for Thanksgiving to visit Daisy. She asked her son to go "charm the nurses" so she could be with her friend, Hoke. As she had trouble with her silverware, he began to feed her pie. She saw him as a friend who had a closer relationship with her than even her own son.

Hanz Zimmer selected wonderful music for this movie when he did Louis Armstrong's "Kiss of Fire," Eartha Kitt's "Santa Baby," and Czech Antonin Dvorak's "Song to the Moon" from his opera *Ruzalka,* wherein a woman asked the moon to remind her prince of how she awaits and loves him. Was Miss Daisy thinking of her dead husband or of a man who would love her like Freeman did?

Critics praised the performances of Tandy and Freeman, but some felt that the racial prejudice of a bossy old lady to her black driver was painful to see.

The budget was $7.5 million, and the box office was $145.8 million.

Other best movie nominees included *Born on the Fourth of July, Dead Poets Society, Field of Dreams,* and *My Left Foot.*

Daniel Day-Lewis (1957- ?) from London won Best Actor for *My Left Foot.* Other contenders were Kenneth Branagh *(Henry V),* Tom Cruise *(Born on the Fourth of July),* Morgan Freeman *(Driving Miss Daisy),* and Robin Williams *(Dead Poets Society).*

Jessica Tandy (1909-1994) from London won Best Actress for *Driving Miss Daisy.* Other contenders were Isabelle Adjani *(Camille Claudel),* Pauline Collins *(Shirley Valentine),* Jessica Lange *(Music Box),* and Michelle Pfeiffer *(The Fabulous Baker Boys).*

Brenda Fricker won Best Supporting Actress for *My Left Foot.*

Denzel Washington won Best Supporting Actor for *Glory.*

Best Song "Under the Sea," w. Dean Pitchford, m. Alan Menken, from *The Little Mermaid*.

Oliver Stone, Director of *Born on the Fourth of July*.

Best Foreign Language Film: *Cinema Paradiso,* director Giuseppe Tornatore, Italy, Italian. A boy who grew up in Sicily became a famous director and returned home after hearing of the death of an old friend. He remembered his childhood and his friend, a projectionist at the Cinema. That friend spent countless hours discussing films and teaching the boy about film making. A scene from Rudolph Valentino and Vilma Banky in the 1926 silent *Son of the Sheik* was shown. The story described the boy's dream of leaving his village to make a career out of cinema, even though many changes were taking place in the film-making world. The nostalgic film was appealing to movie lovers.

British BAFTA awards: Best Film: *Dead Poets Society*. **Director** Kenneth Branagh for *Henry V.* **Best Actor:** Daniel Day-Lewis in *My Left Foot*. **Best Actress:** Pauline Collins in *Shirley Valentine*. **Best Supporting Actor:** Ray McAnally in *My Left Foot*. **Best Supporting Actress:** Michelle Pfeiffer in *Dangerous Liaisons*.

63rd Academy Awards

Ceremony: This event was conducted March 25, 1991, at the Shrine Auditorium in Los Angeles, California, hosted by Billy Crystal. It ran three hours and thirty minutes on ABC television and was viewed by 42.7 million people in the U.S.

The second African American woman to receive an award—Whoopi Goldberg— won Best Supporting Actress for *Ghost*. Sophia Loren, age 57, was given an honorary award as "one of the genuine treasures of world cinema who, in a career rich with memorable performances, has added permanent luster to our art form." Sophia was born in Italy where her sister married the son of Benito Mussolini. Sophia took Allesandra Mussolini under her wing and helped her become an actress. Sophia first starred in *Quo Vadis* at age 16, went on to *Boy on a Dolphin, The Pride and the Passion, Desire Under the Elms, Houseboat, Two Women, Marriage Italian Style, Arabesque* and other films.

Myrna Loy, age 86 who was home sick with cancer that killed her two years later, received an honorary award. Besides acting, she had been involved with UNESCO and welfare for the Red Cross during World War II. She said from her New York apartment, "You've made me very happy. Thank you so much." Myrna began in silent films, such as Al Jolson's *The Jazz Singer* as a young dancer, having been discovered by silent screen idol Rudolph Valentino. She made 120 movies, and thirteen with William Powell.

1990 *Dances with Wolves*

Tagline: "Inside everyone is a frontier waiting to be discovered." This movie was based on the 1988 book of the same name by Michael Blake.

He wrote about a First Lieutenant John Dunbar, wounded in an 1863 battle in Tennessee. Blake based his story about Dunbar meeting and marrying an Indian girl on Cynthia Ann Parker, captured, and raised by Comanches who had Quanah Parker as her son.

This movie is not historic. Kevin Costner had Blake write a screenplay of a Civil War soldier who became involved with Sioux and Lakota Indians. After an injury to his leg and his assumption that he would die, he bravely rode the line being shot at by Confederate soldiers to commit suicide. He was rewarded with the horse that brought him safely through. He wrote in his diary, "The strangeness of this life cannot be measured. In trying to produce my own death, I was elevated to the status of a living hero."

He survived and married a white girl raised by the Sioux. He made notes in a diary of his time tending a post where no additional soldiers arrived. There, he watched a wolf he named "Two Socks," who came to feed and jump around with him. The Lakota gave the soldier the name "Dances with Wolves." He tried to help the Lakota and intervened when U.S. soldiers wanted to take their land. The U.S. military considered the Costner character to be a traitor because he worked on behalf of the Indians and dressed in some ways like an Indian. Tragedies arose as Union soldiers fought Indians and many were lost.

Costner used help from a university Lakota language specialist to have language and subtitles be genuine, but some criticized it as being not quite the words spoken by males. However, the movie was so enjoyable that the budgeted $22 million brought in a box office $424.2 million.

The movie was shot on private ranches in South Dakota and Wyoming, but some locations included Badlands National Park, the Black Hills, Sage Creek Wilderness Area, Belle Fourche River area, and Triple U Buffalo Ranch near Fort Pierre, South Dakota.

Kevin Costner, Mary McDonnell, Graham Greene, and Rodney Grant starred. John Barry did the Oscar-winning score and musician Peter

Buffett, financier Warren Buffett's son, did the "Fire Dance" music. That haunting scene used tympani with booming beats, a theme arising from horns. The wind can be heard as it howls over the plains area. Feelings of love are shown through a harmonica, and soprano choir singing without words to indicate feelings.

The 181-minute movie had a budget of $22 million and an early box office of $184 million increasing to $424.2 million.

Other movie nominees included *Awakenings, Ghost, The Godfather Part III,* and *Goodfellas.*

Jeremy Irons (1948-?) from The Isle of Wight won Best Actor for *Reversal of Fortune.* Other contenders were Kevin Costner *(Dances with Wolves),* Robert De Niro *(Awakenings),* Gerard Depardieu *(Cyrano de Bergerac),* and Richard Harris *(The Field).*

Kathy Bates (1948-?) from Memphis, Tennessee, won Best Actress for *Misery.* Other contenders were Anjelica Huston *(The Grifters),* Julia Roberts *(Pretty Woman),* Meryl Streep *(Postcards from the Edge),* and Joanne Woodward *(Mr. & Mrs. Bridge).*

Whoopi Goldberg won Best Supporting Actress for *Ghost.*

Joe Pesci won Best Supporting Actor for *Goodfellas.*

Best Song "Sooner or Later," w. m. Stephen Sondheim, from *Dick Tracy.*

Kevin Costner, Director of *Dances with Wolves.*

Best Foreign Language Film: *Journey of Hope,* director Xavier Killer, Switzerland, German. A Turkish family saw a photograph of Switzerland and decided it would be better to live there than in their Kurdish community. The father's vote counted most so they went, taking their brightest son with them and leaving the other children with relatives. They were prey to people who offered hope and help but leave them destitute. They finally arrived in Italy where they had to climb mountainous terrain so unsafe that guides refused to take them. They journeyed on but the end suggested that immigrants had more hope than success on their moves to live a better life.

British BAFTA awards: Best Film: *Goodfellas*. **Director** Martin Scorsese. **Best Actor:** Philippe Noiret in *Cinema Paradiso*. **Best Actress:** Jessica Tandy in *Driving Miss Daisy*. **Best Supporting Actor:** Salvatore Cascio in *Cinema Paradiso*. **Best Supporting Actress:** Whoopi Goldberg in *Ghost*.

64th Academy Awards

Ceremony: This event was conducted on March 30, 1992, at the Dorothy Chandler Pavilion in Los Angeles, California, hosted by Billy Crystal and televised by ABC for three hours and thirty-three minutes to 44.4 million viewers. The event opened with Billy Crystal being rolled out wearing a face mask like Anthony (Hannibal Lecter in *The Silence of the Lambs*) Hopkins. This set a funny tone for the evening. The LGBT activists were outside complaining that homosexuals were badly portrayed in movies and had no voice inside the theatre that night.

The Silence of the Lambs was the first horror film to win Best Picture. Actress Jodie Foster, age 28, won for her role in that movie and became the youngest person to win two Oscars. John Singleton was the first African American to be nominated for Best Director for *Boyz n the Hood*. Laura Dern and her mother, Diane Ladd, became the first mother and daughter nominated for acting in the same year.

Director producer Satyajit Ray received an honorary Oscar for his 36 films and for "his rare mastery of the art of motion pictures, and of his profound humanitarian outlook, which has made an indelible influence on filmmakers and audiences throughout the world." The audience saw a video of Ray in a Calcutta hospital where he died 24 days later of heart problems. He said:

Well, it's an extraordinary experience for me to be here tonight to receive this magnificent award; certainly, the best achievement of my movie-making career. When I was a small, small schoolboy, I was terribly interested in the cinema. Became a film fan, wrote to Deanna Durbin. Got a reply, was delighted. Wrote to Ginger Rogers, didn't get a reply.

Then of course, I got interested in the cinema as an art form, and I wrote a 12-page letter to Bill Wilder after seeing *Double Indemnity*. He didn't reply either. Well, there you are. I have learned everything I've learned about the craft of cinema from the making of American films. I've been watching American films very carefully over the years and I love them for what they entertain, and then love them for what they taught. So, I express my gratitude to the American cinema, to the motion picture association who have given me this award and have made me feel so proud. Thank you very, very much.

Steven Spielberg presented the Irving G. Thalberg Memorial Award to George Lucas for changing the look of movies and entertainment. Lucas had done all the *Star Wars* movies. The real space shuttle was photographed with an Oscar floating through the cabin as the crew gave Lucas their thanks.

1991 *The Silence of the Lambs*

Tagline: "To enter the mind of a killer, she must challenge the mind of a madman." This movie is based on Thomas Harris' 1988 novel of the same name. It was about a young FBI trainee, Clarice Starling (Jodie Foster), who is trying to find a serial killer who skins his female victims. She interviewed Hannibal Lecter, a psychiatrist and serial killer in prison (Anthony Hopkins). He commented, "A census taker once tried to test me. I ate his liver with some fava beans and a nice chianti." She and Hannibal shared information about each other, which helped her investigation. Lecter killed his guards, escaped, Starling found the murderer who have been a transsexual, and the movie has an unusual ending. Strangely, the cannibalistic murderer makes the audience like him and that was due to the incredible acting of Hopkins.

First choice for the FBI agent was Gene Hackman, Scott Glenn, Michelle Pfeiffer, Meg Ryan, and Laura Dern, but Jodie Foster's wish to play the character was granted. The Lecter role was considered for Sean Connery, Al Pacino, Robert De Niro, Dustin Hoffman, Derek Jacobi, Daniel Day-Lewis, but Hopkins wanted it badly.

Filming was around Pittsburgh, Pennsylvania, and West Virginia. Most of the music was composed by Howard Shore, who hoped the viewers were unaware of the music but got feelings from the lighting, cinematography, costumes, acting, and sounds. There were a few other songs that Shore used: "American Girl" (1976), "Alone" (1980), "Sunny Day" (1991), "Real Men" (1981), "Goodbye Horses" (1988), "Hip Priest" (1981), "Rock of Ages," Bach's "Goldberg Variations" (1741) and Mozart's "The Magic Flute" (1791).

The 118-minute movie budget was $19 million, and the box office was $272.7 million. It turned out to be a "sleeper hit" akin to *Psycho* and *Halloween*.

Other movie nominees included *Beauty and the Beast, Bugsy, JFK,* and *The Prince of Tides.*

Anthony Hopkins (1937- ?) from Port Talbot, Wales, won Best Actor for *The Silence of the Lambs.* Other contenders were Warren Beatty *(Bugsy),* Robert De Niro *(Cape Fear),* Nick Nolte *(The Prince of Tides),* and Robin Williams *(The Fisher King).*

Jodie Foster won Best Actress for *The Silence of the Lambs.* Other contenders were Geena Davis *(Thelma and Louise),* Laura Dern *(Rambling Rose),* Bette Midler *(For the Boys),* and Susan Sarandon *(Thelma and Louise).*

Mercedes Ruehl won Best Supporting Actress for *The Fisher King.*

Jack Palance won Best Supporting Actor for *City Slickers.*

Best Song "Beauty and the Beast," w. Howard Ashman, m. Alan Menken, from *Beauty and the Beast.*

Jonathan Demme, Director of *The Silence of the Lambs*

Best Foreign Language Film: *Mediterraneo,* director Gabriele Salvatores, Italy, Italian. The tagline of this movie is "Sent to invade a remote Greek island, eight misfit sailors discover a magical place where anything can happen!" A squad of Italian sailors were sent to occupy a Greek island during World War II but suddenly their ship was hit and destroyed. The Italian sailors and the Greek inhabitants come out of hiding and begin to enjoy peaceful lives coexisting with each other. This 96-minute movie is a delight to experience.

British BAFTA awards: Best Film*: The Commitments.* **Director** Alan Parker for *The Commitments.* **Best Actor:** Anthony Hopkins in *The Silence of the Lambs.* **Best Actress:** Jody Foster in *The Silence of the Lambs.* **Best Supporting Actor:** Alan Rickman in *Robin Hood.* **Best Supporting Actress:** Kate Nelligan in *Frankie and Johnny.*

65th Academy Awards

Ceremony: This event was conducted March 26, 1993, at the Dorothy Chandler Pavilion in Los Angeles, hosted by Billy Crystal. It was broadcast on ABC for three hours and thirty-three minutes to 45.7 million viewers, a 3 percent increase from the previous year.

Perhaps the most poignant moment was when Gregory Peck awarded Audrey Hepburn the Jean Hersholt Humanitarian Award posthumously. She had died of an abdominal cancer of the appendix on January 20, 1993. Her first movie had been with him in Rome. Peck learned that a poem by Indian writer Tagore was Hepburn's favorite and read it at her service. Audrey was introduced to future husband Mel Ferrer at a Gregory Peck party, and they were married for 14 years and had one son. She then married an Italian psychiatrist and they had one son. She then lived with the Dutch actor, Robert Wolders, who had been married to Merle Oberon until Merle died. Audrey and Wolders lived together many years. When she died at age 63, he married Henry Fonda's widow, Shirlee.

Anthony Hopkins was introduced as having just received knighthood. He was to present the Best Actress award and it went to his co-star, Emma Thompson, for *Howards End.* Sophia Loren and Marcello Mastroianni presented an honorary Oscar to Federico Fellini for his lifetime of work, and he would die six months after this event. He told his wife, Giulietta Masina, in the audience, to stop crying and thanked Americans for "making me feel at home." Clint Eastwood won for the Best Picture, *Unforgiven,* and said, "This was the Year of the Woman and the greatest woman on the planet is here tonight—my mother."

Angela Lansbury, lifelong friend of Elizabeth Taylor, presented her with the Jean Hersholt Humanitarian Award due to her work on AIDS. She accepted and asked all to love instead of hate people despite their differences.

1992 *Unforgiven*

Tagline: "It's a hell of a thing. Killing a man." Eastwood had to persuade Gene Hackman, who was tired of playing violent roles, that this movie would make a statement against violence. So, Gene agreed to star in it and won an Oscar. When Eastwood called Richard Harris to star as an Englishman in the movie, he was in the Bahamas and was watching an Eastwood movie then. He agreed, telling Eastwood that he loved doing Westerns. Clint decided this would be his last Western.

This was Eastwood's work about an aging killer, fame, courage, heroism, and supposed Western heroes. They were often not the good guy, but just a survivor. The old hero he played, and his friends and opponents were not fearless killers but were cowards, weaklings, liars, and people who believed in revenge. "Deserve's got nothing to do with it." A Western gave Eastwood room to display morals and beliefs by being more truthful about individuals. The search for vengeance is often followed by conscious regret for vengeful acts as the tagline indicated.

When some very bad guys hurt, maimed, and killed prostitutes, the remaining women sought killers to get rid of their enemies. Many came forth for the money but were a sorry lot.

The difficult to watch movie starred Clint Eastwood, Gene Hackman, Morgan Freeman, and Richard Harris. Much of the 131-minute movie was shot in Alberta, Canada, to create a wintry look. The guitar, banjo, harmonica, and honky-tonk piano made it sound western. The music for the movie was composed by Randy Shams and Tim Stithem but the main theme song, "Claudia's Theme," was composed by Eastwood. He was a song and dance man since appearing in the Lerner and Lowe 1969 movie *Paint Your Wagon and* has many song credits. His haunting theme is filled with memories and nostalgia.

This movie was the third Western to win Best Picture after *Cimarron* and *Dances with Wolves.* Although Eastwood has made many western movies, he was allergic to many animals, such as horses, dogs, cats, etc. Their dander produced sneezing, watery eyes, and coughing at times. The budget for *Unforgiven* was $14.4 million and it grossed more than $159 million.

Other movie nominees included *The Crying Game, A Few Good Men, Howards End,* and *Scent of a Woman.*

Al Pacino (1940- ?) from Harlem, New York, won Best Actor for *Scent of a Woman.* Other contenders were Robert Downey, Jr. *(Chaplin),* Clint Eastwood *(Unforgiven),* Stephen Rea *(The Crying Game),* and Denzel Washington *(Malcolm X).*

Emma Thompson (1959- ?) from London won Best Actress for *Howards End.* Other contenders were Catherine Deneuve *(Indochine),* Mary McDonnell *(Passion Fish),* Michelle Pfeiffer *(Love Field),* and Susan Sarandon *(Lorenzo's Oil).*

Marisa Tomei won Best Supporting Actress for *My Cousin Vinny.*

Gene Hackman won Best Supporting Actor for *Unforgiven.*

Best Song "A Whole New World," w. Tim Rice, m. Alan Menken, from *Aladdin.*

Clint Eastwood, Director of *Unforgiven.*

Best Foreign Language Film: *Indochine,* director Regis Wargnier, France, French/Vietnamese. This 160-minute movie was set in 1930 Indochina just as French colonial rule was ending. Catherine Deneuve was a widow with a rubber plantation who adopted a Vietnamese princess as if she was her daughter. They both fall in love with a young French naval officer. The age difference played a part and so did the changing political atmosphere. A slave market, opium, and gambling dens in Saigon, and excellent photography of hidden valleys, provide additional richness to the story.

British BAFTA awards: Best Film: *Howards End*. **Director** James Ivory for *Howards End*. **Best Actor:** Robert Downey in *Chaplin*. **Best Actress:** Emma Thompson in *Howards End*. **Best Supporting Actor:** Gene Hackman in *Unforgiven*. **Best Supporting Actress:** Miranda Richardson in *Damage*. **Outstanding British Film:** *The Crying Game,* director Neil Jordan, producer Stephen Woolley, starring Stephen Rea and Miranda Richardson.

Beginning in 1992, BAFTA decided to have an award for British films each year. It was first named after Alexander Korda but later called **Outstanding British Film**. The requirements to be eligible: The film must have significant creative involvement by individuals who are British or residents in the U.K. for ten years or more.

66th Academy Awards

Ceremony: This event was on March 21, 1994, at the Dorothy Chandler Pavilion in Los Angeles, California, hosted by Whoopi Goldberg. She was the first African American to host the Academy Awards. It was filmed on ABC television for three hours and eighteen minutes with 46.26 million viewers—a 1 percent increase from the previous year.

Tom Cruise introduced Paul Newman as a fellow race car driver, friend, and presented him with the Jean Hersholt Humanitarian Award for his work with young people and the handicapped. He had raised more than $80 million from his home foods dedicated to charity. Newman said the U.S. was the most charitable nation on the planet and that entertainers were the most charitable people.

An honorary Oscar went to English actress Deborah Kerr, who had six nominations but never won an Oscar. She made 44 films and worked three decades in films. With the standing ovation as she walked forward, she said she had been scared to death by this moment but now felt she was "among friends," such as John Huston, Cary Grant, and Robert Mitchum, whom she named.

A memorial tribute to those who died in the last year included Lillian Gish, Myrna Loy, Joseph Cotton, Spanky McFarland, Ruby Keeler, Telly Savalas, Melina Mercouri, Cesar Romero, Alexis Smith, Joseph L. Mankiewicz, Helen Hayes, John Candy, Sammy Cahn, Federico Fellini, Herve Villechaize, Vincent Price, Stewart Granger, River Phoenix, Raymond Burr, Cantinflas, Don Ameche, Audrey Hepburn, Dinah Shore, Fred Gwynne, and Vincent Gardenia.

Tom Hanks won Best Actor in *Philadelphia* and said, "Thanks to Rawley Farnsworth, who was my high school drama teacher, who taught me, 'to act well the part, there all the glory lies,' and former classmate, John Gilkerson--two of the finest gay Americans, two wonderful men that I had the good fortune to be associated with." Holly Hunter won Best Actress for *The Piano* and explained that her parents saw her practice piano on cardboard, bought her a real piano, and she took lessons. Anna Paquin, age 11, became the second youngest to win a competitive acting award and thanked those who cared for her appearance in *The Piano*.

Best Director went to Steven Spielberg for *Schindler's List*. He said this would never have begun without Poldek Pfefferberg, one of Schindler's Jews that was saved. Spielberg, Gerald Molen, and Branko Lustig were presented Oscars for the Best Picture. Spielberg said there were 350,000 Holocaust survivors alive who want to help people remember the Holocaust and teachers everywhere should educate children and people about it. The other two producers spoke and the last was Branko Lustig. He began, "My number was 83317...It is a long way from Auschwitz to this stage. The dying ones left me the legacy to tell—if I survive—how it was." Lustig donated his *Schindler's List* Oscar to Israel's Holocaust memorial in Jerusalem and set up with Spielberg a project at the Shoah Foundation to record the testimony of 50,000-plus Holocaust survivors.

1993 *Schindler's List*

Tagline: "The list is life." The movie was based on the 1982 novel *Schindler's Ark* by Thomas Keneally, who wrote it after meeting Poldek Pfefferberg in 1980. Poldek was one of Schindler's saved Jews and his mission was to get Schindler noted for helping some Jews survive. When Steven Spielberg, Jewish movie producer whose relatives were victims of Nazis, heard of this he felt he wasn't mature enough to make a Holocaust movie properly. But the product helped explain to audiences that despite great evils, people can make choices to be good.

After much time and consideration, Spielberg decided to shoot it in black and white like a documentary, and to show the gradual transformation of a German Nazi party member money-maker into a man who saved more than one thousand Jews. He employed them in his enamel-ware company, which mutated into a company preparing ammunition for Nazis (but deliberately sabotaging their own products).

Spielberg puzzled over the Schindler role and chose a little-known actor, Liam Neeson. He chose the better-known Ralph Fiennes, who gained 28 pounds to play the second lieutenant who shoots Jews whenever he feels like it, and Ben Kingsley was the accountant who compiled the list of Jewish employees who were saved in Schindler's plant.

The character of Schindler began as a man who bribed and praised Germans to get more contracts, fame, and money. He hired Jews because they were cheaper workers and he wanted to get ahead. As he viewed the liquidation of the Polish Jews in the Krakow ghetto, he realized the horror. Partly his realization depended upon watching a 3-year-old little girl in a red coat whom he finally saw on a pile of corpses. Except for candles being lit for a Jewish service in the first scene, the red coat was the only color in the film. The momentary gleam from candles was, according to Spielberg, a bit of hope during a Shabbat before the Nazis destroyed the Jewish ghetto.

Thousands of extras were used in the film, but there was a preference for those who looked more Eastern European. Along the way, Spielberg realized that he wanted the movie to end with actual survivors who owed their lives to Schindler. He searched for and flew them to Schindler's grave in Jerusalem for the final scene. The scheming Schindler turned out to be a savior and wished, when the war ended, that he had done more. The survivors gave him a ring, which bore a Jewish phrase: "Whoever saves one life, saves the world entire."

Spielberg thought of using more German and Polish dialogue but decided not to have viewers looking at subtitles and taking their eyes off the scene. The musical theme repeated throughout the movie was a sad tune played by Itzhak Perlman on the violin. As Perlman played the theme with John Williams conducting the orchestra, he began to cry. His parents, Polish Jews, escaped to what would become Israel but his grandparents were victims of the Nazis.

Perlman, who had polio at age four, sits to play his violin and uses braces and crutches. He suffers from, or enjoys, a disorder called synesthesia. "If I play a B flat on the G string, I will say that the color for me is probably deep forest green. Besides colors, I see shapes. Each note has a shape. I would say that if you play a D on the G string, for me that's round....Music is shape, it's feel and it's color—it's everything... Music is a part of society's soul; that emotional experience when you hear music is something society needs." (See Maureen Seaberg, *Psychology Today*, posted 2/21/2012.)

There is one scene where the ghetto is being attacked when a Jewish folk song, "On the Cooking Stove," was sung by a children's choir. Clarinet solos were also heard as if they were voices somewhere.

The 195-minute movie budget was $22 million but the box office was a very surprising $321.3 million. Spielberg took no salary for the movie. He used the proceeds for the movie to finance other documentaries, such as *Anne Frank Remembered, The Lost Children of Berlin,* and *The Last Days.* After this film, many discussed why the Germans did not do more to help the Jewish victims. Much of the movie was filmed at Schindler's actual factory.

Other movie nominees included *The Fugitive, In the Name of the Father, The Piano,* and *The Remains of the Day.*

Tom Hanks (1956- ?) from Concord, California, won Best Actor for *Philadelphia.* Other contenders were Daniel Day-Lewis *(In the*

Name of the Father), Laurence Fishburne *(What's Love Got to Do with It)*, Anthony Hopkins *(The Remains of the Day)*, and Liam Neeson *(Schindler's List)*.

Holly Hunter (1958-?) from Conyers, Georgia, won Best Actress for *The Piano*. Other contenders were Angela Bassett *(What's Love Got to Do with It)*, Stockard Channing *(Six Degrees of Separation)*, Emma Thompson *(The Remains of the Day)*, and Debra Winger *(Shadowlands)*.

Anna Paquin won Best Supporting Actress for *The Piano*.

Tommy Lee Jones won Best Supporting Actor for *The Fugitive*.

Best Song "Streets of Philadelphia," w. m. Bruce Springsteen, from *Philadelphia*.

Steven Spielberg, Director of *Schindler's List*.

Best Foreign Language Film: *Belle Epoque,* director Fernando Trueba, Spain, Spanish. This was a cute movie about 1931 Spain. A young soldier deserts just as the Second Republic is beginning. He befriended a man with four daughters. He seduced one who just lost her husband and sought solace, another who was lesbian and loved when he dressed like a woman, and a third who was a social climber. The youngest, played by Penelope Cruz, was naïve and was angered by his flirtations with her sisters. He realized she would be the best to marry.

British BAFTA awards: Best Film: *Schindler's List*. **Director:** Steven Spielberg for *Schindler's List*. **Best Actor:** Anthony Hopkins in *The Remains of the Day*. **Best Actress:** Holly Hunter in *The Piano*. **Best Supporting Actor:** Ralph Fiennes in *Schindler's List*. **Best Supporting Actress:** Miriam Margolyes *in The Age of Innocence*. **Outstanding British Film:** *Shadowlands,* director Richard Attenborough, producer Brian Eastman, starring Anthony Hopkins and Debra Winger.

67th Academy Awards

Ceremony: This event took place on March 27, 1995, at the Shrine Auditorium in Los Angeles, California. Hosted by comedian David Letterman. ABC televised the ceremony, which lasted three hours and thirty-two minutes to 48.3 million viewers, a 7 percent increase from the previous year.

The Jean Hersholt Humanitarian Award was awarded to Quincy Jones, the first musician who was ever given this award. He thanked family members and said, "This is the proudest day of my life." He then urged everyone to join the National Endowment for the Arts.

An honorary Academy Award was given to Michelangelo Antonioni. This 83-year-old Italian director had worked with Roberto Rossellini and Carlo Ponti. He did art films about social alienation and ways that people try to connect with each other. Some of his stars were Jeanne Moreau, Marcello Mastroianni, Alain Delon, Vanessa Redgrave, and Jack Nicholson. He had a stroke, could no longer use his right arm, used a cane to walk, and could no longer speak, so his recent films dealt with silence. His wife said he wished to "thank you."

The Irving G. Thalberg Memorial Award went to Clint Eastwood for the lasting value of his body of work. Clint mentioned some who had won the award before, whom he idolized. He said that if Dirty Harry were here and asked if he felt lucky, he'd have said, "You're darn right I do."

The tribute to many who died the last year included Fernando Rey, Cameron Mitchell, Barry Sullivan, Giulietta Masina, Peter Cushing,

Noah Berry Jr., Woody Strode, Jessica Tandy, Tom Ewell, Lionel Stander, Donald Pleasence, Burt Lancaster, Henry Mancini, Martha Ray, George Peppard, Gilbert Roland, Rossano Brazzi, Cab Calloway, Mildred Natwick, Macdonald Carey, David Wayne, and Raul Julia.

Best Actor Tom Hanks for *Forrest Gump* thanked his wife "who taught me what love is." The Best Director and Best Picture were for *Forrest Gump* and one producer, Steve Tisch, said, "It's about humanity, it's about respect, tolerance, and unconditional love."

1994 *Forrest Gump*

Tagline: "Life is like a bunch of chocolates. You never know what you're gonna get." This movie was based on the 1986 novel of the same name by Winston Groom. The stars included Tom Hanks, Robin Wright, Gary Sinise, Mykelti Williamson, and Sally Field. The opening scene is Forrest sitting on a bench waiting for his son to come home on a bus. While waiting, he chatted about his life and his mother's (Sally Field) sayings. "My momma always said, 'Life was like a box of chocolates. You never know what you're gonna get.'" She was a mother who loved Forrest unconditionally, no matter his problems.

Through amazing cinematography, the low intelligence boy lived a life running into famous people through his endurance to be a good person and overcome difficulties. On his first day of school, he met a girl named Jenny (Robin Wright) and they became best friends. He had leg braces to correct a curved spine and when taunted by bullies, learned to run so fast that he won fame. His running accidentally paid off when he ran faster than others on a football field. On an All-American team, he met President John F. Kennedy at the White House.

In the Army he helped a fellow soldier, Bubba (Mykelti Williamson), and they planned to go into the shrimp business after service. Bubba was killed but Forrest saved his lieutenant (Gary Sinise) who lost both legs, so Forrest received a Medal of Honor from President Lyndon B. Johnson.

At an anti-war rally, he ran into Jenny who was living as a hippie. He learned ping-pong and became a competitor against Chinese teams and was interviewed on *The Dick Cavett Show*. He spent New Year's with Lt. Dan, who was bitter over being rescued and living with no legs. Gump met President Richard Nixon and was in the Watergate complex where he saw men with flashlights in the building. He and Lt. Dan finally teamed up and started the shrimp business.

His mother died, and he saw Jenny who was recovering from drug abuse. He proposed and they made love. She left the next morning and, heartbroken, he began a cross-country marathon. Once tired of running, he returned home. He got a letter from Jenny that she wanted to visit and bring his son, Forrest Gump, Jr. She was sick and a disease killed her, but they married before she died. Thus, Forrest is seeing his son off on his first day of school at the picture's end.

Here are some further details about the movie. Those considered for the role of Forrest were John Travolta, Bill Murray, and Chevy Chase but they turned it down. Tom Hanks' younger brother, who bears a strong resemblance, did most of the running by Forrest in the movie. Tom's daughter, Elizabeth, was one of the children on the school bus who did not let Forrest have a seat. Tom and producer Zemeckis learned the studio was ready to close production, so they donated their salaries to keep the project going. The Vietnam scenes were done on a South Carolina Golf Course. Tom Hanks invented the line while sitting on the bench: "My name is Forrest Gump. People call me Forrest Gump." Kurt Russell's voice was dubbed for Elvis Presley, having played Elvis on a TV movie. Some 1,500 extras were used but with help from camera operators, they were multiplied into a crowd that looked like several thousand.

The music featured popular American songs from each era, including Bob Dylan, Elvis Presley, Creedence Clearwater Revival, Aretha

Franklin, Lynryd Skynyrd, Three Dog Night, the Byrds, the Beach Boys, the Jimi Hendrix Experience, the Doors, the Mama and the Papas, the Doobie Brothers, Simon and Garfunkel, Bob Seger, Buffalo Springfield, and an Alan Silvestri score. One feature, a floating feather, began and ended the movie. Nobody knows what the feather represented, but Tom Hanks said it might mean "Our destiny is only defined by how we deal with the chance elements in our life." For many, this movie meant you don't have to be smart or rich to enjoy life because you can find rewards everywhere—like in a box of chocolates.

The 142-minute film budget was $55 million, and the box office was an amazing $683 million.

Other movie nominees included *Four Weddings and a Funeral, Pulp Fiction, Quiz Show,* and *The Shawshank Redemption.*

Tom Hanks won Best Actor for *Forrest Gump.* Other contenders were Morgan Freeman *(The Shawshank Redemption),* Nigel Hawthorne *(The Madness of King George),* Paul Newman *(Nobody's Fool),* and John Travolta *(Pulp Fiction).*

Jessica Lange (1949-?) from Cloquet, Minnesota, won Best Actress for *Blue Sky.* Other contenders were Jodie Foster *(Nell),* Miranda Richardson *(Tom and Viv),* Winona Ryder *(Little Women),* and Susan Sarandon *(The Client).*

Dianne Wiest won Best Supporting Actress for *Bullets Over Broadway.*

Martin Landau won Best Supporting Actor for *Ed Wood.*

Best Song "Can You Feel the Love Tonight," w. Tim Rice, m. Elton John, from *The Lion King.*

Robert Zemeckis, Director of *Forrest Gump.*

Best Foreign Language Film: *Burnt by the Sun,* director Nikita Mihalkov, Russia, Russian. The sun, said the Russian filmmaker, stood for Stalin destroying people, both good and bad. The title came from a popular 1930 song, a Polish tango called "Wearied Sun" and was heard many times during the movie. The movie was shot in Moscow and the dacha was shot in Novgorod. The beauty of this film and the warmth of the characters with each other accompanied by beautiful music made this rise above the other excellent foreign movie nominees.

This remarkable story of a war hero began in 1936, when an Army commander and family went on vacation. His wife's former lover, long-thought dead, showed up at the family dacha. The man seemed friendly but had a secret mission to arrest the commander for his role in a non-existent conspiracy to assassinate Stalin. The story tracked the loving family through the Khrushchev era through trials and tribulations that brought heartbreak to many.

When the filmmaker, Mihalkov, went onstage to collect his Oscar with his little daughter, he apologized for so little English. He said he tried to show the cruel truth in this movie, and because his own daughter was in the movie, he didn't have a problem with actors.

British BAFTA awards: Best Film: *Four Weddings and a Funeral.* **Best Actor:** Hugh Grant in *Four Weddings and a Funeral.* **Best Actress:** Susan Sarandon in *The Client.* **Best Supporting Actor:** Samuel Jackson in *Pulp Fiction.* **Best Supporting Actress:** Kristen Scott Thomas in *Four Weddings and a Funeral.* **Outstanding British Film:** *Shallow Grave,* director Danny Boyle, producer Andrew Macdonald, starring Ewan McGregor and Kerry Fox.

68th Academy Awards

Ceremony: This event was conducted on March 25, 1996, at Dorothy Chandler Pavilion in Los Angeles, hosted by Whoopy Goldberg. ABC televised it for three hours, thirty-nine minutes to 44.8 million viewers, considerably less than the previous year. Before the ceremony, Rev. Jesse Jackson had led an activist group called the Rainbow Coalition protesting underemployed African Americans and other minorities in the film industry. Ceremony producer Quincy Jones and Jackson reached an agreement so the show could go on. Jones noted that racial bias was a problem that permeated everything in the country. "Every facet of America discriminates," he said.

Dancer choreographer Gene Kelly had died on February 2, 1996, and Broadway lights dimmed that evening in honor of him. Tap dancer Savion Glover did a number for the ceremony imitating Kelly, and it was followed by clips of Gene dancing from several of his movies.

Chuck Jones, creator of so many cartoon characters, received an honorary award by Robin Williams, who described his addiction to cartoons. Jones came to the stage with a cane and said that he had made 300 cartons in his 50-plus years in the business. He said, "This Oscar means that you've forgiven me...I was a teacher...and then somebody offered to pay me to draw."

Emma Thompson was the first person to win Oscars for both acting and screenwriting. She had won Best Actress for *Howard's End* and now won Best Adapted Screenplay for *Sense and Sensibility*. Upon receiving the award, she described going to Jane Austen's grave to tell her of her movie's good results. She dedicated her Oscar to director Ang Lee.

Steven Spielberg awarded an honorary Oscar to Kirk Douglas whose Jewish parents came from Belarus. Spielberg described how Douglas had shown courage by playing roles of people with a conscience, and produced, directed, and hammered away the list of supposed communists in Hollywood. He told of a line Douglas said in *The Bad and the Beautiful* movie: "The dark has a life of its own." Kirk, 80 years old, walked after a stroke with no help over to receive the Oscar. One side of his face sagged, and his speech was affected. He said, "I see my four sons. They are proud of the old man. I am proud to be a part of Hollywood for fifty years. This is for my wife. I love you. And I love all of you."

The annual In Memoriam tribute to those who died during the last year included Ginger Rogers, Miklós Rózsa, Dean Martin, Viveca Lindfors, Martin Balsam, Elisha Cook Jr., Ida Lupino, Terry Southern, Haing S. Ngor, and Michael Hordem.

1995 *Braveheart*

Tagline: "Every man dies; not every man really lives." This movie is based on a 15th century poem "The Wallace" by a minstrel called Blind Harry.

It recounted the life of William Wallace, who died in 1305, a freedom fighter in the Wars for Scottish Independence from England. He led a revolt after his beloved was killed. He fought English ruler, Edward the Longshanks, who wanted to wear the crown of Scotland. With the assistance of Robert, the Bruce, Wallace endured savagery and symbolized a free Scotland against English rulers. The title *Braveheart* was derived from Robert the Bruce, who was described in a Scottish poem as *Heart of Bruce*.

Wallace was tried for high treason and was to be hanged, drawn, and quartered. If he hollered "Mercy" he would be given a quick death.

Instead, he hollered "Freedom" and the crowd was moved hearing that cry. Braveheart was a hero who led others with passion, authority, and could speak for his people better than most. Mel Gibson played Wallace and Patrick McGoohan played Longshanks, and a brilliant cast. The movie was not intended to be a historical docudrama but to be a rousing piece of movie with some basis in legends and facts. Some said the movie revived rivalry between Scotland and England, but it was intended to be simply an entertaining movie.

The music was composed and conducted by James Horner and became one of the most commercially successful soundtracks of all time. Costumes and ferocity dominated the unusual features of this movie. Depictions of kilts and bagpipes were inaccurate for this era because they were introduced many generations later. Horner used the Scottish National Anthem, "Scotland the Brave," and the 1917 "The Road to the Isles." One theme was special because he used it in *Titanic in* 1997. Another number was played on an Irish pipe instrument although the movie was about Scotland. Horner arranged for the Choir of Westminster Abbey to be included in music.

This 178-minute movie budget was $78 million and made three or four times that number.

Other movie nominees included *Apollo 13, Babe, The Postman,* and *Sense and Sensibility.*

Nicolas Cage (1964- ?) from Long Beach, California, won Best Actor for *Leaving Las Vegas.* Other contenders were Richard Dreyfuss *(Mr. Holland's Opus),* Anthony Hopkins *(Nixon),* Sean Penn *(Dead Man Walking),* and Massimo Troisi *(The Postman).*

Susan Sarandon (1946- ?) from New York City, New York, won Best Actress for *Dead Man Walking.* Other contenders were Elisabeth Shue *(Leaving Las Vegas),* Sharon Stone *(Casino),* Meryl Streep *(The Bridges of Madison County),* and Emma Thompson *(Sense and Sensibility).*

Mira Sorvino won Best Supporting Actress for *Mighty Aphrodite.*

Kevin Spacy won Best Supporting Actor for *The Usual Suspects.*

Best Song "Colors of the Wind," w. Stephen Schwartz, m. Alan Menken, from *Pocahontas.*

Mel Gibson, Director of *Braveheart.*

Best Foreign Language Film: *Antonia's Line,* director Marleen Gorris, Netherlands, Dutch. Post-World War II, Antonia and her daughter go back to the Dutch home where Antonia's mother left them a farm. They join an unusual community with friends like Crooked Finger and Looney Lips. Strange inhabitants produce opportunities for oppression or victory for their family. Their granddaughter and great-granddaughter help create strong-willed women who improve their community as a line of women who, despite rapes and spites, point to a better future.

British BAFTA awards: Best Film: *Sense and Sensibility.* **Best Actor:** Nigel Hawthorne in *The Madness of King George.* **Best Actress:** Emma Thompson in *Sense and Sensibility.* **Best Supporting Actor:** Tim Roth in *Rob Roy.* **Best Supporting Actress:** Kate Winslet in *Sense and Sensibility.* **Outstanding British Film:** *The Madness of King George,* director Nicholas Hytner, producers Stephen Evans and David Parfitt, starring Nigel Hawthorne and Helen Mirren.

69th Academy Awards

Ceremony: This event was conducted on March 24, 1997, at the Shrine Auditorium in Los Angeles, California, hosted by Billy Crystal. ABC broadcast the show for three hours and thirty-five minutes to 40 million viewers, with a significant 9 percent decrease from the previous year.

The Irving G. Thalberg Memorial Award went to Saul Zaentz, who produced *One Flew Over the Cuckoo's Nest*, *The English Patient*, and *Amadeus*. Saentz said, "Darryl Zanuck, Hal Wallis, David Selznick, Walt Disney, and Samuel Goldwyn…brought passion to their films… Passion moves freely across borders, speaks every language and flourished in every culture. The movement of passion is the most gratifying satisfaction in any moviemaker's life. This happens when you see and hear people all over the world share their laughter, their crying, and their sudden gasps at identical screen moments…This belongs to the many with whom I have shared dream and journeys. My cup is full. Thank you."

When Zaentz won another award for Best Producer, he acknowledged, "I said my cup was full before. Now it runneth over." He described how they had to shut down production of *The English Patient* when they ran out of money, and nobody was being paid. The Weinstein brothers pitched in to help and kept the project going to completion.

The people who died the previous year included Jo Van Fleet, Tupac Shakur, Dorothy Lamour, Stirling Silliphant, Juliet Prowse, Fred Zinnemann, Ben Johnson, Gene Nelson, Joanne Dru, Greer Garson, Albert "Cubby" Broccoli, Lew Ayres, and Pandro Berman.

1996 *The English Patient*

Tagline: "In memory, love lives forever." This movie was based on Michael Ondaatje's 1992 book of the same title. The action involved four people who stayed in an abandoned villa in Italy at the end of World War II. One was a cartographer and surveyor (Ralph Fiennes) who was burned beyond recognition and is dying of his various ailments with his face totally wrapped in bandages. He was revealed to be a Hungarian cartographer who was doing explorations while also assisting the RCMP army. There was in real life a Hungarian explorer who discovered a famous 7,000-year-old cave in the Sahara Desert in 1933. It contained what looked like people swimming and giraffes, dogs, goats, and cows in an area near ancient lakes. A similar picture of the cave is in this movie.

A nurse (Juliette Binoche) was assigned to stay with the surveyor to the end. Willem Dafoe entered the scene to make the cartographer pay for consenting to let foes cut off his thumbs. But after hearing the explorer's story, decided to spare him pain and let the nurse give him morphine.

The complicated story was derived from flashbacks, which depicted a relationship with a married woman (Kristen Scott Thomas) who shared great love with him. She died after she broke her ankle in the famous cave, and he left to seek water and help for her. Her husband was played by Colin Firth. The sad story was interspersed with a loving relationship that developed between the nurse and a Bedouin man who helped the army detect explosives on the roads. That man had also helped the Hungarian explorer's mission by finding the famous cave of swimmers in the Libyan desert.

The unique music for this movie was by Gariel Yared and began with a view of sand dunes as the titles rolled. Yared's music was played during rests to inspire the actors. The old Hungarian tune was a lament in a sad minor key showing that love brings heartache. That set the tone for the entire movie with beautiful background themes. There was a synthesized sound of a Middle Eastern stringed instrument called quanoun, like a large zither with melodramatic tones.

Other movie nominees included *Fargo, Jerry Maguire, Secrets and Lies,* and *Shine.*

Geoffrey Rush (1951-?) from Toowoomba, Australia, won Best Actor for *Shine.* Other contenders were Tom Cruise *(Jerry Maguire),* Ralph Fiennes *(The English Patient),* Woody Harrelson *(The People vs. Larry Flynt),* and Billy Bob Thornton *(Sling Blade).*

Frances McDormand (1957- ?) from Gibson City, Illinois, won Best Actress for *Fargo.* Other contenders were Brenda Blethyn *(Secrets and Lies),* Diane Keaton *(Marvin's Room),* Kristin Scott Thomas *(The English Patient),* and Emily Watson *(Breaking the Waves).*

Juliette Binoche won Best Supporting Actress for *The English Patient.*

Cuba Gooding, Jr. won Best Supporting Actor for *Jerry Maguire.*

Best Song "You Must Love Me, w. Tim Rice, m. Andrew Lloyd Webber, from *Evita.*

Anthony Minghella, Director of *The English Patient.*

Best Foreign Language Film: *Kolya,* director Jan Sverak, Czech Republic, Czech. This film is about the disintegration of the Soviets in 1988 and some Prague inhabitants. A Czech concert cellist played at funerals but was unable to play with the Czech Philharmonic Orchestra because he was blacklisted. A friend offered him money to marry a Soviet woman to allow her to stay in Czechoslovakia. He married her and she was then able to move to West Germany where her boyfriend lived but had to leave behind her 5-year-old son. Through a difficult relationship, a bond formed between the Czech man and the boy, Kolya. Finally, Kolya and his mother were reunited. The cellist fathered a child with his girlfriend as a replacement for the lost boy. He also happily took up his position with the orchestra again.

British BAFTA awards: Best Film: *The English Patient.* **Best Actor:** Geoffrey Rush in *Shine.* **Best Actress:** Brenda Blethyn in *Secrets and Lies.* **Best Supporting Actor:** Paul Scofield in *The Crucible.* **Best Supporting Actress:** Juliet Binoche in *The English Patient.* **Outstanding British Film:** *Secrets and Lies,* director Mike Leigh, producer Simon Channing Williams, starring Timothy Spall and Brenda Blethyn.

70th Academy Awards

Ceremony: This event took place on March 23, 1998, at the Shrine Auditorium in Los Angeles, California, hosted by Billy Crystal. ABC broadcast the show for three hours, forty-seven minutes and it was seen by 57.25 million viewers, a 29 percent increase from the previous year of 40 million viewers.

This ceremony commemorated the 70th anniversary of Academy Awards and 70 former winners were seated onstage. This was the largest gathering of former winners since the 50th ceremony. Canadian actress Fay Wray, age 91, was singled out by Billy Crystal as the "beauty who charmed the beast--King Kong." She was paid $10,000 for the picture that saved RKO from bankruptcy. When Wray died on August 8, 2004, the lights on the Empire State Building in New York City dimmed for 15 minutes. She had been approached to play the aged Rose in the *Titanic* but declined and the role was filled by Gloria Stuart, who began acting in the silent film era.

Martin Scorsese presented an honorary award to Stanley Donen for lifetime achievement. He began as a dancer and created dancing stars in *On the Town, Singin' in the Rain, Seven Brides for Seven Brothers, Charade, Indiscreet, Funny Face,* etc. He was responsible for Gene Kelly dancing in puddles at the right beat and for Fred Astaire dancing up the walls and on ceilings. When handed the Oscar, he sang Irving Berlin's lyrics: "Heaven, I'm in heaven, and my heart beats so that I can hardly speak, and I seem to find the happiness I seek, when we're out together dancing cheek to cheek" and held the Oscar to his cheek. He then did a little dance. Donen lived until 2019, the last twenty years with partner comedian and actress Elaine May.

Whoopi Goldberg presented the memorial tribute to those who had died in the last year and here are many of those: Lloyd Bridges, Richard Jaeckel, William Hickey, Billie Dove, Jacque Cousteau, Stubby Kaye, Red Skelton, Toshiro Mifune, Brian Keith, Chris Farley, Burgess Meredith, J. T. Walsh, Robert Mitchum and James Stewart.

1997 *Titanic*

Tagline: "Nothing on earth could come between them." Screenwriter, producer, director James Cameron loved shipwrecks and after he saw pictures of the *Titanic* wreckage, he decided to do a movie with historic and fictional sides to inform and fascinate audiences. He described it to 20th Century Fox as "Romeo and Juliet on the Titanic." So, he began with divers finding remains of the 1912 ship. An old lady was invited to discuss their work as the bearer of the theme of the movie: Bonding can be so strong that it lasts even after death.

Then he began to write a story to tie fictional dialogue to real characters who either died or survived. For his main survivor who explained to divers what she knew so many years earlier, he wanted an actress from olden days. After considering Fay Wray and Gloria Stuart, he chose the latter. She began in silent movies and went on to talkies in *The Old Dark House* (1932), *Here Comes the Navy* (1934), *Gold Diggers of 1935, The Three Musketeers* (1939), etc. She became the narrator for the movie.

After considering many, Cameron chose Leonardo DiCaprio and Kate Winslet to be the couple who would fall in love and Kate was a survivor played by Gloria Stuart in old age. In a sentimental mood after watching *A Night to Remember* (1958), Cameron chose Bernard Fox to portray survivor Colonel Archibald Gracie. In the 1958 movie, Fox was the actor who said, "Iceberg dead ahead, sir."

Cameron created an incident where DiCaprio and Winslet met just as she tried to kill herself rather than marry somebody whose money would help her family. Despite his lower class in rooms below sea level, their love bloomed. The iceberg caused the ship to go under with 1,500 killed within an hour or so. The dramatic scenery required millions of dollars to provide a correct version of the ship's collapse and people dying or clinging to the few boats.

He added a famous jewel around the neck of the surviving heroine who was drawn in the nude by lover, which was finally cast in the sea by Rose, the aged Gloria Stuart character. The portrait and jewel made the connection between the young girl and the old lady.

Cameron also liked the 1958 portrayal of the ship musicians who played "Nearer My God, to Thee" and enhanced that scene. Cameron, an exacting writer, director, and producer described his work. "If you're smart and you take the ego and the narcissism out of it, you'll listen to the film, and the film will tell you what it needs and what it does not need."

James Horner composed much of the music with the theme song "My Heart Will Go On" sung be Céline Dion. Other music included Irving Berlin's "Alexander's Ragtime Band," Charles Gounod's "Margarite Waltz," Franz von Suppé's "Poet and Peasant," Pyotr Tchaikovsky's "Song without Words," Johann Strauss II's "Blue Danube," and Jacque Offenbach's "Barcarole" and "Orpheus."

Some of the dialogue in the movie illustrated the events. When the DiCaprio character found love with Winslet, on the bow of the ship with arms outstretched he hollered "I'm the king of the world!" When Rose (Winslet) saw the ship architect, she said, "I saw the iceberg and I see it in your eyes… please, tell me the truth." He replied, "The ship will sink…Yes, in an hour or so, all of this will be at the bottom of the Atlantic." DiCaprio told his beloved as they held onto a floating door after leaving the ship, "I don't know about you, but I intend to write a strongly worded letter to the White Star Line about all of this."

Certain passengers were depicted, such as the John Jacob Astor and the "unsinkable Molly Brown," played by Kathy Bates.

This 194-minute movie was the most expensive movie ever made up to that time. The budget was $200 million but the amazing box office was $2.195 billion and more when other countries showed it.

Other movie nominees included *As Good as It Gets, The Full Monty, Good Will Hunting,* and *L.A. Confidential.*

Jack Nicholson won Best Actor for *As Good as It Gets.* Other contenders were Matt Damon *(Good Will Hunting),* Robert Duvall *(The Apostle),* Peter Fonda *(Ulee's Gold),* and Dustin Hoffman *(Wag the Dog).*

Helen Hunt (1963- ?) from Culver City, California, won Best Actress for *As Good as It Gets.* Other contenders were Helen Bonham Carter *(The Wings of the Dove),* Julie Christie *(Afterglow),* Judi Dench *(Mrs. Brown),* and Kate Winslet *(Titanic).*

Kim Basinger won Best Supporting Actress for *L.A. Confidential.*

Robin Williams won Best Supporting Actor for *Good Will Hunting.*

Best Song "My Heart Will Go On," w. Will Jennings, m. James Horner, from *Titanic.*

James Cameron, Director of *Titanic.*

Best Foreign Language Film: *Character,* director Mike van Diem, Netherlands, Dutch. In the 1920s in the Netherlands, Jacob finished law school and argued with a court enforcement officer. He left covered in blood and was arrested the next day. He told police about his life, being bullied at school, and how he stole bread with some boys. When arrested, he called his father, but the man said he did not know the boy. Backtracking, the audience saw that the boy learned to read, became a lawyer, fell in love with a secretary, and in a confusing ending, was found not guilty and was left great wealth. Character appeared to be the key factor in the outcome.

British BAFTA awards: Best Film: *The Full Monty*. **Best Actor:** Robert Carlyle in *The Full Monty*. **Best Actress:** Judi Dench in *Mrs. Brown*. **Best Supporting Actor:** Tim Wilkerson in *The Full Monty*. **Best Supporting Actress:** Sigourney Weaver in *The Ice Storm*. **Outstanding British Film:** *Nil by Mouth,* director Gary Oldman, producers Luc Besson, Gary Oldman, and Douglas Urbanski, starring Ray Winstone and Kathy Burke.

71st Academy Awards

Ceremony: This event was conducted on March 21, 1999, at the Dorothy Chandler Pavilion in Los Angeles, California, hosted by Whoopi Goldberg. It was televised by ABC, lasted four hours and two minutes, and was viewed by 45.1 million viewers. Frank Sinatra had died at the age of 82 on May 14, 1998. When he died, the Empire State building turned its lights blue, the Las Vegas Strip dimmed, and casinos stopped for one minute.

Val Kilmer, who grew up on a dude ranch (Kay El Bar Ranch) in Wickenburg, Arizona, where his mother was part-owner, appeared with a horse onstage. He then did a tribute for cowboy stars who died in 1998—Gene Autry and Roy Rogers.

The Irving G. Thalberg Memorial Award went to Norman Jewison. He had done 26 films, won 12 Oscars, had 41 nominations, and had founded the Canadian Film Institute. Norman came out dancing to *Fiddler on the Roof*, which he produced, and said "Not bad for a goy!" He had done pictures like *In the Heat of the Night, Jesus Christ Superstar, The Russians Are Coming The Russians Are Coming, Moonstruck,* etc. He was glad to be included with all the other greats who had received this award.

An honorary Academy Award went to Elia Kazan, who had written, directed, and produced gems like *Gentlemen's Agreement, Pinky, Streetcar Named Desire, Viva Zapata, On the Waterfront, East of Eden, Splendor in the Grass, The Last Tycoon,* etc. He came out, aged 90, thanked everybody, and said, "I think I can just slip away."

Life Is Beautiful was the second film nominated for Best Picture and Best Foreign Language Film in the same year, the first being *Z* in 1969. Best Actor Roberto Benigni was director for *Life Is Beautiful and* acted in it. That had only been done before by Laurence Olivier in *Hamlet.*

The tribute to those who died in the last year included Dane Clark, Norman Fell, E. G. Marshall, Jerome Robbins, Susan Strasberg, John Derek, Richard Kiley, Maureen O'Sullivan, Gene Raymond, Binnie Barnes, Valerie Hobson, Huntz Hall, Akira Kurosawa, Robert Young, and Roddy McDowall.

1998 *Shakespeare in Love*

Tagline: "A comedy about the greatest love story almost never told." This romantic comedy starred Gwyneth Paltrow, Joseph Fiennes, Geoffrey Rush, Colin Firth, Ben Affleck, and Judi Dench. The fictional story involved Shakespeare, who had a writer's block and sought advice from rival Christopher Marlowe. Meanwhile, the daughter of a wealthy merchant disguised herself as a man to get closer to Shakespeare, but when they began to talk, she ran away. Her parents arranged a betrothal for her (Viola), but when Shakespeare saw her on a balcony, he was attracted and transformed this into *Romeo and Juliet.*

Marlowe was murdered, and Viola feared that Shakespeare was also murdered. The Queen sent Viola to the Colony of Virginia, and as the two lovers bid adieu, he promised to immortalize her in a play. Shakespeare told Viola, "You will never age for me, nor fade, nor die." The music by English film and TV composer Stephen Warbeck was so suitable that many carried on about its perfection for this thought-to-be old-fashioned movie.

The 123-minute movie had a budget of $25 million and did a box office of $289.3 million. It came out when sexual abuse allegations were being pursued against producer Harvey Weinstein. Many cast and crew members distanced themselves and talked little about the film.

Other movie nominees include *Elizabeth, Life is Beautiful, Saving Private Ryan,* and *The Thin Red Line.*

Roberto Benigni (1952-?) from Manciano, Italy, won Best Actor for *Life is Beautiful.* Other contenders were Tom Hanks *(Saving Private Ryan),* Ian McKellen *(Gods and Monsters),* Nick Nolte *(Affliction),* and Edward Norton *(American History X).*

Gwyneth Paltrow (1972- ?) from Los Angeles won Best Actress for *Shakespeare in Love.* Other contenders were Cate Blanchett *(Elizabeth),* Fernanda Montenegro *(Central Station),* Meryl Streep *(One True Thing),* and Emily Watson *(Hilary and Jackie).*

Judi Dench won Best Supporting Actress for *Shakespeare in Love.*

James Coburn won Best Supporting Actor for *Affliction.*

Best Song "When You Believe," w. m. Stephen Schwartz, from *The Prince of Egypt.*

Steven Spielberg, Director of *Saving Private Ryan.*

Best Foreign Language Film: *Life Is Beautiful,* director Roberto Benigni, Italy, Italian/German. This movie idea came to Roberto Benigni, director, writer, and star from two sources. His father spent two years in a World War II German labor camp, and he read *In the End, I Beat Hitler* by Rubino Romeo Salmoni. The story involved a Jewish bookstore owner who married and had a son. In 1944, the family was seized by Nazis and the wife was separated from her husband and son. Her husband tried to make the boy believe everything was a game and if he followed his papa's orders, he would win an army tank. The boy was not to cry, say he's hungry, or complain that he wanted his mother, and he was to hide at some times.

Just as American allies came to the camp, his father told him to stay in a box to win the tank. The Germans killed his father before fleeing, and the boy emerged and rode on an American tank, which he thought he won. He was reunited with his mother. The story moved from comedy to terror with poignancy and love. The message was to stay positive in the face of hardships. The score was composed by Nicola Piovani. The classical "Barcarolle" by Jacques Offenbach was heard as the man wooed his future wife and again as he got onto a prison camp phonograph and played it loudly for his wife as memories of their love.

British BAFTA awards: Best Film: *Shakespeare in Love*. **Best Actor:** Roberto Benigni in *Life Is Beautiful*. **Best Actress:** Cate Blanchett in *Elizabeth*. **Best Supporting Actor:** Geoffrey Rush in *Shakespeare in Love*. **Best Supporting Actress:** Judi Dench in *Shakespeare in Love*. **Outstanding British Film:** *Elizabeth,* director Shekhar Kapur, producers Allson Owen, Eric Fellner, and Tim Beven, starring Cate Blanchett, Geoffrey Rush, John Gielgud, and Richard Attenborough.

72nd Academy Awards

Ceremony: This event was conducted on March 26, 2000, at the Shrine Auditorium in Los Angeles, California, hosted by Billy Crystal. It was on ABC TV for four hours and nine minutes to 46.52 million viewers, a 3 percent increase from the preceding year and an increase in people under age 50.

Best Actress Oscar went to Hilary Swank for *Boys Don't Cry*. She said, "We've come a long way. We couldn't have done this movie three years ago... No one got paid. I dedicate this to Brandon Teena, who inspired us to be ourselves. I look forward to the day when we can celebrate diversity."

Polish director Andrzej Awjda received an honorary award for his trilogy and other movies delivering lessons to young people after the Communist takeover when World War II subsided. Also, the award for Best Foreign Film was made by Antonio Banderas and Penelope Cruz. She had starred in that movie, *All About My Mother,* produced by Pedro Almodovar from Spain.

The Irving G. Thalberg Memorial Award went to actor, director, screenwriter, producer Warren Beatty for his many movies about people taking chances to better their lives. He thanked his parents, wife, and teachers, such as Stella Adler, Elia Kazan, and Sam Goldwyn.

The tribute to those who died during the last year included Sylvia Sidney, Jim Varney, Ernest Gold, Ruth Roman, Henry Jones, Mario Puzo, Rory Calhoun, Hedy Lamarr, Victor Mature, Garson Kanin,

Roger Vadim, Oliver Reed, Ian Bannen, Dirk Bogarde, Lila Kedrova, Charles "Buddy" Rogers, Madeline Kahn, and George C. Scott.

This was an unusual year of movies involved with sexual problems. The Best Movie, *American Beauty*, was about a middle-aged man who fantasized about sex with a girl his daughter's age. The Best Actor, Kevin Spacey, played a man who wanted to be young again and have sex with a daughter-like figure. The Best Actress played a real girl who wanted to be a boy and was raped and murdered for that transgender wish. The Best Supporting Actor played a doctor in a home where abortion and incest were common problems. The Best Supporting Actress played a mental patient committed to a mental institution after attempting suicide following an affair with a friend of her mother. The Best Foreign Film was about people who would today be involved with the LGBT (lesbian, gay, bisexual, and transgender) community. That movie also dealt with various medical problems, such as AIDS and donor organs.

1999 American Beauty

Tagline: "Look closer." Alan Ball was inspired by the publicity of the Amy Fisher trial to write this story. Amy was 16 when she had sex with an older married man, and she went to the man's home and shot his wife. She desired publicity for what, she said, had been done to her. After her prison time, she sought publicity again. Ball wrote about a middle-aged husband (Kevin Spacey) married to a materialistic wife (Annette Bening), who suddenly quit his dull job. His teenage daughter (Thora Birch) had a girlfriend (Mena Suvari) whom he fantasized about, picturing her in a bath with rose petals. He got a job in a fast-food diner and began buying marijuana from the next-door neighbor's son.

When that neighbor (Chris Cooper) saw his son accept money from the Spacey character, he assumed it was for sex. That riled the ex-Marine, who had fought off homosexuality but had made a slight sexual pass at the Spacey character himself. The Bening character was having an affair and their home life was askew. When she caught her husband masturbating, it seemed to him like a mother scolding a son and he began to regard her as motherly.

Spacey learned from a conversation between his daughter and her girlfriend that he might look more attractive if he were more fit, so he began to work out (Spacey really did begin to work on his own body during the making of the movie).

In a scene that required permission from the parents of young Suvari, he was finally about to have sex with the young girl. The vulnerable girl lacked self-confidence and tried to use her looks to make someone like her. When she admitted that this was her first time to have sex, everything changed. Ball wrote this scene so that the older man did not take advantage of the girl. Suddenly, the Spacey character became fatherly and helped the girl build up her waning self-confidence. However, the neighbor, wrestling with worries that his son was having sex with Spacey and having his own battles with sexuality, shot the Spacey character just as he was feeling redeemed.

The focus in the movie was on appearances and beauty in a materialistic society, and how it monopolized fantasies. One line is: "Sometimes there's so much beauty in the world, I feel like I can't take it and my heart is just going to cave in." The movie is told, like *Sunset Boulevard*, by a dead man.

Only the music and the cinematography with red in many scenes resolving toward rain and gray near the end hinted that all would not be well. Much pulsing energy by percussion instruments excited all. It was like Spacey wanting to be young again. The soundtrack included songs by Thomas Newman, Bobby Darin, The Who, Free, Eels, The Guess Who, Bill Withers, Betty Carter, Peggy Lee, The Folk Implosion,

Gomez, Bob Dylan, Beatles, and Neil Young's "Don't Let It Bring You Down".

The 122-minute movie was mainly shot in Sacramento and Torrance, California. The $15 million budget made low payouts for some major actors but surprisingly brought in $356.3 million.

Until the last scene, such as in *Casablanca,* the audience is uncertain whether the more emotional male will be a restrained hero or will allow lust to rule his life.

Other movie nominees included *The Cider House Rules, The Green Mile, The Insider,* and *The Sixth Sense.*

Kevin Spacey (1959- ?) from South Orange, New Jersey, won Best Actor for *American Beauty.* Other contenders were Russell Crowe *(The Insider),* Richard Farnsworth *(The Straight Story),* Sean Penn *(Sweet and Lowdown),* and Denzel Washington *(The Hurricane).*

Hillary Swank (1974-?) from Lincoln, Nebraska, won Best Actress for *Boys Don't Cry.* Other contenders were Annette Bening *(American Beauty),* Janet McTeer *(Tumbleweeds),* Julianne Moore *(The End of the Affair),* and Meryl Streep *(Music of the Heart).*

Angelina Jolie won Best Supporting Actress for *Girl, Interrupted.*

Michael Caine won Best Supporting Actor for *The Cider House Rules.*

Best Song "You'll Be in My Heart," w. m. Phil Collins, from *Tarzan.*

Sam Mendes, Director of *American Beauty.*

Best Foreign Language Film: *All About My Mother,* director Pedro Almodovar, Spain, Spanish. This unusual movie dealt with faith, homosexuals, people who have AIDS, and a young man whose mother deals with donor organ transplants at a hospital. There is a complicated storyline and the movie was shot in the unique city of Barcelona, Spain. Using a smart script and references to American movies, it does not become depressing because it focuses on resilience and good humor. It evokes empathy for people in difficult circumstances despite their life choices.

British BAFTA awards: Best Film: *American Beauty.* **Best Actor:** Kevin Spacey in *American Beauty.* **Best Actress:** Annette Bening in *American Beauty.* **Best Supporting Actor:** Jude Law in *The Talented Mr. Ripley.* **Best Supporting Actress:** Maggie Smith in *Tea with Mussolini.* **Outstanding British Film:** *East Is East,* director Damien O'Donnell, producer Leslee Udwin.

73rd Academy Awards

Ceremony: This event was conducted on March 25, 2001, at the Shrine Auditorium in Los Angeles, California, hosted by Steve Martin. It was televised by ABC for three hours and twenty-three minutes, received by 42.9 million people, which was 7 percent less than the previous year.

To celebrate the science fiction film *2001: A Space Odyssey*, the astronauts in the International Space Station appeared at the beginning of the telecast by satellite to introduce host Martin. The orchestra performed versions of "Also Sprach Zarathustra" from the movie, and 83-year-old science fiction writer Arthur C. Clarke presented the Best Adapted Screenplay from his home in Sri Lanka. The stage was designed to resemble a space capsule.

Jack Cardiff, age 87, received the first ever cinematography award. He had begun as an actor in silent films, became a cinematographer, and eventually a director. Cardiff said this was a dream come true. An honorary award went to 84-year-old Ernest Lehman, screenwriter, for so many hits. The Irving G. Thalberg Memorial Award went to 81-year-old Dino De Laurentis, Italian film producer, who hoped that young Italians would keep up the industry in Italy with their works.

The tribute to those who died in the last year included Douglas Fairbanks Jr., Marie Windsor, Julius Epstein, George Montgomery, Ring Lardner Jr., Steve Reeves, Jean Peters, Vittorio Gassman, Jean-Pierre Aumont, Dale Evans, Gwen Verdon, Stanley Kramer, Harold Nicholas, Howard W. Koch, Loretta Young, Richard Farnsworth, John Gielgud, Jason Robards Jr., Claire Trevor, Alec Guinness, and Walter Matthau.

2000 *Gladiator*

Tagline: "A gladiator defied an emperor." The movie was inspired by Daniel Mannix's 1958 book entitled *Those About to Die*. Ridley Scot was approached by producers who showed him a copy of an 1872 painting by Jean-Leon Gerome entitled "Thumbs Down." Ridley was then absorbed with making a more accurate depiction of the life of gladiators than had been shown in earlier movies. A main gladiator character was created, and some characters were drawn from historical texts for the year of A.D. 180. A crew was hired consisting of Russell Crowe, Joaquin Phoenix, Oliver Reed, Richard Harris, and Djimon Hounsou. The latter actor is from Benin, a French-speaking West African nation, and former Dahomey Kingdom.

The film was made in Morocco and Malta and a half-size colosseum was built. Some 2,000 people were hired to be viewed as if they were many thousands involved in fights between gladiators and some animals.

The story involved a beloved Roman general Maximus and the famous Marcus Aurelius near the end of his life. He chose Maximus (Crowe) over his son Commodus (Phoenix) to rule. However, the son learned of this and planned to kill Maximus and his family. Maximus survived but arrived too late to save his family. He became a captive and was put into gladiator games with people trained to fight and die. He spent years trying to rise to the top so he could exact revenge upon Commodus. The gladiators were trained by Proximus (Reed) to please the crowd so that Commodus might allow them to live with a thumbs up signal.

Maximus worked with the other gladiators to unite them and fight together to overcome their lot in life. As he slew animals and men, he became a hero to the Romans. Commodus decided to regain his own popularity by personally fighting the famed gladiator, but secretly wounded him in the back before the fight so that he was slowly bleeding to death. He died and was buried nobly after killing Commodus, so the gladiators were freed. One line about the gladiators was: "What we do in life echoes in eternity."

Midway through filming the movie in Malta, Oliver Reed died. He earlier had a bar brawl and a bad cut requiring 36 stitches, so was a known risk. But he had been well received in *Oliver!* playing Bill Sykes. However, he promised Ridley Scott not to drink on the set nor on weekdays. Sunday morning, May 2, 1999, he went into The Pub, began to drink, and challenged arriving sailors to drink and arm-wrestle him. After some hours of this, he fell to the floor saying, "I need your help," and died. His body was flown to Ireland for burial. His role in *Gladiator* was filled by using shots of his face and digital reconstruction of his body, altogether costing an extra $3 million. The pub where he died was renamed Ollie's Last Pub. In the script, he was supposed to live but in view of his death, his character was allowed to die.

German composer Hans Zimmer liked women singing and rhythmic battle songs for movies like *Gladiator*. Sometimes, he picked Wagnerian themes and major opera singers for mighty battles. He did not name some sources, but the music was extremely suited to the story depicted in this movie. He influenced many other movie composers who did make similar choices.

The 155-minute movie budget was $103 million but the movie made nearly four times the budget at the box office.

Other movie nominees included *Chocolat; Crouching Tiger, Hidden Dragon; Erin Brockovich;* and *Traffic*.

Russell Crowe (1964- ?) from Wellington, New Zealand, won Best Actor for *Gladiator*. Other contenders were Javier Bardem *(Before Night Falls)*, Tom Hanks *(Cast Away)*, Ed Harris *(Pollock)*, and Geoffrey Rush *(Quills)*.

Julia Roberts (1967- ?) from Smyrna, Georgia, won Best Actress for *Erin Brockovich*. Other contenders were Joan Allen *(The Contender)*, Juliette Binoche *(Chocolat)*, Ellen Burstyn *(Requiem for a Dream)*, and Laura Linney *(You Can Count on Me)*.

Marcia Gay Harden won Best Supporting Actress for *Pollock*.

Benicio del Toro won Best Supporting Actor for *Traffic*.

Best Song "Things Have Changed," w. m. Bob Dylan, from *Wonder Boys*.

Steven Soderbergh, Director of *Traffic*.

Best Foreign Language Film: *Crouching Tiger, Hidden Dragon,* Ang Lee, Taiwan, Mandarin. This movie was directed and produced by Ang Lee and was filmed in Mandarin Chinese. The title came from an old Chinese idiom describing a situation that is full of unnoticed special people. The movie was set in 19th century China toward the end of the Qing dynasty. There was a famous swordsman who called his 400-year-old sword Green Destiny. He trusted an extraordinary female warrior and asked her to take his sword to Governor Yu. Once there, a daring masked thief stole it. As the burglar was tracked and found to be a woman, many things arose, such as various loves, passions, poisons, a search for freedom, and extraordinary martial arts skills practiced by many characters. The music featured ancient Chinese instruments playing Chinese opera music, Japanese kabuki music, and famous cellist Yo-Yo Ma.

British BAFTA awards: Best Film: *Gladiator*. **Best Actor:** Jamie Bell in *Billy Elliot*. **Best Actress:** Julia Roberts in *Erin Brockovich*. **Best Supporting Actor:** Benicio del Toro in *Traffic*. **Best Supporting Actress:** Julie Walter in *Billy Elliot*. **Outstanding British Film:** *Billy Elliot*. director Stephen Daldry, producers Greg Brenman and Jon Finn, starring Gary Lewis, Jamie Draven, and Jamie Bell.

74th Academy Awards

Ceremony: This event was conducted at the Kodak Theatre in Hollywood, California, on March 24, 2002, hosted by Whoopi Goldberg. ABC aired it for four hours and twenty-three minutes to 41.82 million viewers. That was 3 percent less than the previous year. The September 11, 2001, attacks on the New York World Trade Centers caused some to consider cancelling festivities but the Academy decided that would signal to all that "the terrorists have won."

Tom Cruise opened the show with a montage of movie memories and salute to besieged New York led by Woody Allen and Nora Ephron. Cruise said, "Now, more than ever, if we break through some line or learn something that makes us a little bit better, we should celebrate it."

A new category, making 24, was added to honor animated movies of at least seventy minutes in length. Before this category, three Disney films, 1937 *Snow White and the Seven Dwarfs*, 1988 *Who Framed Roger Rabbit*, and 1995 *Toy Story*, were given Special Achievement Academy Awards.

A tribute to Sidney Poitier, Best Actor Award to Denzel Washington and Halle Berry (first African American to win Best Actress) was historic for racial recognition. Poitier said he arrived in Hollywood at 22 and saw that there were few ways to get recognition. He thanked filmmakers for taking chances and thought African Americans and all Americans benefitted from their daring choices. He accepted the honorary Oscar for all African American actors and actresses who came before him. Denzel Washington said, "God is good, God is great. There is nothing I'd rather do, Sidney, than chase you. I try to be the best that I can be." Halle Berry cried and said, "This is so much bigger than me." She named earlier African American movie stars and thanked her mother and husband and director. Music crowded to rush her, but she said, "After 74 years [of Academy Awards] I've got to take the time to thank more." And included Oprah Winfrey as a role model and Warren Beatty.

The Jean Hersholt Humanitarian Award was presented to Arthur Hiller who created 45 or more charity organizations. He said, "It is embarrassing to receive an award for something you should be doing, which I learned from my parents." Robert Redford received an honorary award for his lifetime filming and directing and setting up the Sundance Institute for new artists. He reflected on those before him and thanked those who supported him in times of need.

The Best Picture Oscar went to Ron Howard and Brian Grazer for *A Beautiful Mind*. Grazer thanked Russell Crowe for his profound dedication, Horner for his haunting score, and hoped the movie would help us treat mentally ill people better. Dr. John Nash and wife Alicia were present when the ceremony took place. Sadly, he and wife Alicia died in a taxi accident May 23, 2015, upon his return from Norway for the Abel Prize, which he earned in addition to the Nobel Prize for game theory, geometry, and differential equations.

The memorial tribute to those who died in the past year included Jack Lemmon, Nigel Hawthorne, Beatrice Straight, Eileen Heckart, Ann Southern, Harold Russell, Kim Stanley, William Hanna, Chuck Jones, Carroll O'Connor, George Harrison, and Anthony Quinn. Then a moment of silence was requested for the victims of the September 11 attacks.

2001 *A Beautiful Mind*

Tagline: "He saw the world in a way no one could have imagined." This movie was inspired by the Pulitzer Prize-nominated 1997 book of the same title by Sylvia Nasar. This German-born journalist did a story of the famous mathematician, John Nash, and his mental illness. Tom Cruise was considered for the lead role, but director Ron Howard chose Russell Crowe, who doggedly tried to get his portrayal right. His wife was played by Jennifer Connelly, but the math scientist's real wife was from El Salvador.

It was difficult for film makers to demonstrate his problems. He did not see things as some paranoid schizophrenics do, but he heard voices, and some were critical. The creative version of schizophrenia in the movie has imaginary figures but his feelings of persecution were not quite as depicted. He became well enough to teach and work later, and finally decided not to take psychotropic medicines or any more insulin therapy shock treatments.

"Perhaps it is good to have a beautiful mind. But an even greater gift is to discover a beautiful heart." This movie quotation indicated how the mathematician's intentions were to help others. James Horner developed a music score that featured a young girl's voice and shadowed Nash's quick-moving mind with beautiful sound patterns that could help him be understood. Since it is very difficult to show the disease of schizophrenia, director Howard worked with music director and composer James Horner to help communicate for Nash in the movie. After the first screening of the movie, Howard and Horner talked about how to depict the ever-changing character. Horner chose a Welsh singer to sing soprano vocals to attain a balance between a child and an adult voice. He wanted to show the humanity of the voice through pure, bright voice and instruments.

Since some mathematicians describe their sudden ideas as "flashes of light," cinematographers used a flash of light appearing over an object or person to show Nash's mind and creativity. In addition, much of the work was filmed at Princeton University, Fairleigh Dickinson University, Vanderbilt University, and Manhattan College. When sick,

Nash thought he was to decode enemy communications and imagined that he was working for the U.S. Department of Defense. The problems for a spouse and the children of schizophrenics are numerous and long-lasting, which was hard to display.

Just as paranoid people often believe they are more important than others, the characters depicted as imagined U.S. agents or family members made the patient feel that he was being studied, copied, spied upon, and cared about. Those fantasies of importance and brilliance are part of what propelled him to achieve breakthroughs and solve problems.

The 135-minute film budget was $58 million, and the box office was six times that amount.

Other movie nominees included *Gosford Park, In the Bedroom, The Lord of the Rings: The Fellowship of the Ring,* and *Moulin Rouge!*

Denzel Washington (1954-?) from Mt. Vernon, New York, won Best Actor for *Training Day.* Other contenders were Russell Crowe *(A Beautiful Mind),* Sean Penn *(I Am Sam),* Will Smith *(Ali),* and Tom Wilkinson *(In the Bedroom).*

Halle Berry (1966-?) from Cleveland, Ohio, won Best Actress for *Monster's Ball.* Other contenders were Judy Dench *(Iris),* Nicole Kidman *(Monster's Ball),* Sissy Spacek *(In the Bedroom),* and Renee Zellweger *(Bridget Jones's Diary).*

Jennifer Connelly won Best Supporting Actress for *A Beautiful Mind.*

Jim Broadbent won Best Supporting Actor for *Iris.*

Best Song "If I Didn't Have You," w. m. Randy Newman, from *Monsters, Inc.*

Ron Howard, Director of *A Beautiful Mind.*

Best Foreign Language Film: *No Man's Land,* director Danis Tanovic, Bosnia and Herzegovina, Bosnian/French/English. This movie was made in a co-production between Bosnia, Herzegovina, Slovenia, Italy, France, Belgium, and the United Kingdom. The stars are probably not recognizable, but their actions are incredibly tense and well-done, making the 98-minute movie spellbinding to watch.

Three soldiers wound up in a trench together as day turned to night. The Bosniak (Ciki) and the Bosnean Serv (Nino) were wounded and struggled to survive by trading insults with each other. Meanwhile, a wounded Bosniak soldier (Cera) awoke, and all realized he was on a land mine, which would explode if he moved. An English reporter arrived and tried to bring help from the United Nations commanders to save the three. Once Ciki and Nino were rescued, their anger escalated and Ciki shot Nino, who was then shot by a peacekeeper. The land mine could not be defused so the authorities lied to reporters saying that Cera was saved. He was left alone in the trench and authorities passed information to troops on both sides making them believe that their enemies would use artillery barrages, a subterfuge to cover the explosion which would kill Cera and obliterate the evidence. The result was the well-known phrase, "War is hell!"

British BAFTA awards: Best Film: *The Lord of the Rings: The Fellowship of the Ring*. **Best Actor:** Russell Crowe in *A Beautiful Mind*. **Best Actress:** Judi Dench in *Iris*. **Best Supporting Actor:** Jim Broadbent in *Moulin Rouge*. **Best Supporting Actress:** Jennifer Connelly in *A Beautiful Mind*. **Outstanding British Film:** *Gosford Park,* director Robert Altman, producers Bob Balaban and David Levy, starring Maggie Smith, Michael Gambon, and Kristin Scott Thomas.

75th Academy Awards

Ceremony: This event was conducted on March 23, 2003, at the Kodak Theatre in Hollywood, California, hosted by Steve Martin. ABC televised it for three hours and thirty minutes seen by 33.04 million. It had a 21 percent decrease from the previous year and was the lowest viewing for Academy Awards since television statistics began. People apparently watched other stations because the invasion of Iraq was more important than seeing celebrities celebrate themselves.

Some Oscar winners commented about the war, such as Adrien Brody for *The Pianist,* who expressed the wish for American soldiers to return home. Roman Polanski won Best Director for *The Pianist* but could not travel to the U.S. because of an arrest warrant for statutory rape. A very pregnant Catherine Zeta-Jones came to receive her Best Supporting Actress award for *Chicago.* She had been pregnant during part of the filming for that movie.

Peter O'Toole received an honorary award for his 40 years in movies, seven acting nominations, and his movie about *Lawrence of Arabia.* O'Toole told a standing ovation, "Always a bridesmaid, never a bride, but now I have my very own 'til death do us part."

Olivia de Havilland announced celebration of the 75th anniversary of awards with 59 actors who had received awards seated onstage. She spoke of Louise Rainier as the oldest (age 92). Olivia herself was the oldest living Oscar recipient until her death at 104 years of age on July 26, 2020.

The tribute to those who died during the last year included Eddie Bracken, Katy Jurado, Dudley Moore, Rod Steiger, Horst Buchholz, Leo McKern, Milton Berle, Signe Hasso, Richard Crenna, Rosemary Clooney, Kim Hunter, Adolph Green, Alberto Sordi, Marvin Mirisch, James Coburn, and Billy Wilder.

2002 *Chicago*

Tagline: "With the right song and dance, you can get away with murder." This story was based on a 1926 Broadway play about two actual Jazz-era females who murdered men. The next version was a 1975 Broadway musical that audiences found rather cynical but Bob Fosse, a choreographer with many musicals under his belt, inserted his style of dancing. Some of that was in a 1996 revival that held records for the longest-running musical on Broadway due to Fosse's influence. The film credits acknowledged Fosse, who died in 1987.

This movie starred Renee Zellweger, Catherine Zeta-Jones, Richard Gere, Queen Latifah, and John C. Reilly as well as a great supporting cast. From the opening scene, the movie popped with sights, dancing, songs, and sounds that had some audiences wanting to dance in the aisles. One popular song line was, "You can like the life you're living. You can live the life you like." Another quote was, "No, I'm no one's wife, but oh, I love my life and all that jazz."

Songs told the story of wife (Zellweger) who shot her lover but got her husband (Reilly) to take the blame. Later she said she was pregnant (but her husband couldn't calculate that impossibility). The other woman (Zeta-Jones) shot her husband when he was having sex with her sister. The murderesses vied for a lawyer (Gere) to get them off for their crimes. Meanwhile, their corrupt prison matron (Latifah) wanted pay for her efforts to help the girls. Later, when exonerated, the two began their own musical show together.

Some snappy song titles gave more clues to the movie: "All That Jazz," "Funny Honey," "When You're Good to Mama," "Cell Block Tango," "All I Care About," "We Both Reached for the Gun," "Roxie," "I Can't Do It Alone," "Mister Cellophane," "Razzle Dazzle," etc. Rob Marshall choreographed the film and Bill Condon adapted the screenplay. One star from the 1975 Chicago musical was Chita Rivera, who originated the role played by Zeta-Jones, and she played Nicky, a prostitute in a cameo role in this movie. Many, like Richard Gere, had to learn to tap dance or dance and sing.

Each murder suspect had a word in the songs: "Pop! Six! Squish! Uh-uh! Cicero! Lipschitz!" The first woman killed her husband because of his bubble gum popping habit. The second woman killed her Mormon husband once he took his sixth wife. The third woman's husband accused her of an affair with the milkman and he ran squish into her knife ten times. The fourth woman was Hungarian whose only word in English when charged was uh-uh, so she was hanged. The fifth woman killed her husband when she found him doing acrobatics with her sister in Cicero, Illinois. The sixth woman, Mona Lipschitz, killed her husband when she found out he cheated on her with several women and one man.

The songs by John Kander and lyrics by Fred Ebb matched the masterful screenwriting and choreography for a witty portrayal that made audiences want to see the movie repeatedly. The movie's success spurred development of more musicals, such as *Beauty and the Beast, Mamma Mia: Here We Go Again, The Lion King, La La Land, Bohemian Rhapsody,* and many others.

The 113-minute movie was shot in Toronto, Ontario, Canada at the Osgoode Hall, Queen's Park, a former distillery, Elgin Theater, Union Station, Canada Life Building, Danforth Music Hall, and Old City Hall. The budget was $45 million, and the box office was some six times that amount.

Other movie nominees included *Gangs of New York, The Hours, The Lord of the Rings: The Two Towers,* and *The Pianist.*

Adrien Brody (1973-?) from New York, New York, won Best Actor for *The Pianist.* Other contenders were Nicolas Cage *(Adaptation),* Michael Caine *(The Quiet American),* Daniel Day-Lewis *(Gangs of New York),* and Jack Nicholson *(About Schmidt).*

Nicole Kidman (1967-?) from Honolulu, Hawaii, won Best Actress for *The Hours.* Other contenders were Salma Hayek *(Frida),* Diane Lane *(Unfaithful),* Julianne Moore *(Far from Heaven),* and Renee Zellweger *(Chicago).*

Catherine Zeta-Jones won Best Supporting Actress for *Chicago.*

Chris Cooper won Best Supporting Actor for *Adaptation.*

Best Song "Lose Yourself," w. Eminem, m. Jeff Bass, Eminem, and Luis Resto, from *8 Mile.*

Roman Polanski, Director of *The Pianist.*

Best Foreign Language Film: *Nowhere in Africa,* director Caroline Link, Germany/English/Swahili. This unusual movie was based on the autobiography of Stefanie Zweig. She described the life of her German Jewish family who fled persecution in Germany by moving to Kenya. Her father, a former lawyer, changed life to become a farmer. Her mother was used to big city life but slowly adapted to changes with a possible lover. The daughter learned the new language and adapted easily. However, as time passed the marriage crumbled, both parents blamed each other and began moving in different directions.

In a stunning move, the parents were imprisoned by the British as aliens and alienations grew. When released, the father joined the British Army, but later applied to Germany and was accepted as a judge. Ready to leave, his wife and daughter were not. A locust invasion reunited the family to stave off crop failures. The mother became pregnant again by her husband and the narration as the daughter told the story implied that her family prevailed.

The 141-minute movie has received excellent reviews from Americans and is the first German Academy Award for Best Foreign Language film.

British BAFTA awards: Best Film: *The Pianist*. **Best Actor:** Daniel Day-Lewis in *Gangs of New York*. **Best Actress:** Nicole Kidman in *The Hours*. **Best Supporting Actor:** Christopher Walken in *Catch Me If You Can*. **Best Supporting Actress:** Catherine Zeta-Jones in *Chicago*. **Outstanding British Film:** *The Warrior*, director Asif Kapadia, producer Bertrand Falvre, starring Irrfan Khan, Puru Chibber, and Aino Annuddin.

76th Academy Awards

Ceremony: This event took place on February 29, 2004, at the Kodak Theatre in Hollywood, California, hosted by Billy Crystal. ABC broadcast the ceremony for three hours and forty-five minutes to 43.56 million people—a 26 percent increase from the previous year. Sofia Coppola was awarded Best Director, becoming the first American woman and the third woman to be nominated in that category. Her grandfather, Carmine Coppola, and her father, Francis Ford Coppola, had won Oscars making her a three-generation winner. The only other three-generation family to win Oscars were Walter, John, and Angelica Huston.

Former Oscar host Bob Hope stood up in the audience and waved to all. Actress Katherine Hepburn, who died at age 96 on June 29, 2003, having won a record four Oscars for Best Actress, was honored. Blake Edwards gained an honorary award for making movies that made us happy. He rode out on a motorized wheelchair with a bandaged foot. But he got up and walked back to thank everyone, including his parents and wife, Julie Andrews.

The Best Supporting Actress Oscar went to Renee Zellweger, who said, "I want to thank my immigrant parents." Her mother, a midwife, moved to Texas from Norway to care for a Norwegian family. Her father, from Switzerland, moved to Katy, Texas.

The award for Best Supporting Actor went to Tim Robbins. Since he played a sexually abused character in *Mystic River,* he encouraged people who were victims of such experiences to seek help.

A tribute to those who died in the last year used glorious music composed by Miklós Rózsa from *The Thief of Bagdad*. The list included Gregory Peck, Wendy Hiller, David Hemmings, Hope Lange, Charles Bronson, Art Carney, Elia Kazan, Leni Riefenstahl, Buddy Ebsen, Ray Stark, John Ritter, Hume Cronyn, Buddy Hackett, Robert Stack, Alan Bates, Gregory Hines, Jack Elam, Jeanne Crain, Ann Miller, and Donald O'Connor.

2003 *The Lord of the Rings: The Return of the King*

Tagline: "There can be no triumph without loss." This was the third of a movie trilogy but can be seen as an all-in-one movie if desired. The series is a long fairy tale with good and bad special effects creatures who fight each other a lot. Along the way, there are wonderful landscapes, humor, tension, bonding, and many characters who mutate one into another. This kind of hero appears to be human but lives in a world of unrealities.

Why do people love this series and these movies? They are exciting, inspiring, and awesome. They depict people in love, tragedy, and heroism, almost akin to a Wagnerian opera. Some may fret over whether there are changes from J. R. R. Tolkien's *The Lord of the Rings*, but the changes maintain the same high quality of story-telling. Director Peter Jackson did a complete representation of his fantasy world with miniatures that miniature teams spent 1,000 days of shooting for the final digital effects of the ring's destruction to be shown.

Howard Shore composed seven minutes of music per day to keep up with the shootings. He composed the Oscar-winning song "Into the West" with lyrics inspired by the premature death of a New Zealand filmmaker who had befriended director Jackson. The musical score was done by the London Philharmonic Orchestra, featuring vocal soloists, many timpani and trumpets, choirs, bands, and unusual instruments.

One instrument was invented using a violin with four pairs of strings. In addition to famous singers, there was also living legend Sir James Galway, the Irish flautist who played the flute and whistle as Frodo and Sam climbed Mount Doom.

The movie was made in New Zealand, a land of contrasts and enthusiastic inhabitants. It was the perfect place for such a film, as the producers and directors realized. Here is one passionate quotation from the movie: "How do you pick up the threads of an old life? How do you go on, when in your heart you begin to understand there is no going back? There are some things that time cannot mend. Some hurts that go too deep, that have taken hold."

The cast included Elijah Wood, Ian McKellen, Liv Tyler, Viggo Mortensen, Sean Astin, Cate Blanchett, John Rhys-Davis, Ian Holm, and others who create vigorous roles. The 201-minute movie budget was $94 million, and the box office was more than ten times the budget.

Other movie nominees included *Lost in Translation, Master and Commander: The Far Side of the World, Mystic River,* and *Seabiscuit.*

Sean Penn (1960- ?) from Santa Monica, California, won Best Actor for *Mystic River.* Other contenders were Johnny Depp *(Pirates of the Caribbean),* Ben Kingsley *(House of Sand and Fog),* Jude Law *(Cold Mountain),* and Bill Murray *(Lost in Translation).*

Charlize Theron (1975- ?) from Benoni, South Africa, won Best Actress for *Monster.* Other contenders were Keisha Castle-Hughes *(Whale Rider),* Diane Keaton *(Something's Gotta Give),* Samantha Morton *(In America),* and Naomi Watts *(21 Grams).*

Renee Zellweger won Best Supporting Actress for *Cold Mountain.*

Tim Robbins won Best Supporting Actor for *Mystic River.*

Best Song "Into the West," w. m. Annie Lennox, Howard Shore and Fran Walsh, from *The Lord of the Rings: The Return of the King.*

Peter Jackson, Director of *The Lord of the Rings: The Return of the King.*

Best Foreign Language Film: *The Barbarian Invasions,* director Denys Arcand, Canada, French. This Canadian French comedy-drama is the story of a terminally ill professional who is a womanizer. Since he was dying, writer and director Arcand alluded to the September 11, 2001, attacks on the World Trade Towers and Pentagon and the deaths. Was that the beginning of modern barbarian invasions? The sick professor traveled to obtain care and heroin in both Quebec and Vermont in the U.S. before his death among loved ones. The emotional depth shown by excellent actors and views of the current world made this film seem evocative and intelligent.

British BAFTA awards: Best Film*: The Lord of the Rings: The Return of the King.* **Best Actor:** Bill Murray in *Lost in Translation.* **Best Actress:** Scarlett Johansson in *Lost in Translation.* **Best Supporting Actor:** Bill Nighy in *Love Actually.* **Best Supporting Actress:** Renee Zellweger in *Cold Mountain.* **Outstanding British Film:** *Touching the Void,* director Kevin Macdonald, producer John Smithson, starring Brendan Mackey, Nicholas Aaron, and Ollie Ryall.

77th Academy Awards

Ceremony: This event was at the Kodak Theatre in Hollywood, California, on February 27, 2005, hosted by Chris Rock and broadcast by ABC for three hours and fourteen minutes to 42.14 million viewers. This was a 3 percent decrease from the previous year. Chris Rock paid tribute to television host Johnny Carson, who died a month earlier at age 79.

An honorary award went to Sidney Lumet's lifetime achievement as a director for 50 years. Lumet thanked the Academy and said he owed so much to so many. Director Martin Scorsese presented the Jean Hersholt Humanitarian Award to film executive Roger Mayer saying, "whose love for all of us" caused him to provide for the preservation of films and provide for the health of people in the industry. Mayer said he wanted to thank so many and singled out Ted Turner, who kept those provisions going financially.

Best Actress Hillary Swank said, "I'm just a girl from a trailer park who had a dream." She thanked her parents, her trainers "down to the last pound," and Clint Eastwood. "You are my makushla," she told Clint, using the last line in *Million Dollar Baby*. Best Actor award went to Jamie Fox for portraying Ray Charles. He thanked Ray for living and said, "Let's have this African American dream." He thanked Oprah Winfrey for helping him know Sidney Poitier, who asked Ray to carry the responsibility for black actors to work. He thanked his grandmother, who "told me to be a southern gentleman and talk sense," but now he could only talk to her in his dreams. He ended by telling her, "I can't wait to go to sleep tonight 'cause we've got a lot to talk about. I love you."

Best Picture award went to Clint Eastwood and cohorts for *Million Dollar Baby*. Clint thanked his wife and 96-year-old mother in the audience. He spoke about the challenge of making that movie in only 37 days. He said he was lucky to still be working but after hearing Lumet say he was 80, "I'm just a kid." Eastwood was the oldest winning Best Director in Oscar history.

2004 *Million Dollar Baby*

Tagline: "Beyond their journey, there is a love." A young lady (Maggie played by Hillary Swank) wanted to be the best boxer she could be so she sought the best trainer (Frankie played by Clint Eastwood). He had no interest in a female boxer, but she was not deterred. She used his workout gym and trained relentlessly, with the aid of Morgan Freeman who worked there. The lonely Eastwood character, estranged from his daughter, gradually found joy in the successes of the determined young lady in early fights.

He was of Irish background and had a cape made for her with an Irish slogan on it. She was going to the top and he decided to help her. She came to the biggest match of all, but due to Eastwood moving a chair to the wrong place, she fell on it resulting in a life-threatening injury. She became paralyzed from the neck down and asked him one last favor. He granted it and whispered to her that the Irish saying was "You're my blood, my pulse."

Clint's son, Kyle Eastwood, played electric bass guitar and double bass. In addition to his own albums, he has contributed to nine of his father's films: *The Rookie, Mystic River, Million Dollar Baby, Flags of Our Fathers, Letters from Iwo Jima, Changeling, Gran Torino, Invictus,* and *J. Edgar.* For this movie, he composed "Boxing Baby," "Solferino," and "Blue Diner," with Michael Stevens.

The movie was very hard on Swank, who had to learn to box and gain much muscle in a short time for the role. The 132-minute movie had a budget of $30 million and a box office of some seven times that amount.

Other movie nominees included *The Aviator, Finding Neverland, Ray,* and *Sideways.*

Jamie Foxx (1967- ?) from Terrell, Texas, won Best Actor for *Ray.* Other contenders were Don Cheadle *(Hotel Rwanda),* Johnny Depp *(Finding Neverland),* Leonardo DiCaprio *(The Aviator),* and Clint Eastwood *(Million Dollar Baby).*

Hilary Swank (1974-?) from Lincoln, Nebraska, won Best Actress for *Million Dollar Baby.* Other contenders were Annette Bening *(Being Julia),* Catalina Sandino Moreno *(Maria Full of Grace),* Imelda Staunton *(Vera Drake),* and Kate Winslet *(Eternal Sunshine of the Spotless Mind).*

Cate Blanchett won Best Supporting Actress for *The Aviator.*

Morgan Freeman won Best Supporting Actor for *Million Dollar Baby.*

Best Song "Al Otro Lado del Rio," w. m. Jorge Drexler, from *The Motorcycle Diaries.*

Clint Eastwood, Director of *Million Dollar Baby.*

Best Foreign Language Film: *The Sea Inside,* director Alejandro Amenabar, Spain, Spanish. This 126-minute movie covered the life of Spaniard Ramon Sampedro (Javier Bardem), who jumped into a rocky river causing paralysis from the neck down. He, just as *Million Dollar Baby,* wanted assisted suicide since he could not do it himself. His death, after 29 years of requests, involved people with whom he had been funny, flirtatious, and deadly serious. It was filmed on TV and became a topic of euthanasia for Spain as it had in many other countries. Bardem, who seems to delight in dark comedy, made the deadly subject tolerable and the theme of love pervaded the movie.

Beethoven's "Prisoners' Chorus" from *Fidelio* was an appropriate choice for a movie where the main character was a prisoner in his own body.

British BAFTA awards: Best Film: *The Aviator*. **Best Actor:** Jamie Foxx in *Ray*. **Best Actress:** Imelda Staunton in *Vera Drake*. **Best Supporting Actor:** Clive Owen in *Closer*. **Best Supporting Actress:** Cate Blanchett in *The Aviator*. **Outstanding British Film:** *My Summer of Love,* director Pawel Pawlikowski, producers Tanya Seghatchian and Chris Collins, starring Natalie Press, Emily Blunt, and Paddy Considine.

78th Academy Awards

Ceremony: This event took place on March 5, 2006, at Kodak Theatre in Hollywood, California, hosted by Jon Stewart. ABC broadcast the ceremony for three hours and thirty-three minutes to 38.94 million viewers. That was an 8 percent decrease from the previous year.

There were montages of film noir, political films, and epic films. Robert Altman was presented with an honorary Oscar because he repeatedly reinvented the art form and inspired film makers and audiences.

Phillip Seymour Hoffman received the Best Actor award for *Capote,* and he thanked his mother in the audience for bringing up four kids alone. George Clooney won the Best Supporting Actor award for *Syriana.* He said he was proud to be part of the organization that finally awarded Hattie McDaniel with an Oscar like this in 1939 when she had to sit in the back of the theater. The producers of Best Picture *Crash* said they tried to produce a film about love, tolerance, and truth.

The tribute to those who died the previous year was accompanied by theme music from *Now Voyager* composed by Max Steiner, who won an Oscar for this work. Those people included Teresa Wright, Pat Morita, Dan O'Herlihy, Vincent Schiavelli, Moira Shearer, Sandra Dee, Anthony Franciosa, Barbara Bel Geddes, Chris Penn, John Mills, Simone Simon, Brock Peters, Ernest Lehman, Shelley Winters, Anne Bancroft, Eddie Albert, Ismail Merchant, Robert Wise, and Richard Pryor.

2005 *Crash*

Tagline: "You think you know who you are. You have no idea." Events lasting 1.5 days in Los Angeles depict how some lives intertwined with each other. Things go very badly for some but work out surprisingly well by the end of the movie. The cast included Sandra Bullock, Don Cheadle, Tony Danza, Keith David, Matt Dillon, Terrence Howard, and many others. Racial stereotypes are the focus of this movie seen through interactions of Hispanics, Caucasians, blacks, and Muslims. Prejudices complicate problems but after 112 minutes, the audience sees that everybody had both a good and a bad side in this surprising movie.

This fierce story came to Canadian writer/director Paul Haggis after his car was abducted in Los Angeles just after 9/11. Much can be learned about prejudice from this film to promote empathy between people of different backgrounds and even people in the same family. The budget was $6.5 million and box office was more than ten times the budget. One quote is: "In L.A., nobody touches you. We're always behind this metal and glass. I think we miss that touch so much, that we crash into each other, just so we can feel something."

Music was mainly composed by Mark Isham, but one old favorite by Merle Haggard was "Swinging Doors." Isham had done music for many movies and TV and brought out the drama in movies like this with background effects that make the viewer's heart race. But he knew how to calm the viewer for the many scenes of resolution in *Crash*.

Other movie nominees included *Brokeback Mountain, Capote, Good Night, and Good Luck,* and *Munich.*

Philip Seymour Hoffman (1967-2014) from Fairport, New York, won Best Actor for *Capote*. Other contenders were Terrence Howard *(Hustle and Flow),* Heath Ledger *(Brokeback Mountain),* Joaquin Phoenix *(Walk the Line),* and David Strathairn *(Good Night, and Good Luck).*

Reese Witherspoon (1976- ?) from New Orleans, Louisiana, won Best Actress for *Walk the Line.* Other contenders were Judi Dench *(Mrs. Henderson Presents),* Felicity Huffman *(Transamerica),* Keira Knightley *(Pride and Prejudice),* and Charlize Theron *(North Country).*

Rachel Weisz won Best Supporting Actress for *The Constant Gardener.*

George Clooney won Best Supporting Actor for *Syriana.*

Best Song "It's Hard Out Here for a Pimp," w. m. Frayser Boy, Juicy J & DJ Paul, from *Hustle and Flow.*

Ang Lee, Director of *Brokeback Mountain.*

Best Foreign Language Film: *Tsotsi,* director Gavin Hood, South Africa, Zulu/Zhosa/Afrikaans. The tagline of this movie is "In this world… redemption just comes once." A young thug in Johannesburg has killed and robbed people. One day he shot a woman to steal her car and later found there was a baby in the back seat. He tried to feed the baby, who was as helpless as he may have been as a child from bad parenting. His criminal behavior did not cease but the audience saw him gradually change.

British BAFTA awards: Best Film: *Brokeback Mountain.* **Best Actor:** Philip Seymour Hoffman in *Capote.* **Best Actress:** Reese Witherspoon in *Walk the Line.* **Best Supporting Actor:** Jake Gyllenhaal *in Brokeback Mountain.* **Best Supporting Actress:** Thandie Newston in *Crash.* **Outstanding British Film:** *Wallace and Gromit: The Curse of the Were-Rabbit.* Directors Nick Park and Steve Box, producers Claire Jennings, David Sproxton, and Bob Baker, starring Peter Sallis, Helena Bonham Carter, and Ralph Fiennes.

79th Academy Awards

Ceremony: This event took place on February 25, 2007, at the Kodak Theatre in Hollywood, California, hosted by Ellen DeGeneres. It was televised by ABC for three hours and fifty-one minutes to 39.92 million viewers, a 2.5 percent increase from the previous year.

An honorary award was given to Ennio Morricone by Clint Eastwood. Clint had been in many spaghetti westerns where Italian Morricone, composer, and orchestrator, did the music. Morricone also did music for horror and drama films and his style was copied by many film composers. He was also one of the world's best chess players.

Former U.S. Vice President Al Gore was present and his climate change documentary, called *An Inconvenient Truth,* won an Oscar. Gore and Leonardo DiCaprio gave an announcement about the Academy's new efforts to help the environment showing that the Academy had "gone green."

Martin Scorsese won Best Director for *The Departed.* He said, "Double check the envelope" because he was so surprised. Martin was an Italian boy with asthma and couldn't play sports so watched movies (*The Red Shoes, Tales of Hoffman,* etc.). He expected to be a priest but failed after the first year of seminary. He changed his major and learned the film business.

Forrest Whitaker was shocked to win the award for Best Actor. He said he first watched movies sitting in the back seat of his parent's car in East Texas. He became an operatic tenor but wanted to go into movies. He thanked the people of Uganda and God for enabling him to play his role as Idi Amin in *The Last King of Scotland.*

The memorial tribute to those who died the previous year included Glenn Ford, Alida Valli, Betty Comden, Jane Wyatt, Don Knotts, Red Buttons, Darren McGavin, Sven Nykvist, Joseph Barbera, June Allyson, Maureen Stapleton, Carlo Ponti, Peter Boyle, Jack Palance, Jack Warden, and Robert Altman.

2006 *The Departed*

Tagline: "Lies. Betrayal. Sacrifice. How far will you take it?" This riveting story involved the Boston state police war against Irish American organized criminals. Undercover policeman Costigan (Leonardo DiCaprio) was to infiltrate the mob run by Costello (Jack Nicholson). Meanwhile, a young criminal (Matt Damon) has infiltrated the state police informing the mob from his position with the investigation unit. DiCaprio and Damon are living double lives. Both groups realize there is a mole in their organization. The cat and mouse game comes down to who will turn on who.

Others in the formidable cast included Mark Wahlberg, Martin Sheen, and Alec Baldwin. Production began in 2003 with Brad Grey, Brad Pitt, William Monahan, and Martin Scorsese. The Nicholson character was based on Irish American Whitey Bulger. Howard Hawks' *Scarface* (1932) used an X to foreshadow death. Scorsese used an X in this movie's taped window, hallway carpet, and elevator behind Costigan's head in the site where he would die. The movie becomes a search for a rat. In the final scene, the rat about to be killed says, "Okay." Then a rat is shown crawling across the fence behind him.

Howard Shore's score added popular songs from Roger Waters, The Beach Boys, The Rolling Stones, Roy Buchanan, The Allman Brothers, Dropkick Murphys, The Human Beinz, LaVern Baker, and Patsy Cline. The main theme was written by Shore and performed by guitarists.

Scorsese described that theme as a dangerous and lethal tango that used the zither from *The Third Man* as inspiration.

The 151-minute movie had a budget of $90 million and a box office of some twenty times the budget.

Other movie nominees included *Babel, Letters from Iwo Jima, Little Miss Sunshine,* and *The Queen.*

Forest Whitaker (1961-?) from Longview, Texas, won Best Actor for *The Last King of Scotland.* Other contenders were Leonardo DiCaprio *(Blood Diamond)*, Ryan Gosling *(Half Nelson)*, Peter O'Toole *(Venus)*, and Will Smith *(The Pursuit of Happiness).*

Helen Mirren (1945- ?) from London won Best Actress for *The Queen.* Other contenders were Penelope Cruz *(Volver)*, Judi Dench *(Notes on a Scandal)*, Meryl Streep *(The Devil Wears Prada)*, and Kate Winslet *(Little Children).*

Jennifer Hudson won Best Supporting Actress for *Dreamgirls.*

Alan Arkin won Best Supporting Actor for *Little Miss Sunshine.*

Best Song "I Need to Wake Up," w. m. Melissa Etheridge, from *An Inconvenient Truth.*

Martin Scorsese, Director of *The Departed.*

Best Foreign Language Film: *The Lives of Others,* director Florian Henckel von Donnersmarck, Germany, German. The director thought about a conversation when author Maxim Gorky met Vladimir Lenin, who said his favorite piece was Beethoven's *Appassionata.* Then Lenin said:

But I can't listen to music often. It affects my nerves, it makes me want to say sweet nothings and pat the heads of people who, living in a filthy hell, can create such beauty. But today we mustn't pat anyone on the head or we'll get our hand bitten off; we've got to hit them on the heads, hit them without mercy, though in the ideal we are against doing any violence to people. Hmmm—it's a hellishly difficult office.

So, the German director set out to capture hidden thoughts and secret desires of East German people just before the fall of the Berlin Wall. The 137-minute film depicted an East German secret policeman bugging and listening to a couple and gradually intervening to protect them. It recorded political changes in life at the time. Music included Brahms' haunting *Verrat* performed by the City of Prague Philharmonic Orchestra.

British BAFTA awards: Best Film*: The Queen.* **Best Actor:** Forest Whitaker in *The Last King of Scotland.* **Best Actress:** Helen Mirren in *The Queen.* **Best Supporting Actor:** Alan Arkin in *Little Miss Sunshine.* **Best Supporting Actress:** Jennifer Hudson in *Dreamgirls.* **Outstanding British Film***: The Last King of Scotland,* director Kevin Macdonald, producers Andrea Calderwood, Lisa Bryer, Charles Steel, and Peter Morgan, starring Forest Whitaker, James McAvoy, and Gillian Anderson.

80th Academy Awards

Ceremony: This event was conducted on February 24, 2008, at the Kodak Theatre in Hollywood, California, hosted by Jon Stewart and televised by ABC for three hours and twenty-one minutes to 31.7 million viewers, a 21 percent decrease from last year. That was the lowest viewership since 1974.

Robert F. Boyle, film art director and production designer, received an honorary award for sketches, collages, and structures for movies beginning with Cecile B. DeMille's 1936 *The Plainsman* starring Gary Cooper. He did stellar work on many movies, such as *The Thomas Crown Affair, Fiddler on the Roof, Saboteur, Marnie, North by Northwest,* etc. The latter film showed Mt. Rushmore heads of Washington, Jefferson, Theodore Roosevelt, and Abraham Lincoln, made by Boyle. A 40-minute documentary about Boyle's work was made called *The Man on Lincoln's Nose.* He was the oldest person to receive an honorary award at age 98. He was determined to walk (with a cane and assistance) from his wheelchair. He thanked several, including Alfred Hitchcock, who introduced him to his wife.

Javier Bardem won Best Supporting Actor and commented about wearing the most horrible haircut ever in *No Country for Old Men.*

The memorial tribute to those who died in the last year included Roscoe Lee Browne, Barry Nelson, Kitty Carlisle Hart, Betty Hutton, Calvin Lockhart, Jane Wyman, Jack Valenti, Michael Kidd, Monty Westmore, Lois Maxwell, Miyoshi Umeki, Laraine Day, Jean-Pierre Cassel, Suzanne Pleshette, Deborah Kerr, Ingmar Bergman, and Heath Ledger.

2007 *No Country for Old Men*

Tagline: "You can't stop what's coming!" Therein lies the terror of this movie as Javier Bardem flips coins with people about whether to kill them or not. The story is told through the lines from the sheriff (Tommy Lee Jones). There is little other dialogue by actors. The film was taken from Cormac McCarthy's 2005 novel of the same name and notable for its short sentences and lack of punctuation. McCarthy also wrote *All the Pretty Horses*.

A few other characters are Woody Harrelson, Barry Corbin, and Tess Harper. Despite being surrounded by excellent actors, however, the movie belongs to Javier Bardem. His character does not appear in dark scenes but in sunlit scenes, sometimes scraping the blood off his boots after a killing. The bad guy comes looking for the good guys and he makes the choices about who dies, even though he gives them a bit of a choice by having them flip a coin.

Bardem has a killing weapon that almost invited the victim to be part of the murder. Unlike *High Noon* with a song that says, "Do not forsake me oh my darlin'," this movie has a minimized score with sounds, squeaks, and one song. That was a traditional Mexican birthday song (Las Mañanitas) about the flowers blooming when someone is born and was performed by Lola Beltrán. This movie should not be seen by children because it grabs you by the throat and doesn't let you go even after the ending. It is unforgettable but indescribable.

One interesting quote was: "I always figured when I got older, God would sorta come into my life somehow. And he didn't. I don't blame him. If I was him, I would have the same opinion of me that he does." This exemplifies the Coen brothers' use of themes about fate, pessimism, circumstances, and a little humor to make the 122 minutes tolerable. The Coen brothers also liked suspense and didn't want music to guide the audience so only used wind, boots, caliche, shootouts, beeps, engines, and natural sounds. Thus, it was a scarier movie because music did not give a hint about what was coming next.

Other movie nominees included *Atonement, Juno, Michael Clayton,* and *There Will Be Blood.*

Daniel Day-Lewis (1957-?) from London won Best Actor for *There Will Be Blood.* Other contenders were George Clooney *(Michael Clayton),* Johnny Depp *(Sweeney Todd: The Demon Barber of Fleet Street),* Tommy Lee Jones *(In the Valley of Elah),* and Viggo Mortensen *(Eastern Promises).*

Marion Cotillard (1975-?) from Paris won Best Actress for *La Vie en Rose.* Other contenders were Cate Blanchett *(Elizabeth: The Golden Age),* Julie Christie *(Away from Her),* Laura Linney *(The Savages),* and Ellen Page *(Juno).*

Tilda Swinton won Best Supporting Actress for *Michael Clayton.*

Javier Bardem won Best Supporting Actor for *No Country for Old Men.*

Best Song "Falling Slowly," w. m. Glen Hansard and Market Irglova, from *Once.*

Joel Coen and Ethan Coen, Directors of *No Country for Old Men.*

Best Foreign Language Film: *The Counterfeiters,* director Stefan Ruzowitzky, Austria, German. The Austrians filmed a true story of the largest counterfeit operation ever, by Nazis using Jews in a concentration camp. Jews counterfeiting pound notes and dollars were given better living quarters. The best counterfeiter was living the good life until his arrest. He was ordered to weaken Germany's opponents by producing fake foreign currency. When Germany fell, the Jewish team leader bet his fake money and lost it gambling. When a lady consoled him for losing, they begin to dance and he said, "We can always make more." The 99-minute movie has operas in the background and an Argentine tango during a dance scene. There is violence, frontal nudity, and foul language.

British BAFTA awards: Best Film: *Atonement*. **Best Actor:** Daniel Day-Lewis in *There Will be Blood*. **Best Actress:** Marion Cotillard in *La Vie en Rose*. **Best Supporting Actor:** Javier Bardem in *No Country for Old Men*. **Best Supporting Actress:** Tilda Swinton in *Michael Clayton*. **Outstanding British Film**: *This Is England*, director Shane Meadows, producer Mark Herbert, starring Thomas Turgoose, Stephen Graham, and Jo Hartley.

81st Academy Awards

Ceremony: This event was conducted on February 22, 2009, at the Kodak Theatre in Hollywood, California, hosted by Hugh Jackman. It was televised by ABC for three hours and thirty minutes to 36.94 million viewers, a 13 percent increase from the previous year.

This show had some firsts. The orchestra performed on stage instead of in a pit. A montage of upcoming 2009 films was shown over the closing credits. Film historian, host of Turner Classic Movies (TCM), 77-year-old author Robert Osborne greeted guests entering the festivities. As a struggling young actor appearing with Lucille Ball and Desi Arnaz, Lucy told him to leave acting and write about movies, so he did that and hosted TCM until his death in 2017.

Heath Ledger won the award for Best Supporting Actor for *The Dark Knight*. His parents and sister accepted the award on stage on his behalf. The 28-year-old Australian died of an overdose the previous month. He was the second performer to win a posthumous acting Oscar, the first being English-Australian actor Peter Finch.

The memorial to those who died in the last year was done with the background song, "I'll Be Seeing You," from the 1944 movie of the same name. This list included Cyd Charisse, Bernie Mac, Van Johnson, Isaac Hayes, Ricardo Montalban, Michael Crichton, Nina Foch, Pat Hingle, Harold Pinter, Roy Scheider, Evelyn Keyes, Richard Widmark, Jules Dassin, Paul Scofield, James Whitmore, Charlton Heston, Sydney Pollack, and Paul Newman.

2008 *Slumdog Millionaire*

Tagline: "The boy who had the answer to every question." What a surprise that India would yield such splendid stories amidst poverty and corruption. The 18-year-old boy played by Dev Patel did so well on the TV quiz show that he was arrested for cheating. As an orphan living in the slums of Mumbai, how could he expect to win 20 million rupees with the whole country watching the TV show? As the movie proceeded, the audience learned why he knew answers due to his background. However, major problems stemming from poverty in India were seen and made the movie unsuitable for children because eyes were gouged to make peddlers gain more sympathy from passersby.

Early in life, the boy grew up with gangs, but one girl, Latika, won him over. His little band of friends were called the Three Musketeers. As he grew older, he found that Latika had been taken in by bad people but watched a particular TV show. After much searching, he decided the only way she could find him was if he was on television winning each weekly round. One quote was: "I thought we'd be together only in death." He connected with her in a final question where he could call a friend to answer who was the third musketeer. She called and they found each other with a little money thrown in. The message may be that life can be beautiful if you work hard and learn as much as possible, even when things are difficult.

Director Danny Boyle disliked sentimental themes so declared there would be no cellos in the score. A. R. Rahman used twenty days to put together a combination of modern and old Indian culture with strong nervous music heard from beginning to end. That picked up the nervous contestant trying to answer questions correctly, to win money and his girlfriend. It has been called a fairy-tale ending, but fairy tales always have some bad people in them. The movie was based on a 2005 book called *Q & A* by Vikas Swarup.

Director Danny Boyle enabled this 120-minute movie to be an international hit due to the idea of a TV show about "Who wants to be a millionaire?" After the finale and finding his lost love, the cast danced and sang down the street while the credits were running.

Other movie nominees included *The Curious Case of Benjamin Button, Frost/Nixon, Milk,* and *The Reader.*

Sean Penn won Best Actor for *Milk.* Other contenders were Richard Jenkins *(The Visitor),* Frank Langella *(Frost/Nixon),* Brad Pitt *(The Curious Case of Benjamin Button,* and Mickey Rourke *(The Wrestler).*

Kate Winslet won Best Actress for *The Reader.* Other contenders were Anne Hathaway *(Rachel Getting Married),* Angelina Jolie *(Changeling),* Melissa Leo *(Frozen River),* and Meryl Streep *(Doubt).*

Penelope Cruz won Best Supporting Actress for *Vicky Cristina Barcelona.*

Heath Ledger won Best Supporting Actor for *The Dark Knight.*

Best Song "Jai Ho, w. Gulzar, m. A. R. Rahman, from *Slumdog Millionaire.*

Danny Boyle, Director of *Slumdog Millionaire.*

Best Foreign Language Film: *Departures,* director Yojiro Takita, Japan, Japanese. The tagline of this movie was "The gift of last memories." A young married cellist learned his orchestra must let people go so he applied for other jobs. Through an error in an ad, he thought he was applying for a travel job, but it was a job to help people travel from life to death as an undertaker. Though hesitant, he learned the rituals to prepare the body, console the mourners, handle grief, and final reconciliations with loved ones. He didn't want to tell his wife, but one older man was helpful. With surprising humor and realization of the important role he played to people at their most critical time, he became proud of himself. The 130-minute film was well acted and directed, and one section was enhanced by the evocative Beethoven's "Symphony No. 9 in D Minor, the Choral."

British BAFTA awards: Best Film: *Slumdog Millionaire*. **Best Actor:** Mickey Rourke in *The Wrestler*. **Best Actress:** Kate Winslet in *The Reader*. **Best Supporting Actor:** Heath Ledger in *The Dark Knight*. **Best Supporting Actress:** Penelope Cruz in *Vicky Cristina Barcelona*. **Outstanding British Film**: *Man on Wire,* director James Marsh, producer Simon Chinn, starring Philippe Petit, Jean Francois Heckel, and Jen-Louis Blondeau.

82nd Academy Awards

Ceremony: This event was conducted on March 7, 2010, at the Kodak Theatre in Hollywood, California, hosted by Alec Baldwin and Steve Martin. ABC broadcast it for three hours and thirty-seven minutes to 41.62 million viewers, a 13 percent increase since the previous year.

Roger Corman was awarded an honorary Oscar for his rich engendering of films and filmmakers. Some who worked with Corman were Francis Ford Coppola, Martin Scorsese, Ron Howard, Peter Bogdanovich, James Cameron, and John Sayles. He made career breaks for Jack Nicholson, Peter Fonda, Bruce Dern, Charles Bronson, Dennis Hopper, Talia Shire, Sandra Bullock, Robert DeNiro, and David Carradine. Some followers awarded him cameos in films like *The Godfather Part II, The Silence of the Lambs, Apollo 13,* and *Rachel Getting Married.*

Lauren Bacall, 86-years-old, received an honorary award in recognition of her central place in the golden age of motion pictures. She took the statuette and said, "A man, at last! I've been very lucky, at age 19, to have been chosen by Howard Hawks to star with Humphrey Bogart, an extraordinary actor and man. He changed my life for sixty years, amazing when you consider how young I am! I've worked with some of the best. Greg Peck--his wife got in the way but what can you do? Kirk Douglas said, 'Never fear, Kirk is here'… Now I'm going to have a two-legged man in my room, and I can hardly stand it. I'm still alive. Some of you are surprised, aren't you?"

Her children were in the audience -- Leslie Howard Bogart, Stephen Humphrey Bogart, and Sam Robards. Leslie, a nurse, was so named because Bogart was so grateful to actor Leslie Howard. He insisted Humphrey play in the movie *Petrified Forest,* which began Bogart's film career.

Gordon Willis received an award for his mastery of light, shadow, color, and motion. He worked with Woody Allen, Alan Pakula, Francis Ford Coppola, and others to make storytelling visual. He used light, black, and shadows to show morals of characters in movies. He transposed the written screenplay into moving pictures that told a story.

The Irving G. Thalberg Memorial Award went to John Calley. This film studio producer was photographed sick in bed and died the following year. He said about producing films, "You're very unhappy for a long period of time, and you don't experience joy. At the end, you experience relief, if you're lucky." He was responsible for films like *The Americanization of Emily, The Sandpiper, The Cincinnati Kid, Catch-22, Fat Man and Little Boy, The Remains of the Day, The DaVinci Code, The Birdcage, Postcards from the Edge, The Exorcist, Superman,* etc.

This was the first year that a female director won the award for Best Director. Kathryn Bigelow directed and won Best Picture for *The Hurt Locker.* She thanked all who wear a uniform and risk their lives for us whether in the military, police, fire, etc. She wished that all come home safe.

The memorial pictures of those who died the previous year showed while the Beatles song "In My Life" played. They included Patrick Swayze, Maurice Jarre, Monte Hale, Betsy Blair, Joseph Wiseman, Jean Simmons, David Carradine, Dom DeLuise, Ron Silver, Brittany Murphy, Lou Jacobi, Kathryn Grayson, Roy Disney, Larry Gelbart, Horton Foote, Budd Schulberg, Michael Jackson, Natasha Richardson, Jennifer Jones, and Karl Malden.

2009 *The Hurt Locker*

Tagline: "You don't have to be a hero to do this job, but it helps." This movie depicted soldiers who disarmed bombs at the battle site. The sergeant who trained men in Iraq to do this acted as if he did not fear death. The intensity began from the first scene and continued to the last moment. Someone said, "The rush of battle is often a potent and lethal addiction, for war is a drug."

Director Kathryn Bigelow made macho men the tragic heroes, who sometimes couldn't return to normal life. They must have their fix so they re-up leaving their family behind. Relationships between men were intense and were built more on survival than on friendship. She chose less known actors so that we watched them as soldiers instead of stars. There were some relationships between Iraqis and American soldiers, such as buying DVDs. Death was a constant encounter that brought distancing and numbness in many soldiers. Sometimes, enemies wearing bombs changed their minds and we saw the results when Americans risked their lives to defuse bombs.

Marco Beltranic and Buck Sanders did the music for this film. It was like a horror film with a bomb that could go off any minute, so the audience was made anxious. But this thriller was due to the actors whose excitement came from danger. Real life has no music so one might say this is how we really live with little music but much noise. This tense movie brought home the message that soldiers sometimes feel—it's so exciting that the high must continue. This 131-minute movie had a budget of $15 million and the box office was three times that.

Other movie nominees included *Avatar, The Blind Side, District 9, An Education, Inglourious Basterds, Precious, A Serious Man, Up,* and *Up in the Air.*

Jeff Bridges (1949- ?) from Los Angeles won Best Actor for *Crazy Heart.* Other contenders were George Clooney *(Up in the Air),* Colin Firth *(A Single Man),* Morgan Freeman *(Invictus),* and Jeremy Renner *(The Hurt Locker).*

Sandra Bullock (1964- ?) from Arlington County, Virginia, won Best Actress for *The Blind Side.* Other contenders were Helen Mirren

(The Last Station), Carey Mulligan *(An Education)*, Gabourey Sidibe *(Precious)*, and Meryl Streep *(Julie and Julia)*.

Mo'Nique won Best Supporting Actress for *Precious.*

Christoph Waltz won Best Supporting Actor for *Inglourious Basterds.*

Best Song "The Weary Kind," w. m. Ryan Bingham and T. Bone Burnett, from *Crazy Heart.*

Kathryn Bigelow, Director of *The Hurt Locker.*

Best Foreign Language Film: *The Secret in Their Eyes,* director Juan Jose Capanella, Argentina, Spanish. The tagline is "The secret of their lives is about to be revealed." A retired federal justice worker in Argentina can't forget a woman who was raped and killed and her husband who went to the train station every day to spot the killer by his eyes. Actors did more with looks than words. There were silences and feelings that took time to be understood. The director and the actors carefully gave this 129-minute movie a depth that made it quite unique.

British BAFTA awards: Best Film*: The Hurt Locker.* **Best Actor:** Colin Firth in *A Single Man.* **Best Actress:** Carey Mulligan in *An Education.* **Best Supporting Actor:** Christof Waltz in *Inglourious Basterds.* **Best Supporting Actress:** Mo'Nique in *Precious.* **Outstanding British Film***:* *Fish Tank,* director Andrea Arnold, producers Kees Kasander, Nick Laws, and Andrea Arnold, starring Katie Jarvis, Michael Fassbender, and Kierston Wareing.

83rd Academy Awards

Ceremony: This event was conducted on February 27, 2011, at the Kodak Theatre in Hollywood, California, hosted by James Franco and Anne Hathaway. ABC broadcast it for three hours and sixteen minutes to 37.9 million viewers, a 9 percent decrease from the previous year. To revitalize interest, the Academy voted to have up to ten nominees for Best Picture, but some years had eight or nine.

Honorary awards were made to Kevin Brownlow, British film historian, who saved and restored movies. Jean-Luc Godard was awarded an honorary Oscar for passion, confrontation, and a new kind of cinema. Beginning with the 1960 *Breathless,* he helped establish a new wave of movies and was a filmmaker whose movies showed how people make sense of the world.

Eli Wallach received an honorary award for a lifetime of indelible screen characters. His first stage role was with Walter Cronkite when they attended the University of Texas. Eli went on to Broadway and Cronkite to journalism but information about both men is held in the library of the University of Texas. Eli played in *Baby Doll; The Misfits; The Good, the Bad and the Ugly; How the West Was Won; The Godfather Part III; Wall Street: Money Never Sleeps,* etc.

Francis Ford Coppola was awarded the Irving G. Thalberg Memorial Award. He enjoyed symphony music, which made him immensely interested in the music in his *Godfather* films.

When Colin Firth won Best Actor for *The King's Speech,* he said, "I think my career has just peaked." He and the producers thanked Harvey Weinstein for his commitment to make the film.

Charlie Chaplin's song "Smile" played while the tribute to those who died showed their pictures. Here are most of those stars: John Barry, Tony Curtis, Tom Mankiewicz, Gloria Stuart, Lionel Jeffries, Leslie Nielsen, Robert Boyle, Lynn Redgrave, Anne Francis, Arthur Penn, Susannah York, David Wolper, Patricia Neal, Robert Culp, Jill Clayburgh, Dennis Hopper, Dino De Laurentiis, Blake Edwards, Kevin McCarthy, and Lena Horne.

Halle Berry paid special tribute to Lena Horne and introduced a clip of her singing "Stormy Weather." Lena was mother-in-law to Sidney Lumet, who married her daughter. (See *The Hornes: An American Family* by Gail Lumet Buckley published in 1986.) The ceremony ended with a children's choir performing "Over the Rainbow" from *The Wizard of Oz.*

2010 *The King's Speech*

Tagline: "When his nation needed a leader, when the people needed a voice, an ordinary man would help him find the courage." The writer (David Seidler) was a stutterer and read about the king's problem and his therapist. He wanted to do this story earlier, but the Queen Mother (married to the King) asked that he wait until she died, which happened in 2002. Then daughter, Queen Elizabeth, gave permission. Seidler had contacted Lionel Logue's son, who lent his father's notebooks to the author. The king's letter of thanks to Logue had also surfaced.

Colin Firth was the third choice to play this role and prepared by going to speech therapists and watching films of the King speaking. When Geoffrey Rush was chosen to be the therapist, he poured his own money into the film production. This movie described Prince

Albert (Colin Firth) who had to take the throne after his older brother married an American lady. Albert's speech impediment scared and overwhelmed him. He said, "If I'm King, where's my power? Can I form a government? Can I levy a tax, declare a war? No! And yet I am the seat of all authority. Why? Because the nation believes that when I speak, I speak for them. But I can't speak."

His wife (Helena Bonham Carter) hired an Australian speech therapist and actor to help him. The methods used involved breathing exercises, singing, cursing, smoking, etc. The first important speech Albert (called Bertie) had to make was when England entered World War II. His coach (Geoffrey Rush) worked long and hard with him to accomplish this goal.

On September 3, 1939, this speech was delivered slowly, paced by the King, who overcame his stammer by his therapist who would become his lifelong friend. The background of Beethoven's 7th *Symphony, II Allegreto* revised by Alexandre Desplat accompanied it brilliantly. Desplat focused on helping the sound of the voice through his music. The music made this movie a winner. This conductor used his hands to convey pathos to clarinets, oboes, bassoons, flutes, violins, bass fiddles, cellos, and tympani indicating how to play it.

As the King slowly spoke, a lower sad tune in a minor key played while a major key was heard above it, gradually ascending and finally sounding loud and victorious as it overcame the lower sadness. Here are a few words of that speech:

In this grave hour, perhaps the most fateful in our history, I send to every household of my peoples, both at home and overseas, this message, spoken with the same depth of feeling for each one of you as if I were able to cross your threshold and speak to you myself… The task will be hard. There may be dark days ahead, and war can no longer be confined to the battlefield… With God's help, we shall prevail. May He bless and keep us all."

Speech professionals were thrilled by this movie. It brought more people to seek help for this discouraging and humiliating problem. Some well-known people stutter, like President Joseph Biden, Mel Tillis, James Earl Jones, Jack Paar, Julia Roberts, Marilyn Monroe, Herschel Walker, Ken Venturi, Mrs. John (Annie) Glenn, Winston Churchill, and Andrew Lloyd Weber. Permission was given for use of Ely Cathedral, St. James Palace, and Lancaster House in London. The 118-minute film had a budget of $15 million and made many times that amount.

Other movie nominees included *127 Hours, Black Swan, The Fighter, Inception, The Kids Are All Right, The Social Network, Toy Story 3, True Grit,* and *Winter's Bone.*

Colin Firth (1960- ?) from Grayshott, England, won Best Actor for *The King's Speech.* Other contenders were Javier Bardem *(Biutiful),* Jeff Bridges *(True Grit),* Jesse Eisenberg *(The Social Network),* and James Franco *(127 Hours).*

Natalie Portman (1981- ?) from Jerusalem, Israel, won Best Actress for *Black Swan.* Other contenders were Annette Bening *(The Kids Are All Right),* Nicole Kidman *(Rabbit Hole),* Jennifer Lawrence *(Winter's Bone),* and Michelle Williams *(Blue Valentine).*

Melissa Leo won Best Supporting Actress for *The Fighter.*

Christian Bale won Best Supporting Actor for *The Fighter.*

Best Song "We Belong Together," w. m. Randy Newman, from *Toy Story 3.*

Tom Hooper, Director of *The King's Speech.*

Best Foreign Language Film: *In a Better World,* director Susanne Bier, Denmark, Danish. The tagline for this movie is "A better life, a better world." This movie is about a Danish physician who tended the sick in the Sudan but had a rocky marriage with his doctor wife in Denmark due to an affair he had. They had two sons and one, Elias, was bullied at school until a new friend (Christian) defended him. As they bonded, Christian told how he just lost his mother to cancer and was very angry that his father promised she would not die. Meanwhile, the doctor treated a warlord, and he was taken from hospital and killed. Everybody appeared to want revenge on somebody, which was the theme of the movie. Some motives were resolved with a better outcome for most of the characters. This 118-minute movie was done with affection so that empathy for the characters built in viewers as well as in the characters.

British BAFTA awards: Best Film: *The King's Speech*. **Best Actor:** Colin Firth in *The King's Speech*. **Best Actress:** Natalie Portman in *Black Swan*. **Best Supporting Actor:** Geoffrey Rush in *The King's Speech*. **Best Supporting Actress:** Helena Bonham Carter in *The King's Speech*. **Outstanding British Film**: *The King's Speech*, director Tom Hooper, producers Tom Hooper, Iain Canning, Emilie Sherman, and Gareth Unwin, starring Colin Firth, Geoffrey Rush, and Helena Bonham Carter.

84th Academy Awards

Ceremony: This event took place on February 26, 2012, at Hollywood and Highland Center Theatre in Hollywood, California, hosted by Billy Crystal. ABC broadcast the 3-hours, 13-minute program to 39.46 million viewers, a 4 percent increase from the previous year. This year there were ten nominees for Best Picture.

Honorary Oscars were awarded to two people. Dick Smith was awarded for his unparalleled mastery of texture, shade, form, and illusion. Shaken by the award, he said while crying that he had loved doing make-up all his life and this was the crown on top of that.

James Earl Jones was awarded for his consistent excellence and uncommon versatility. He was in London just finishing playing *Driving Miss Daisy* on the stage with Vanessa Redgrave. She announced that he would receive an Oscar and invited Ben Kingsley to present it to him, saying, "You're always so damn good!" Jones said an actor's worst fear was that he'll be buck naked or forget his lines, but he had his clothes and remembered his lines, so this was "an actor's wet dream. I've learned a new word here in England—gobsmacked, so I am gobsmacked." James began to stutter at age 6 but at 14 began talking by learning poetry and reading it aloud. His father, actor Robert Earl Jones, left him to be raised by grandparents while starring in black movies made by Oscar Micheaux and produced by Alfred Sack beginning in 1939. Later, he was in movies like *The Sting, Trading Places,* and *Witness.*

Oprah Winfrey was presented with the Jean Hersholt Humanitarian Award for her work and regular programs that benefited the entertainment industry. She said, "You have voted for what I believe is the essence of why we're all here. We're all here to help each other."

Meryl Streep accepted the Best Actress award and said that it's the friends she's made that make this career so worthwhile. Jean Dujardin accepted Best Actor award and said, "I love your country" and "Merci beaucoup." Christopher Plummer accepted the award for Best Supporting Actor thanking his fellow nominees and was the oldest (age 83) to win that award. Octavia Spencer took the Oscar in her hand and said, "Thank you for putting me with the hottest guy in the room. I'm freaking out." Directors and producers of *The Artist* thanked the Board of Governors of the Academy for the award for Best Picture and expressed great thanks to director and producer Billy Wilder who had died ten years earlier.

The Memorial tribute to those who died in the last year showed pictures while Louis Armstrong's "What a Wonderful World" was sung by a children's chorus. They included Jane Russell, John Calley, Farley Granger, Whitney Houston, Peter Falk, Cliff Robertson, Sidney Lumet, Jackie Cooper, Gilbert Cates, Ben Gazzara, and Elizabeth Taylor.

2011 *The Artist*

Tagline: "When silent movies are golden once more." The movie was set in 1927 as a silent film except for 12 words at the end. The main character was played by Jean Dujardin, who acted like a Douglas Fairbanks swashbuckler hero of silent films. The bottom line was that talking movies ruined the star's career. He became nearly suicidal, but a female fan and co-star pulled him out of it. He was not ready to talk in films but unlike other male actors whose voices were bad, the audience only heard a fine voice with a French accent. Other actors included John Goodman, James Cromwell, and Ed Lauter. This film was made from a love of early movies and geniuses. The fact that it was photographed in black and white was nostalgic of times long gone.

Love scenes included the music from *Vertigo* by Bernard Hermann (who worked with Alfred Hitchcock) and "Pennies from Heaven." This was the first non-talking film to win the Academy Award Best Picture since the original two movies that won for the first Academy Awards (*Wings* and *Sunrise*). The 100-minute film had a budget of $15 million and a box office of ten times that amount.

Other movie nominees included *The Descendants, Extremely Loud and Incredibly Close, The Help, Hugo, Midnight in Paris, Moneyball, The Tree of Life,* and *War Horse.*

Jean Dujardin (1972-?) from Rueil-Malmaison, France, won Best Actor for *The Artist.* Other contenders were Demian Bichir *(A Better Life)*, George Clooney *(The Descendants)*, Gary Oldman *(Tinker Tailor Soldier Spy)*, and Brad Pitt *(Moneyball)*.

Meryl Streep won Best Actress for *The Iron Lady.* Other contenders were Glenn Close *(Albert Nobbs)*, Viola Davis *(The Help)*, Rooney Mara *(The Girls with the Dragon Tattoo)*, and Michelle Williams *(My Week with Marilyn)*.

Octavia Spencer won Best Supporting Actress for *The Help.*

Christopher Plummer won Best Supporting Actor for *Beginners.*

Best Song "Man or Muppet," w. m. Bret McKenzie, from *The Muppets.*

Michel Haznavicius, Director of *The Artist.*

Best Foreign Language Film: *A Separation,* director Asghar Farhadi, Iran, Persian. This film was about a wife who wanted to live abroad for their 14-year-old daughter's greater opportunities. Her husband stayed in Iran to tend to his father with Alzheimer's. When they tried to divorce, there was insufficient evidence to allow divorce. The court went over subtle acts and nuances that made things more complicated. The court left the decision to the daughter about which parent to live with. The audience identified with all characters in this 123-minute movie.

British BAFTA awards: Best Film: *The Artist*. **Best Actor:** Jean Dujardin in *The Artist*. **Best Actress:** Meryl Streep in *The Iron Lady*. **Best Supporting Actor:** Christopher Plummer in *Beginners*. **Best Supporting Actress:** Octavia Spencer in *The Help*. **Outstanding British Film**: *Tinker Tailor Soldier Spy*, director Tomas Alfredson, producers Tomas Alfredson, Eric Fellner, Bridget O'Connor, Peter Straughan, Robyn Slovo, and Tim Bevan, starring Gary Oldman, Colin Firth, and Tom Hardy.

85th Academy Awards

Ceremony: This event was conducted at the Dolby Theatre in Hollywood, California, on February 24, 2013, hosted by actor Seth MacFarlane and actress Emma Stone. ABC broadcast the awards on ABC for three hours and thirty-five minutes to 40.38 million viewers, a 3 percent increase from the previous year. There were nine nominees for Best Picture this year.

Quvenzhane Wallis, age 9, was the youngest nominee for Best Actress and Emmanuelle Riva, age 85, was the oldest nominee for Best Actress but neither won. An honorary Oscar was awarded to stuntman and stunt director Hal Needham. The only other stuntman to receive an award was Yakima Canutt. Needham died of cancer eight months later. Another honorary Oscar went to George Stevens Jr., a tireless champion of the arts in America and especially that most American of arts—the Hollywood film. He founded the American Film Institute, was a writer, director, producer, and arranged the Kennedy Center honors program. The Jean Hersholt Humanitarian Award went to Jeffrey Katzenberg of Walt Disney Studios. Animated films had raised money for education, the arts, and health issues benefitting the motion picture industry.

An honorary Oscar went to D. A. Pennebaker, who redefined the language of film and taught a generation of filmmakers to look to reality for inspiration. He chronicled the 1960s and rock artists using hand-held cameras. In his acceptance speech he mentioned the following, "We were in Monterey. Nobody is gonna be interested in this music. So, I said you guys go film Ravi Shankar music... It was the most exciting thing that we'd done there. I tell students to watch that sequence and you'll see two people learning how to be filmmakers in less than an hour."

Argo won Best Picture and Ben Affleck, George Clooney, Alan Arkin, and others were on stage to receive Oscars for this political film. Affleck thanked everybody involved with this film. Michelle Obama, directly from the White House, thanked all for their help in educating and lifting the spirits of people to believe in themselves. She read the winner from the envelope.

The In Memoriam segment of those who had died showed a montage from *Out of Africa* as Barbra Streisand sang "The Way We Were." These people were included in the list: Ernest Borgnine, Jack Klugman, Celeste Holm, Charles Durning, Nora Ephron, Herbert Lom, Ray Bradbury, Richard Zanuck, and Marvin Hamlisch.

2012 *Argo*

Tagline: "Based on the declassified true story." In 1979, Iranians stormed the U.S. embassy in Tehran because President Jimmy Carter gave the Shah asylum in the U.S. Sixty-six embassy staff members were taken as hostages but six escaped to stay with the Canadian ambassador. Their escape was secret, and the U.S. tried to bring them home by Central Intelligence Agency specialists. While one CIA consultant (Tony Mendez) talked with his son long-distance, the boy described the *Battle for the Planet of the Apes* that he was watching on television.

Suddenly, the idea of getting the six people out by pretending they were making a movie in Iran occurred to Mendez. The CIA had no better idea so made up fake Canadian passports and identities and just needed someone to connect with the Canadian ambassador and the Americans. That person was played by Ben Affleck—producer, director, and actor for this movie. The story was written by Chris Terrio using a 2007 article published in *Wired* entitled "How the CIA used a Fake Sci-Fi Flick to Rescue Americans from Tehran."

Affleck's tense version of events with some made-up events brought the movie to life. Other characters were played well by Bryan Cranston, Alan Arkin, John Goodman, and many other excellent actors. Some complained that there were stereotypes of Iranians and others. Popular songs by several groups made it seem more current and enjoyable to the younger generation.

Songs were not important in this movie. Mark Isham did some composing, and some songs were done by Bobbie Short, Mick Jagger, Keith Richards, Van Halen, and Rupert Holmes. Many complained that the movie made it seem like Americans were the heroes, but Canadians helped arrange the escape of Americans. But the 120-minute-movie was exciting and nearly true, so it won. The budget was $44.5 million but the box office was a surprising six times the budget.

Other movie nominees included *Amour, Beasts of the Southern Wild, Django Unchained, Les Misérables, Life of Pi, Lincoln, Silver Linings Playbook,* and *Zero Dark Thirty.*

Daniel Day-Lewis won Best Actor for *Lincoln.* Other contenders were Bradley Cooper *(Silver Linings Playbook),* Hugh Jackman *(Les Misérables),* Joaquin Phoenix *(The Master),* and Denzel Washington *(Flight).*

Jennifer Lawrence (1990-?) from Indian Hills, Kentucky, won Best Actress for *Silver Linings Playbook.* Other contenders were Jessica Chastain *(Zero Dark Thirty),* Emmanuelle Riva *(Amour),* Quvenzhane Wallis *(Beasts of the Southern Wild),* and Naomi Watts *(The Impossible).*

Anne Hathaway won Best Supporting Actress for *Les Misérables.*

Christoph Waltz won Best Supporting Actor for *Django Unchained.*

Best Song "Skyfall," w. m. Adele and Paul Epworth, from *Skyfall.*

Ang Lee, Director of *Life of Pi.*

Best Foreign Language Film: *Amour,* director Michael Haneke, Austria, French. This beautiful movie about an old couple was written for the husband to be played by 82-year-old Jean-Louis Trintignant. He was earlier featured with Brigette Bardot in *And God Created Woman* as well as in *Z* and other important movies. His wife, played by Emmanuelle Riva, had been featured in the famous movie *Hiroshima Mon Amour.*

The retired couple had been music teachers. She had strokes and he must care for her in this passionately acted movie. She begged him not to send her elsewhere for care. The loving relationship between the two brought out great performances and a special movie. The British Academy of Film and Television Arts voted Riva the best actress for her performance in *Amour,* thus the oldest ever voted Best Actress.

The 127-minute movie was photographed well and songs such as Franz Schubert's "Opus 90" and poignant dialogue made it a winner. One line of dialogue showed the gentle conversations. She said, "What would you say if no one came to your funeral?" He said, "Nothing, presumably."

British BAFTA awards: Best Film*: Argo.* **Best Actor:** Daniel Day-Lewis in *Lincoln.* **Best Actress:** Emmanuelle Riva in *Amour.* **Best Supporting Actor:** Christoph Waltz in *Django Unchained.* **Best Supporting Actress:** Anne Hathaway for *Les Misérables.* **Outstanding British Film***: Skyfall,* director Sam Mendes, producers Sam Mendes, Michael G. Wilson, Barbara Broccoli, Neal Purvis, Robert Wade, and John Logan, starring Daniel Craig, Javier Bardem, and Naomie Harris.

86th Academy Awards

Ceremony: This event took place on March 2, 2014, at the Dolby Theatre in Hollywood, California, hosted by Ellen DeGeneres. ABC broadcast it for three hours and thirty-four minutes to 43.74 million viewers. That was a 6 percent increase from the previous year making this the most watched Oscar ceremony since 2000. This year, there were nine nominees for Best Picture.

Lupita Nyong'o won Best Supporting Actress for *12 Years a Slave*. She accepted the Oscar and said, "It does not escape me that so much joy in my life was from so much pain in others.... No matter where you're from, your dreams are valid." The central theme of this movie was slavery, and the terrible acts humans perpetrate on the helpless.

Cate Blanchett won Best Actress for *Blue Jasmine*. When she got up, she said to the audience, "Sit down. You're too old to be standing." She thanked Woody Allen for casting her and said there's a feeling that movies with women don't do well but "they earn money."

Jared Leto won Best Supporting Actor for *Dallas Buyers Club*. He said, "There was a teenage girl, a high school dropout, who was pregnant—a single mom. That's my mother, who is here tonight. I love you and you are my best friend...For the 36 million who lost the battle to AIDS, if you ever felt injustice for who you are, tonight I stand with you." Matthew McConaughey won Best Actor for *Dallas Buyers Club*. He thanked the 6,000 members of AMPAS and said there are four things he needed each day: "God, my family where I learned what it means to be a man, my mother's lesson to respect yourself so you can respect others, and to chase someone. I am chasing someone I want to be ten years from now."

Angelina Jolie received the Jean Hersholt award for her endeavors to help others. She donated $1 million to the UN refugee program, was an advocate for them and for wildlife, had donated and represented immigrant education and prevention of sexual violence to women. She has adopted several refugee children. She said about her mother, "Whenever what I did had meaning, she made a point of telling me, 'That is what film is for.' She was very clear that nothing would mean anything if I didn't live a life of use to others." Angelina was the daughter of actor Jon Voight and Marcheline Bertrand, who died of cancer at age 56 when Angelina was 32.

Angela Lansbury, age 88, received an honorary award "as an entertainment icon who has created some of the cinema's most memorable characters, inspiring generations of actors." Robert Osborne, narrator for Turner Classic Movies, presented her award saying, "Angela has been adding class, talent, beauty, and intelligence to the movies ever since her film debut in 1944." She added, "I thank you, TCM. After Peter [her husband] died, you helped me get back on track." She described her beginning in *Gaslight,* the many stars she worked with, until she got to her role of the mother in *The Manchurian Candidate.* She said she couldn't top that role so went to Broadway *(Sweeney Todd)* and then television with the hit show *Murder, She Wrote.*

The In Memoriam pictures of people who died the previous year included James Gandolfini, Karen Black, Hal Needham, Eileen Brennan, Paul Walker, Deanna Durbin, Annette Funicello, Peter O'Toole, Sid Caesar, Robert Ebert, Shirley Temple Black, Joan Fontaine, Harold Ramis, Eleanor Parker, Ray Dolby, Julie Harris, Maximilian Schell, Esther Williams, and Philip Seymour Hoffman.

2013 *12 Years a Slave*

Tagline: "The extraordinary true story of Solomon Northup." This movie was based on the 1853 autobiography of Northrup. The theme is slavery and the terrible acts that people did to blacks. Slave owners were played by Michael Fassbender, Benedict Cumberbatch, and others. This film is very hard to watch but is important because it is the true story of a real man.

Northrup (Chiwetel Ejiofor) was a free man from New York who was kidnapped after being drugged with alcohol and sold into slavery. He learned from others how to survive. He was intelligent, could read, write, and play the violin. He encountered both good and bad slave owners, and saw the damage done to others besides himself. One other female slave, played by Lupita Nyongo'o, received unbelievable cruelty as a mistress and slave before she begged Northrup to kill her. The movie ended with his freedom, reunion with his family, and his unsuccessful suits against slave owners. Christians using the *Bible* to justify slavery was an important issue in this movie.

Finally, a meeting with Canadian abolitionist (Brad Pitt) led to his freedom. Hans Zimmer created an emotional score with original violin music and classical and American music. That included Franz Schubert's "Trio in B-flat," "Run, Nigger, Run" by John and Alan Lomax, and a John Legend soundtrack called "Roll, Jordan, Roll."

Britisher Steve McQueen did this picture creating torture that matched Spanish painter Goya's depictions, which demanded a viewer's attention. This 134-minute movie (which should not be seen by children because of cruelty) had a budget of just more than $20 million and a box office of nine times the budget. It was filmed at four antebellum plantations but mainly Magnolia in Schriever, Louisiana. Some scenes took place at the Column's Hotel and Madame John's

Legacy in the French Quarter of New Orleans. The performances gave the story a very special nobility.

Other movie nominees included *American Hustle, Captain Phillips, Dallas Buyers Club, Gravity, Her, Nebraska, Philomena,* and *The Wolf of Wall Street.*

Matthew McConaughey (1969- ?) from Uvalde, Texas, won Best Actor for *Dallas Buyers Club.* Other contenders were Christian Bale *(American Hustle),* Bruce Dern *(Nebraska),* Leonardo DiCaprio *(The Wolfe of Wall Street),* and Chiwetel Ejiofor *(12 Years a Slave).*

Cate Blanchett (1969- ?) from Ivanhoe, Austria, won Best Actress for *Blue Jasmine.* Other contenders were Amy Adams *(American Hustle),* Sandra Bullock *(Gravity),* Judy Dench *(Philomena),* and Meryl Streep *(August: Osage County).*

Lupita Nyong'o won Best Supporting Actress for *12 Years a Slave.*

Jared Leto won Best Supporting Actor for *Dallas Buyers Club.*

Best Song "Let It Go," w. m. Kristen Anderson-Lopez and Robert Lopez, from *Frozen.*

Alfonso Cuaron, Director of *Gravity.*

Best Foreign Language Film: *The Great Beauty,* director Paolo Sorrentino, Italy, Italian. This was about a 65-year-old journalist who lived the good life in Rome for years. Then, he re-examined that lifestyle and his friends. So many had tragic ends, but a few were beautiful and good. His life of writing was revived when he met a nun and helped with a shipwreck. His next novel was created as he found the "great beauty" in his life. The 142-minute movie was a hit but did not have actors well-known to Americans. Star, Toni Servillo, was considered a fine Italian actor.

British BAFTA awards: Best Film: *12 Years a Slave*. **Best Actor:** Chewetel Ejiofor in *12 Years a Slave*. **Best Actress:** Cate Blanchett in *Blue Jasmine*. **Best Supporting Actor:** Barkhad Abdi in *Captain Phillips*. **Best Supporting Actress:** Jennifer Lawrence in *American Hustle*. **Outstanding British Film**: *Gravity*, director Alfonso Cuaron, producers Alfonso Cuaron, David Heyman, and Jonas Cuaron, starring Sandra Bullock and George Clooney.

87th Academy Awards

Ceremony: This event took place February 22, 2015, in the Dolby Theatre in Hollywood, California, hosted by Neil Patrick Harris. ABC televised for three hours and forty-three minutes to 37.26 million viewers, a 15 percent decrease from the previous year. There were eight nominees for Best Picture.

Robert Duvall, age 84, oldest male acting nominee ever in Oscar history, lost to Best Supporting Actor J.K. Simmons for *Whiplash*. Patricia Arquette won for Best Supporting Actress in *Boyhood*. She said as she took the Oscar, "It's time for equal rights for women in America."

Eddie Redmayne won Best Actor for *The Theory of Everything*, which portrayed the life of Stephen Hawking, who suffered from ALS (Amyotrophic Lateral Sclerosis or Lou Gehrig's Disease). He said, "I am a lucky man. This belongs to people suffering from ALS." Julianne Moore won Best Actress for *Boyhood*. She said that she valued the movie because it shed a light on Alzheimer's disease and that might help others.

The Best Picture was *Birdman or the Unexpected Virtue of Ignorance*. Mexican director/producer Alejandro G. Iñárritu accepted the award on behalf of his crew and said he dedicated the Oscar to building "a Mexican government that we deserve."

Jean-Claude Carrière received an honorary Oscar for his "elegantly crafted screenplays that elevated the art of screenwriting to the level of literature." He wrote 80-plus screenplays, worked with Jacques Tati, Luis Buñuel, Umberto Eco, and developed a French film school where he taught screenplay writing. Hayao Miyazaki received an honorary Oscar as a Japanese "master storyteller whose animated artistry has inspired filmmakers and audiences." His themes were environmentalism, anti-war, feminist, and a sense of wonder in young people.

Maureen O'Hara received an honorary Oscar as "one of Hollywood's brightest stars, whose inspiring performances glowed with passion, warmth, and strength." She came out on a wheelchair. Liam Neeson, also from Ireland, said his first crush was on her. She said Charles Laughton was responsible for her career, signing her first and "that old devil John Ford" and John Wayne came later. She left with the old Irish phrase: "May the road rise up to meet you. May the wind be always at your back. May the sun shine warm upon your face."

Harry Belafonte was awarded the Jean Hersholt Humanitarian Award for "a lifetime of demonstrating how art is ennobled by ceaseless courage and conscience." Belafonte's acceptance speech was the boldest statement of problems for blacks ever spoken at the Oscars. Thus, much of his speech is included here:

America has come a long way since Hollywood in 1915 gave the world the film *Birth of a Nation*. By all measure, this cinematic work was considered the greatest film ever made. After the release of this film, American citizens went on a murderous rampage. The film also gained the distinction to be the first film ever screened at the White House. The then-presiding President Woodrow Wilson openly praised the film, and the power of this presidential anointing validated the film's brutality and its grossly distorted view of history. This, too, further inflamed the nation's racial divide.

In 1935, at the age of 8, sitting in a Harlem theater, I watched in awe and wonder the incredible feats of the white superhero *Tarzan of the Apes*. This white liberator, who could speak no language, swinging from tree to tree, saving Africa from the tragedy of destruction by a black indigenous population of inept, ignorant, void-of-any-skills population governed by ancient superstitions, with no heart for Christian charity. Through this film, the virus of racial inferiority, of never wanting to be identified with anything African, swept into the psyche of its youthful observers for black children in their Harlem theaters to cheer Tarzan and boo Africans. Native Americans, our Indian brothers and sisters, fared no better.

I came upon fellow artists, like the great actor and my hero, singer-humanist Paul Robeson, painter Charles White, dancer Katherine Dunham, historian's superior academic mind Dr. W.E.B. Du Bois, social strategist and educator Eleanor Roosevelt, writers Langston Hughes, and Maya Angelou and James Baldwin. They were also my moral compass.

Robeson said, 'Artists are the gatekeepers of truth. They are civilization's radical voice.' For my life of activism and commitment to social change, the opposition has been fiercely punitive. Some who've controlled institutions of culture and commentary have at times used their power to not only distort truth, but to punish the truth-seekers. Hollywood, too, has sadly played its part in these tragic scenarios. And on occasion, I have been one of its targets.

Today's cultural harvest yields a sweeter fruit: *Defiant Ones, Schindler's List, Brokeback Mountain, 12 Years a Slave,* and many more.

Approaching 88 years of age, how truly poetic that as I joyfully glow with my fellow honorees, we should have in our midst as one of our celebrators a man who did so much in his own life to redirect the ship of racial hatred and American culture. Ladies and gentlemen, I refer to my friend — my elderly friend — Sidney Poitier. (Poitier was one year older than Belafonte.)

I thank the Academy and its Board of Governors for this honor. I really wish I could be around for the rest of this century to see what Hollywood does with the rest of the century. After all, Paul Robeson said, 'Artists are the radical voice of civilization.' Perhaps we as artists and as visionaries, for what's better in the human heart and the human soul, could influence citizens everywhere in the world to see the better side of who and what we are as a species. Thank you very much.

The pictures and list of those who died in the last year included Mickey Rooney, Geoffrey Holder, James Garner, Edward Herrmann, Maya Angelou, James Shigeta, Anita Ekberg, Virna Lisi, Louis Jourdan, Richard Attenborough, Ruby Dee, Samuel Goldwyn Jr., Martha Hyer, Robin Williams, Rod Taylor, Luise Rainer, Herb Jeffries, Eli Wallach, Gabriel Garcia Marquez, Bob Hoskins, and Mike Nichols.

2014 *Birdman or The Unexpected Virtue of Ignorance*

Tagline: "The Expected Wickedness of Knowing Everything." This suggested that viewers would learn too much about someone or even themselves. Alejandro Iñárritu read Raymond Carver's short story entitled *What We Talk About When We Talk About Love*. Much of that story happened offstage. A lot is left out of his story, so the character's vulnerabilities are laid bare. That brings an awareness of our own selves that nobody else might know.

Iñárritu tried to make a different kind of movie to capture that experience so he decided to do it almost as if a camera were the main character running for hours without stopping. It made the movie seem as if the camera was on and the audience learned everything about one person—Birdman. The concept challenged the cinematographer, director, actors, and audience. The main cast were Michael Keaton as Birdman, Zach Galifianakis, Edward Norton, and Emma Stone.

The Keaton character had gained fame playing a superhero called Birdman in TV and movies. He was like Don Quixote, who believed himself to be a chivalrous knight or Icarus who believed he could fly until his wax wings melted near the sun. Birdman continued to live within the character of the former actor, taunting him to be more than he could be. He tried to put on a show about the superhero but got negative reviews. The audience now watched him living without editing just as real people live, said Director Iñárritu. Viewers experienced much while watching him try to soar again as he once soared when *Birdman* was a big hit.

Making the movie like one long take required special small cameras, natural light, tiny hand-held cameras, and lengthy actor portrayals without breaks. The movie was shot in New York City and used St. James Theatre and The Rum House on 47th Street for some scenes. Music was mainly solo jazz percussion performances. Some classical pieces from Mahler and Tchaikovsky and some modern composers were used in certain scenes.

The movie is surrealistic with dark humor. The thrilling end is left to the imagination of the viewer so readers could supply their own endings. The 119-minute film had a budget of $18 million and the box office was at least six times the budget.

Other movie nominees included *American Sniper, Boyhood, The Grand Budapest Hotel, The Imitation Games, Selma, The Theory of Everything,* and *Whiplash.*

Eddie Redmayne (1982- ?) from London won Best Actor for *The Theory of Everything.* Other contenders were Steve Carell *(Foxcatcher),* Bradley Cooper *(American Sniper),* Benedict Cumberbatch *(The Imitation Game),* and Mikael Keaton *(Birdman).*

Julianne Moore (1960- ?) from Ft. Bragg, North Carolina, won Best Actress for *Still Alice.* Other contenders were Marion Cotillard *(Two Days, One Night),* Felicity Jones *(The Theory of Everything),* Rosamund Pike *(Gone Girl),* and Reese Witherspoon *(Wild).*

Patricia Arquette won Best Supporting Actress for *Boyhood.*

J. K. Simmons won Best Supporting Actor for *Whiplash.*

Best Song "Glory," w. m. Common and John Legend, from *Selma.*

Alejandro G. Iñárritu, Director of *Birdman.*

Best Foreign Language Film: *Ida,* director Pawel Pawlikowski, Poland, Polish. A Catholic nun was about to take vows but was required to see her relatives before that happened. Anna visited her only living relative, an aunt who showed her where her Jewish relatives were buried. Aunt Ida told her to try some sins before taking vows. Anna had no interest in men, only in her family roots. Her aunt's musical collection was played by the two ladies and one Bach selection played in a minor key made a lasting impression. Another unusual selection was the Russian communist theme song, "The Internationale." The aunt had been a communist and finally committed suicide. The nun went to her funeral, left the convent, and began a life that resembled her aunt's life.

British BAFTA awards: Best Film*: Boyhood.* **Best Actor:** Eddie Redmayne in *The Theory of Everything.* **Best Actress:** Julianne Moore in *Still Alice.* **Best Supporting Actor:** J. K. Simmons in *Whiplash.* **Best Supporting Actress:** Patricia Arquette in *Boyhood.* **Outstanding British Film***: The Theory of Everything,* director James Marsh, producers Tim Bevan, Eric Fellner, Lisa Bruce, and Anthony McCarten, starring Eddie Redmayne, Felicity Jones, and Tom Prior.

88th Academy Awards

Ceremony: This event was conducted on February 28, 2016, at the Dolby Theatre in Hollywood, California, hosted by Chris Rock. ABC broadcast it for three hours and thirty-seven minutes to 34.42 million viewers, a 4 percent decrease from the previous year. There were eight nominees for Best Picture.

All twenty of the acting nominees and four of the five directors nominated were Caucasian. On the same day, civil rights activist Al Sharpton held a nearby protest saying, "This will be the last night of an all-white Oscar."

Spike Lee was awarded an honorary Oscar as a "filmmaker, educator, motivator, iconoclast, and artist." However, he chose not to come and attended a Knicks basketball game in New York. He was upset that his movie *Do the Right Thing* lost to *Driving Miss Daisy*.

Debbie Reynolds was awarded the Jean Hersholt Humanitarian Award "for her charitable contributions and tireless efforts towards mental health," but she could not attend. She died ten months later December 28, 2016, a day after her daughter Carrie died.

Vice President Joe Biden appeared and supported Lady Gaga and Diane Warren in their efforts to combat sexual assault on America's university campuses. "We must and can change the culture so that no abused women or men like the survivors you see here tonight ever feel like they have to ask themselves 'What did I do?' They did not do anything wrong." All were urged to take the pledge to intervene in situations when consent has not or cannot be given.

Leonardo DiCaprio's acceptance as Best Actor noted that "climate change is real" and that we need to support leaders who will speak for the indigenous populations who will be most affected. He ended, "Let us not take this planet for granted."

Morgan Freeman announced the winner of Best Picture, *Spotlight*. The spokesperson said, "This movie gave a voice to survivors that we hope will resonate all the way to the Vatican."

The memorial tribute to those who died the previous year included Wes Craven, Stan Freberg, Lizabeth Scott, Christopher Lee, Theodore Bikel, Robert Loggia, Maureen O'Hara, Omar Sharif, Dean Jones, Richard Corliss, James Horner, Holly Woodlawn, David Bowie, Vilmos Zsigmond, Daniel Gerson, and Leonard Nimoy.

2015 *Spotlight*

Tagline: "Break the story, break the silence." This important movie described the *Boston Globe's* Pulitzer-Prize-winning investigation of priests abusing children and the cover-ups by the Catholic Church. The Spotlight Team characters were played by Mark Ruffalo, Michael Keaton, Rachel McAdams, Brian d'Arcy, and their *Globe* leaders Liev Schreiber and John Slattery. The most important additional character was Stanley Tucci, who played the attorney representing victims of sexual abuse in a stellar performance.

The movie was a startling realization that there were so many pedophile priests, who were simply moved from one church to another when discovered. The *Globe* investigation led to changes that rocked and improved the Catholic churches from their very seat of power in the Vatican. It left viewers with the feeling that journalism was very important as a search for truth.

Howard Shore composed most of the music in the film. A few extra pieces included the following, which set the serious tone of this story: Bach's *Brandenburg Concerto* No. 3, 3rd movement, Handel's *Concerto Grosso* No. 1 in G Major Opus 6 and *Concerto Grosso* No. 2 in F Major, Opus 6, Randolph Coleman Hawkins "Bean's Blues" and "Silent Night."

Other movie nominees included *The Big Short, Bridge of Spies, Brooklyn, Mad Max: Fury Road, The Martian, The Revenant*, and *Room*.

Leonardo DiCaprio (1974-?) from Los Angeles, California, won Best Actor for *The Revenant*. Other contenders were Bryan Cranston *(Trumbo)*, Matt Damon *(The Martian)*, Michael Fassbender *(Steve Jobs)*, and Eddie Redmayne *(The Danish Girl)*.

Brie Larson (1989- ?) from Sacramento, California, won Best Actress for *Room*. Other contenders were Cate Blanchett *(Carol)*, Jennifer Lawrence *(Joy)*, Charlotte Rampling *(45 Years)*, and Saoirse Ronan *(Brooklyn)*.

Alicia Vikander won Best Supporting Actress for *The Danish Girl*.

Mark Rylance won Best Supporting Actor for *Bridge of Spies*.

Best Song "Writing's on the Wall," w. m. Jimmy Napes and Sam Smith from *Spectre*.

Alejandro G. Iñárritu, Director of *The Revenant*.

Best Foreign Language Film: *Son of Saul,* director Laszlo Nemes, Hungary, Hungarian. This complex film is about a man who cleaned up remains of people who were killed in gas chambers. One day, a boy (perhaps his own illegitimate son), who was barely alive, was seen and he searched for a rabbi to do a proper burial. One thing led to another, and the man and the boys were thought to be allies. It was filmed in a suburb of Budapest. A haunting musical background made the shocking movie a lasting memory.

British BAFTA awards: Best Film*: The Revenant.* **Best Actor:** Leonardo DiCaprio in *The Revenant.* **Best Actress***:* Brie Larson in *Room.* **Best Supporting Actor:** Mark Rylance in *Bridge of Spies.* **Best Supporting Actress:** Kate Winslet in *Steve Jobs.* **Outstanding British Film***: Brooklyn,* director John Crowley, producers John Crowley, Finola Dwyer, Amanda Posey, and Nick Hornby, starring Saoirse Ronan, Emory Cohen, and Domhnall Gleeson.

89th Academy Awards

Ceremony: This event was conducted on February 26, 2017, at the Dolby Theatre in Hollywood, California, hosted by comedian Jimmy Kimmel. ABC televised it for three hours and forty-nine minutes to 33 million viewers, 4 percent less than the previous year. There were nine nominees for Best Picture and many complaints about blacks, Latinos, and Asians being ignored by the Academy in earlier awards. Thus, this year many were nominated, and some won.

Mahershala Ali won Best Supporting Actor for *Moonlight* and had been a rapper. He said he had learned that attention for roles was not about who you are but about the characters you play. He thanked his wife, who stood by him, and announced that they had a daughter born four days earlier. Viola Davis won Best Supporting Actress for *Fences* and thanked Denzel Washington, as she said this was the only profession that celebrated what it meant to live a life.

Emma Stone won Best Actress for *La La Land* and described how much she admired co-star Ryan Gosling. Casey Affleck won for *Manchester by the Sea* and hugged brother Ben Affleck as he walked to the stage. He also thanked Denzel Washington for teaching him how to act. Warren Beatty and Faye Dunaway were to limit the award for Best Picture but were handed the envelope for Emma Stone. Once announced, the *La La Land* producers went to the stage and made some quick acceptance comments. Presenters were handed the correct envelope, which showed that *Moonlight* won. One winner said he hoped the movie inspired little black boys.

President Donald Trump had placed an immigration ban on people, which was called "inhumane" by Firouz Naderia, former director at NASA. An Iranian director, Asghar Farhadi, won the award for the Best Foreign Language Film but was unable to travel to the event. Academy President Cheryl Boone Isaacs said, "Every one of us knows that there are some empty chairs in this room, which has made Academy artists into activists."

The tribute to those who died in the last year included Bill Paxton, who died the day before the ceremony, Arthur Hiller, Bill Nunn, George Kennedy, Gene Wilder, Patty Duke, Garry Marshall, Mary Tyler Moore, Prince, Kenny Baker, John Hurt, Pat Conroy, Nancy Davis Reagan, Ken Howard, Zsa Zsa Gabor, Debbie Reynolds, and Carrie Fisher.

2016 *Moonlight*

Tagline: "This is the story of a lifetime." The book was based on a semi-autobiographical 3-part play, *In Moonlight Black Boys Look Blue*, by Tarell Alvin McCraney. He wrote that in 2003 to cope with his mother's death from AIDS. The book took the main character, Chiron, and his friend, Kevin, through adolescence, mid-teens, and young adulthood with three actors for each character's age. A constant figure is drug dealer Juan (played by Mahershala Ali), who both protected Chiron but created problems because of drug dealing. One might think this movie is irrelevant to whites but it increased understanding of others—empathy, which leads to acceptance. It helped explain that since arrival in America, black men had to be tough with little care and loving, so couldn't easily offer that to others.

Juan told Chiron he learned as a kid that black boys appeared blue in moonlight. He built up Chiron, who was ashamed of his color and being gay. Juan said, "No place you can go in the world ain't got no black people. We were the first on this planet." Many scenes contained moonlight and water, which helped Chiron develop his identity.

Chiron was neglected by his mother, who didn't love him because he "walked funny" and was effeminate. In her final treatment center for AIDS, she apologized but the damage was done. Chiron was only fulfilled by his relationship with Kevin, whose life headed elsewhere after he got a girl pregnant. Chiron turned to building up his body to look more masculine and selling drugs as his only protector, Juan, had done.

Most of the music was contemporary with one classical number, Mozart's "Laudate Dominum" from *Vesperae Solennes de Confessore*, K. 339. This movie exposed problems of black men about masculinity, vulnerability, and living in a white-oriented critical society. Though difficult to endure, it is very worthy of attention. This 111-minute movie filmed mainly in a Miami housing project had a budget of less than $4 million and a box office of more than eight times the budget.

Other movie nominees included *Arrival, Fences, Hacksaw Ridge, Hell or High Water, Hidden Figures, La La Land, Lion,* and *Manchester by the Sea.*

Casey Affleck (1975- ?) from Falmouth, Massachusetts, won Best Actor for *Manchester by the Sea*. Other contenders were Andrew Garfield *(Hacksaw Ridge),* Ryan Gosling *(La La Land),* Viggo Mortensen *(Captain Fantastic),* and Denzel Washington *(Fences).*

Emma Stone (1988- ?) from Scottsdale, Arizona, won Best Actress for *La La Land*. Other contenders were Isabelle Huppert *(Elle),* Ruth Negga *(Loving),* Natalie Portman *(Jackie),* and Meryl Streep *(Florence Foster Jenkins).*

Viola Davis won Best Supporting Actress for *Fences.*

Mahershala Ali won Best Supporting Actor for *Moonlight.*

Best Song "City of Stars," w. Benj Pasek and Justin Paul, m. Justin Hurwitz, from *La La Land.*

Damien Chazelle, Director of *La La Land.*

Best Foreign Language Film: *The Salesman,* director Asghar Farhadi, Iran, Persian. This Iranian movie was a takeoff on *Death of a Salesman.* A young couple performed the Miller play but had to move as their apartment crumbled. His wife was attacked because she stayed in a room that had belonged to a prostitute. The husband left to track down the man who hurt his wife and planned revenge on him. Their real life carried some of the same problems as Miller's play. When the movie won, Trump's ban on seven "Muslim" nations prevented Farhadi's coming. Farhadi asked the first female space tourist, a former director of Solar System Exploration at NASA, to represent him. Anousheh Ansari took the stage saying some of his words: "My absence is out of respect for the people of my country and those of the other six nations who have been disrespected by the inhumane law that banned entry of immigrants to the U.S."

British BAFTA awards: Best Film*: La La Land.* **Best Actor:** Casey Affleck in *Manchester by the Sea.* **Best Actress:** Emma Stone in *La La Land.* **Best Supporting Actor:** Dev Patel in *Lion.* **Best Supporting Actress:** Viola Davis in *Fences.* **Outstanding British Film***: I, Daniel Blake,* director Ken Loach, producers Ken Loach, Rebecca O'Brien, and Paul Laverty, starring Dave Johns and Hayley Squires.

90th Academy Awards

Ceremony: This event was conducted on March 4, 2018, at the Dolby Theatre in Hollywood, California, hosted by Jimmy Kimmel. ABC televised it for three hours and fifty-three minutes to 26.5 million viewers, making it the second least watched ceremony since records were kept. This year, there were nine nominees for Best Picture.

Honorary awards went to Agnes Varda, 89, "whose compassion and curiosity informs a uniquely personal cinema" and worked to bring about the French New Wave of the 1950s and 1960s and Charles Burnett as "a resolutely independent and influential film pioneer, who has chronicled the lives of black Americans with eloquence and insight." His focus was family structure and self-identity among African Americans. The other honorary award went to Owen Roizman "whose expansive visual style and technical innovation have advanced the art of cinematography." He was the president of the American Society of Cinematography. He had polio as a child but learned his art in a wheelchair and worked with directors who were fast and careful, like Sidney Lumet. Some of his movies were *Network, Tootsie, Absence of Malice, The French Connection*, and *The Exorcist*.

A Special Achievement Academy Award was presented to Alejandro G. Iñárritu "for Carne y Arena virtual reality installation, in recognition of a visionary and powerful experience in storytelling." Carne y Arena means present but not visible, like flesh and sand. This showed a method of using virtual reality technology to help viewers walk in the bodies of those they are viewing. As Iñárritu said, "If you don't understand, you can't love." He thought this kind of movie might unite people by understanding each other better. He made a special point that movie images without sound do nothing because sound promotes storytelling and emotions. Donald Sutherland was honored for a "lifetime of indelible characters, rendered with unwavering truthfulness."

Gary Oldham won Best Actor for *Darkest Hour* playing Prime Minister Winston Churchill. He saluted Churchill and described his time in the United States as having been so good. He then told his nearly 99-year-old mom in England, "Put on the kettle. I'm bringing Oscar home." Francis McDormand won Best Actress and said to producers about women, "We all have stories to tell, projects, so invite us in."

The Shape of Water won. Director Guillermo del Toro said he grew up in Mexico and admired foreign films, so he dedicated his Oscar to youth who had dreams, such as he did.

The list of those who died over the past year included Chuck Berry, Robert Osborne, Harry Dean Stanton, John Heard, Martin Landau, Roger Moore, Sam Shepard, Jeanne Moreau, Joseph Bologna, Don Rickles, Bernie Casey, Shashi Kapoor, Danielle Darrieux, and Jerry Lewis.

2017 *The Shape of Water*

Tagline: "Experience a connection beyond words." The story involved a secret experiment in a government laboratory around 1962. The story, direction, and production were by Guillermo del Toro. He saw *Creature from the Black Lagoon* as a kid and wanted the monster to end up with the female. So, his movie made that happen.

Elisa was a mute played by Sally Hawkins, who prepared by watching silent comedians like Charlie Chaplin, Buster Keaton, Harold Lloyd, and Stan Laurent from Laurel and Hardy. They all were mute in silent movies and conveyed emotions by their actions. Richard Jenkins played Elisa's friend as a gay neighbor. Guillermo del Toro created the

Jenkins character around gay filmmaker James Whale, who directed *Frankenstein, The Invisible Man,* and *Bride of Frankenstein,* but could not work later due to his sexual orientation.

Elisa cleaned and worked in the laboratory with a co-worker (Octavia Spencer) who became an interpreter for Elisa to others. When the laboratory received a strange creature from a South American river, they studied it for possible help in the space race with the Russians. When it seemed he was to be killed, Elisa had become enamored in their special understanding without words. Despite her efforts, he was wounded but had special healing skills. He took Elisa with him and was able to help her survive under water.

This fantastical movie has been called mesmerizing because it transports us to the unbelievable world of fantasy and love without words. A few words for the monster were done by del Toro, himself. The score was done by Alexandre Desplat, who used water as a theme for his songs and background. He also used cute songs like Glenn Miller's band doing "I Know Why," Carmen Miranda doing "Chica Chica Boom Chick," "Babalu," Andy Williams doing "A Summer Place," and "You'll Never Know." He even used "I Went to Market" from Stephen Foster's "My Old Kentucky Home," used by Bill "Bojangles" Robinson in the 1935 movie with Shirley Temple called *The Little Colonel.*

The movie was filmed mainly in Ontario and Toronto. The 123-minute movie had a budget of $19 million and box office world gross of ten times more.

Other movie nominees included *Call Me by Your Name, Darkest Hour, Dunkirk, Get Out, Lady Bird, Phantom Thread, The Post,* and *Three Billboards Outside Ebbing, Missouri.*

Gary Oldham (1958- ?) from London won Best Actor for *Darkest Hour.* Other contenders were Timothee Chalamet *(Call Me by Your*

Name), Daniel Day-Lewis *(Phantom Thread)*, Daniel Kaluuya *(Get Out)*, and Denzel Washington *(Roman J. Israel, Esq)*.

Frances McDormand won Best Actress for *Three Billboards Outside Ebbing, Missouri*. Other contenders were Sally Hawkins *(The Shape of Water)*, Margot Robbie *(I, Tonya)*, Saoirse Ronan *(Lady Bird)*, and Meryl Streep *(The Post)*.

Allison Janney won Best Supporting Actress for *I, Tonya*.

Sam Rockwell won Best Supporting Actor for *Three Billboards Outside Ebbing, Missouri*.

Best Song "Remember Me," w. m. Kristen Anderson-Lopez and Robert Lopez, from *Coco*.

Guillermo del Toro, Director of *The Shape of Water*.

Best Foreign Language Film: *A Fantastic Woman,* director Sebastian Lelio, Chile, Spanish. This rare movie is about a transgender young woman who aspired to be a singer in Chile. She met an older married man at a bar, and they had a most passionate sexual encounter, but the man died soon after. She was questioned by police, the ex-wife, and son, and her dog was taken. She endured the loss of the man, humiliation, and respect. Actress Daniela Vega played this complex role well and the movie ended with getting her dog back and singing in an opera recital.

The award won for this 104-minute movie helped Chilean LBGTQ activists discuss a gender identity bill with politicians. That was successful and since 2018 transgender people above the age of 14 can change their name and their gender. Winning this movie resulted in Daniela Vega becoming the first transgender woman to be a 2018 presenter at the Academy Awards.

British BAFTA awards: Best Film*: Three Billboards Outside Ebbing, Missouri*. **Best Actor:** Gary Oldman in *Darkest Hour*. **Best Actress:** Frances McDormand in *Three Billboards Outside Ebbing, Missouri*.

Best Supporting Actor: Sam Rockwell in *Three Billboards Outside Ebbing, Missouri*. **Best Supporting Actress:** Allison Janney in *I, Tonya*. **Outstanding British Film***: Three Billboards Outside Ebbing, Missouri*, director Martin McDonagh, producers Martin McDonagh, Graham Broadbent, and Peter Czermin, starring Frances McDormand, Woody Harrelson, and Sam Rockwell.

91st Academy Awards

Ceremony: This event was conducted on February 24, 2019, at the Dolby Theatre in Hollywood, California, with no host. ABC broadcast the ceremony for three hours and twenty-one minutes to 29.56 million, a 12 percent increase from the previous year. This year, there were eight nominees for Best Picture. The aim of the Academy was to limit the ceremony to three hours by having some awards given during ads, but this was not done.

An honorary award went to Marvin Levy "for an exemplary career in publicity that has brought films to the minds, hearts, and souls of audiences all over the world." He worked with Steven Spielberg on campaigns for *Close Encounters of the Third Kind, Back to the Future, Schindler's List,* and *Jurassic Park.* Lalo Schifrin was also given an honorary award "in recognition of his unique musical style, compositional integrity and influential contribution to the art of film scoring." An Argentinian jazz aficionado, he wrote for TV and movies, including themes for *Mission Impossible, Mannix, Cool Hand Luke, Bullitt,* and *Coogan's Bluff.* Cicely Tyson, 93, "whose unforgettable performances and personal integrity have inspired generations of filmmakers, actors and audiences" got her an honorary award. She thanked her mother, Oprah Winfrey, and Whoopi Goldberg. Some of her movies were *Sounder, The Autobiography of Miss Jane Pittman, Diary of a Mad Black Woman, The Help,* and *How to Get Away with Murder.*

The Irving G. Thalberg Memorial Award went to husband-wife team Kathleen Kennedy and Frank Marshall as "creative producers whose bodies of work reflect a consistently high quality of motion picture production." They produced movies such as *E. T., The Color Purple, The Money Pit, Empire of the Sun, Jurassic Park, Paper Moon, Raiders of the Lost Ark, Poltergeist, Cape Fear, The Sixth Sense, Snow Falls on Cedars, The Bourne Identity* series, *Seabiscuit, Indiana Jones and the Kingdom of the Crystal Skull, The Curious Case of Benjamin Button, Sully,* etc.

Rami Malek, who won Best Actor, said he was a first generation Egyptian. He proudly said, "We made a movie about a gay man, an immigrant, a man who was unapologetically himself." The In Memoriam included many who died the previous year, including Michel Legrand, Margot Kidder, Neil Simon, Burt Reynolds, Miloš Forman, Penny Marshall, Stan Lee, Tab Hunter, and Albert Finney.

2018 *Green Book*

Tagline: "Inspired by a true friendship." The story was written by Nick Vallelonga, son of the chauffeur for black pianist Dr. Don Shirley. The title is named for a 1936 book written by Harlem-based postman Victor H. Green called the *Green Book,* used for safe dining, hotels, and travel for blacks until passage of the Civil Rights Act in the 1960s ending legal segregation.

Bouncer (played by Viggo Mortensen) was out of a job when the Copacabana nightclub was being renovated. He got a job driving a famous pianist (played by Mahershala Ali) for engagements in southern states. They had trouble adjusting but eventually became friends. The chauffeur wrote letters to his wife, which the pianist helped him make more romantic, and he defended the black pianist who was attacked by whites. The pianist was not permitted to dine in the restaurant where he was to entertain. The pianist was to be arrested when he was found having sex with a white man. Dr. Shirley placed a call to the White House for help. He and his chauffeur parted but remained friends after their tour until they both died in 2013.

Mortensen had to gain 50 or so pounds for the role. Mahershala had to learn basic piano skills even though score composer Kris Bowers' hands were shown in playing numbers. Casting was notable for using family members of the Vallelonga family, as well as writer and co-producer Brian Currie, who played the Maryland State Trooper who helped out during a snowstorm. Jazz artist Quincy Jones knew Don Shirley and believed he was one of America's greatest pianists.

The music included classical pieces, such as a Chopin's "Etude" and old popular songs like "Pretty L'il Thing" and "Goodbye, My Lover, Goodbye." The 130-minute movie budget was $23 million, and the box office was well more than that amount.

Other movie nominees included *Black Panther*, *Black Klansman*, *Bohemian Rhapsody*, *The Favorite*, *Roma*, *A Star Is Born*, and *Vice*.

Rami Malek (1981- ?) from Los Angeles won Best Actor for *Bohemian Rhapsody*. Other contenders were Christian Bale *(Vice)*, Bradley Cooper *(A Star Is Born)*, Willem Dafoe *(At Eternity's Gate)*, and Viggo Mortensen *(Green Book)*.

Olivia Colman (1974-?) from Norwich, England, won \Best Actress for *The Favourite*. Other contenders were Yalitza Aparicio *(Roma)*, Glenn Close *(The Wife)*, Lady Gaga *(A Star Is Born)*, and Melissa McCarthy *(Can You Ever Forgive Me?)*.

Regina King won Best Supporting Actress for *If Beale Street Could Talk*.

Mahershala Ali won Best Supporting Actor for *Green Book*.

Best Song "Shallow," w. m. Lady Gaga, Mark Ronson, Anthony Rossomando, and Andrew Wyatt, from *A Star Is Born*.

Alfonso Cuaron, Director of *Roma*.

Best Foreign Language Film: *Roma,* director Alfonso Cuaron, Mexico, Spanish and Mixtec. The tagline of this movie is: "There are periods in history that scar societies and moments in life that transform us as individuals." The story is of two maids in Mexico City who served an aristocratic family. One maid, Cleo, told her boyfriend she was pregnant, and he ran off. The manor lady took Cleo and her children to a fiesta, but a fire started during the New Year's celebration and all suffered trying to contain it. The manor's husband had a girlfriend, and his wife tried to keep that from their children. When Cleo was ready to deliver, Sofia took her shopping. Gunmen invaded the store and held Cleo at gun point. Her water broke. The child was stillborn. Doom seemed inevitable as audiences tensed up. In real life, during filming there was an attack by thieves. Some wound up in hospital and valuable personal articles were stolen. Director Alfonso Cuaron thanked fellow Mexican filmmakers in the final credits: Gael Garcia Bernal, Guillermo del Toro, Alejandro G. Iñárritu, and Emmanuel Lubezki.

British BAFTA awards: Best Film*: Roma.* **Best Actor:** Rami Malek in *Bohemian Rhapsody.* **Best Actress:** Olivia Colman in *The Favourite.* **Best Supporting Actor:** Mahershala Ali in *Green Book.* **Best Supporting Actress:** Rachel Weisz in *The Favourite.* **Outstanding British Film***: The Favourite,* director Yorgos Lanthimos, producers Yorgos Lanthimos, Ceci Dempsey, Ed Guiney, Lee Magiday, Deborah Davis, and Tony McNamara, starring Olivia Colman, Emma Stone, and Rachel Weisz.

92nd Academy Awards

Ceremony: This event took place on February 9, 2020, at Dolby Theatre in Hollywood, California, with no host. ABC's broadcast showed it for three hours and thirty-six minutes to 23.64 million viewers, a 20 percent decrease from the previous year. There were nine nominees for Best Picture.

AMPAS Board of Directors changed the name of Best Foreign Language Film category to Best International Feature Film. During the performance of the nominees for Best Song, Eimear Noone became the first woman to conduct the orchestra during an Oscar ceremony. Tom Hanks announced that the Academy Museum of Motion Pictures would open before the end of 2020.

The Jean Hersholt Humanitarian Award went to Geena Davis "for her work fighting for gender parity in media through her Geena Davis Institute on Gender in Media." She said that women are presented in the media as one-dimensional in so many cases that it sends a message to children that men are more important than women, yet they make up half of civilization. She invited filmmakers to look at their projects and rethink whether a woman playing the role of a man could happen. Hanks said as a grandfather of three little girls, he thanked her on their behalf. He also added that Geena was an Olympic-caliber archer with bow and arrows.

David Lynch, dubbed "Renaissance man of American filmmakers," won an honorary award for "fearlessly breaking boundaries in pursuit of his singular cinematic vision." A filmmaker, artist, musician, writer, director, producer, he worked with films like *Eraserhead, The Elephant*

Man, Blue Velvet, Twin Peaks, and television series. He founded the David Lynch Foundation for transcendental meditation for the homeless, veterans, refugees, prisoners, schools, etc.

Wes Studi was the first Native American to win an acting Academy Award and was recognized for "the power and craft he brought to his indelible film portrayals and for his steadfast support of the Native American community." He appeared in 30 films using linguistic skills in numerous Native tribal languages. His familiar face was in movies including *Avatar* and *Dances of Wolves*.

Lina Wertmuller, age 91, received an award for "her provocative disruption of political and social norms delivered with bravery through her weapon of choice, the camera lens." The little Italian was supported to stand by 86-year-old Sophia Loren and others. Lina said that the Oscar should have a woman's name like "Anna." She asked women to holler out a feminine name for Oscar (and some did). She said the next time she would come naked to the Academy Awards. She said Sophia had made a pact with the devil because she's still so beautiful. Lina was involved with *Seven Beauties, The Seduction of Mimi, Love and Anarchy, Swept Away*, etc.

Brad Pitt won Best Supporting Actor and gave recognition to stunt players and coordinators. Laura Dern won Best Supporting Actress for a movie about love and our planet. She thanked her parents, actors Bruce Dern and Diane Ladd. Joaquin Phoenix won Best Actor and wanted to use his voice for the voiceless in their fight against an injustice and a call for help with the environment. He thanked everyone for giving him a second chance. He added that his deceased brother, actor River Phoenix, wrote a song lyric hoping for love and peace.

Renee Zellweger won Best Actress for *Judy* and the orchestra played "Over the Rainbow." She said, "Our heroes unite us" and named all kinds of heroes. She said that Judy Garland never won this award so she held it up and said, "This is for you."

Parasite became the first non-English language film to win Best Picture. When the winning film was announced, and the Korean filmmakers walked to the stage, the audience began a Hurrah chant. Through a translator, the filmmaker thanked everybody who helped make *Parasite* and thanked the Korean film audience.

The tribute to those who died the previous year included Kobe Bryant, Rip Torn, Diahann Carroll, Terry Jones, Agnes Varda, Danny Aiello, Buck Henry, Stanley Donen, Robert Forster, D. A. Pennebaker, Fernando Luhan, Andre Previn, Sylvia Miles, Bibi Andersson, Doris Day, Rutger Hauer, Franco Zefferelli, John Witherspoon, Peter Fonda, and Kirk Douglas.

2019 *Parasite*

Tagline: "Act like you own the place!" The Kims were a poor family living in a cramped basement apartment in Seoul, Korea. They even smelled poor to some who lived in higher society, like the Parks. The Parks' modern house was large, comfy, and had an outdoor area in the sun amidst crowded city tenements. The Kims begin to pretend they knew more than they did and gradually replaced the hired help in the Parks' house, one by one.

When the Parks went camping, one former maid knocked on the door and told the Kims that she left something important in the basement when fired. It was her husband who was living there to avoid loan sharks. She brought him food and assured him that he would be tended.

Just as the Kims were having a wonderful time in the large house, the Parks suddenly came back because of a storm. The Kims hid in the living room and the Parks smelled them. The Kims were determined to somehow take over the house for themselves. The Parks were rather dumb and relied on the Kims until a party took place. A horrible scene with killings displayed the revenge the poor people took on the rich family.

This movie was about parasites who lived off each other due to class conflict and the consequences of capitalism. Even when the Parks' house was bought by Germans, the tale wasn't over because the basement was still used. The Kims' dreamt of when they would be back.

Bong Joon-ho, the director, had been a tutor for the son of a wealthy family in Seoul as a young man. He felt he was infiltrating the private lives of strangers. He wanted his friends to see the house. Then he fleshed out the story about a poor family infiltrating a rich house of people who couldn't wash dishes or drive themselves without a poor person's help. So, he decided there were two kinds of parasites—the rich and the poor—who use each other.

The music was mainly piano pieces and light percussion to create a tense atmosphere. There is one excerpt from Act II of Handel's opera *Rodelinda* and the Italian song "Mio Caro Bene" sung by Gianni Morandi. The Korean film composer was Jung Jaeil.

Other movie nominees included *Ford v Ferrari, The Irishman, Jojo Rabbit, Joker, Little Women, Marriage Story, 1917,* and *Once Upon a Time in Hollywood.*

Joaquin Phoenix (1974- ?) from San Juan, Puerto Rico, won Best Actor for *Joker.* Other contenders were Antonio Banderas *(Pain and Glory),* Leonardo DiCaprio *(Once Upon a Time in Hollywood),* Adam Driver *(Marriage Story),* and Jonathan Pryce *(The Two Popes).*

Renee Zellweger(1969-?) from Katy, Texas, won Best Actress for *Judy.* Other contenders were Cynthia Erivo *(Harriet),* Scarlett Johansson *(Marriage Story),* Saoirse Ronan *(Little Women),* and Charlize Theron *(Bombshell).*

Laura Dern won Best Supporting Actress for *Marriage Story.*

Brad Pitt won Best Supporting Actor for *Once Upon a Time in Hollywood.*

Best Song "I'm Gonna Love Me Again," w. Bernie Taupin, m. Elton John, from *Rocketman.*

Bong Joon-ho, Director of *Parasite.*

Best International Feature Film: *Parasite,* director Bong Joon-ho, South Korea, Korean and English.

British BAFTA awards: Best Film*: 1917.* **Best Actor:** Joaquin Phoenix in *Joker.* **Best Actress:** Renee Zellweger in *Judy.* **Best Supporting Actor:** Brad Pitt in *Once Upon a Time in Hollywood.* **Best Supporting Actress:** Laura Dern in *Marriage Story.* **Outstanding British Film***: 1917,* director Sam Mendes, producers Yorgos Sam Mendes, Pippa Harris, Jayne-Ann Tenggren, Callum McDougall, Krysty Wilson-Cairns, starring Dean-Charles Chapman, George MacKay, and Daniel Mays.

93rd Academy Awards

Ceremony: This event took place on April 25, 2021, in Los Angeles, California at both Union Station and the Dolby Theatre with no single host. *ABC* broadcast it for three hours and nineteen minutes. The awards were impacted by many months of closed theatres, movies that lacked actor or name recognition, and declining interest in Oscar ceremonies for some years.

This ceremony was delayed due to the COVID-19 pandemic. Attendees were limited to 170, rotated in and out through the show. Those attendees were required to take a temperature check upon entry, at least three COVID-19 tests prior to attendance, get vaccinated prior to attendance, and wear face masks when not on-camera. Table settings achieved social distances by being on different levels with no more than four persons per table. Travel was minimized due to COVID-19 so some nominees and winners, such as Anthony Hopkins for Best Actor, were not present. He was the oldest, age 83, ever to win in the acting category.

Several other differences from previous ceremonies occurred. There were no honorary awards, only 23 categories were used with sound mixing and sound categories merged and voting for the Best International Feature Film was open to all voting members of the Academy. In addition, the Best Original Songs were not done during the ceremony at Union Station but before the ceremony at the new Academy Museum of Motion Pictures on the rooftop terrace. "Fight for You" from *Judas and the Black Messiah* won Best Song. Also, the

Best Actor and Best Actress were awarded after the Best Picture was announced. There were nine nominees for Best Picture.

Chloé Zhao won Best Director for *Nomadland.* She hailed from China and did that film "for those who hold onto the goodness in ourselves." Frances McDormand won Best Actress for *Nomadland* and recommended that everyone go to the largest screen they could to view the movies nominated for Best Picture. She, the director, and the cast went to live in vans with some 40 actual nomads who live in vans moving from one place to another over time as in the movie. Yuh-Jung Youn won Best Supporting Actress for *Minari.* She was from Korea, didn't believe in competition, felt she had a bit of luck, and thanked her two boys, who made her go out to work.

Perhaps the most moving moment of the evening came with the winner for *Another Round,* the Best International Feature Film. This film from Denmark meant "binge drinking" and Thomas Vinterberg wrote the play. He told his daughter he was thinking of doing the movie. Ida told her father about the drinking culture within the Danish youth and thought he should do it. He intended to put her in the picture but four days into filming she was talking on a cell phone while driving and died in a crash. He held up the Oscar and said, "This is for you!"

There were two recipients for the Jean Hersholt Humanitarian Award: Tyler Perry for his philanthropy and charitable endeavors and efforts to address homelessness and economic difficulties by African Americans, and The Motion Picture and Television Fund for the emotional and financial relief services offered to members of the entertainment industry.

The In Memoriam segment included Cicely Tyson, Ian Holm, Max von Sydow, Chloris Leachman, Yaphet Kotto, Olivia de Havilland, Christopher Plummer, George Segal, Wilford Brimley, Marge Champion, Shirley Knight, Rhonda Fleming, Fred Willard, Hal Holbrook, Ennio Morricone, Carl Reiner, Larry McMurtry, Lynn Stalmaster, Brian Dennehy, Diana Rigg, Jerry Stiller, and Sean Connery.

2020 *Nomadland*

Tagline: "Surviving America in the Twenty-First Century." In 2011, Fern (McDormand) loses her job in a small Nevada town and decided to sell everything and purchase a van to travel about searching for work. Her husband had recently died, and she first found a short job at an Amazon fulfillment center. She met a co-worker who invited her to an Arizona community of vans with fellow nomads. Slowly, they taught her skills for the road. That friend was dying of cancer but expected good friends and memories on the road to be a better way to die than in a hospital.

Fern became a camp host at one van campground and ran into a man she liked. He became ill, had surgery, but later they traveled together. She learned his wife was pregnant and wanted him to meet his grandchild. That visit resulted in him staying with his wife and ended his wandering.

Fern moved on but her van broke down and she went to see her sister. When reproached, she took a loan from her sister to repair her van. She traveled back to the Arizona community where she learned her friend had died of cancer. She returned to her original Nevada town, disposed of things held in storage, and returned to the road. The cast lived in vans with real van nomads who played various parts in this unique movie.

Director Zhao went looking for classical music inspired by nature. She found Italian Ludovico Einaudi's music about walking in the Alps. She wanted Fern's inner dialogue in different landscapes to show the audience how she changed, and it worked well. The movie ran 108 minutes, had a budget of $5 million and box office was considerably more than was spent.

Other best picture nominees were *The Father, Judas and the Black Messiah, Mank, Minari, Promising Young Woman, Sound of Metal,* and *The Trial of the Chicago 7.*

Anthony Hopkins won Best Actor for *The Father*. Other contenders were Riz Ahmed *(Sound of Metal)*, Chadwick Boseman *(Ma Rainey's Black Bottom)*, Gary Oldman *(Mank)*, and Steven Yeun *(Minari)*.

Francis McDormand won Best Actress for *Nomadland*. Other contenders were Viola Davis *(Ma Rainey's Black Bottom)*, Andra Day *(The United States vs. Billie Holiday)*, Vanessa Kirby *(Pieces of a Woman)*, and Carey Mulligan *(Promising Young Woman)*.

Youn Yuh-jung (1947-?) from North Korea, won Best Supporting Actress for *Minari*.

Daniel Kaluuya (1989-?) from London, England, won Best Supporting Actor for *Judas and the Black Messiah*.

Best Song "Fight for You" from *Judas and the Black Messiah* w. H.E.R. and Tiara Thomas, m. D'Mile and H.E.R.

Chloé Zhao, Director of *Nomadland*

Best International Feature Film: *Another Round*, director Thomas Vinterberg, Denmark, Sweden and Holland. This film was called *Druk* ("binge drinking") in Danish. Teachers and colleagues meet at a gym and discussed unmotivated students and how their own professional lives felt stale. They began to discuss a psychiatrist who theorized that a blood alcohol content (BAC) of 0.05 made people more creative and relaxed. They decided to test the theory by drinking at work.

They agreed to rules that BAC should never be below 0.05 and that they would have no drinks after 8 p.m. That helped all four members of the group so much that they increased the BAC to 0.10. After some fun nights coming home drunk, two men were confronted by their families. Martin's wife had an affair, he left her, and the group abandoned the experiment. Later, Tommy was binge drinking so much that he boarded his boat with his dog, sailed away, and drowned.

At the funeral, the rest were reluctant to drink. Martin's wife sent word that she would give their marriage another chance. He celebrated, danced, and the movie ended as he jumped into the water with a final picture of him in mid-air.

The director's daughter wanted her father to make this film because she knew of heavy drinking among her young crowd. However, she died, and the film was dedicated to her. The movie ran 117 minutes and is in Danish. The cast was unknown to most Americans.

British BAFTA awards: Best Film: *Nomadland.* **Best Actor:** Anthony Hopkins in *The Father.* **Best Actress:** Frances McDormand in *Nomadland.* **Best Supporting Actor:** Daniel Kaluuya in *Judas and the Black Messiah.* **Best Supporting Actress:** Youn Yuh-jung in *Minari.* **Outstanding British Film**: *Promising Young Woman.* director Emerald Fennell, starring Carey Mulligan, Bo Burnham, Alison Brie, and Clancy Brown.

Made in the USA
Coppell, TX
18 January 2024

27870792R00246